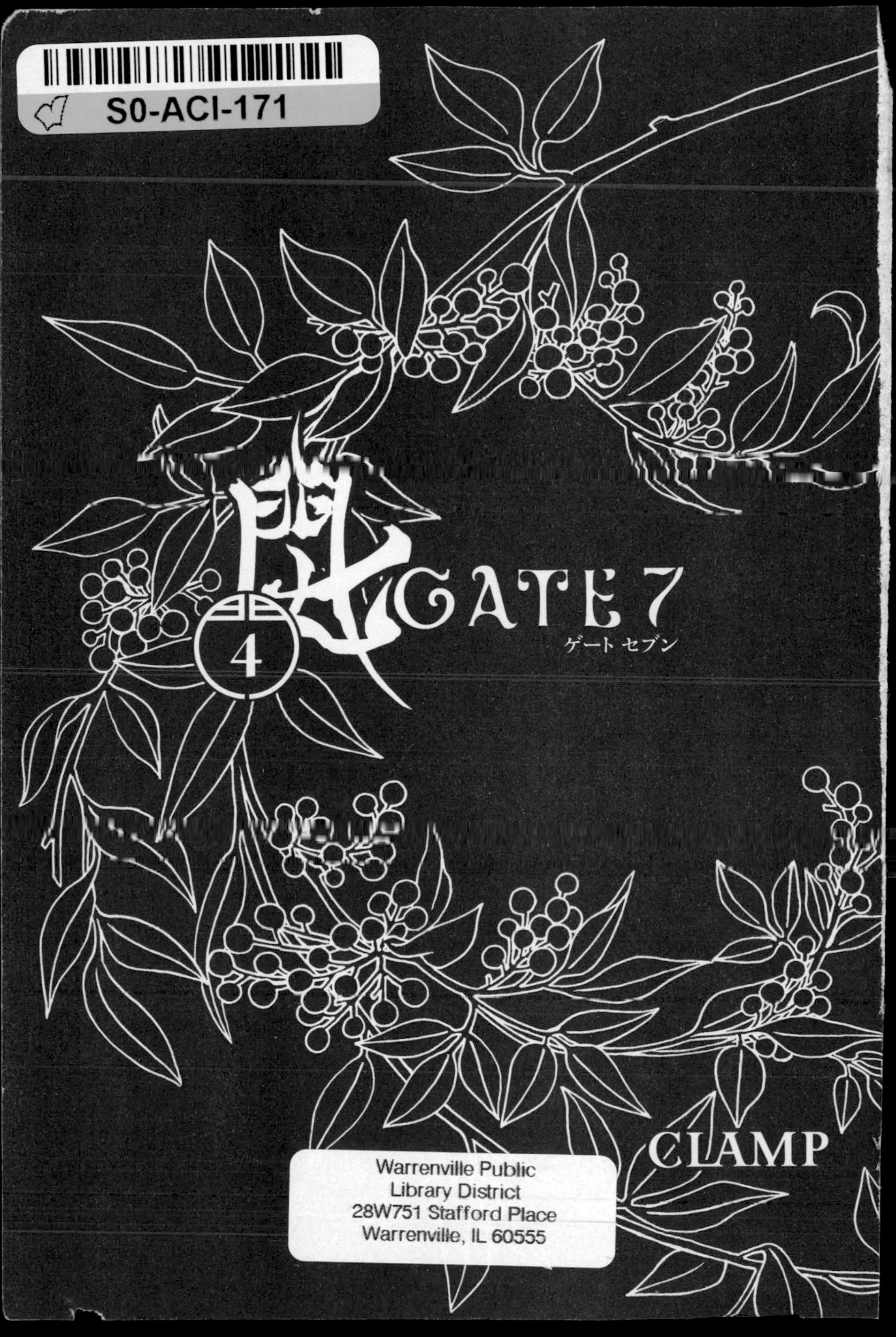
GATE 7
ゲート セブン
4
CLAMP

PUBLISHER **MIKE RICHARDSON**

EDITOR **PHILIP R. SIMON**

ASSISTANT EDITOR **EVERETT PATTERSON**

COLLECTION DESIGNER **TINA ALESSI**

DIGITAL PRODUCTION **RYAN JORGENSEN**

Special thanks to Michael Gombos, Annie Gullion, and Carl Gustav Horn.

GATE 7 VOLUME 4

Dark Horse Manga, a division of Dark Horse Comics, Inc.
10956 SE Main Street, Milwaukie, OR 97222
DarkHorse.com

To find a comics shop in your area, call the Comic Shop Locator Service toll-free at 1-888-266-4226.

First edition: July 2013
ISBN 978-1-59582-961-0
1 2 3 4 5 6 7 8 9 10

Printed in the United States of America

GATE 7 ④

TRANSLATION BY WILLIAM FLANAGAN
ENGLISH ADAPTATION BY WILLIAM FLANAGAN & PHILIP R. SIMON
LETTERING BY STEVE DUTRO

CONTENTS

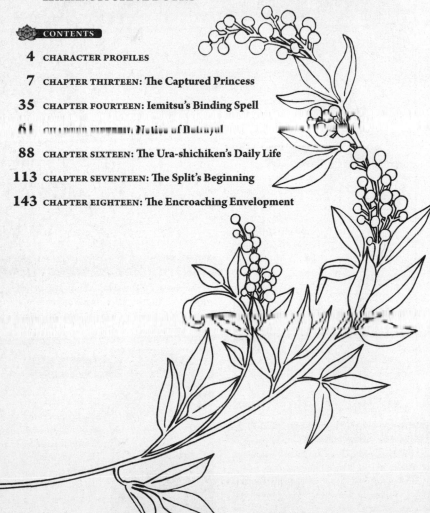

MAIN CHARACTERS

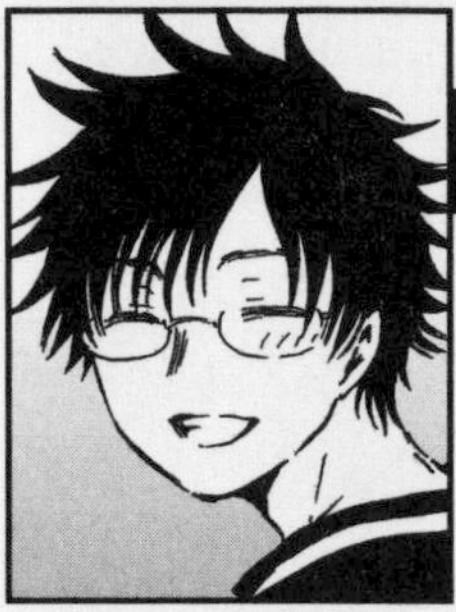

CHIKAHITO TAKAMOTO

A high-school student who loves everything about Kyoto, including its history, shrines, temples, and cuisine. He met Hana and the others on a sightseeing trip to Kyoto.

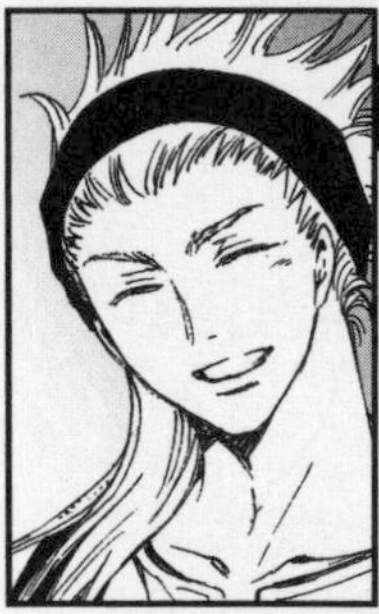

SAKURA

A member of the Ura-shichiken who acts as the controller of all shadow-based elemental weapons. He is easygoing and treats Chikahito with kindness.

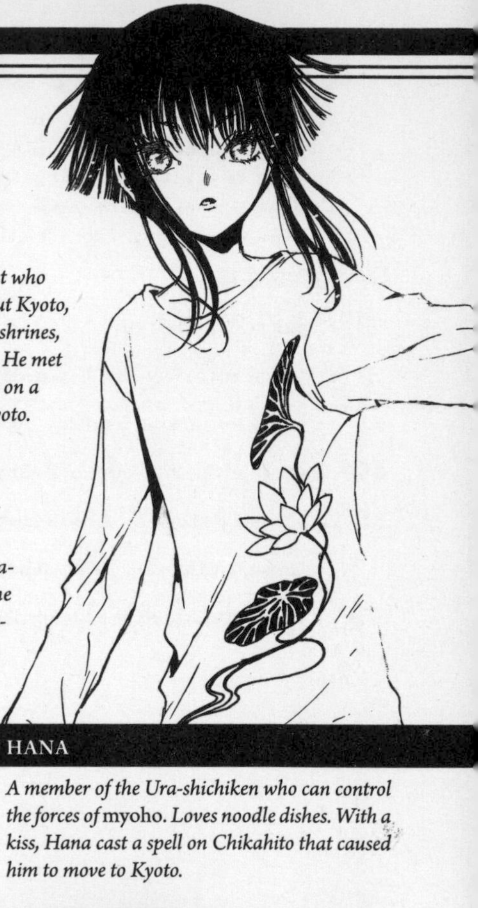

HANA

A member of the Ura-shichiken who can control the forces of myoho. *Loves noodle dishes. With a kiss, Hana cast a spell on Chikahito that caused him to move to Kyoto.*

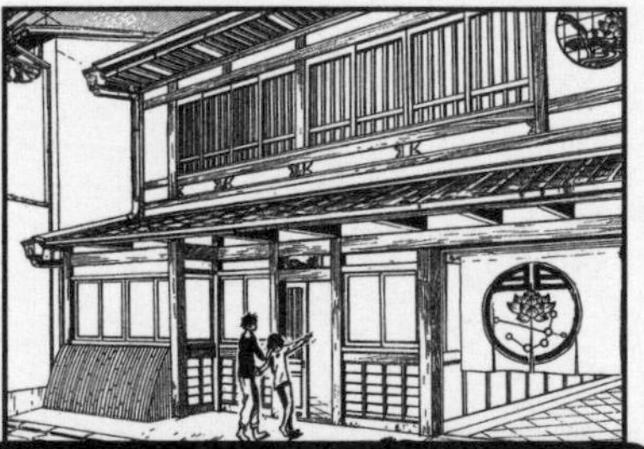

URA-SHICHIKEN

*A district located near the Kitano Tenmangu Shrine that is home to a group of people—also called the Ura-shichiken, followers of the Toyotomi clan—who have paranormal talents (*inou*) and are enlisted to protect the local area and Toyotomi interests.*

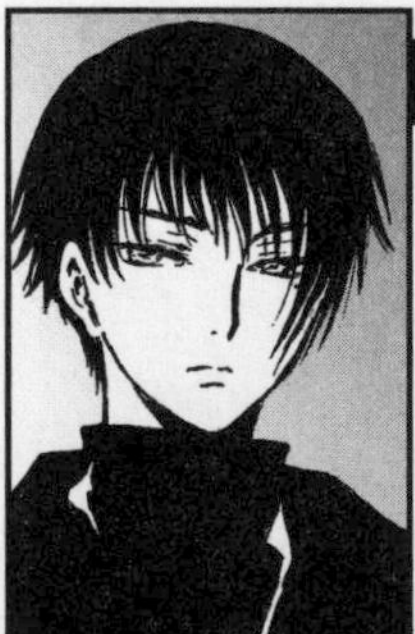

TACHIBANA

A member of the Ura-shichiken who acts as the controller of all light-based elemental weapons. He is always very protective of Hana and brusque toward Chikahito.

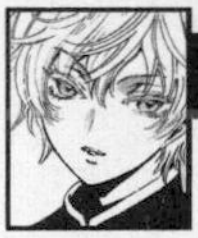

IEMITSU TOKUGAWA

The Tokugawa leader currently holding the most power in the clan. He is in a blood contract with the oni Mitsuha, who eats humans.

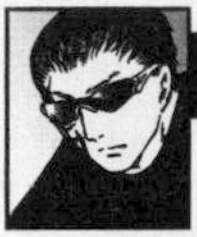

TENKAI

A vassal of Iemitsu who can mystically envelop areas at will.

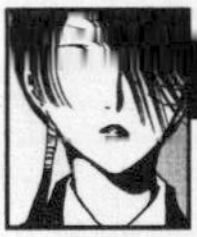

MITSUYOSHI YAGYUU

A vassal of Iemitsu who is usually referred to as Jyubee.

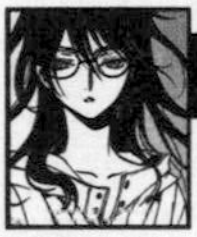

YUKIMURA SANADA

A nursery-school teacher who can merge with the oni Engetsu in order to wield its full strength.

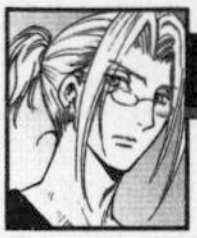

SASUKE SARUTOBI

A member of Yukimura Sanada's Ten Braves. Along with Saizou, he is a loyal vassal of Sanada's.

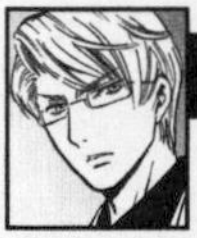

SAIZOU KIRIGAKURE

Another member of Sanada's Ten Braves, he has vowed unwavering loyalty to Sanada.

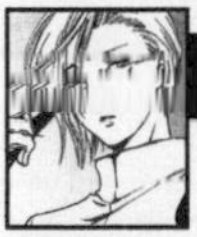

MITSUHIDE AKECHI

A man who is after the powerful oni called Dairokutenmaoh. Mitsuhide's oni is named Enka.

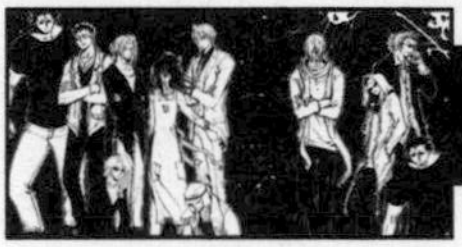

SANADA'S TEN BRAVES

Ten warriors who act on Yukimura Sanada's orders.

ONI *Beings who honor blood contracts with humans in order to grant them great strength and special powers. A blood contract with an oni can only be inherited by the descendant with the strongest blood relationship to the original contract holder.*

STORY SO FAR

While on a sightseeing trip to Kyoto, high-school student Chikahito Takamoto stumbles onto a paranormal battle taking place in a dark, strangely enveloped space. The fight involves Hana, Sakura, and Tachibana—three members of the Ura-shichiken. Three months later, Chikahito finds himself transferring to Kyoto and reuniting with the group. After being defeated by Sakura in a desperate battle, Yukimura Sanada becomes a Toyotomi ally. On the first day at his new school, Chikahito makes friends with a student, but in reality his new friend is the reincarnation of Toyotomi enemy Iemitsu Tokugawa. Almost as bad, Mitsuhide Akechi is a teacher at the school. On his way home, Chikahito meets Masamune Date and they are confronted by the reincarnation of Gracia Hosokawa, leading to a vicious battle of oni. Masamune defeats Gracia and gains control of her oni, Nigemizu. Chikahito and Hana later meet up with Sakura to report the day's events . . . but what is that tiger-looking thing that suddenly appears?!

CHAPTER THIRTEEN: THE CAPTURED PRINCESS

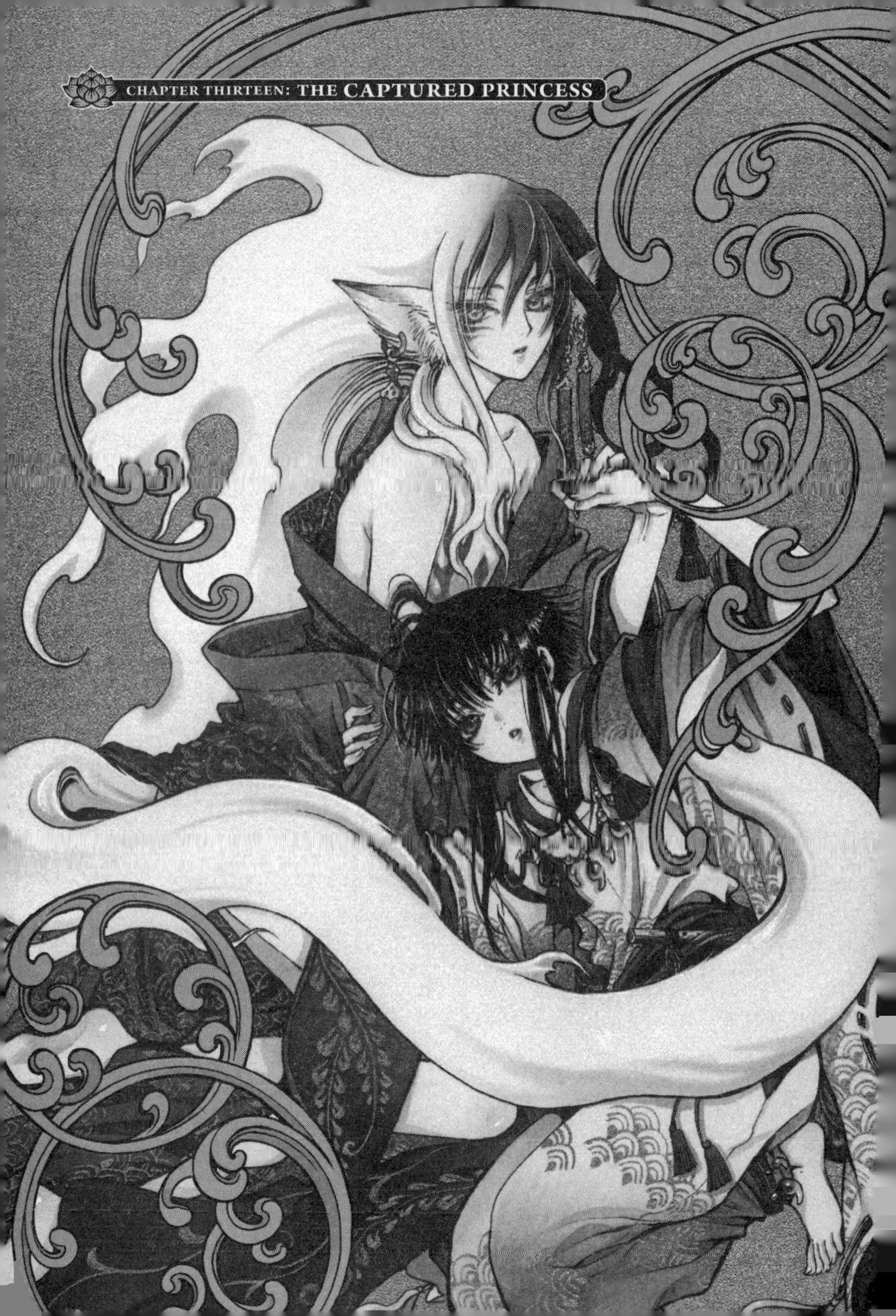

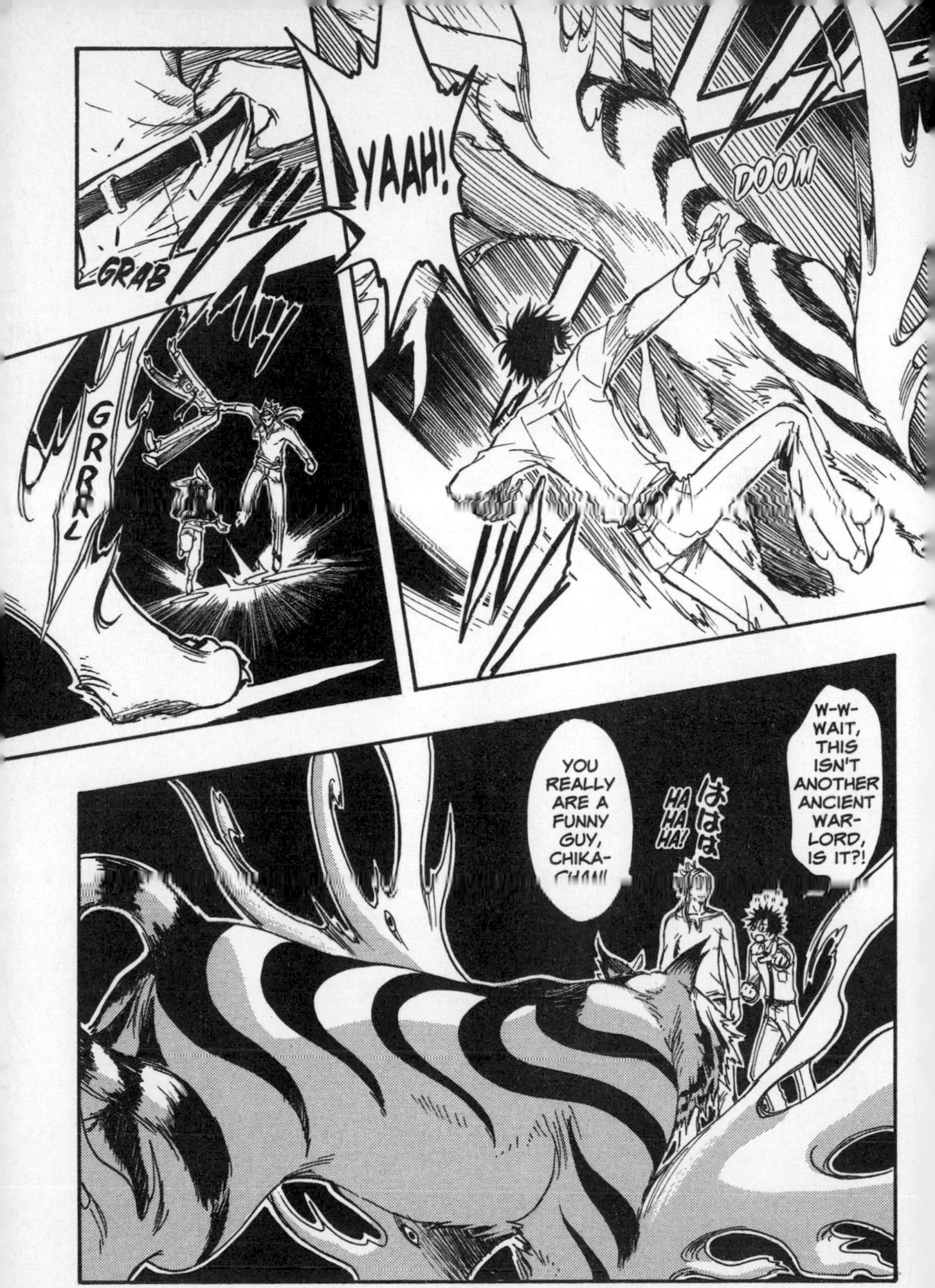
YAAH!
DOOM
GRAB
GRRRRL
W-W-WAIT, THIS ISN'T ANOTHER ANCIENT WAR-LORD, IS IT?!
はは
HA HA HA!
YOU REALLY ARE A FUNNY GUY, CHIKA-CHAN!

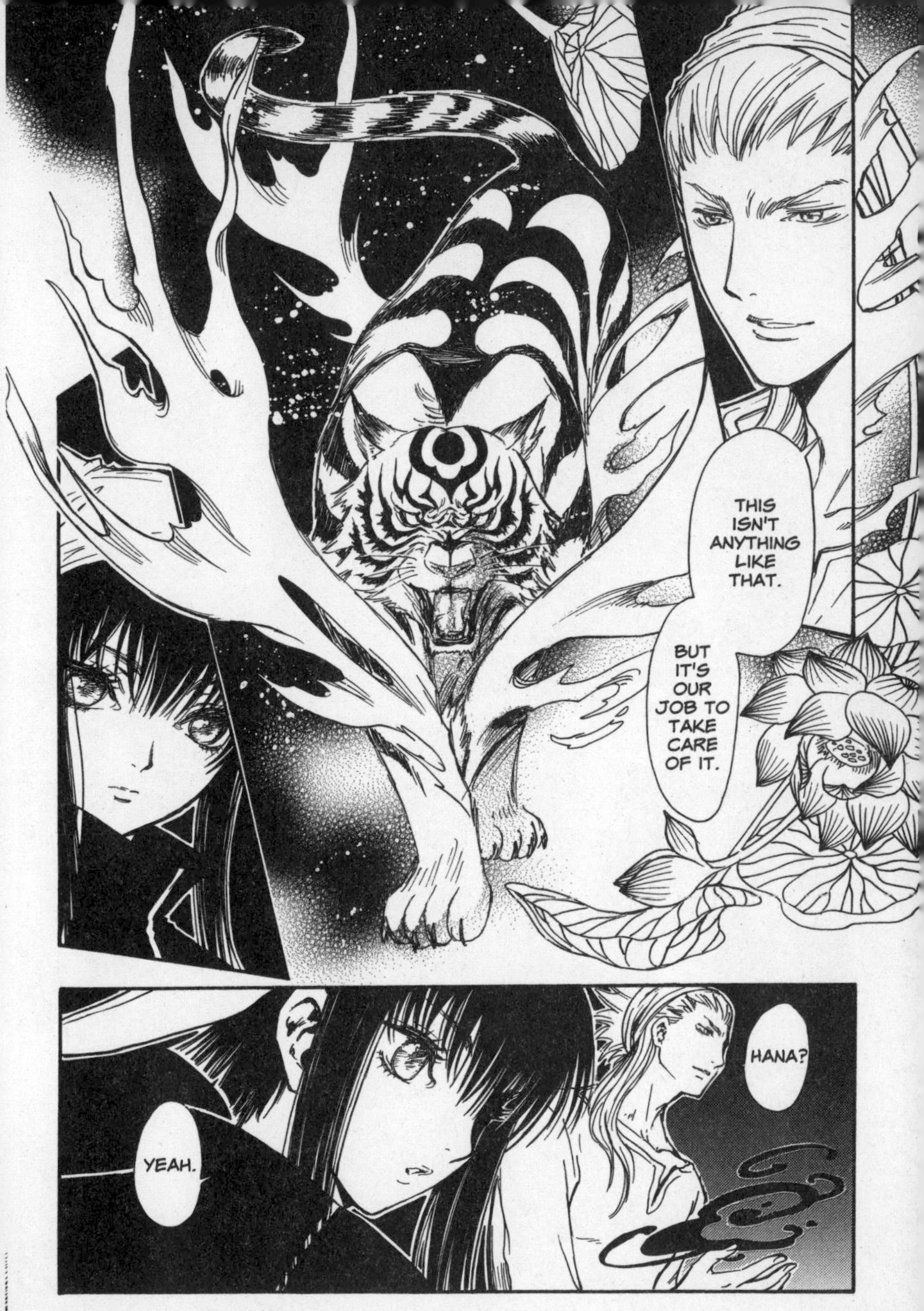
THIS ISN'T ANYTHING LIKE THAT.
BUT IT'S OUR JOB TO TAKE CARE OF IT.
HANA?
YEAH.

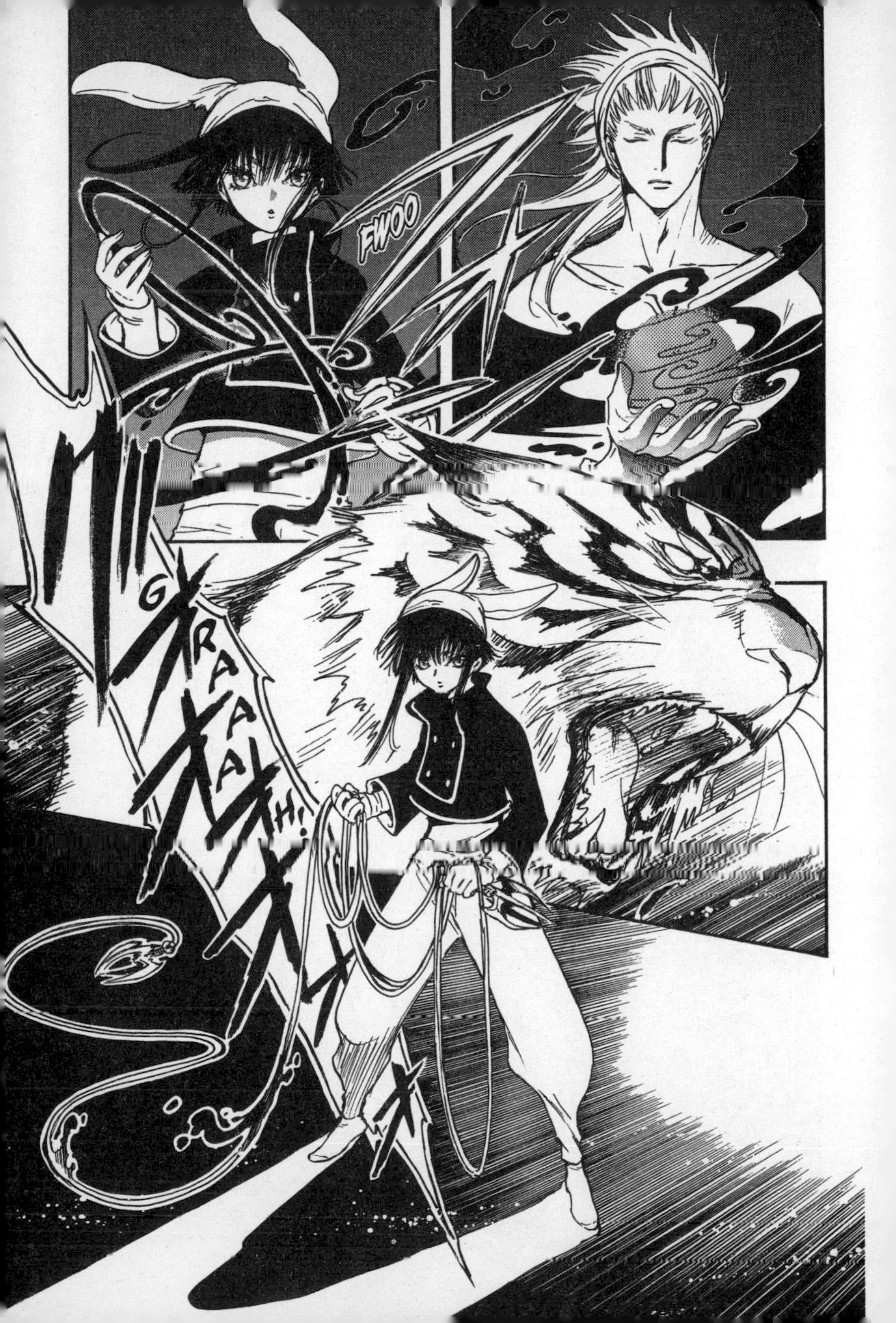
FWOO
GRAAAAH!

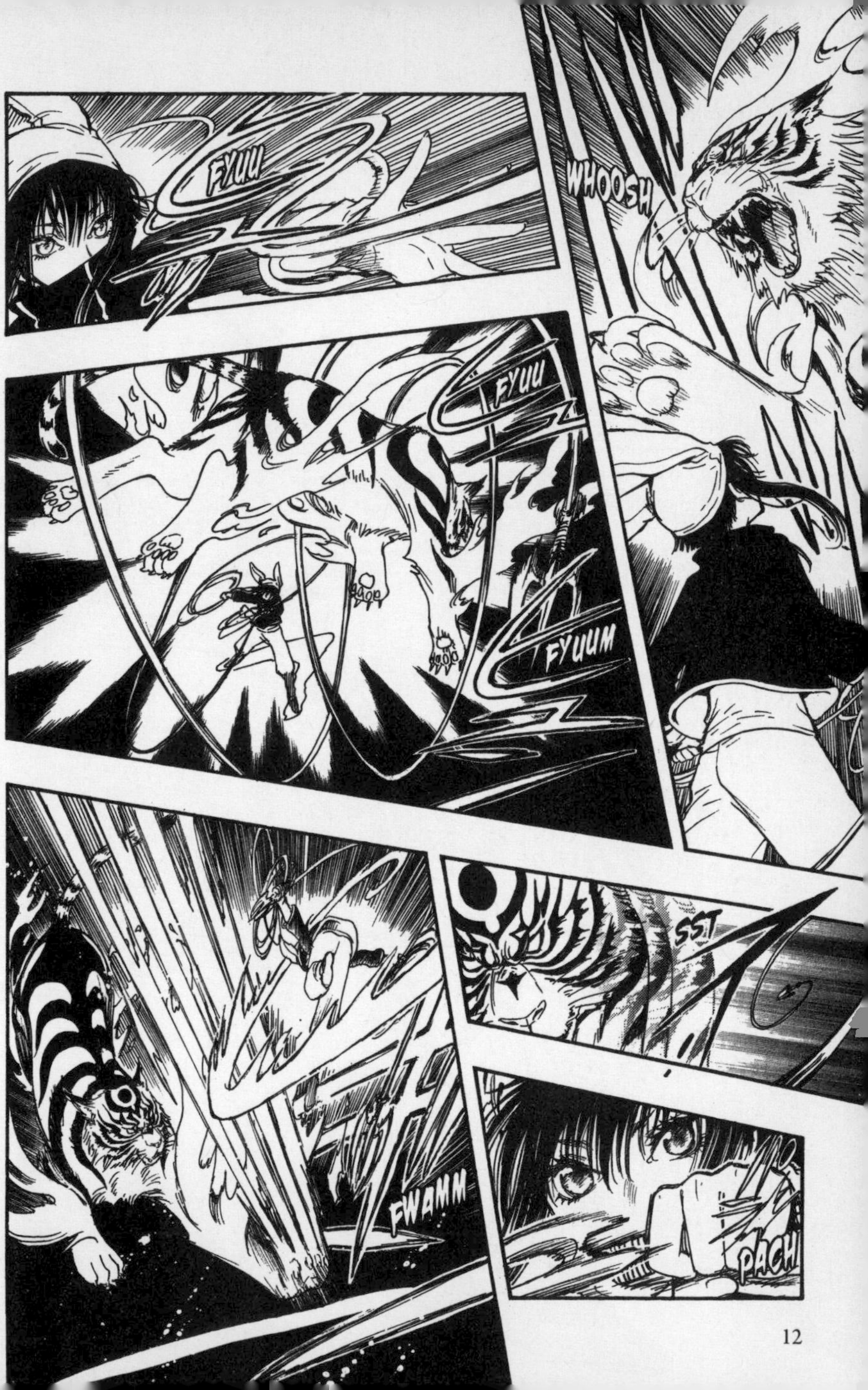
WHOOSH
FYUU
FYUU
FYUUM
SST
PACH
FWAMM

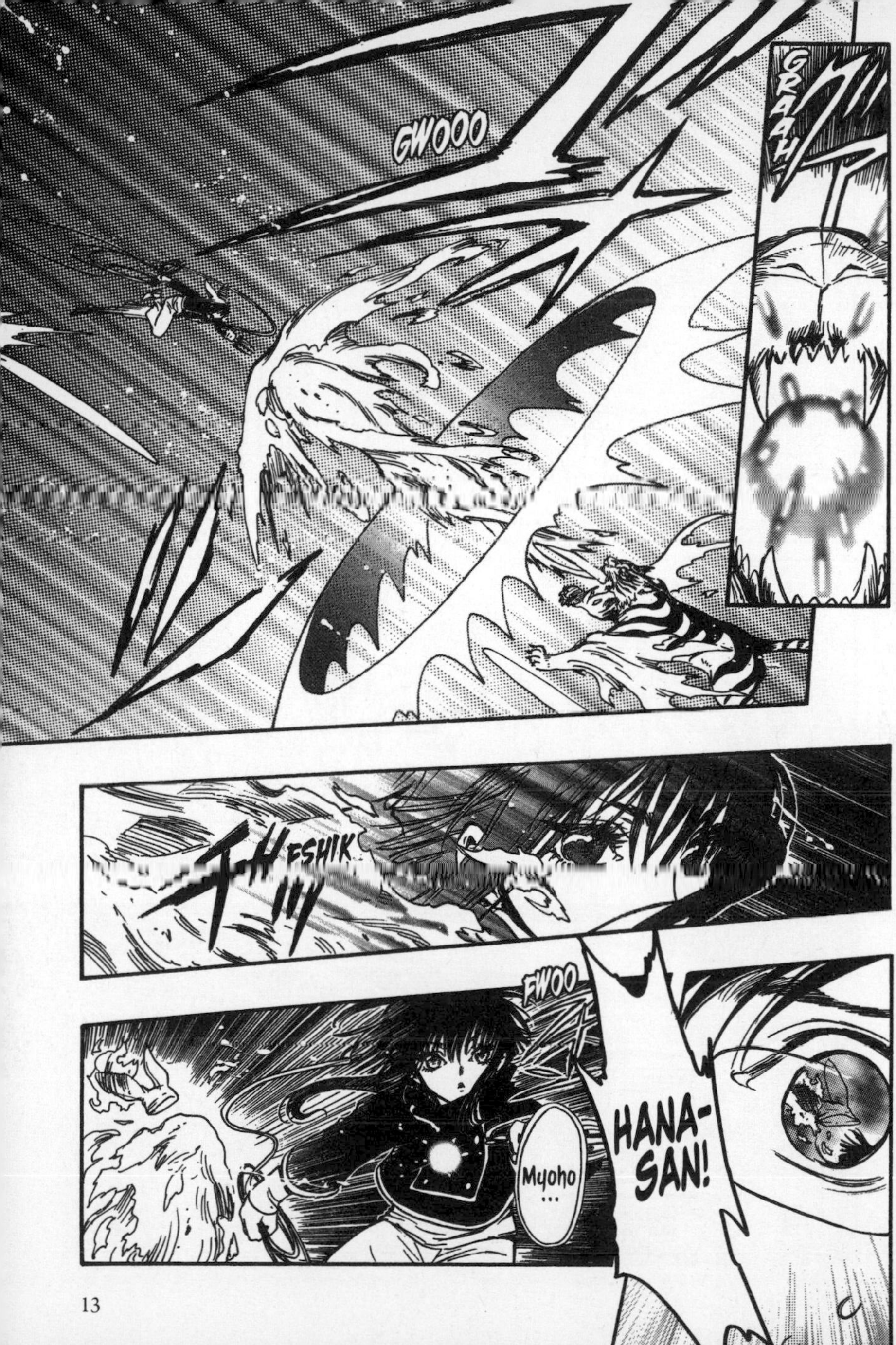
GRAAH
GWOOO
HESHIK
HANA-SAN!
FWOO
Myoho...

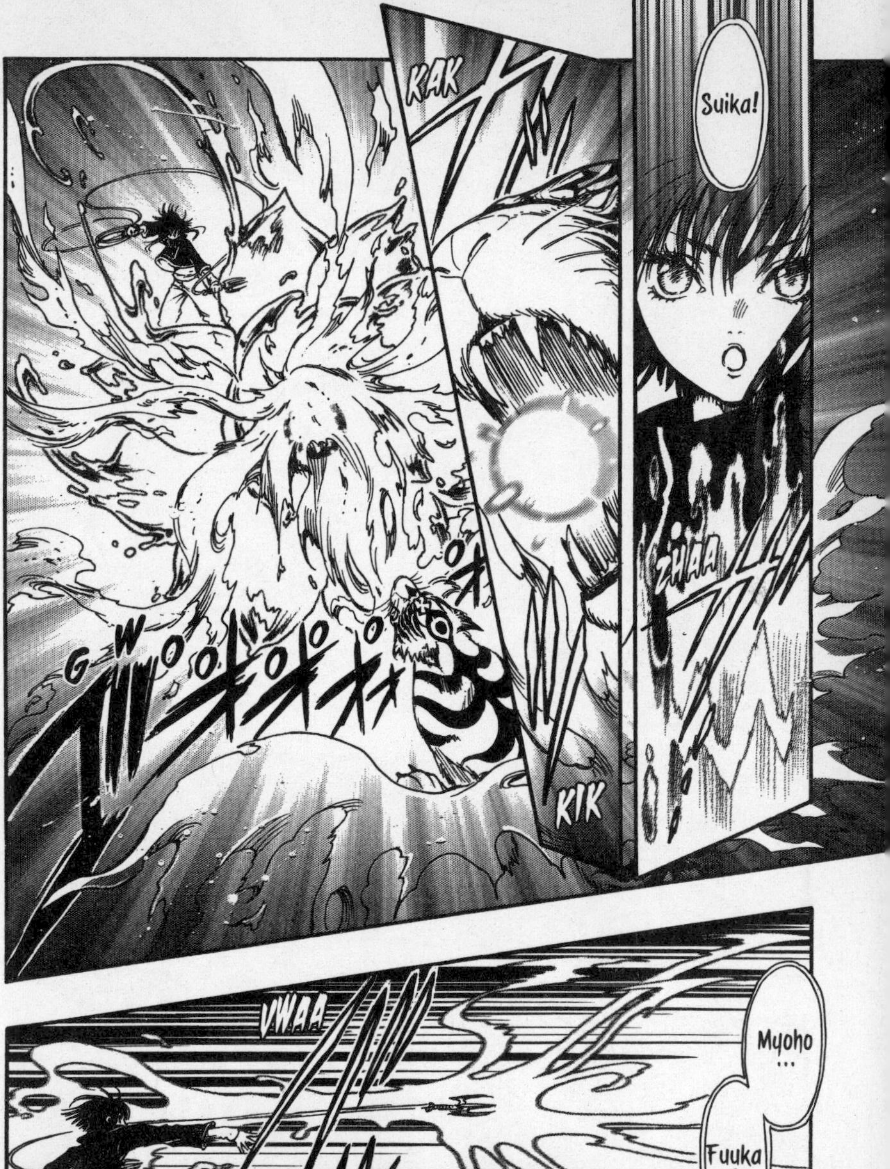
Suika!
ZHAA
KAK
KIK
GWOOOOOOO
Myoho...
Fuuka!
VWAA

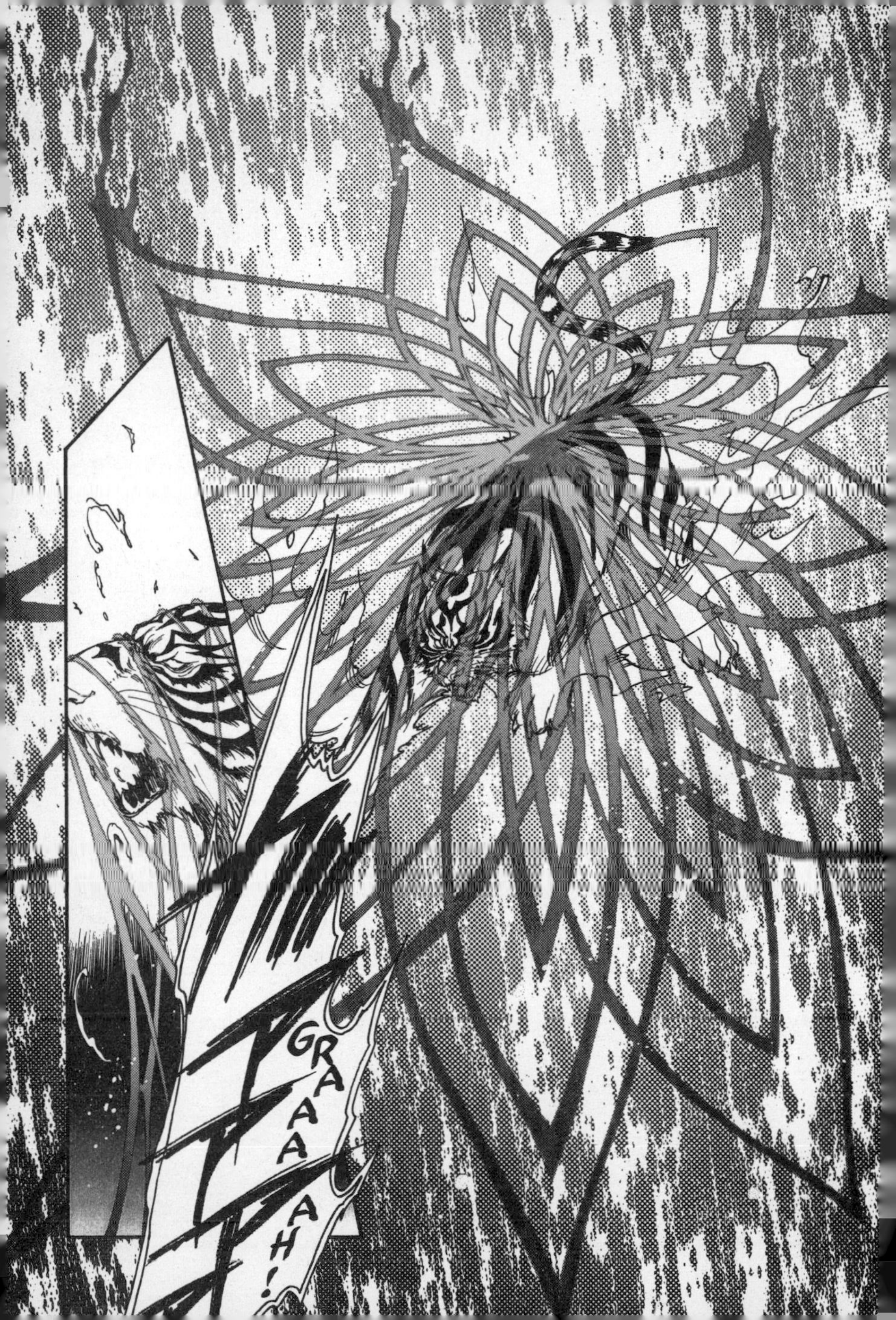
GRAAAAH!!

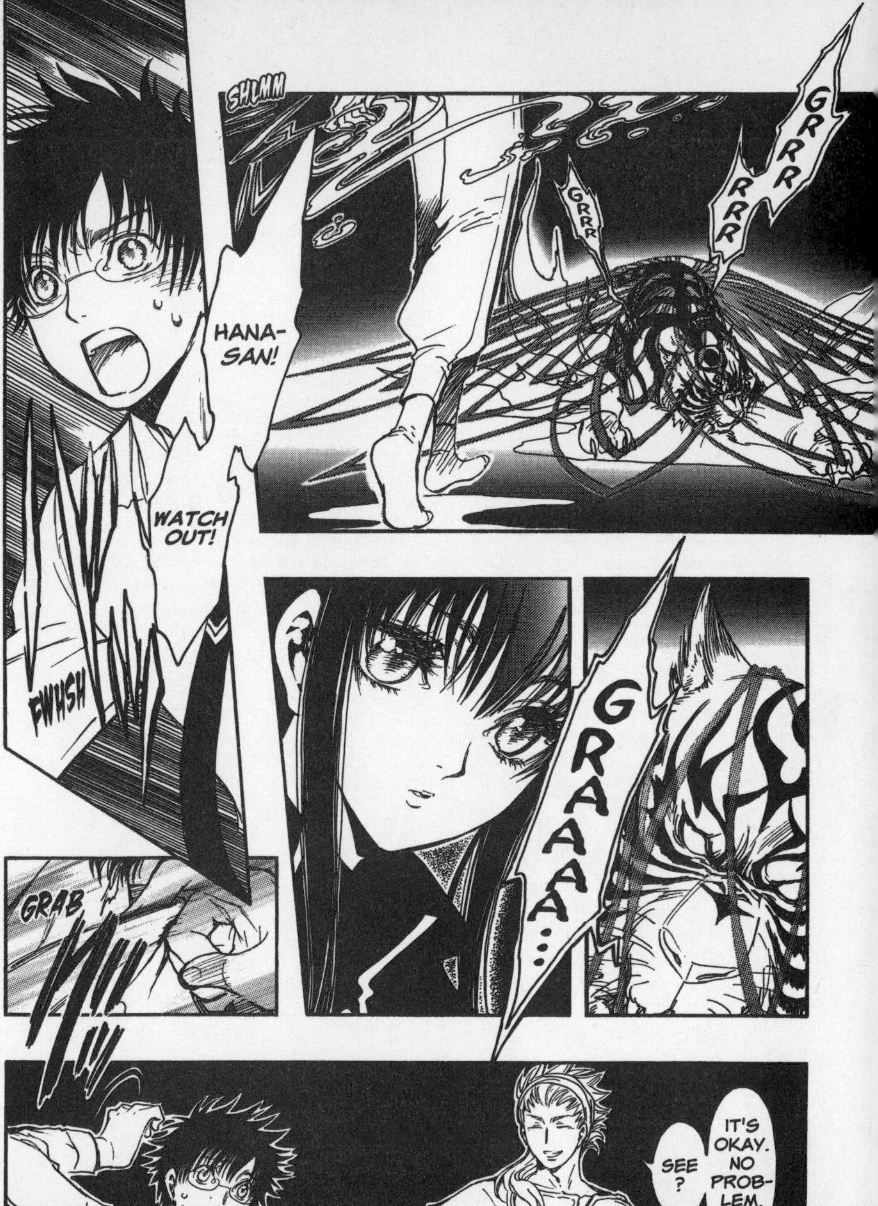
SHLMM
GRRR
GRRRRRR
GRAAAA...
HANA-SAN!
WATCH OUT!
FWHSH
GRAB
IT'S OKAY. NO PROBLEM.
SEE?

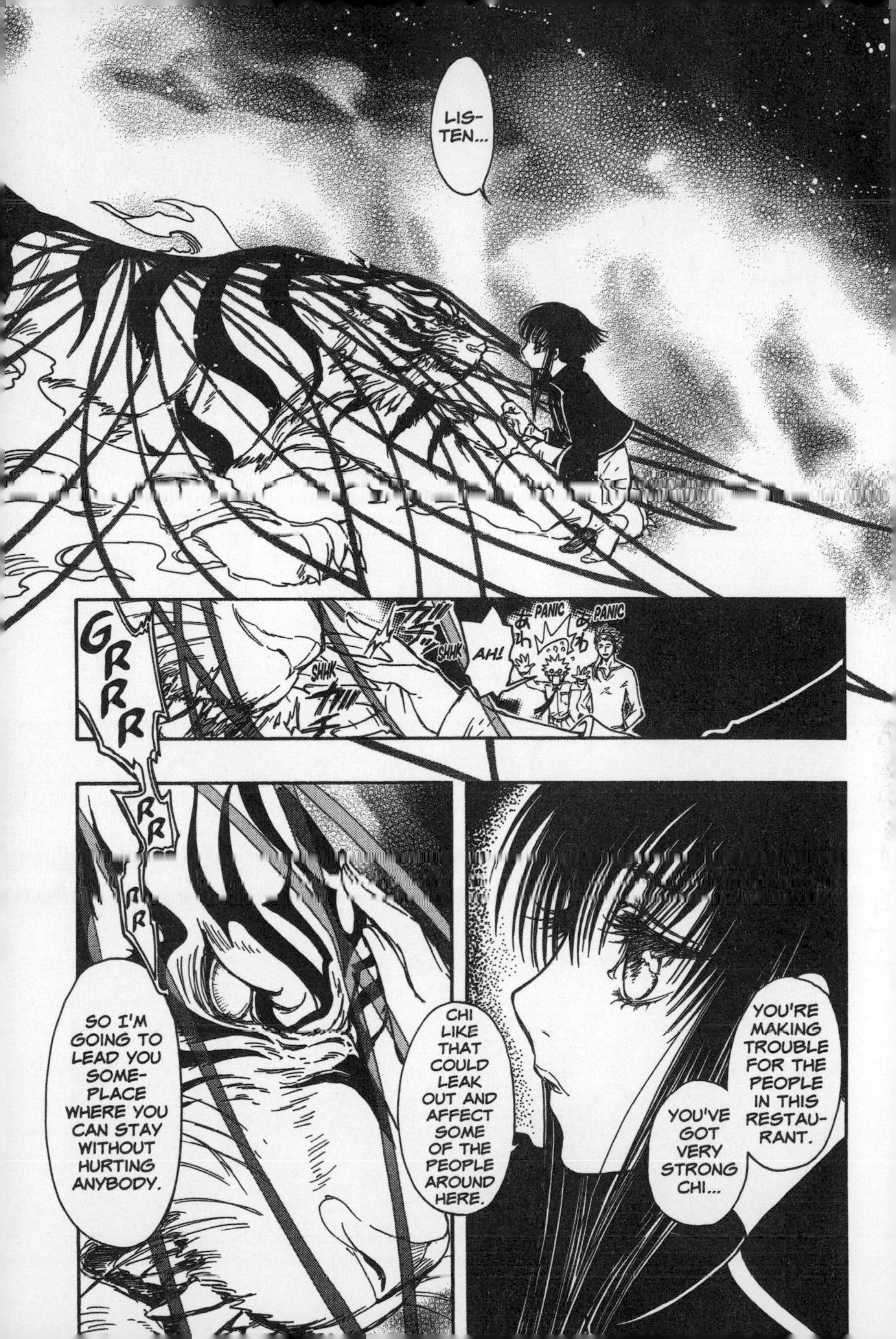

LIS-TEN...
PANIC
PANIC
AH!
SHHK
SHHK
GRRRRRRRR
YOU'RE MAKING TROUBLE FOR THE PEOPLE IN THIS RESTAU-RANT.
YOU'VE GOT VERY STRONG CHI...
CHI LIKE THAT COULD LEAK OUT AND AFFECT SOME OF THE PEOPLE AROUND HERE.
SO I'M GOING TO LEAD YOU SOME-PLACE WHERE YOU CAN STAY WITHOUT HURTING ANYBODY.

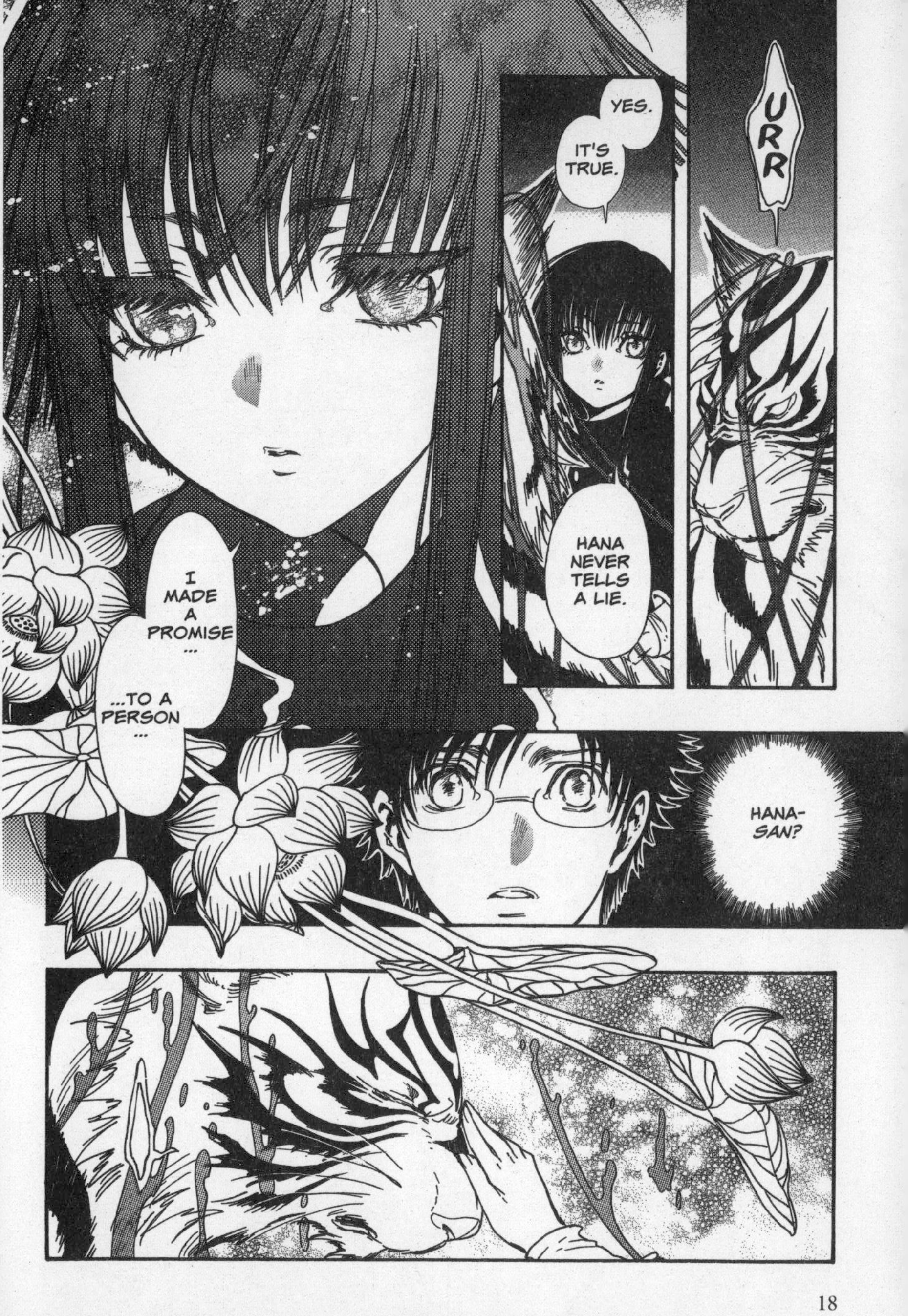
URR
YES.
IT'S TRUE.
HANA NEVER TELLS A LIE.
I MADE A PROMISE ...
...TO A PERSON ...
HANA-SAN?

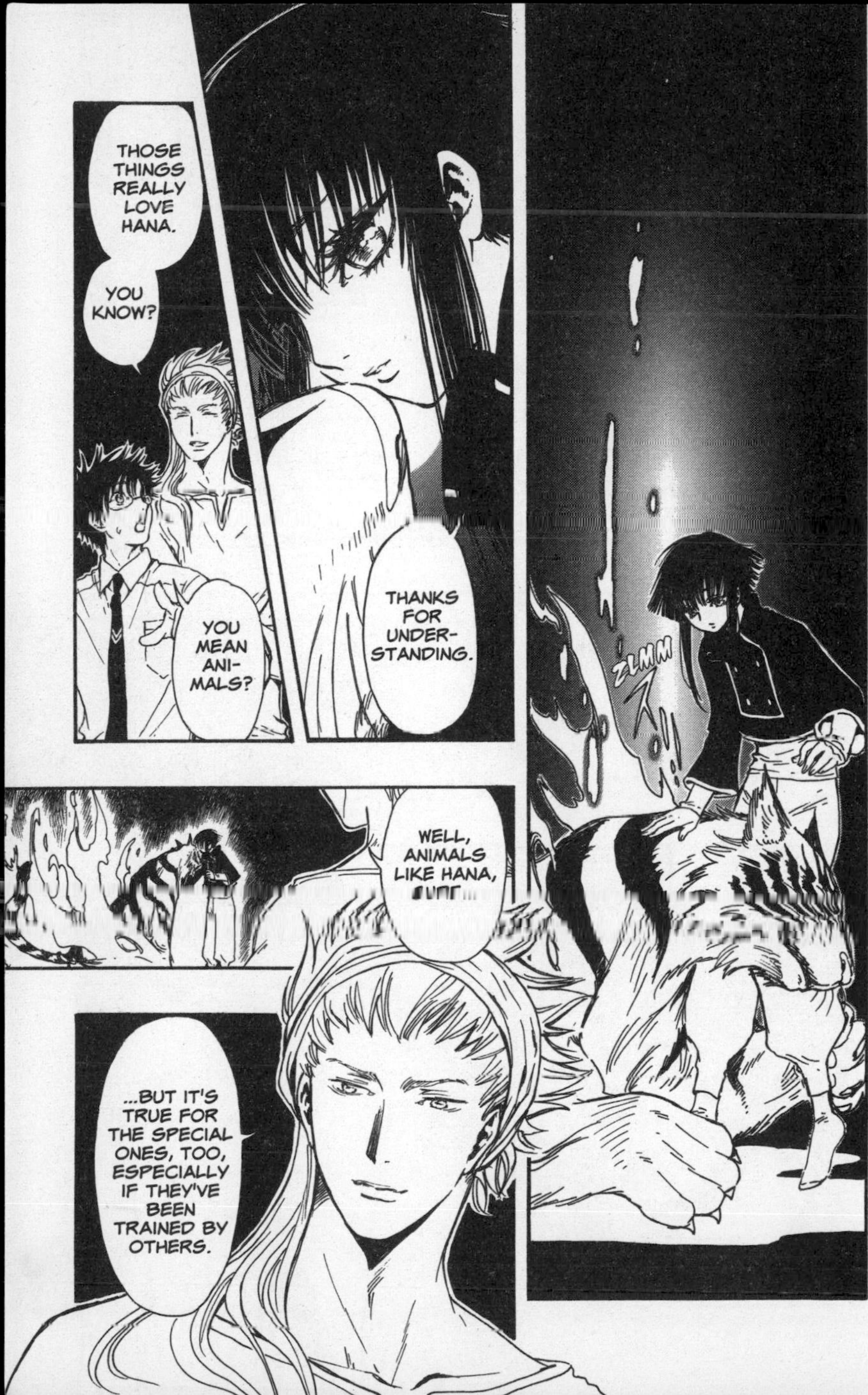
ZLMM
THANKS FOR UNDER-STANDING.
THOSE THINGS REALLY LOVE HANA.
YOU KNOW?
YOU MEAN ANI-MALS?
WELL, ANIMALS LIKE HANA,
...BUT IT'S TRUE FOR THE SPECIAL ONES, TOO, ESPECIALLY IF THEY'VE BEEN TRAINED BY OTHERS.

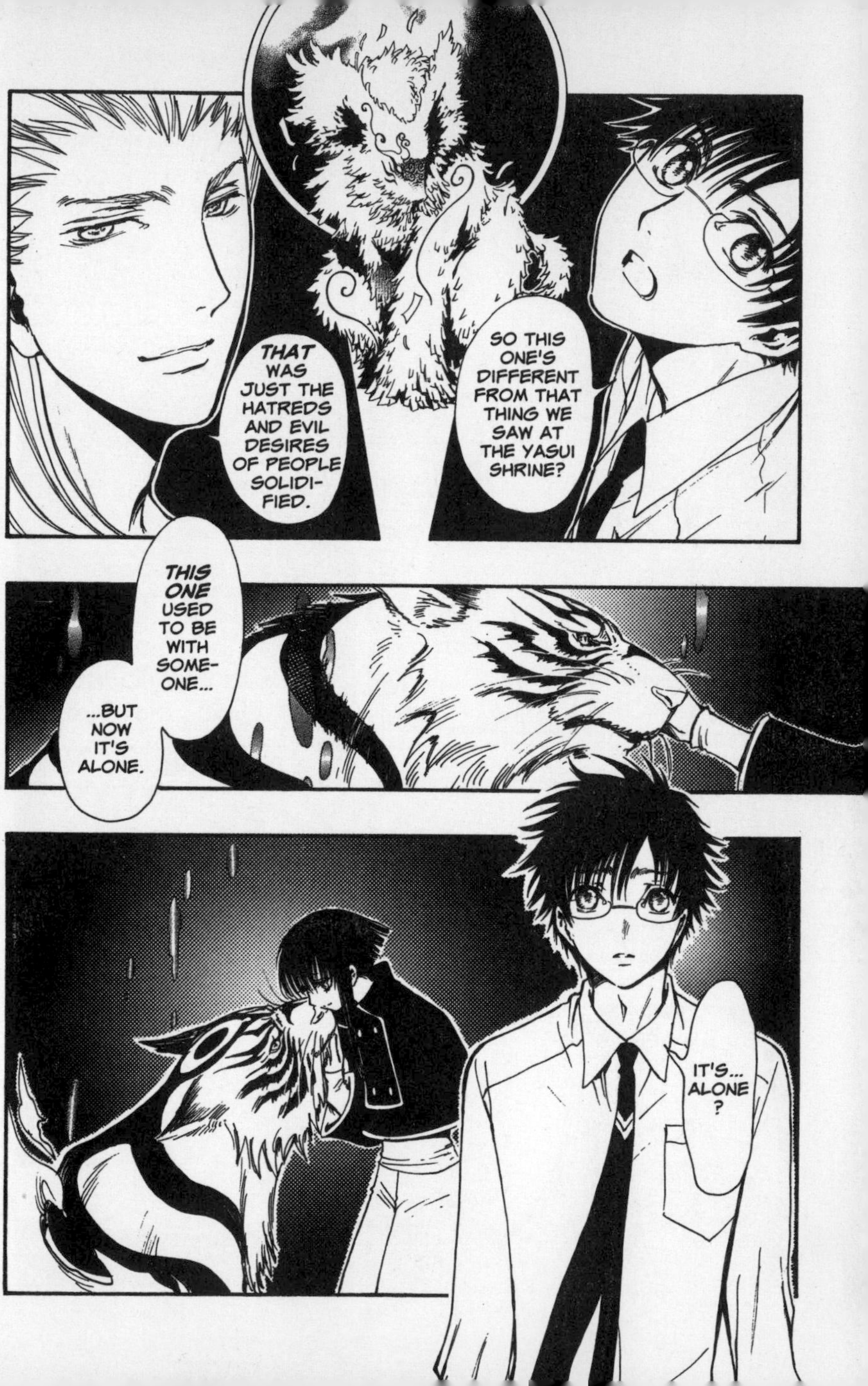
SO THIS ONE'S DIFFERENT FROM THAT THING WE SAW AT THE YASUI SHRINE?
THAT WAS JUST THE HATREDS AND EVIL DESIRES OF PEOPLE SOLIDIFIED.
THIS ONE USED TO BE WITH SOMEONE...
...BUT NOW IT'S ALONE.
IT'S... ALONE?

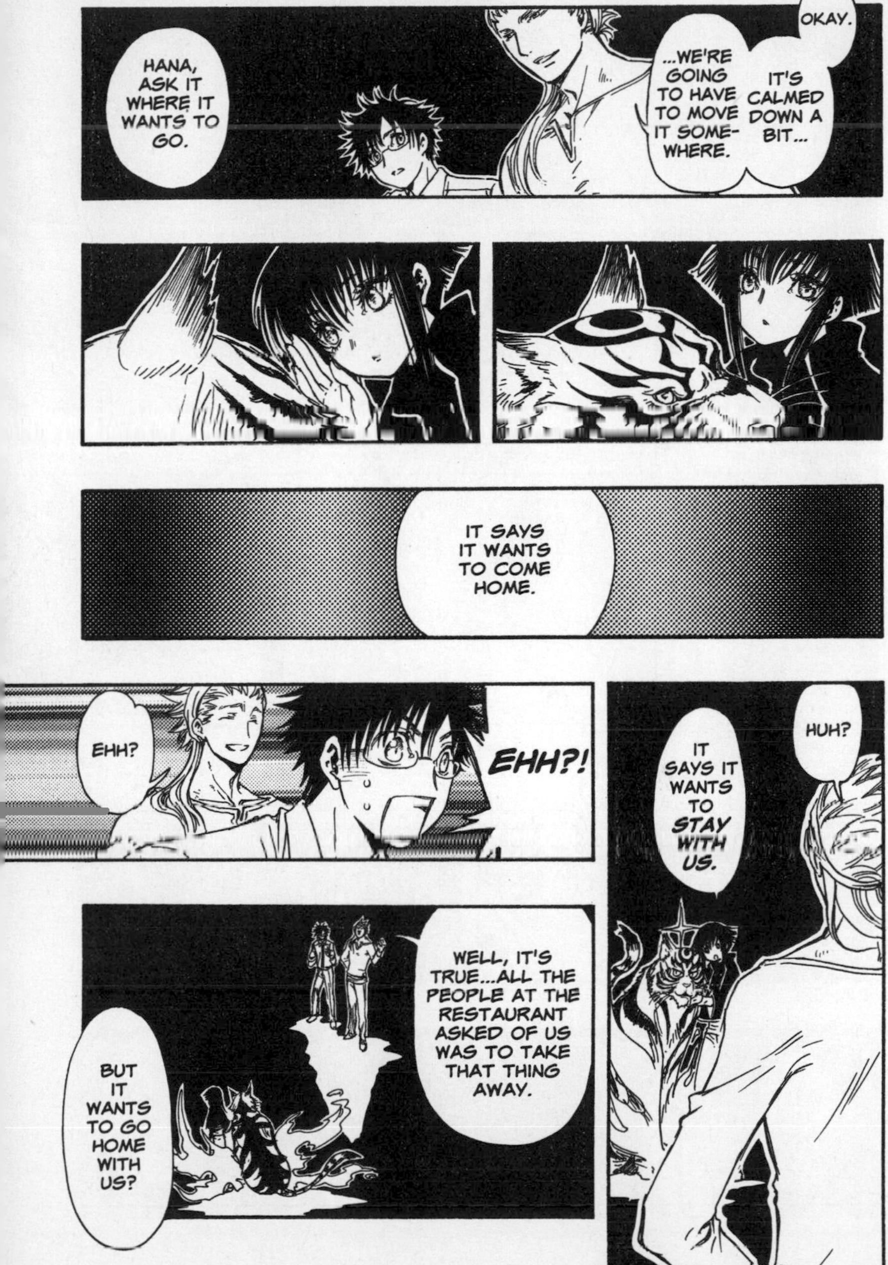
OKAY.
IT'S CALMED DOWN A BIT...
...WE'RE GOING TO HAVE TO MOVE IT SOME-WHERE.
HANA, ASK IT WHERE IT WANTS TO GO.
IT SAYS IT WANTS TO COME HOME.
HUH?
IT SAYS IT WANTS TO *STAY WITH US.*
EHH?!
EHH?
WELL, IT'S TRUE...ALL THE PEOPLE AT THE RESTAURANT ASKED OF US WAS TO TAKE THAT THING AWAY.
BUT IT WANTS TO GO HOME WITH US?

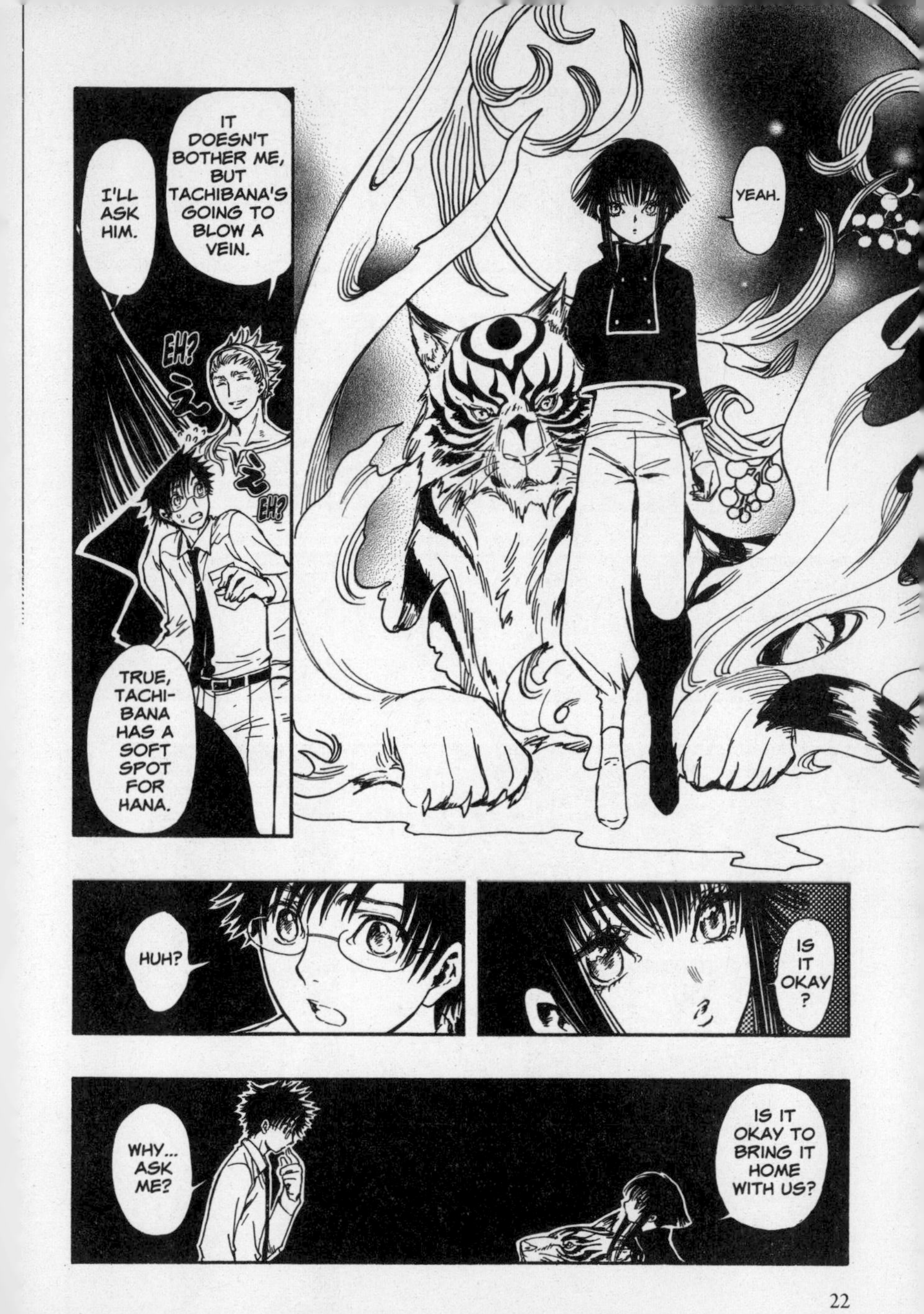
YEAH.
IT DOESN'T BOTHER ME, BUT TACHIBANA'S GOING TO BLOW A VEIN.
I'LL ASK HIM.
EH?
EH?
TRUE, TACHIBANA HAS A SOFT SPOT FOR HANA.
IS IT OKAY?
HUH?
IS IT OKAY TO BRING IT HOME WITH US?
WHY... ASK ME?

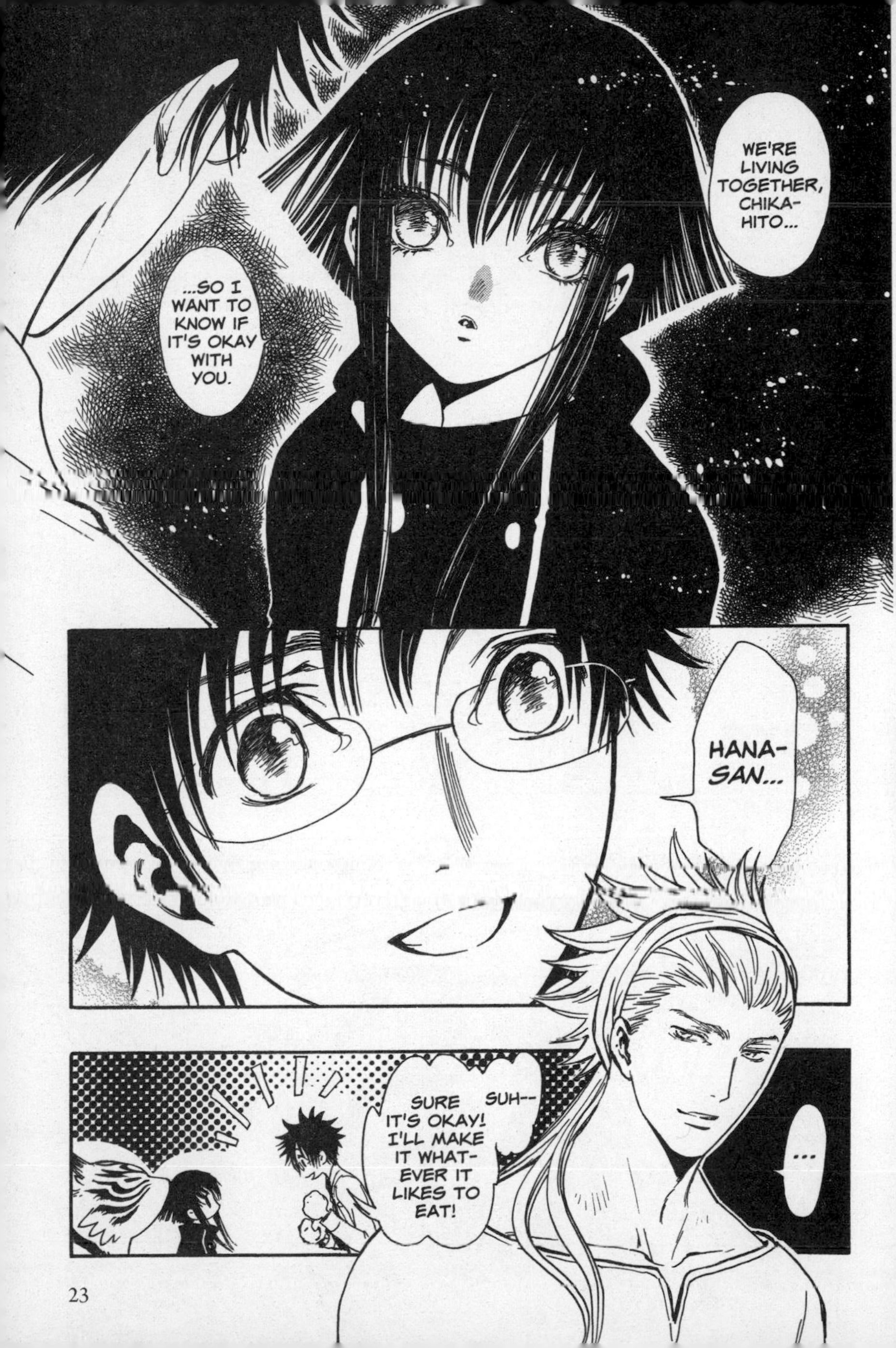
WE'RE LIVING TOGETHER, CHIKA-HITO...
...SO I WANT TO KNOW IF IT'S OKAY WITH YOU.
HANA-SAN...
...
SUH--
SURE IT'S OKAY! I'LL MAKE IT WHAT-EVER IT LIKES TO EAT!

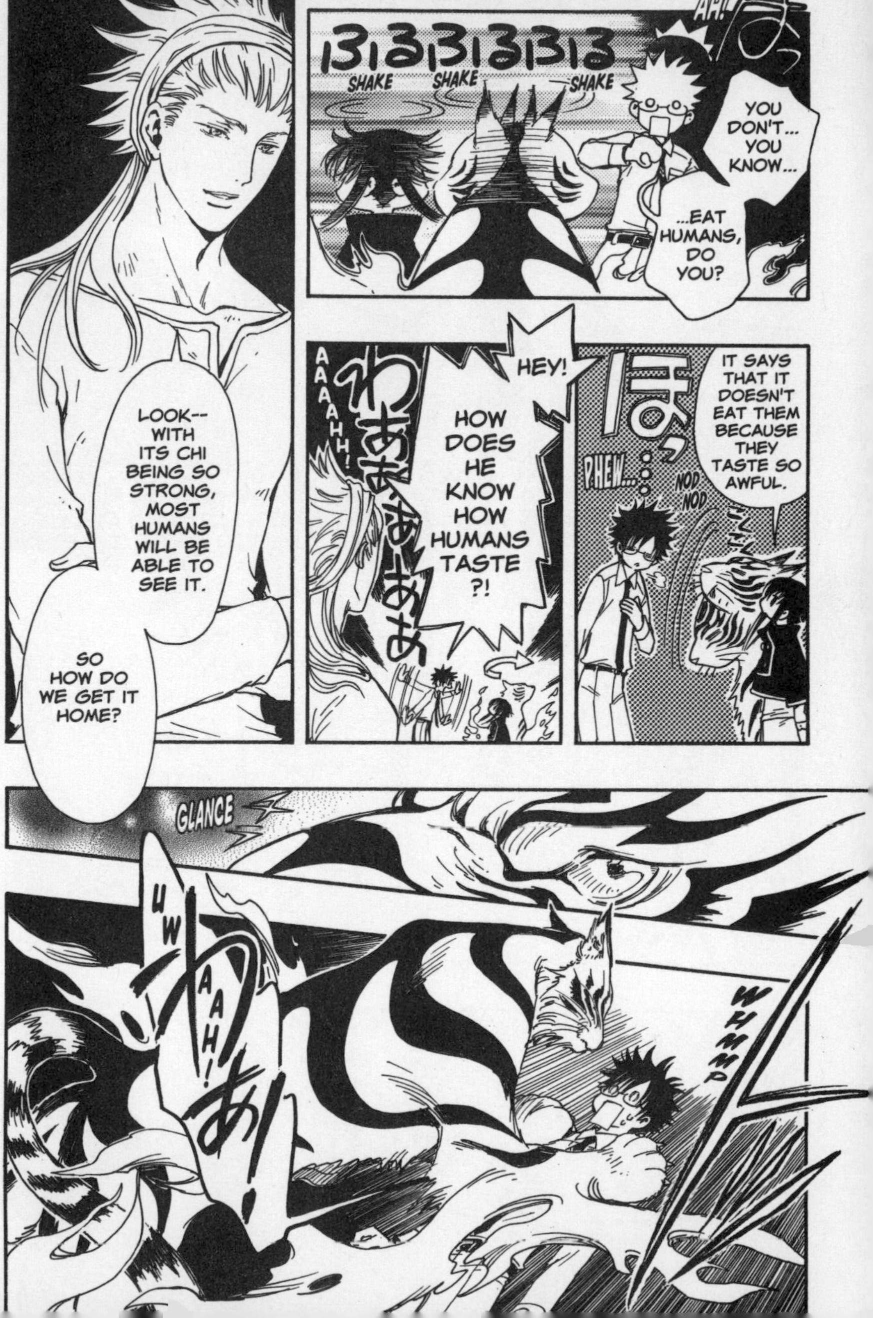
AH! はっ
YOU DON'T... YOU KNOW...
...EAT HUMANS, DO YOU?
ふるふるふるふるふるふる
SHAKE SHAKE SHAKE
IT SAYS THAT IT DOESN'T EAT THEM BECAUSE THEY TASTE SO AWFUL.
ほっ
PHEW...
NOD NOD
HEY!
HOW DOES HE KNOW HOW HUMANS TASTE ?!
わあああああ
AAAAAHH!
LOOK-- WITH ITS CHI BEING SO STRONG, MOST HUMANS WILL BE ABLE TO SEE IT.
SO HOW DO WE GET IT HOME?
GLANCE
WHUMMP
わあ!
UWAAAH!

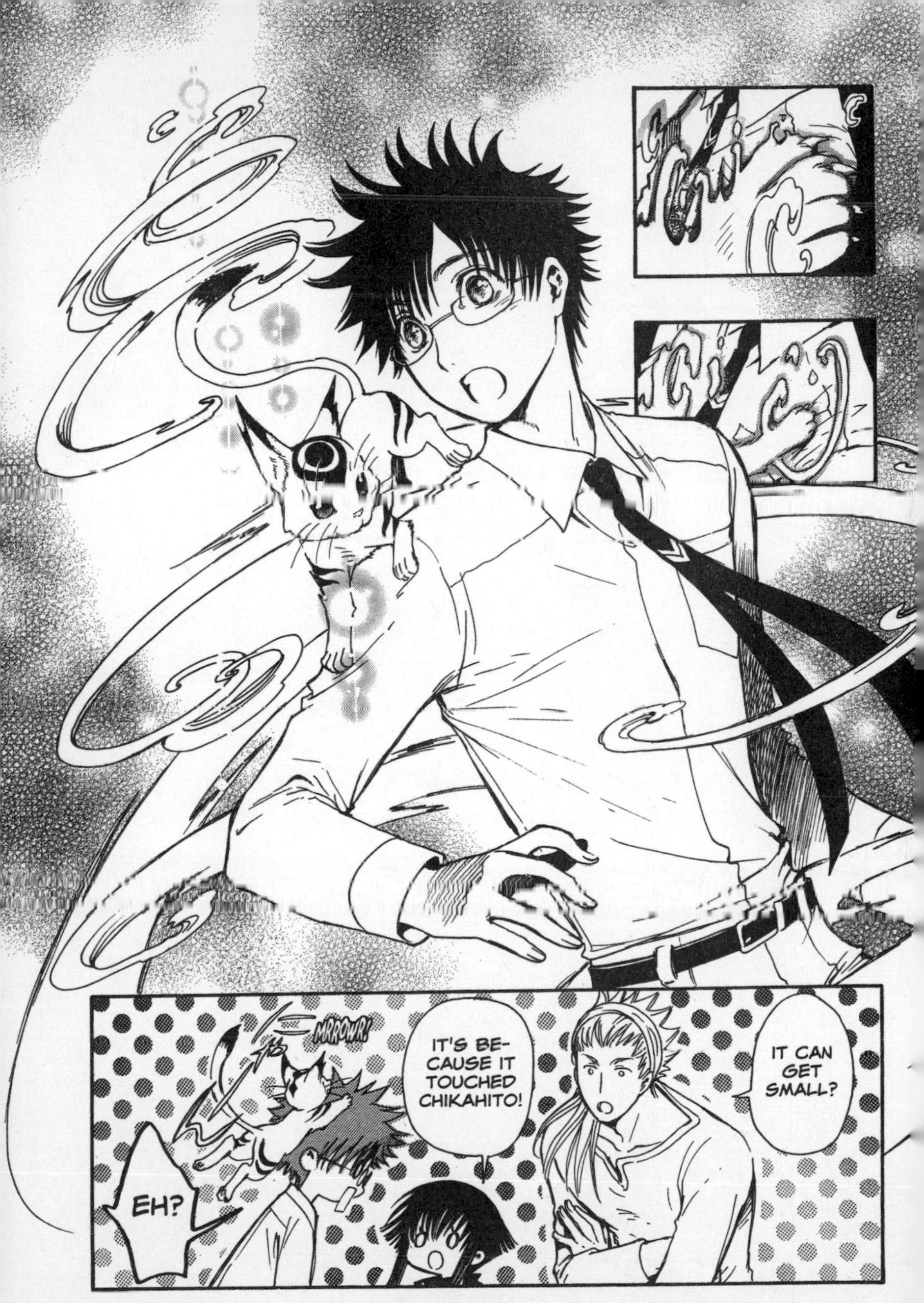
IT CAN GET SMALL?
IT'S BE-CAUSE IT TOUCHED CHIKAHITO!
MRROWR!
EH?

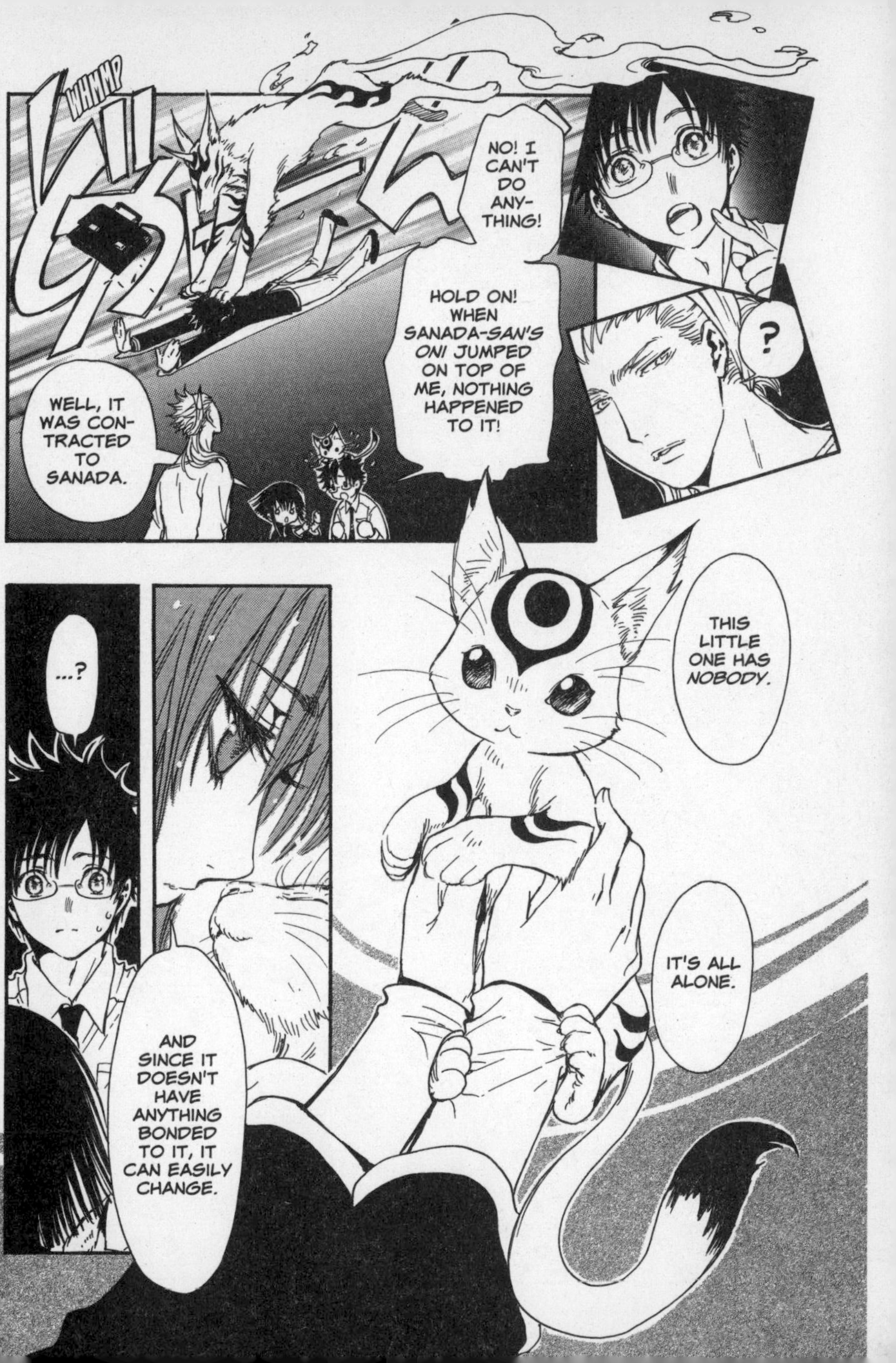
NO! I CAN'T DO ANY-THING!
HOLD ON! WHEN SANADA-SAN'S *ONI* JUMPED ON TOP OF ME, NOTHING HAPPENED TO IT!
?
WHMMP
WELL, IT WAS CON-TRACTED TO SANADA.
THIS LITTLE ONE HAS *NOBODY*.
IT'S ALL ALONE.
AND SINCE IT DOESN'T HAVE ANYTHING BONDED TO IT, IT CAN EASILY CHANGE.
...?

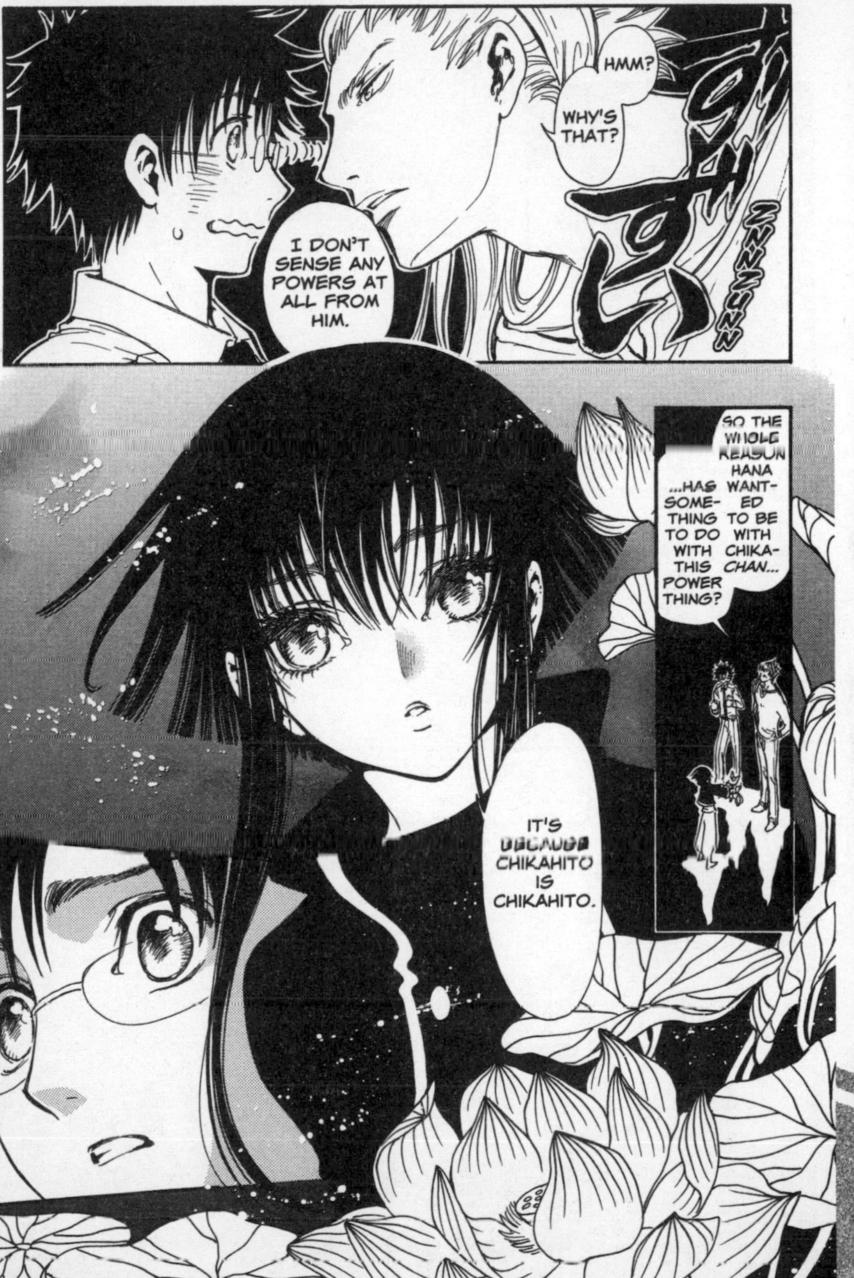
HMM?
WHY'S THAT?
ZUNNZUNN
I DON'T SENSE ANY POWERS AT ALL FROM HIM.
SO THE WHOLE REASON HANA WANTED TO BE WITH CHIKA-CHAN...
...HAS SOMETHING TO DO WITH THIS POWER THING?
IT'S BECAUSE CHIKAHITO IS CHIKAHITO.

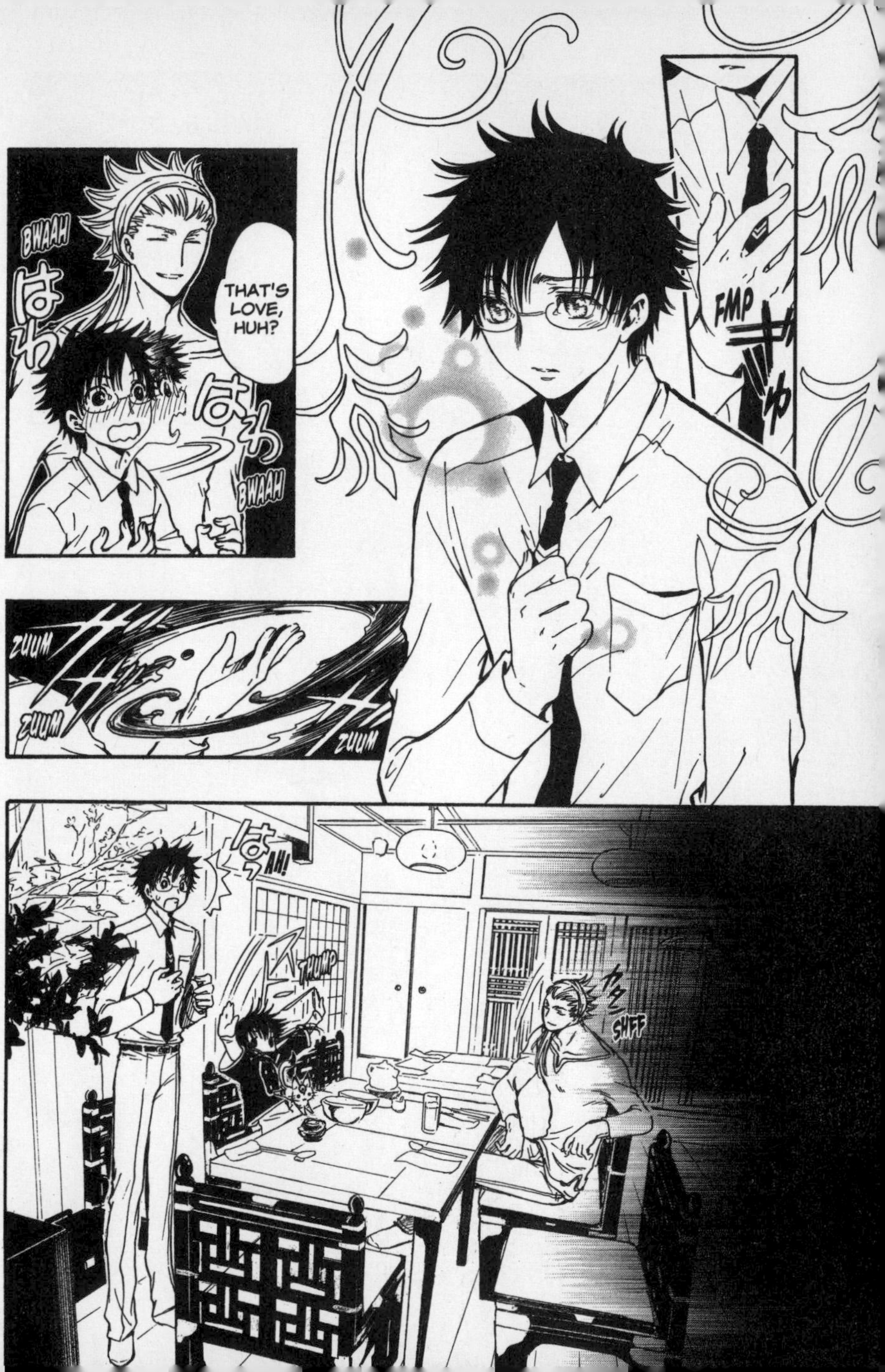
FMP
ぎゅ
THAT'S LOVE, HUH?
BWAAH
はわ
はわ
BWAAH
ZUUM
ZUUM
ZUUM
はっ
AH!
THUMP
カタ
SHFF

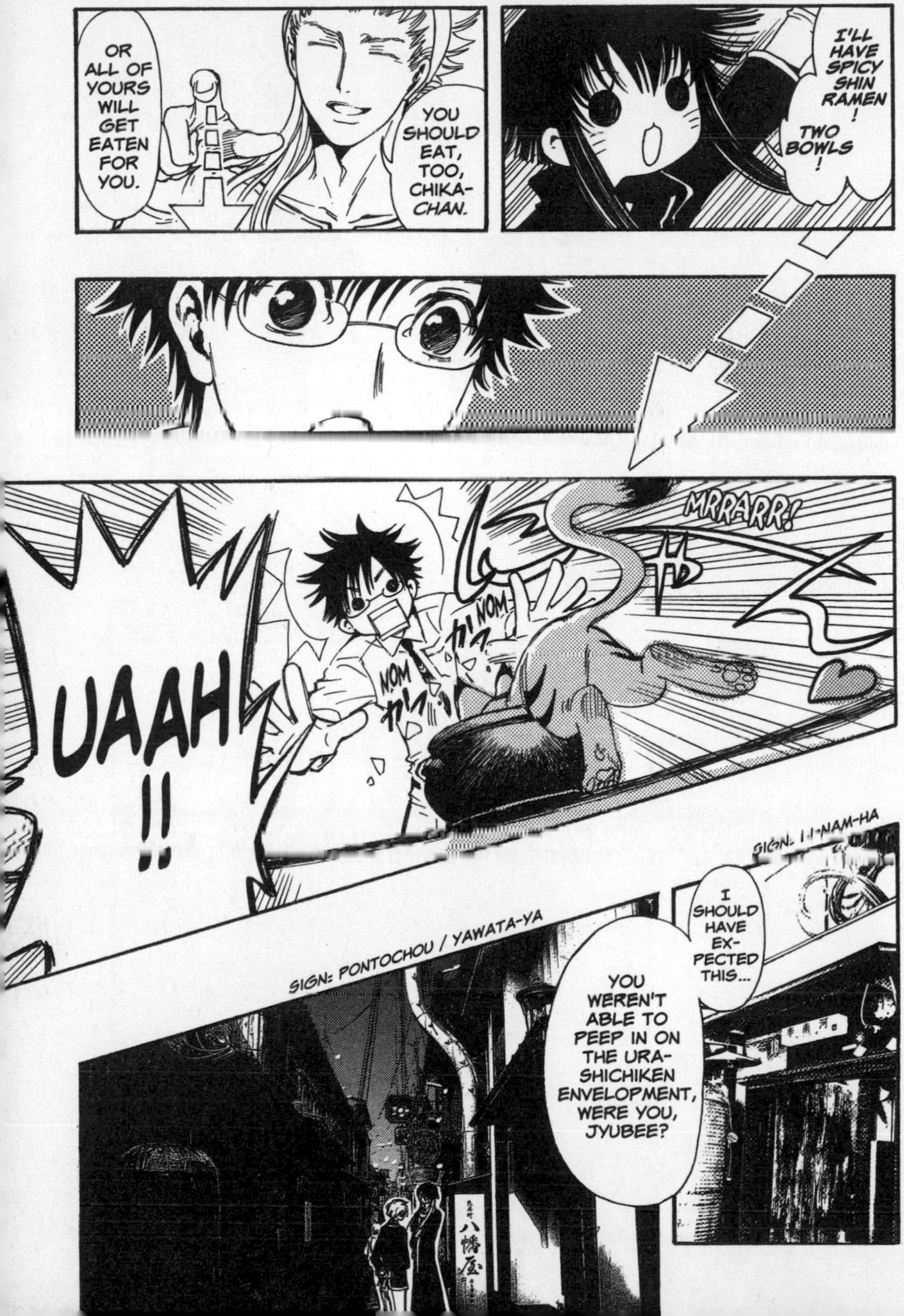
I'LL HAVE SPICY SHIN RAMEN! TWO BOWLS!
YOU SHOULD EAT, TOO, CHIKA-CHAN.
OR ALL OF YOURS WILL GET EATEN FOR YOU.
MRRARR!
NOM NOM
UAAH!!
SIGN: LI-NAM-HA
I SHOULD HAVE EXPECTED THIS...
YOU WEREN'T ABLE TO PEEP IN ON THE URA-SHICHIKEN ENVELOPMENT, WERE YOU, JYUBEE?
SIGN: PONTOCHOU / YAWATA-YA

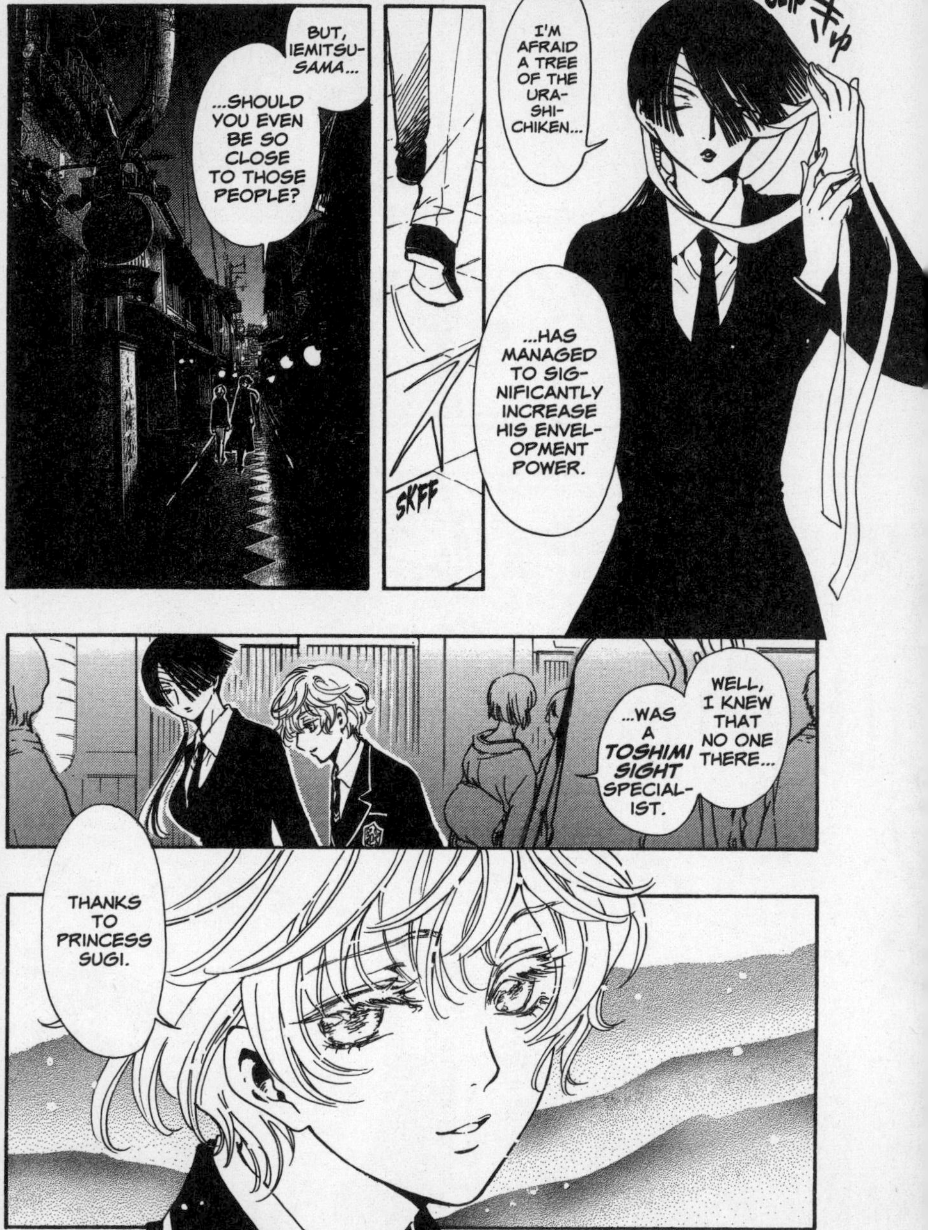
SLIP
I'M AFRAID A TREE OF THE URA-SHI-CHIKEN...
...HAS MANAGED TO SIG-NIFICANTLY INCREASE HIS ENVEL-OPMENT POWER.
SKFF
BUT, IEMITSU-SAMA...
...SHOULD YOU EVEN BE SO CLOSE TO THOSE PEOPLE?
WELL, I KNEW THAT NO ONE THERE...
...WAS A TOSHIMI SIGHT SPECIAL-IST.
THANKS TO PRINCESS SUGI.

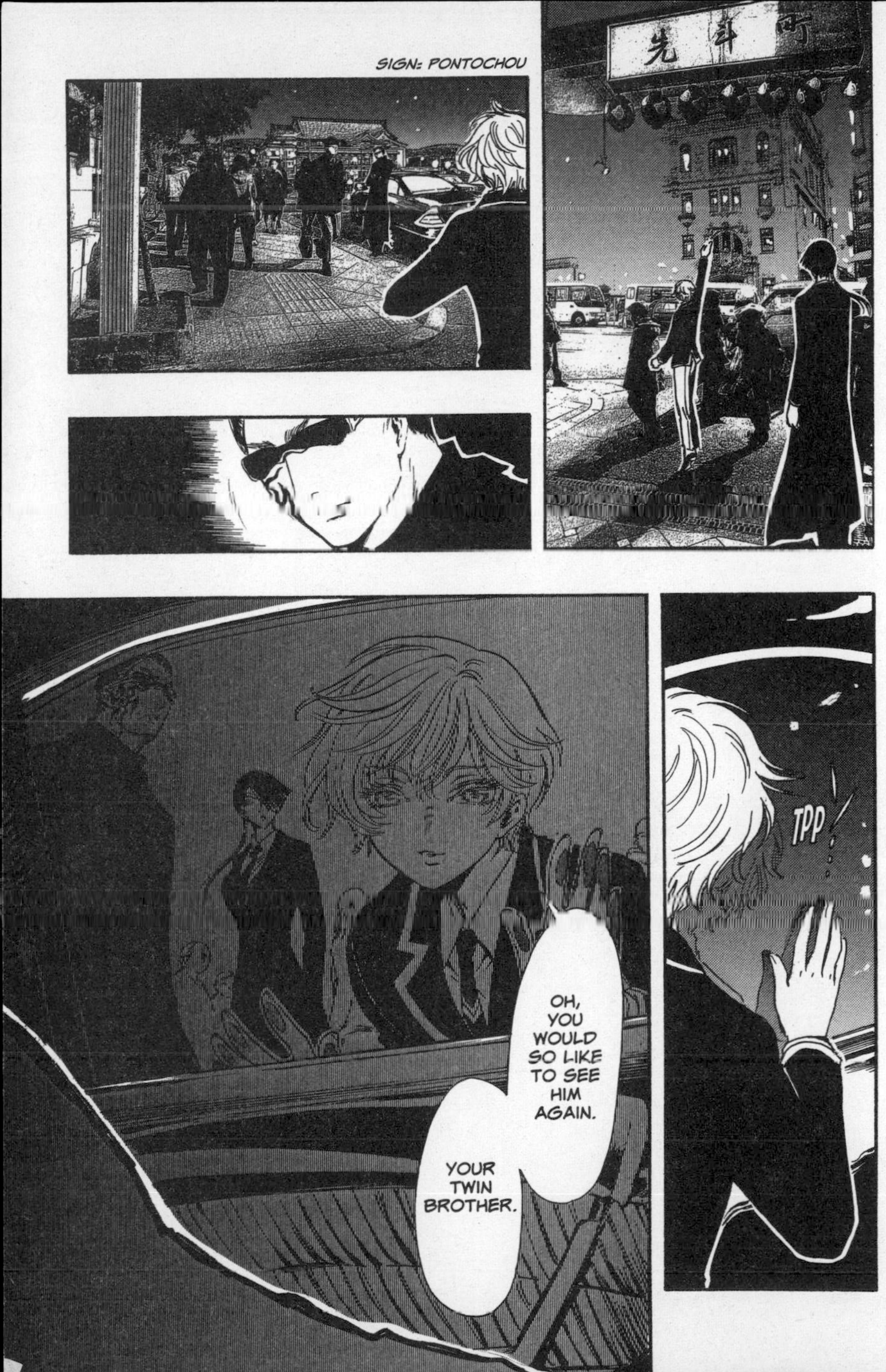
先斗町
SIGN: PONTOCHOU
TPP
OH, YOU WOULD SO LIKE TO SEE HIM AGAIN.
YOUR TWIN BROTHER.

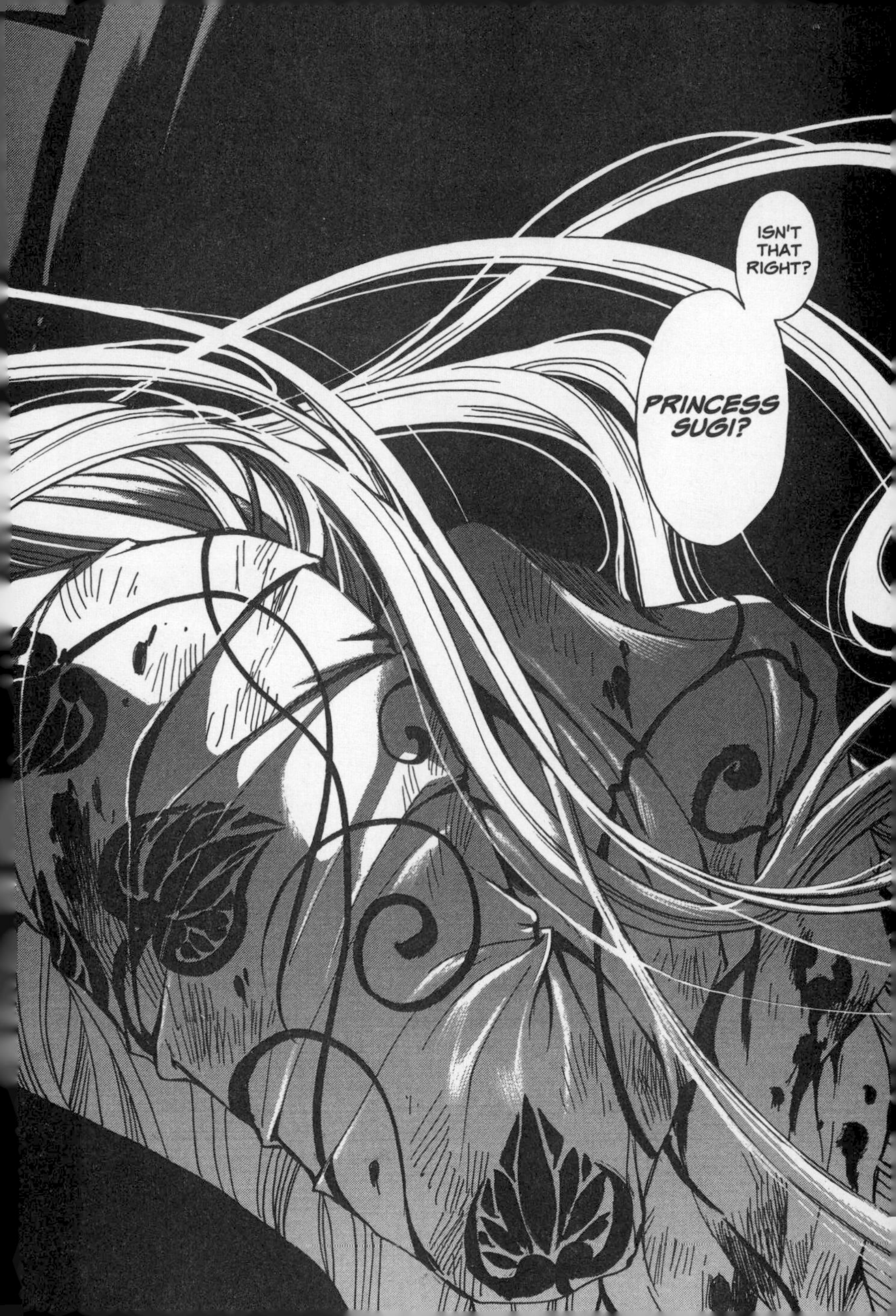
ISN'T THAT RIGHT?
PRINCESS SUGI?

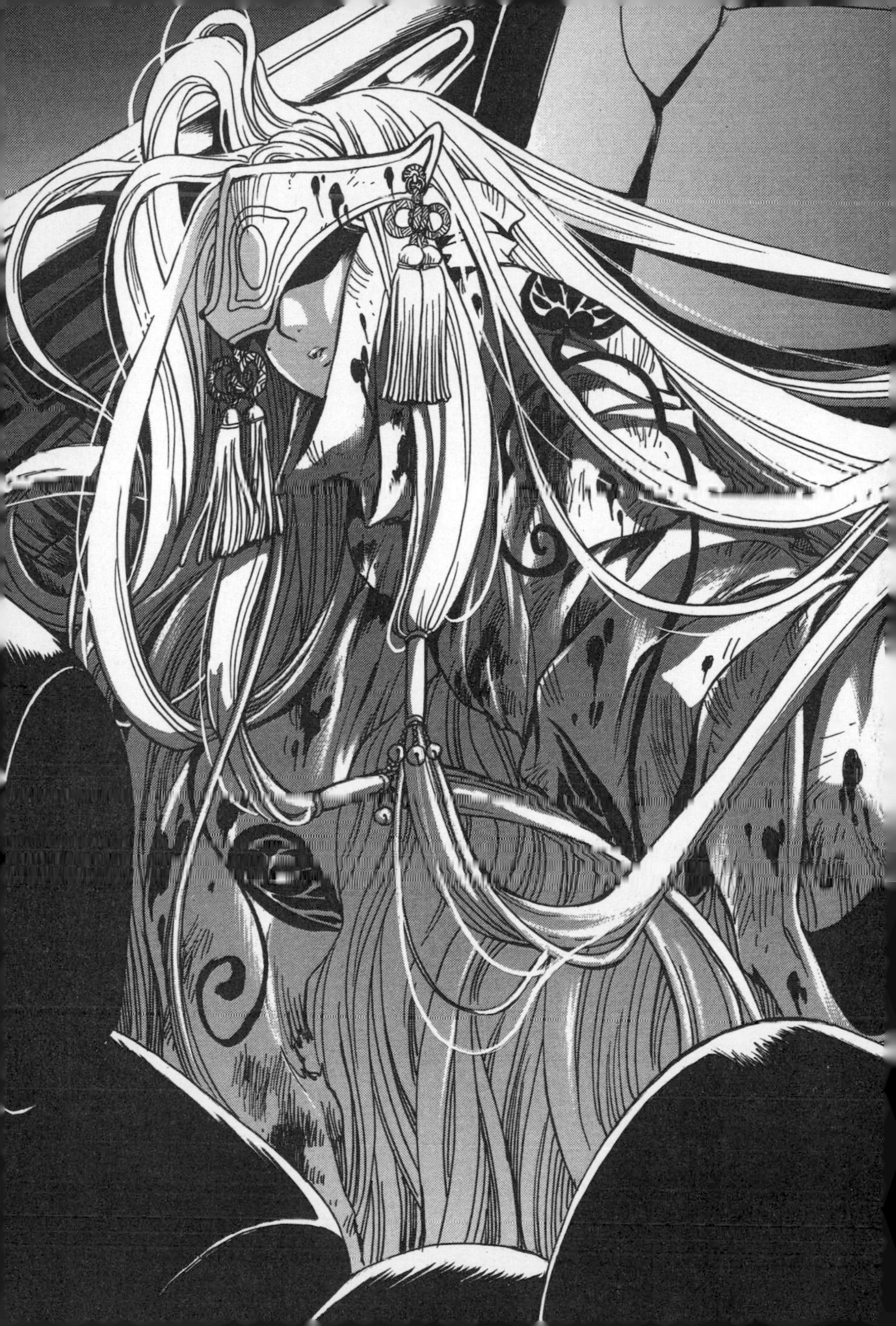

GATE 7
ゲート セブン

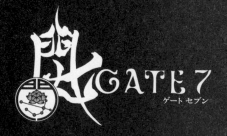

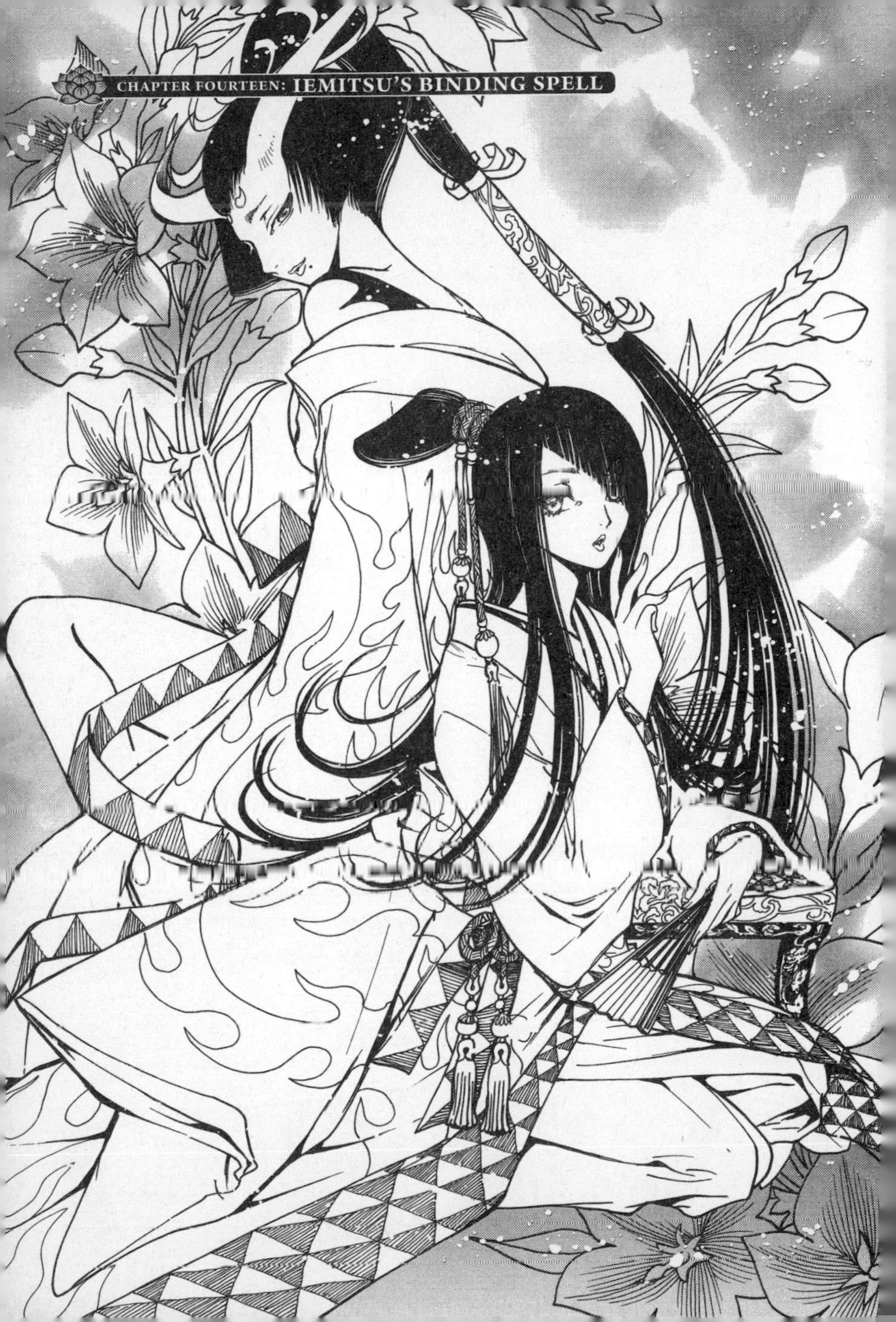
CHAPTER FOURTEEN: IEMITSU'S BINDING SPELL

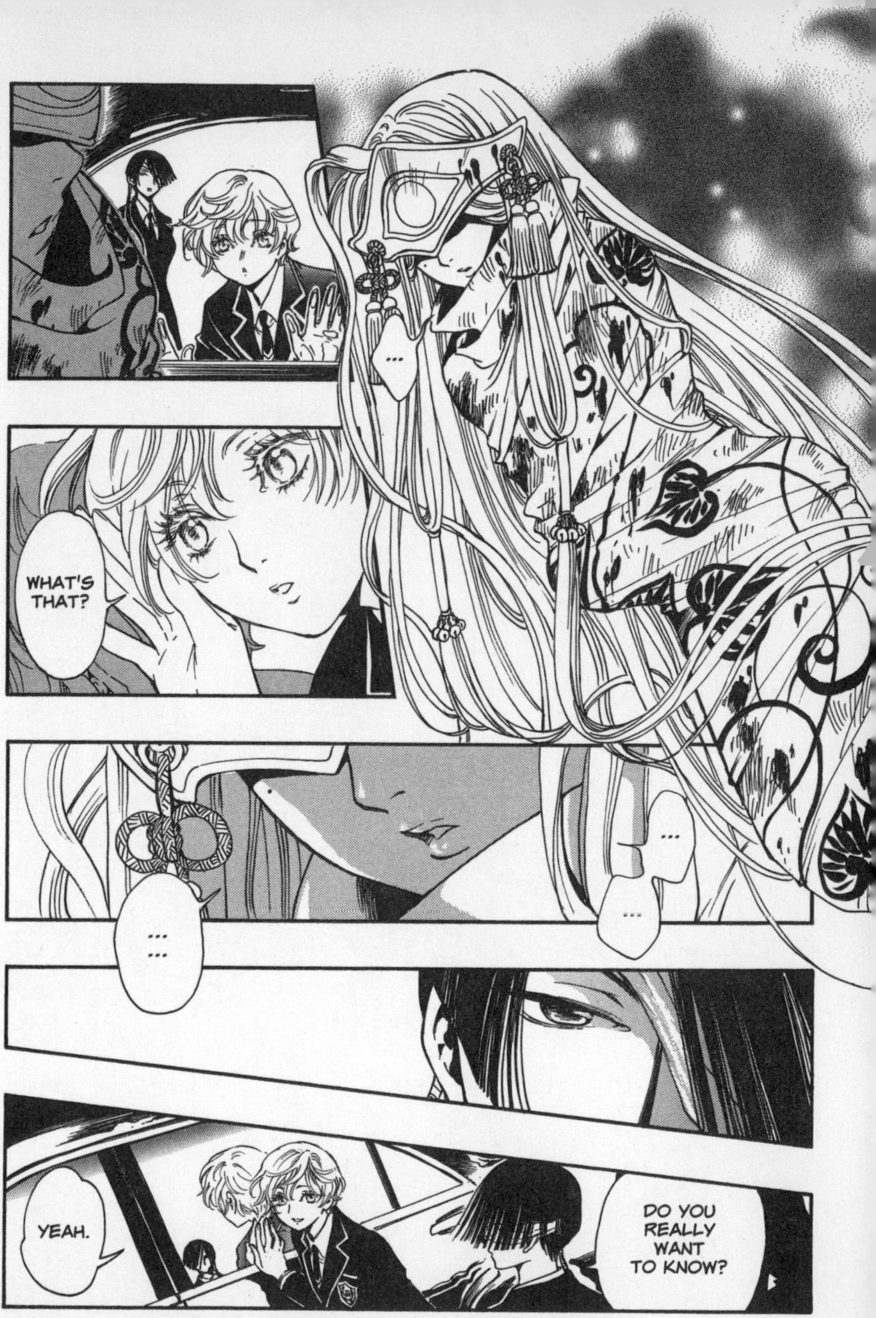
...
WHAT'S THAT?
...
...
...
...
DO YOU REALLY WANT TO KNOW?
YEAH.

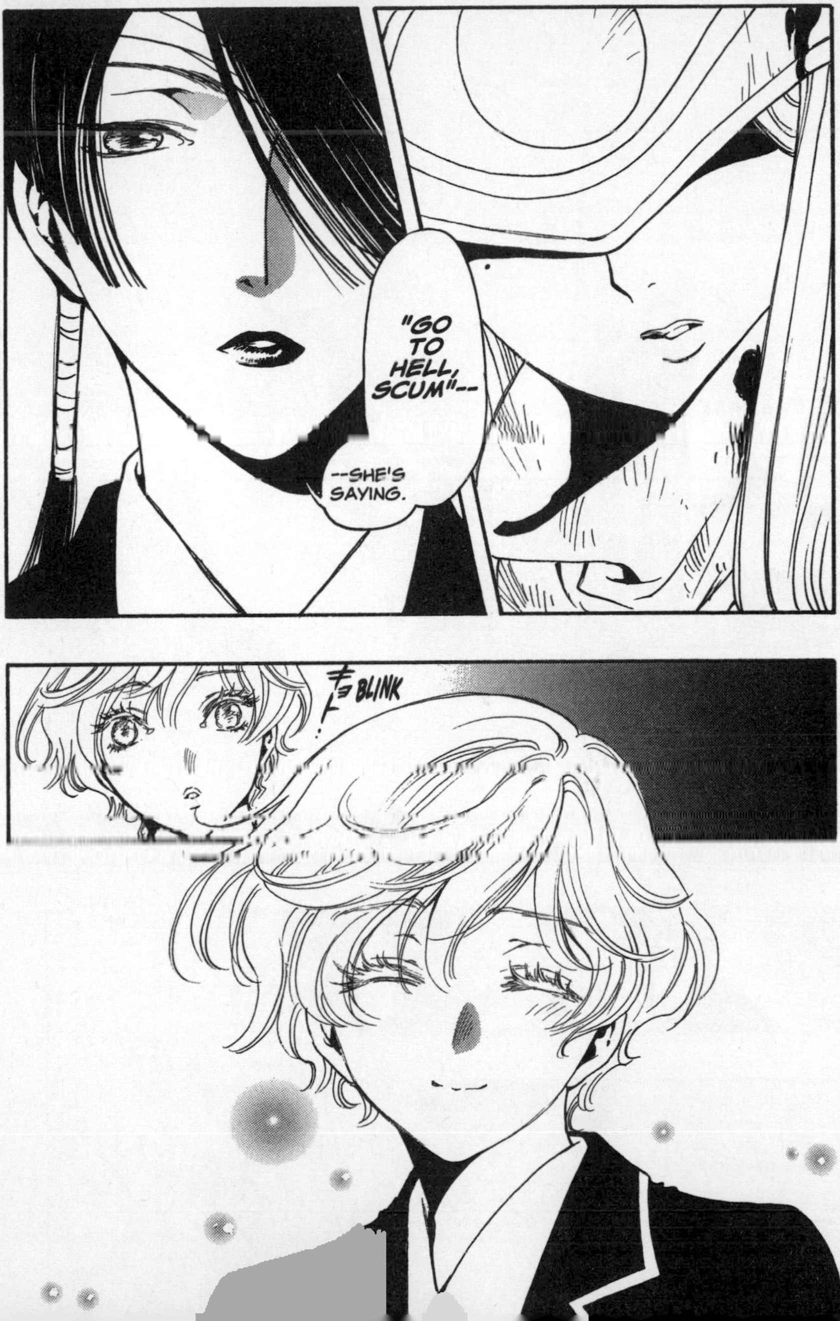
"GO TO HELL, SCUM"--
--SHE'S SAYING.
BLINK

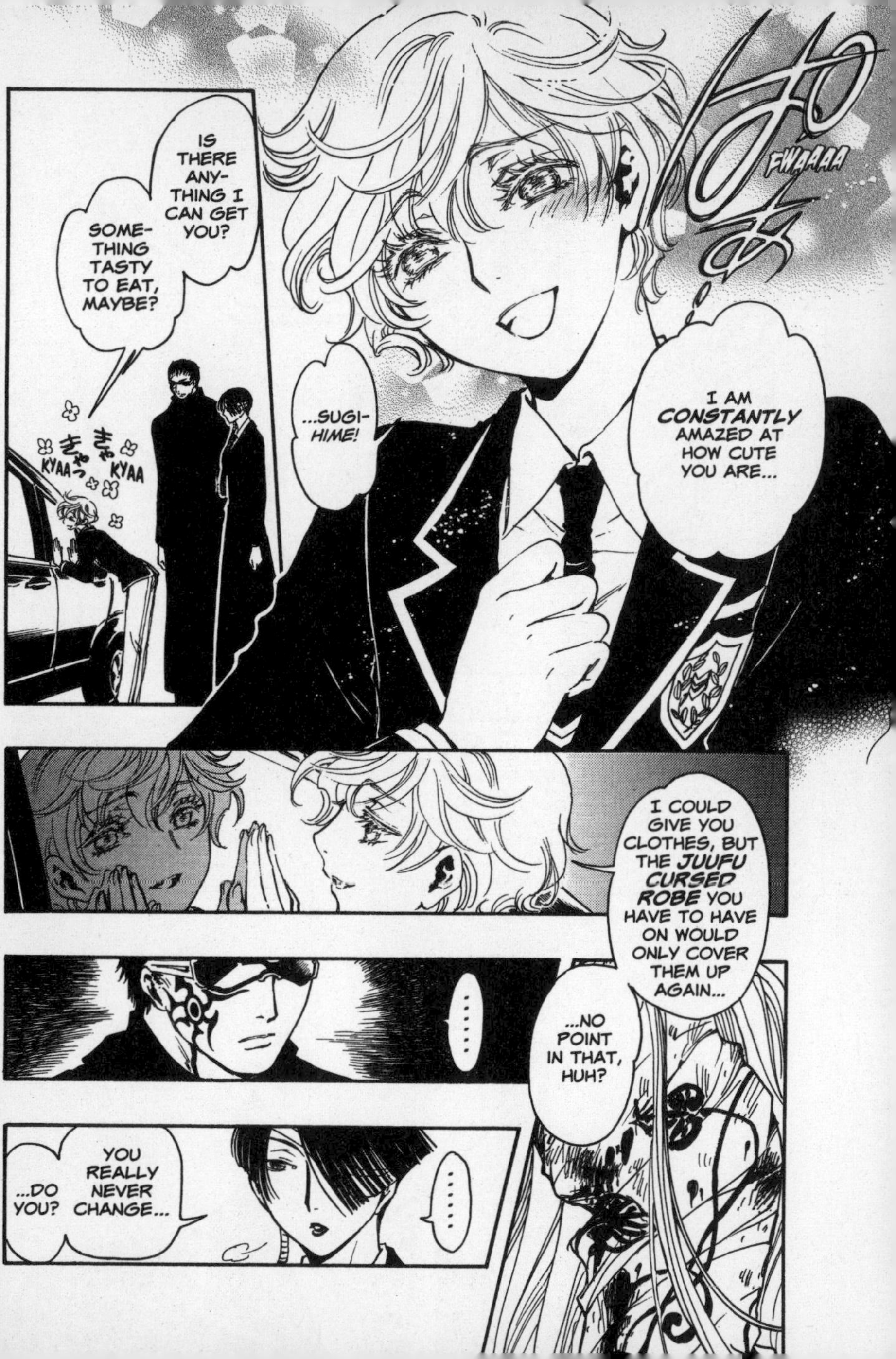
FWAAAA
...SUGI-HIME!
I AM CONSTANTLY AMAZED AT HOW CUTE YOU ARE...
IS THERE ANYTHING I CAN GET YOU?
SOMETHING TASTY TO EAT, MAYBE?
KYAA KYAA
I COULD GIVE YOU CLOTHES, BUT THE JUUFU CURSED ROBE YOU HAVE TO HAVE ON WOULD ONLY COVER THEM UP AGAIN...
......
...NO POINT IN THAT, HUH?
......
YOU REALLY NEVER CHANGE...
...DO YOU?

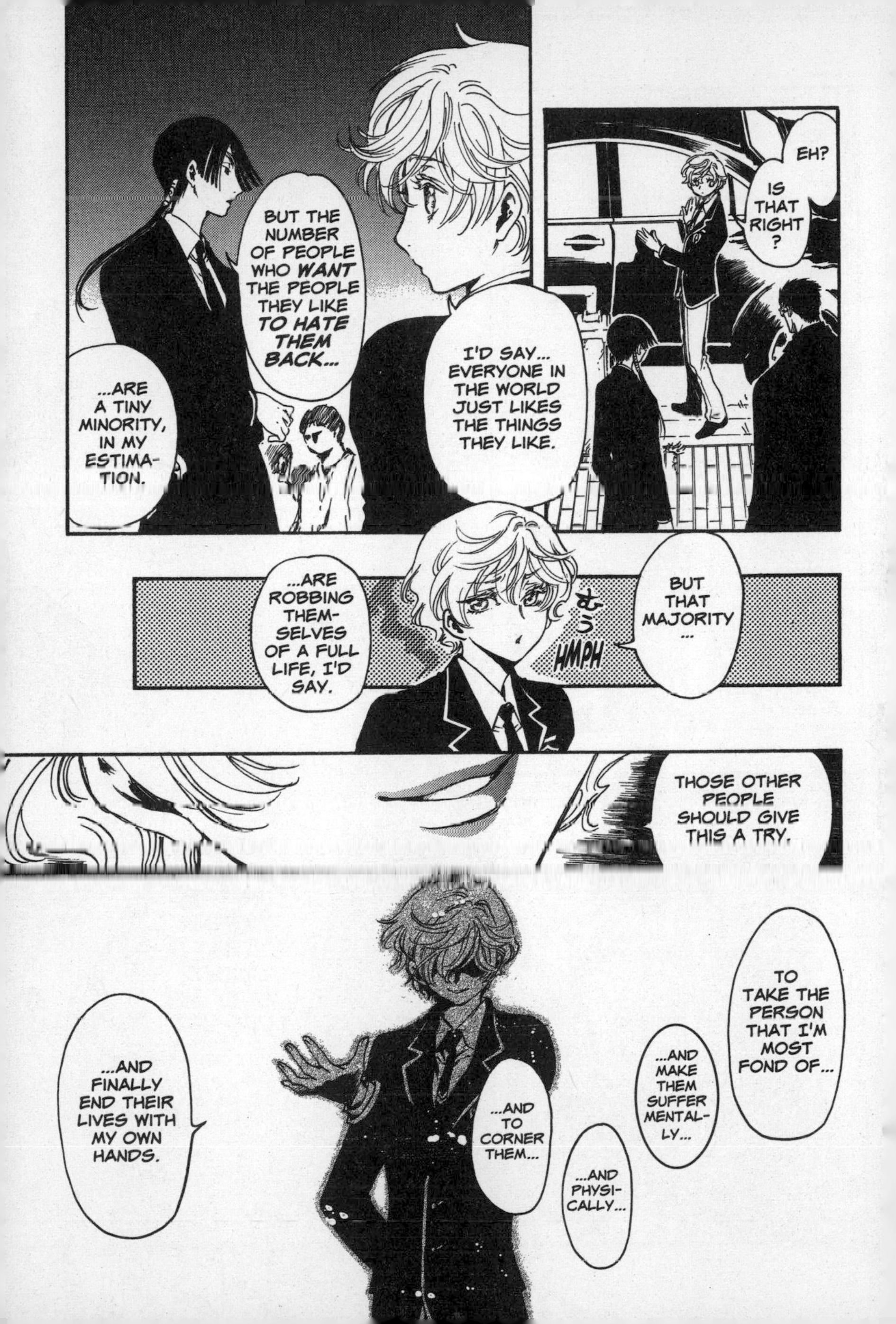
EH? IS THAT RIGHT?
I'D SAY... EVERYONE IN THE WORLD JUST LIKES THE THINGS THEY LIKE.
BUT THE NUMBER OF PEOPLE WHO WANT THE PEOPLE THEY LIKE TO HATE THEM BACK...
...ARE A TINY MINORITY, IN MY ESTIMATION.
BUT THAT MAJORITY...
HMPH
...ARE ROBBING THEMSELVES OF A FULL LIFE, I'D SAY.
THOSE OTHER PEOPLE SHOULD GIVE THIS A TRY.
TO TAKE THE PERSON THAT I'M MOST FOND OF...
...AND MAKE THEM SUFFER MENTALLY...
...AND PHYSICALLY...
...AND TO CORNER THEM...
...AND FINALLY END THEIR LIVES WITH MY OWN HANDS.

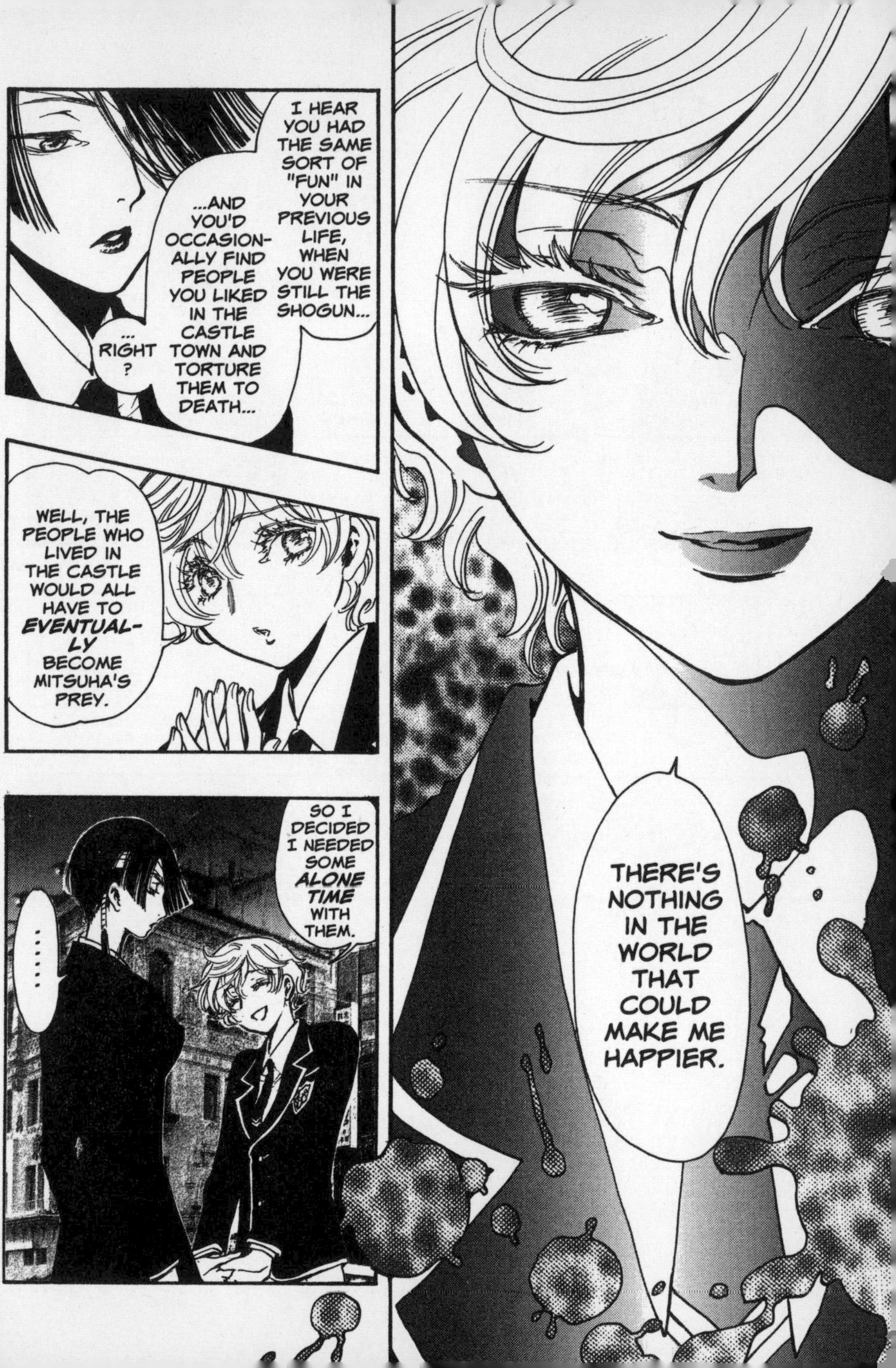
THERE'S NOTHING IN THE WORLD THAT COULD MAKE ME HAPPIER.
I HEAR YOU HAD THE SAME SORT OF "FUN" IN YOUR PREVIOUS LIFE, WHEN YOU WERE STILL THE SHOGUN...
...AND YOU'D OCCASION-ALLY FIND PEOPLE YOU LIKED IN THE CASTLE TOWN AND TORTURE THEM TO DEATH...
...RIGHT?
WELL, THE PEOPLE WHO LIVED IN THE CASTLE WOULD ALL HAVE TO ***EVENTUAL-LY*** BECOME MITSUHA'S PREY.
SO I DECIDED I NEEDED SOME ***ALONE TIME*** WITH THEM.
......

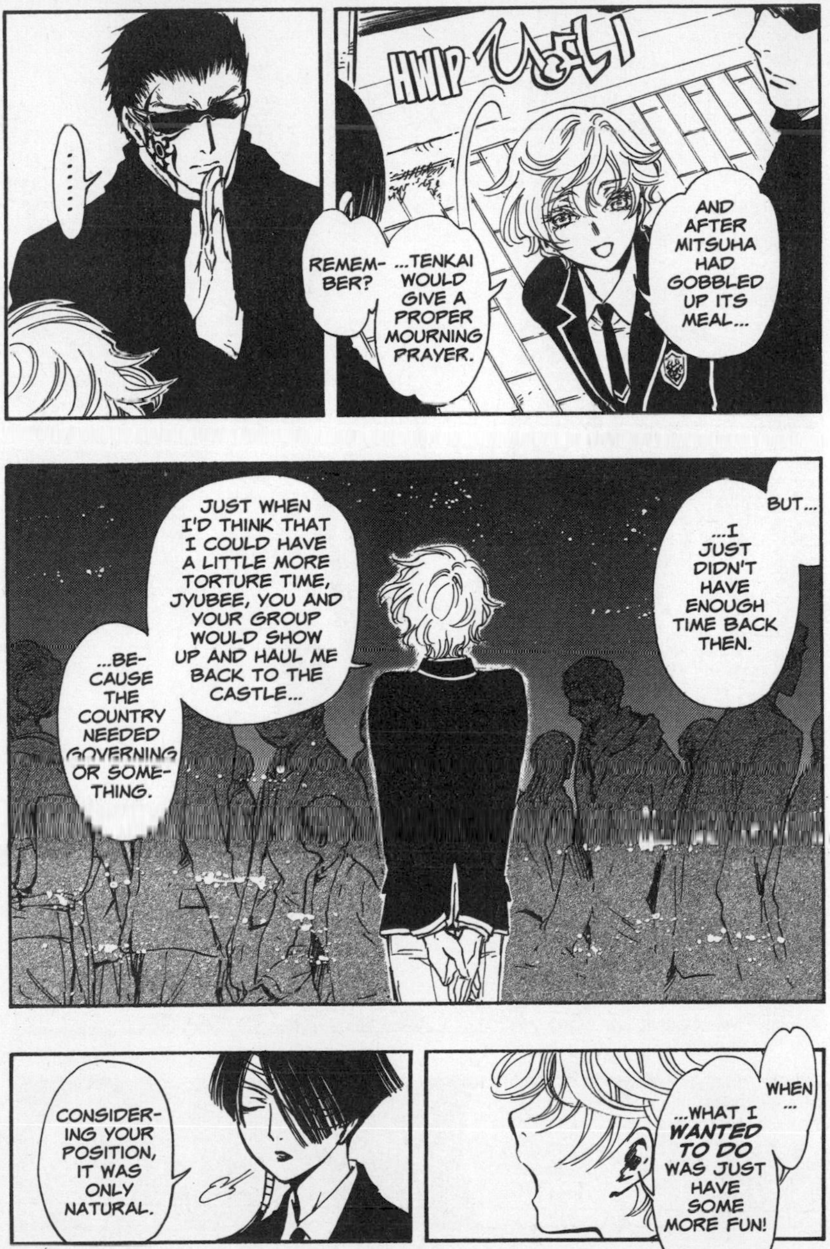
HWIP
AND AFTER MITSUHA HAD GOBBLED UP ITS MEAL...
...TENKAI WOULD GIVE A PROPER MOURNING PRAYER.
REMEM-BER?
......
BUT...
...I JUST DIDN'T HAVE ENOUGH TIME BACK THEN.
JUST WHEN I'D THINK THAT I COULD HAVE A LITTLE MORE TORTURE TIME, JYUBEE, YOU AND YOUR GROUP WOULD SHOW UP AND HAUL ME BACK TO THE CASTLE...
...BE-CAUSE THE COUNTRY NEEDED GOVERNING OR SOME-THING.
WHEN...
...WHAT I *WANTED TO DO* WAS JUST HAVE SOME MORE FUN!
CONSIDER-ING YOUR POSITION, IT WAS ONLY NATURAL.

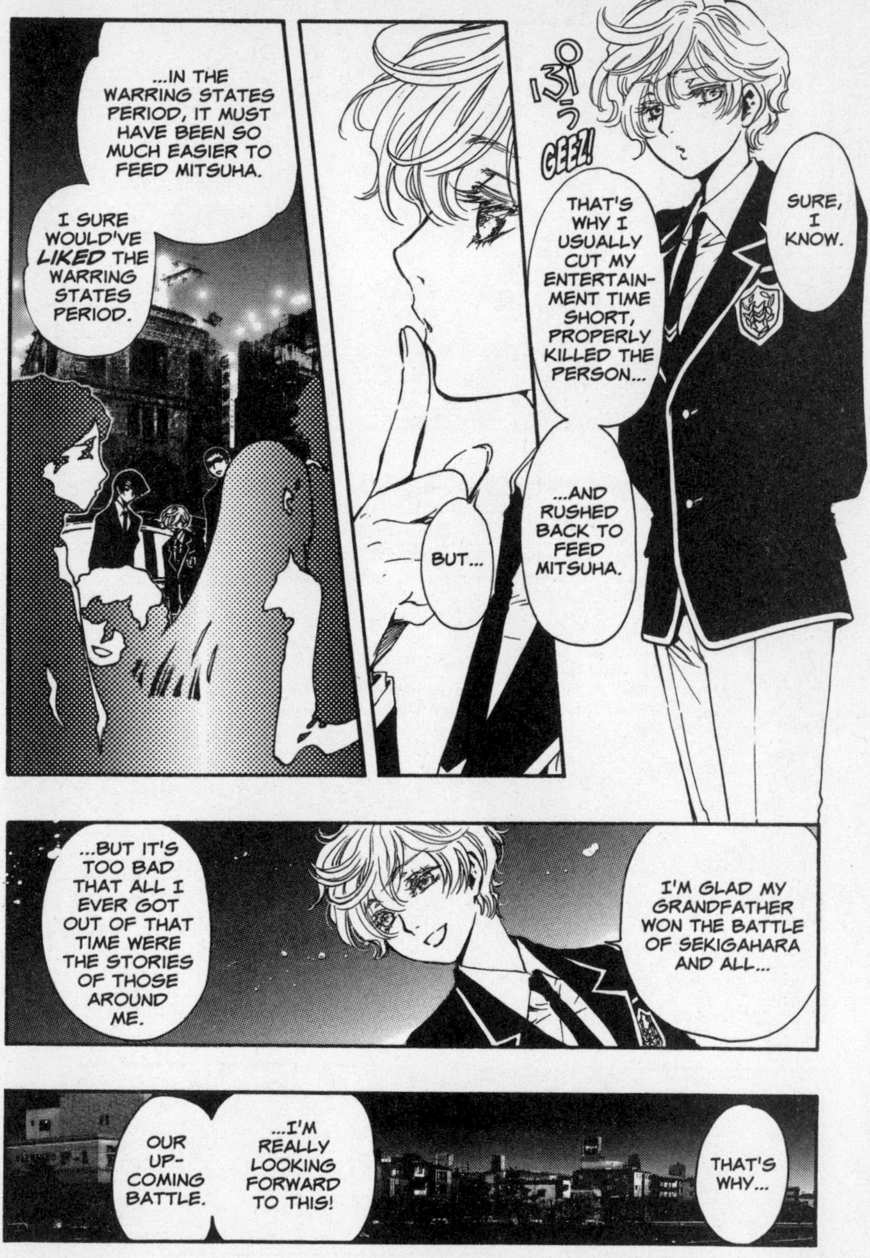
SURE, I KNOW.
ぷう
GEEZ!
THAT'S WHY I USUALLY CUT MY ENTERTAIN-MENT TIME SHORT, PROPERLY KILLED THE PERSON...
...AND RUSHED BACK TO FEED MITSUHA.
BUT...
...IN THE WARRING STATES PERIOD, IT MUST HAVE BEEN SO MUCH EASIER TO FEED MITSUHA.
I SURE WOULD'VE *LIKED* THE WARRING STATES PERIOD.
I'M GLAD MY GRANDFATHER WON THE BATTLE OF SEKIGAHARA AND ALL...
...BUT IT'S TOO BAD THAT ALL I EVER GOT OUT OF THAT TIME WERE THE STORIES OF THOSE AROUND ME.
THAT'S WHY...
...I'M REALLY LOOKING FORWARD TO THIS!
OUR UP-COMING BATTLE.

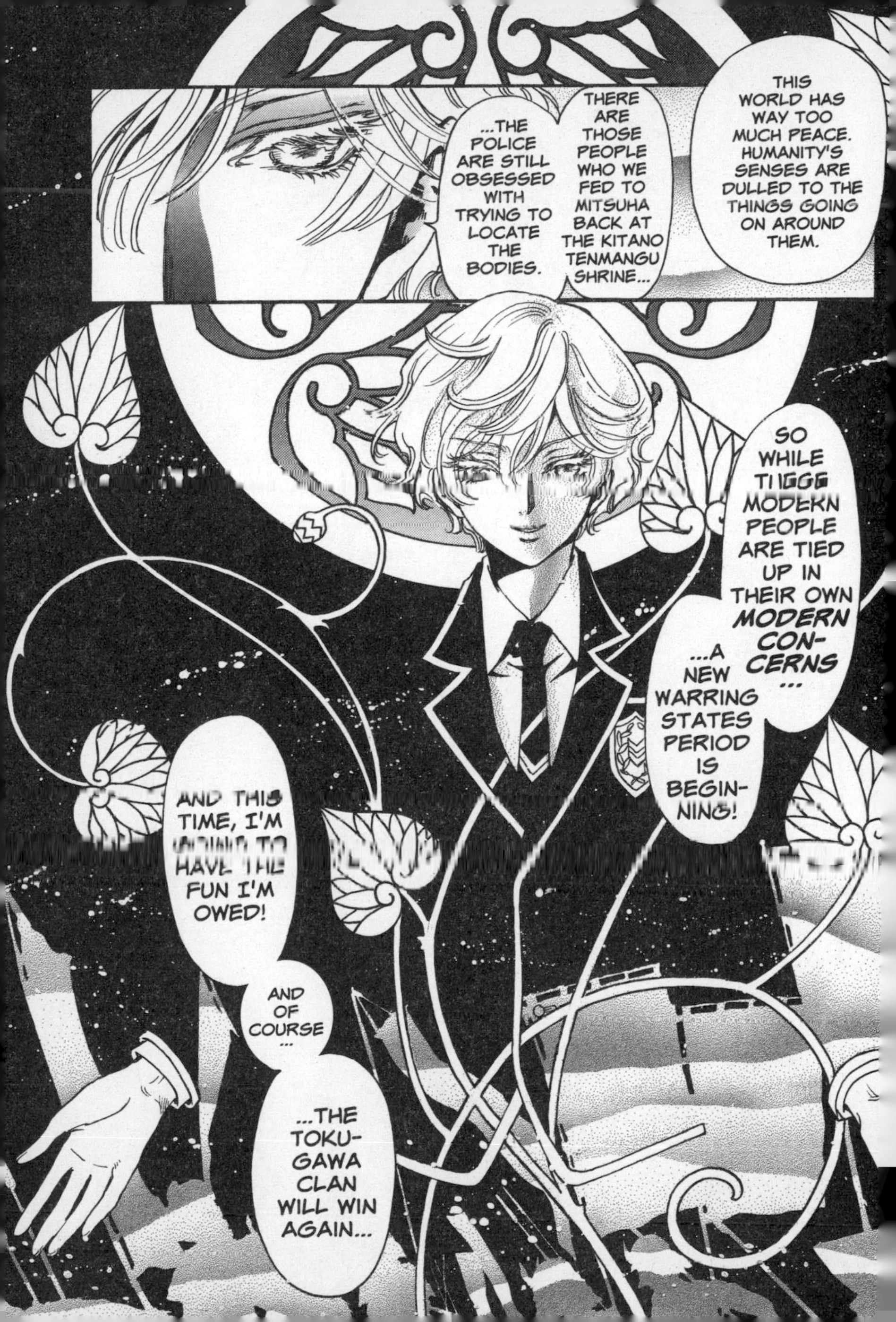
THIS WORLD HAS WAY TOO MUCH PEACE. HUMANITY'S SENSES ARE DULLED TO THE THINGS GOING ON AROUND THEM.
THERE ARE THOSE PEOPLE WHO WE FED TO MITSUHA BACK AT THE KITANO TENMANGU SHRINE...
...THE POLICE ARE STILL OBSESSED WITH TRYING TO LOCATE THE BODIES.
SO WHILE THESE MODERN PEOPLE ARE TIED UP IN THEIR OWN *MODERN CONCERNS*...
...A NEW WARRING STATES PERIOD IS BEGINNING!
AND THIS TIME, I'M GOING TO HAVE THE FUN I'M OWED!
AND OF COURSE...
...THE TOKUGAWA CLAN WILL WIN AGAIN...

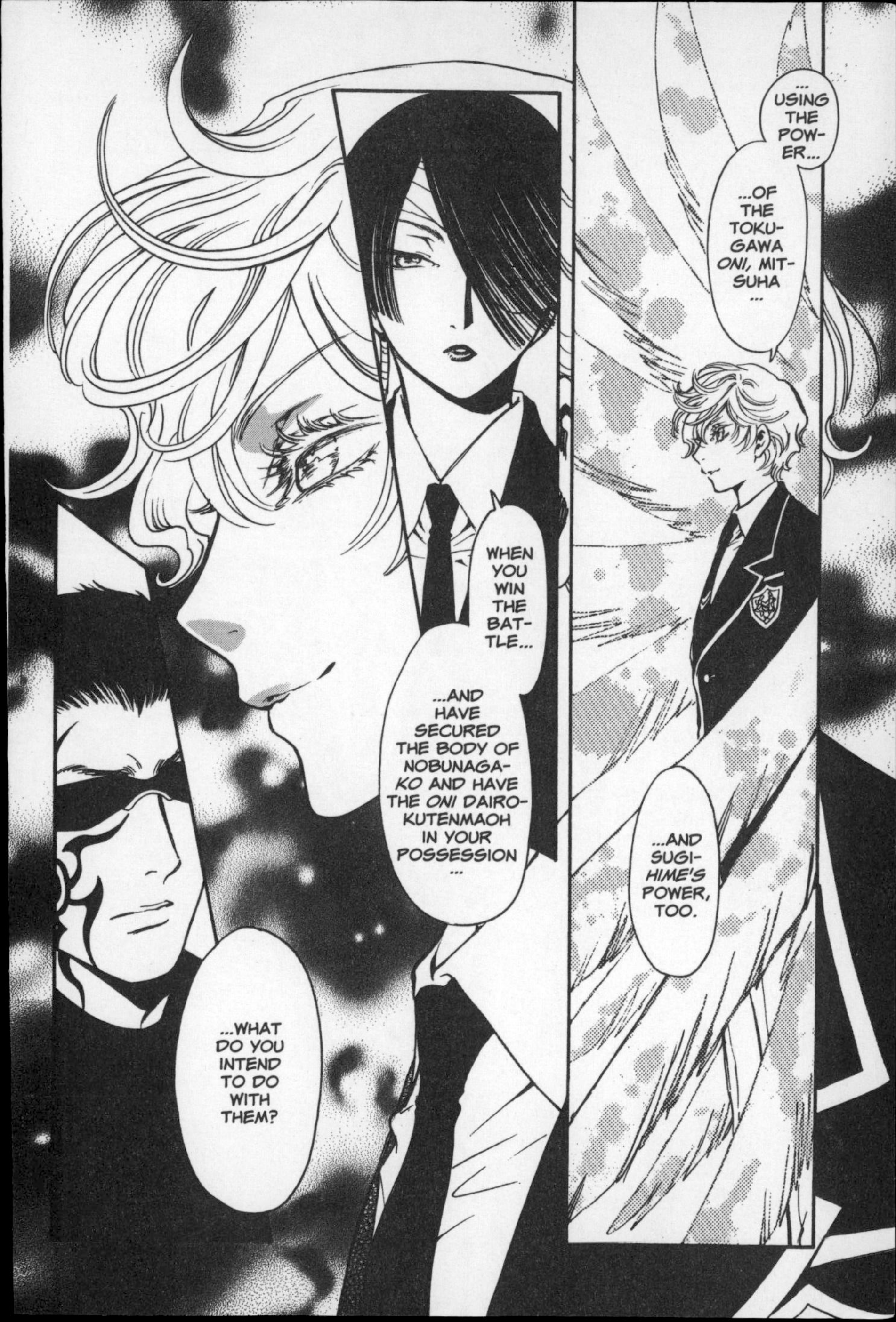
...USING THE POWER...
...OF THE TOKUGAWA *ONI*, MITSUHA ...
...AND SUGIHIME'S POWER, TOO.
WHEN YOU WIN THE BATTLE...
...AND HAVE SECURED THE BODY OF NOBUNAGAKO AND HAVE THE *ONI* DAIROKUTENMAOH IN YOUR POSSESSION ...
...WHAT DO YOU INTEND TO DO WITH THEM?

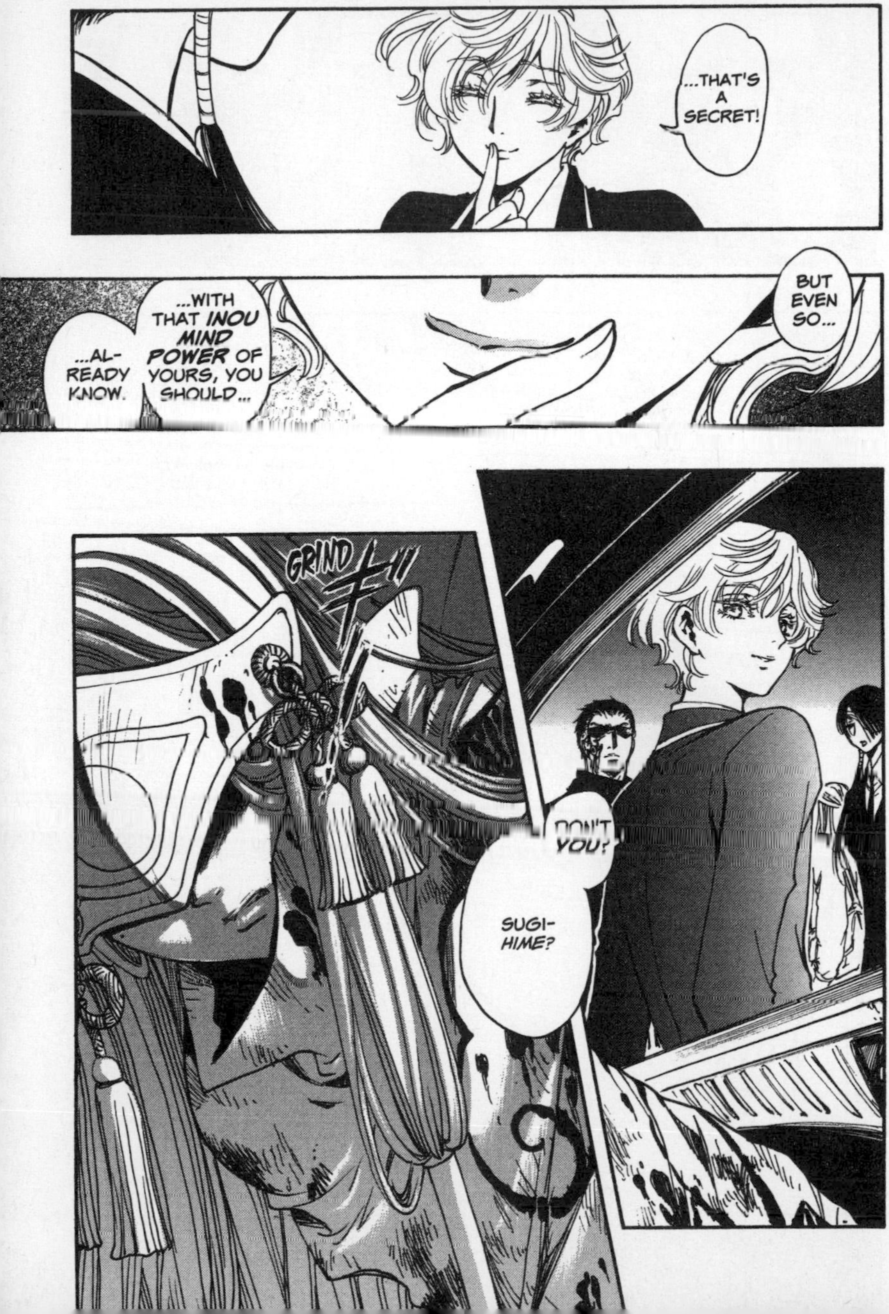
...THAT'S A SECRET!
BUT EVEN SO...
...WITH THAT INOU MIND POWER OF YOURS, YOU SHOULD...
...AL-READY KNOW.
DON'T YOU?
SUGI-HIME?
GRIND

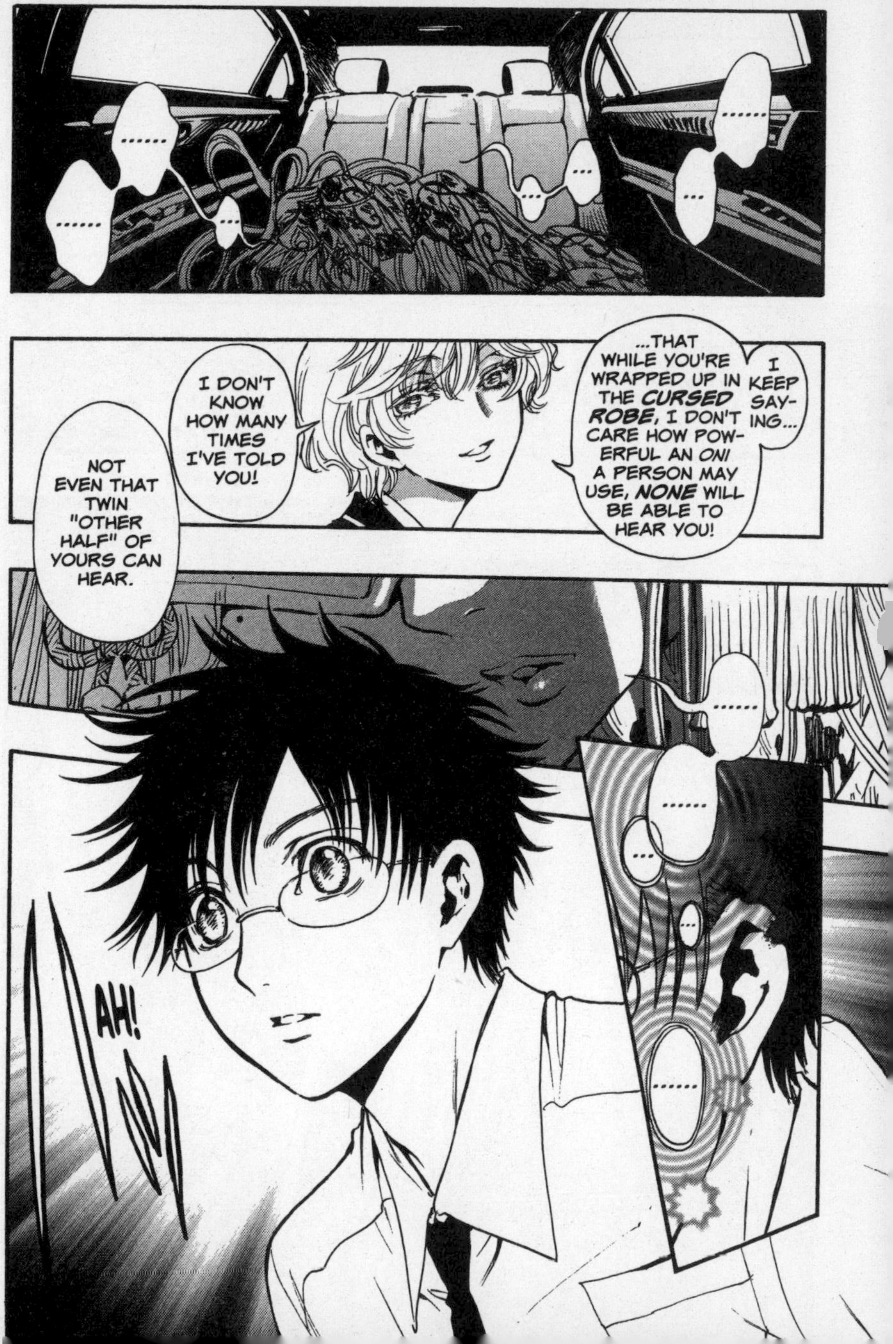
......
...
...
......
......
...
I KEEP SAYING...
...THAT WHILE YOU'RE WRAPPED UP IN THE *CURSED ROBE*, I DON'T CARE HOW POWERFUL AN *ONI* A PERSON MAY USE, *NONE* WILL BE ABLE TO HEAR YOU!
I DON'T KNOW HOW MANY TIMES I'VE TOLD YOU!
NOT EVEN THAT TWIN "OTHER HALF" OF YOURS CAN HEAR.
......
......
...
...
......
AH!

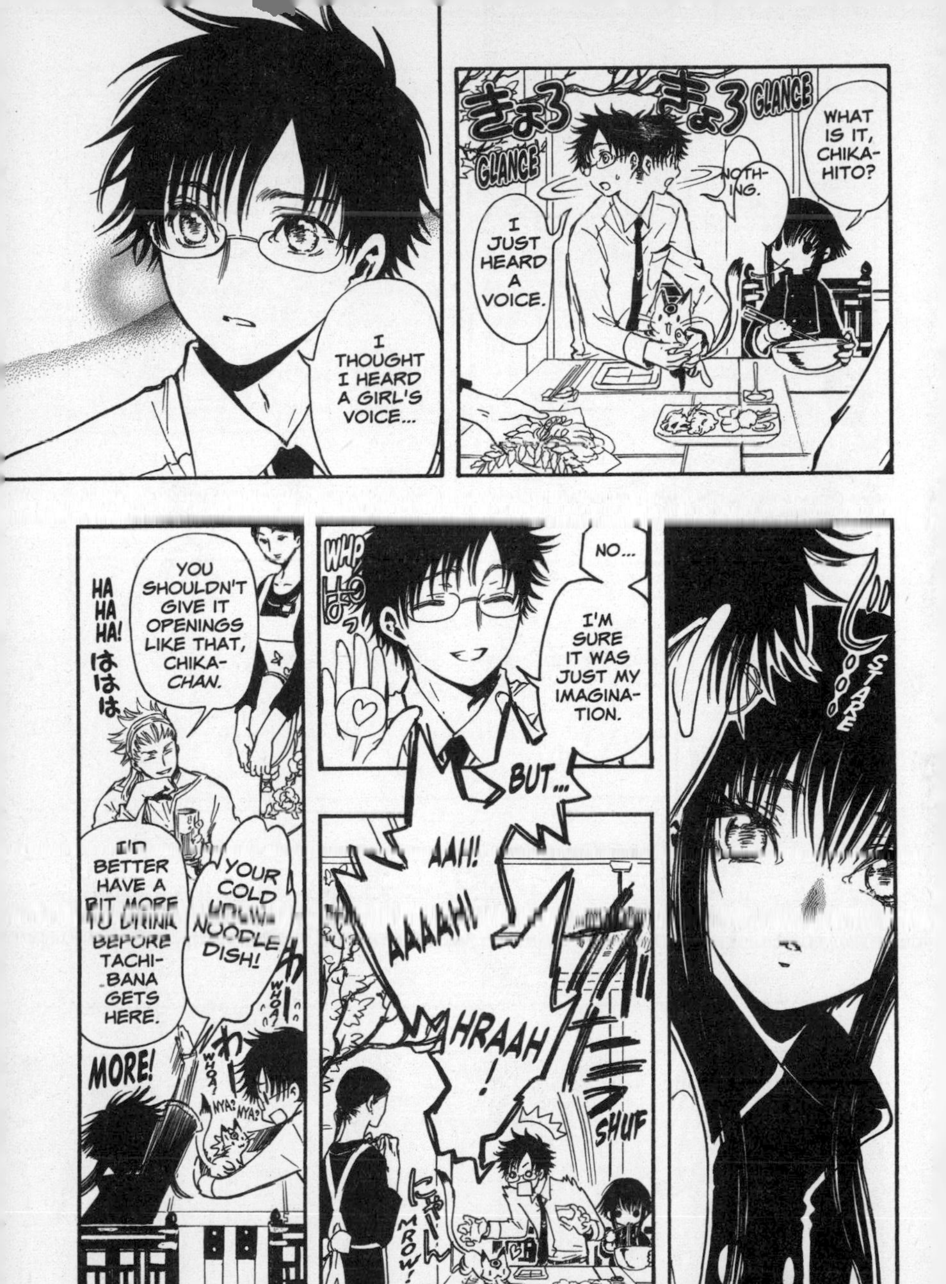

きょろ きょろ
GLANCE
GLANCE
WHAT IS IT, CHIKAHITO?
NOTHING.
I JUST HEARD A VOICE.
I THOUGHT I HEARD A GIRL'S VOICE...
STARE
WHP
はっ
NO...
I'M SURE IT WAS JUST MY IMAGINATION.
BUT...
AAH!
AAAAH!
HRAAH!
SHUF
MROW!
にゃ~ん
HA HA HA!
ははは
YOU SHOULDN'T GIVE IT OPENINGS LIKE THAT, CHIKA-CHAN.
YOUR COLD UDON NOODLE DISH!
I'D BETTER HAVE A BIT MORE TO DRINK BEFORE TACHIBANA GETS HERE.
WHOA!
WHOA!
MORE!
NYA?
NYA?

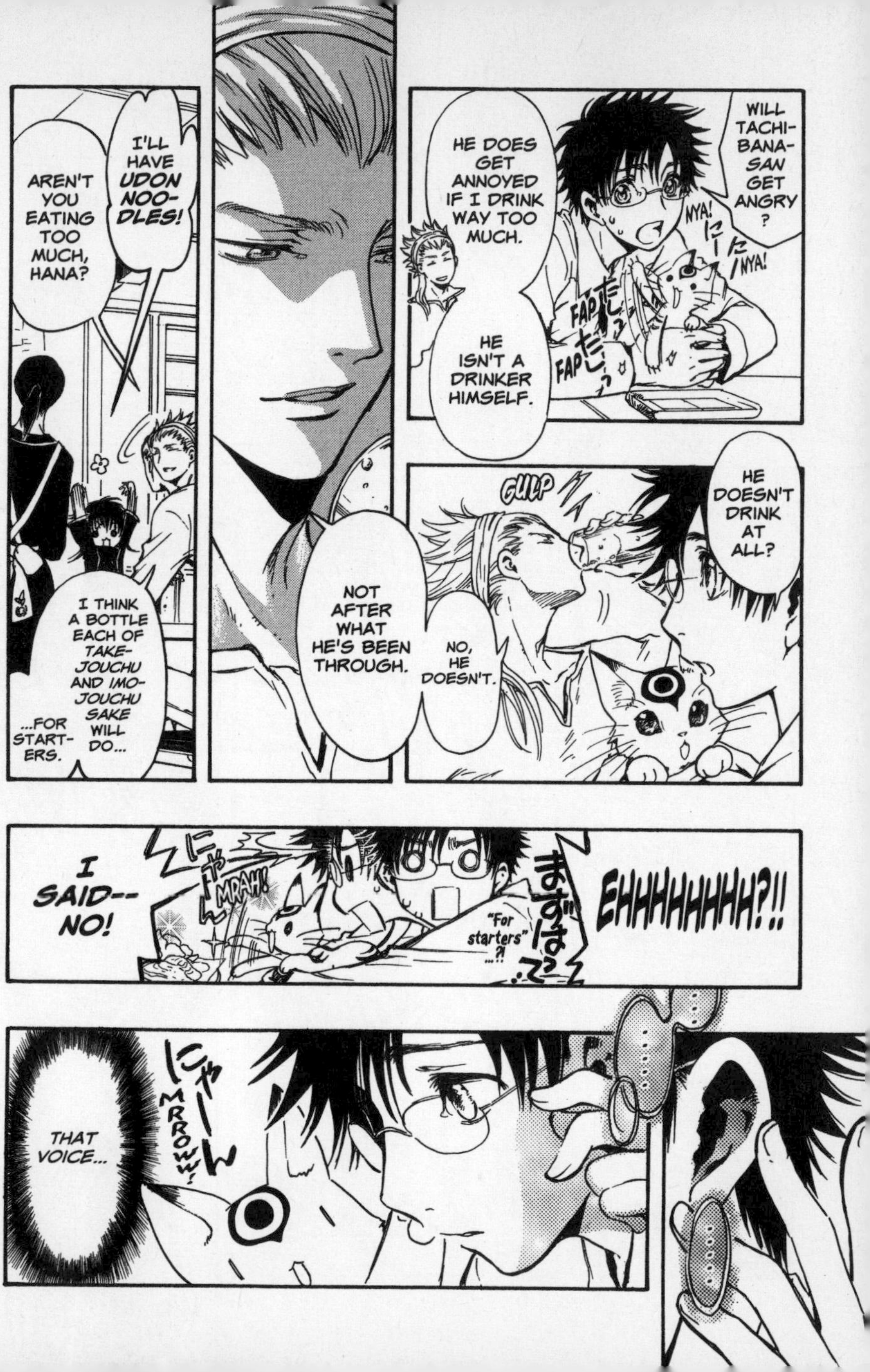
WILL TACHIBANA-SAN GET ANGRY?
NYA!
NYA!
HE DOES GET ANNOYED IF I DRINK WAY TOO MUCH.
FAP
FAP
HE ISN'T A DRINKER HIMSELF.
HE DOESN'T DRINK AT ALL?
GULP
NO, HE DOESN'T.
NOT AFTER WHAT HE'S BEEN THROUGH.
I'LL HAVE UDON NOODLES!
AREN'T YOU EATING TOO MUCH, HANA?
I THINK A BOTTLE EACH OF TAKE-JOUCHU AND IMO-JOUCHU SAKE WILL DO...
...FOR STARTERS.
EHHHHHHHH?!!
"For starters" ...?!
MRAH!
I SAID-- NO!
MRROWW!
THAT VOICE...

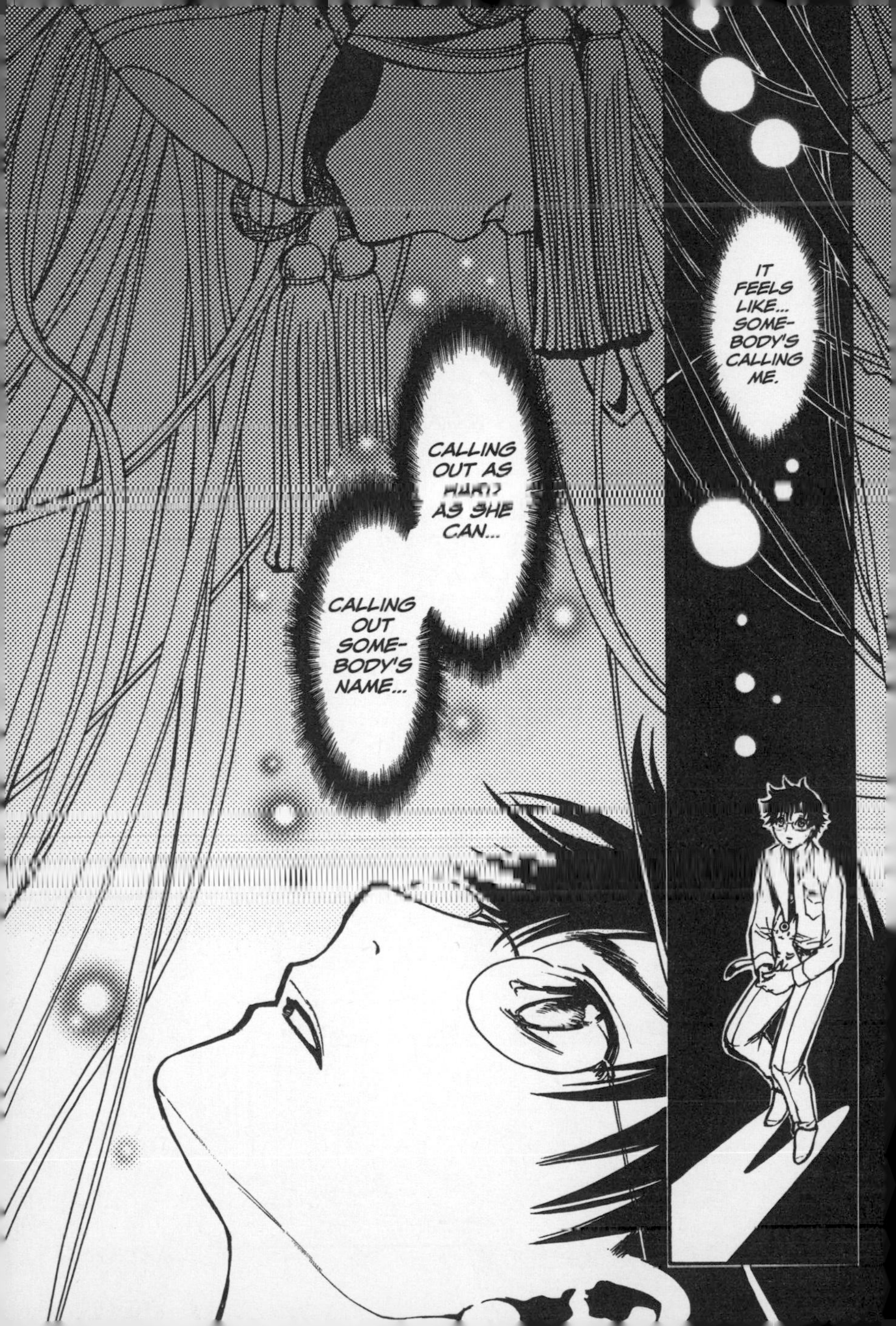
IT FEELS LIKE... SOMEBODY'S CALLING ME.
CALLING OUT AS HARD AS SHE CAN...
CALLING OUT SOMEBODY'S NAME...

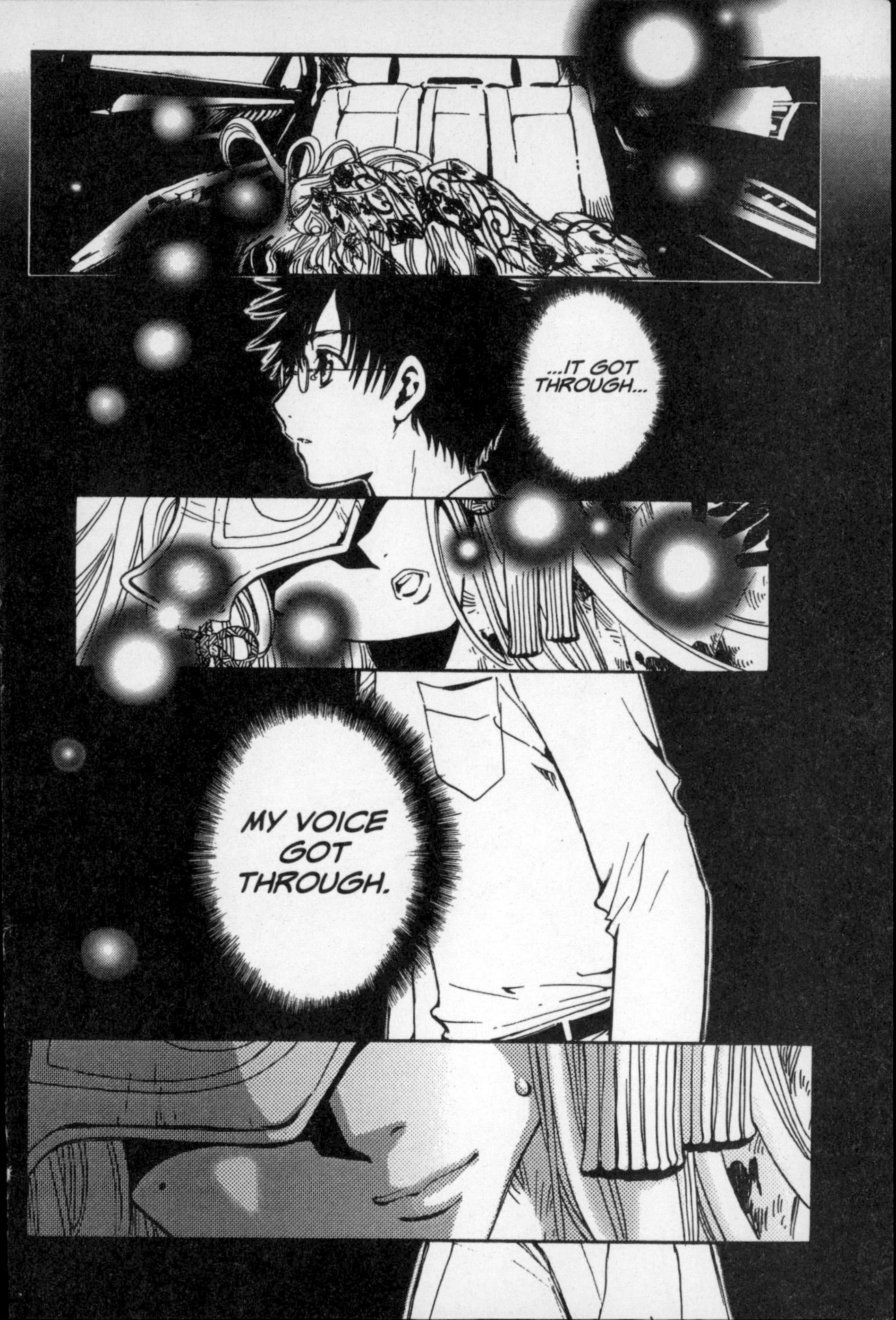
...IT GOT THROUGH...
MY VOICE GOT THROUGH.

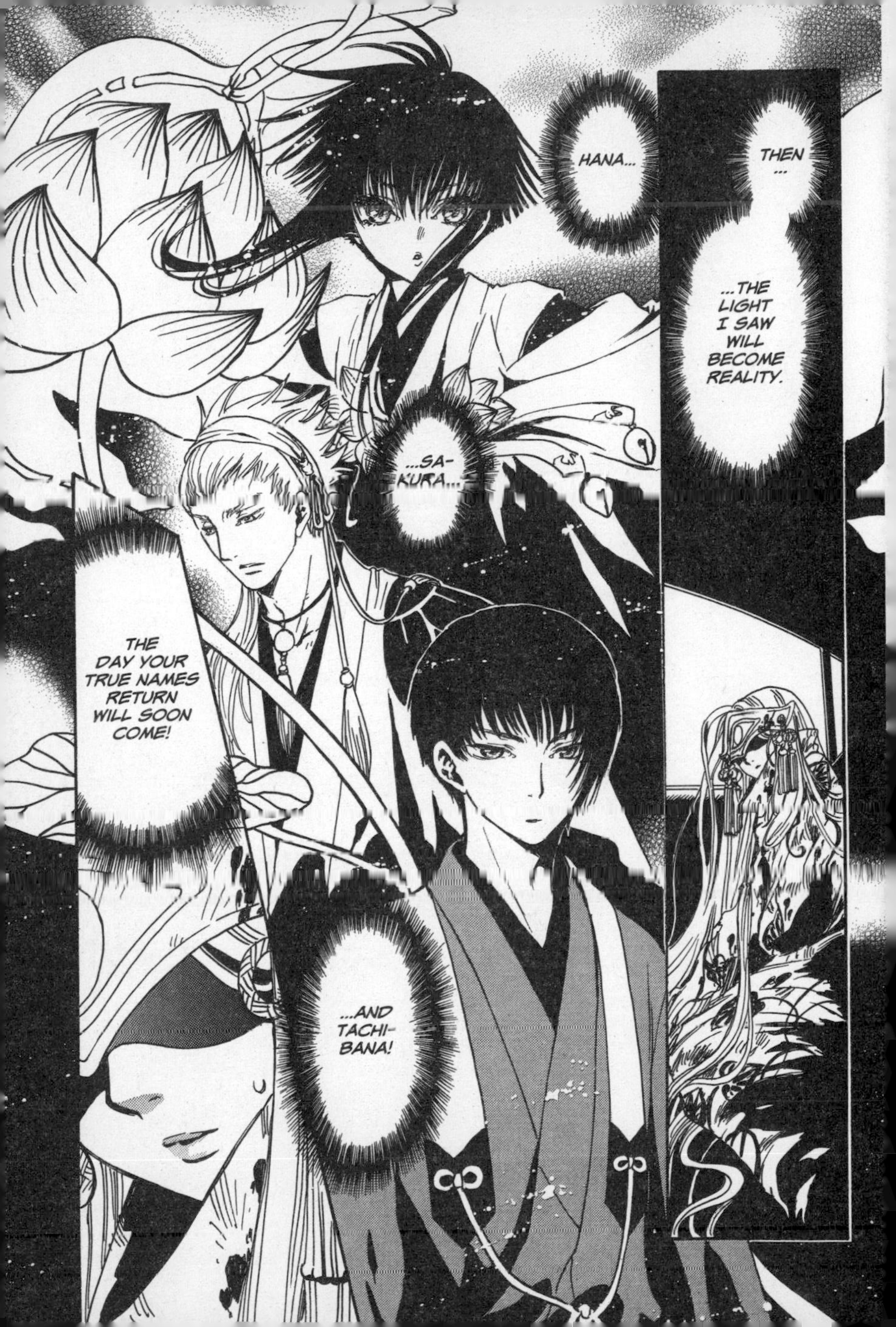
THEN ...
...THE LIGHT I SAW WILL BECOME REALITY.
HANA...
...SA-KURA...
THE DAY YOUR TRUE NAMES RETURN WILL SOON COME!
...AND TACHI-BANA!

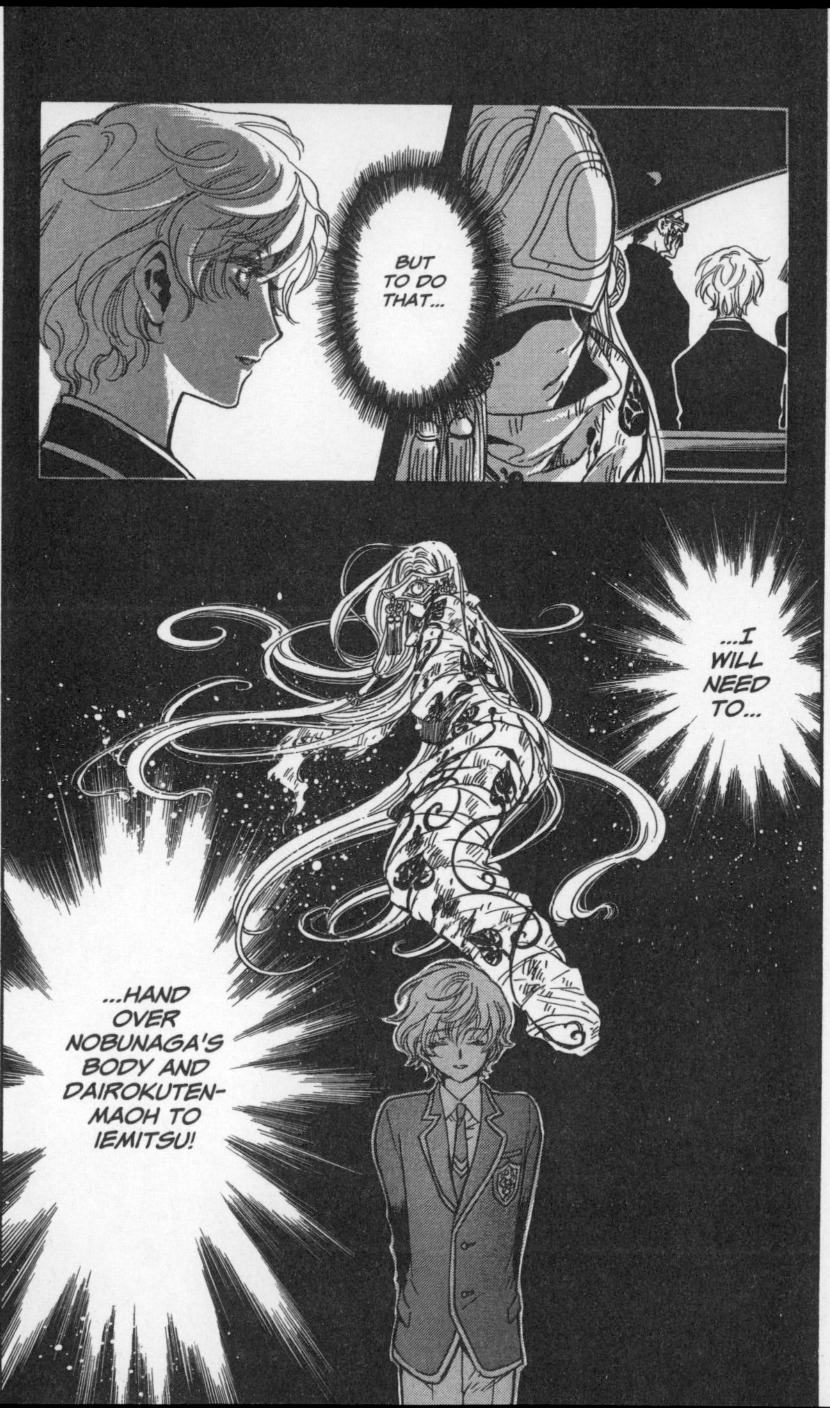
BUT TO DO THAT...
...I WILL NEED TO...
...HAND OVER NOBUNAGA'S BODY AND DAIROKUTEN-MAOH TO IEMITSU!

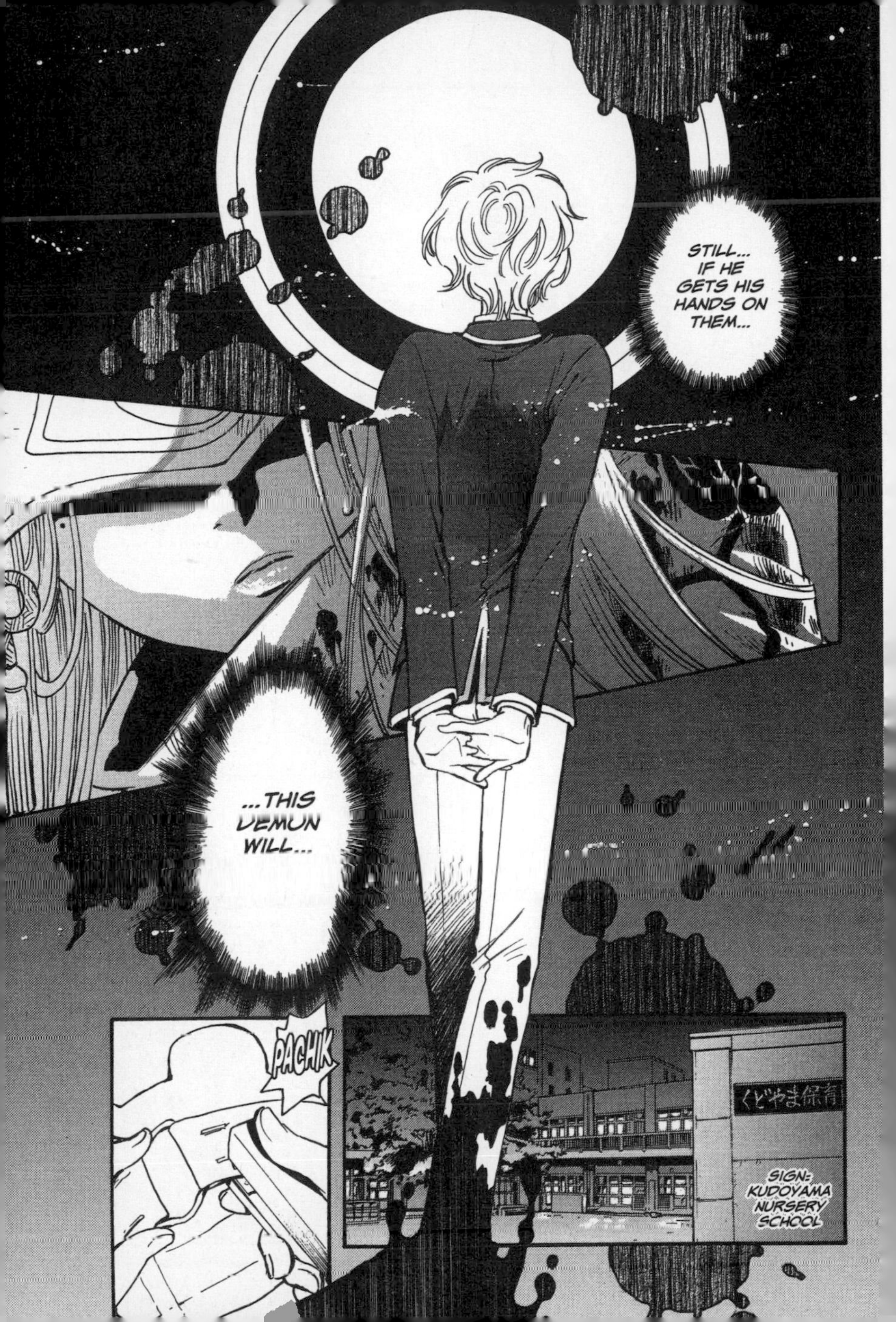
STILL... IF HE GETS HIS HANDS ON THEM...
...THIS DEMON WILL...
くどやま保育
SIGN: KUDOYAMA NURSERY SCHOOL
PACHIK

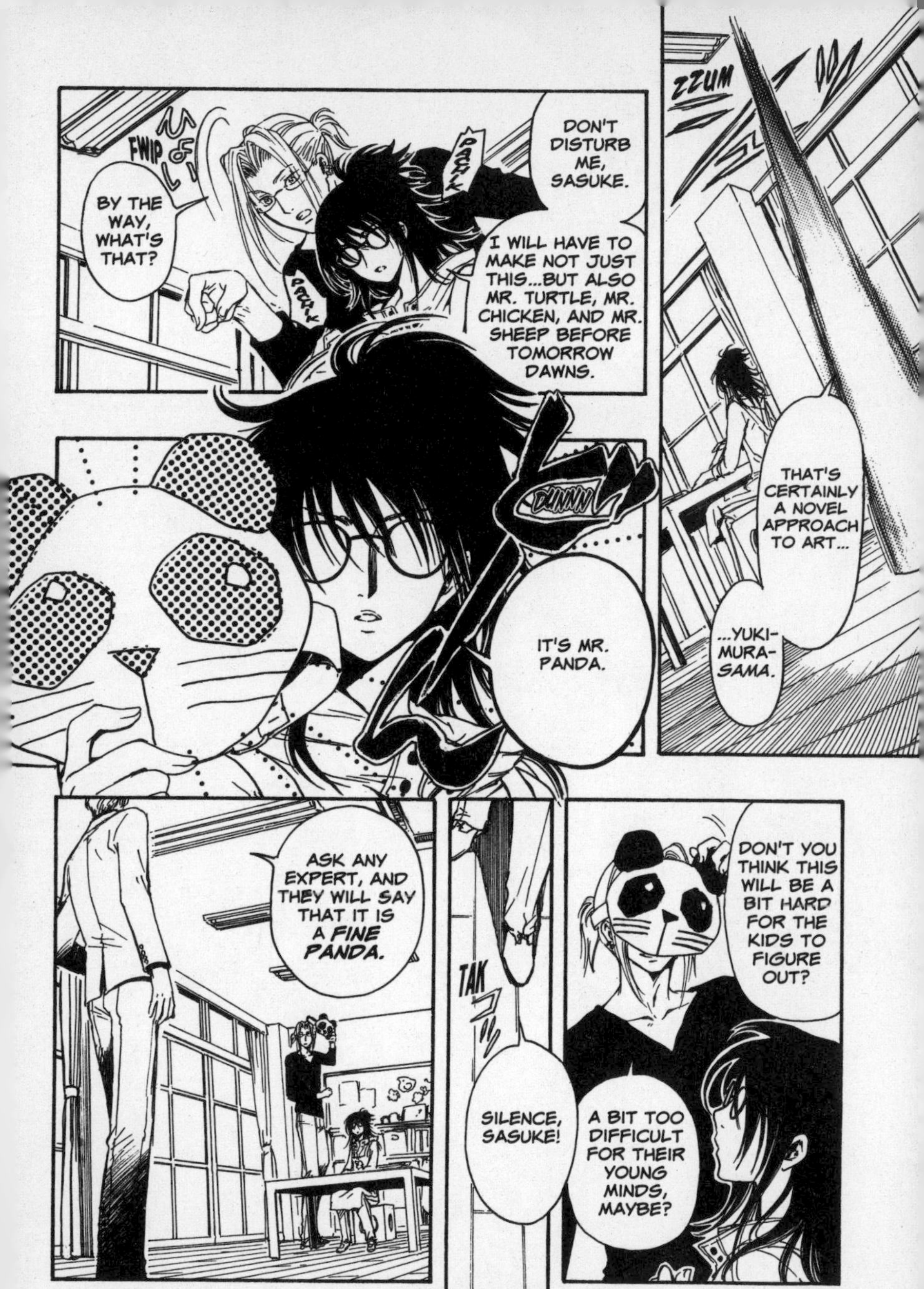
ZZUM
THAT'S CERTAINLY A NOVEL APPROACH TO ART...
...YUKIMURA-SAMA.
DON'T DISTURB ME, SASUKE.
PACHIK
I WILL HAVE TO MAKE NOT JUST THIS...BUT ALSO MR. TURTLE, MR. CHICKEN, AND MR. SHEEP BEFORE TOMORROW DAWNS.
FWIP
BY THE WAY, WHAT'S THAT?
PACHIK
DUNNN
IT'S MR. PANDA.
DON'T YOU THINK THIS WILL BE A BIT HARD FOR THE KIDS TO FIGURE OUT?
A BIT TOO DIFFICULT FOR THEIR YOUNG MINDS, MAYBE?
SILENCE, SASUKE!
TAK
ASK ANY EXPERT, AND THEY WILL SAY THAT IT IS A *FINE PANDA.*

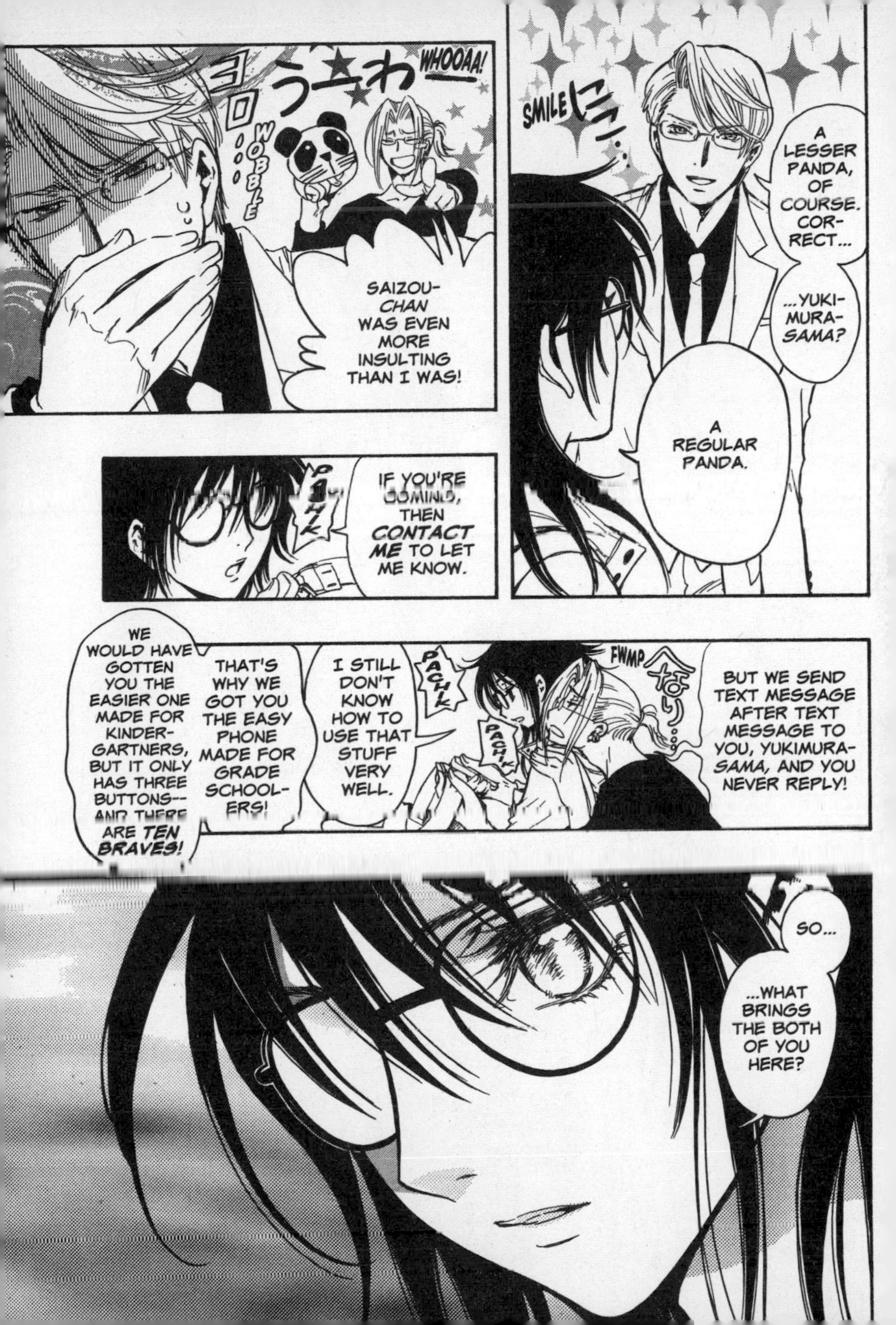
SMILE
A LESSER PANDA, OF COURSE. CORRECT...
...YUKIMURA-SAMA?
A REGULAR PANDA.
WHOOAA!
WOBBLE
SAIZOU-CHAN WAS EVEN MORE INSULTING THAN I WAS!
PACHIK
IF YOU'RE COMING, THEN CONTACT ME TO LET ME KNOW.
BUT WE SEND TEXT MESSAGE AFTER TEXT MESSAGE TO YOU, YUKIMURA-SAMA, AND YOU NEVER REPLY!
FWMP
PACHIK
PACHIK
I STILL DON'T KNOW HOW TO USE THAT STUFF VERY WELL.
THAT'S WHY WE GOT YOU THE EASY PHONE MADE FOR GRADE SCHOOLERS!
WE WOULD HAVE GOTTEN YOU THE EASIER ONE MADE FOR KINDERGARTNERS, BUT IT ONLY HAS THREE BUTTONS--AND THERE ARE TEN BRAVES!
SO...
...WHAT BRINGS THE BOTH OF YOU HERE?

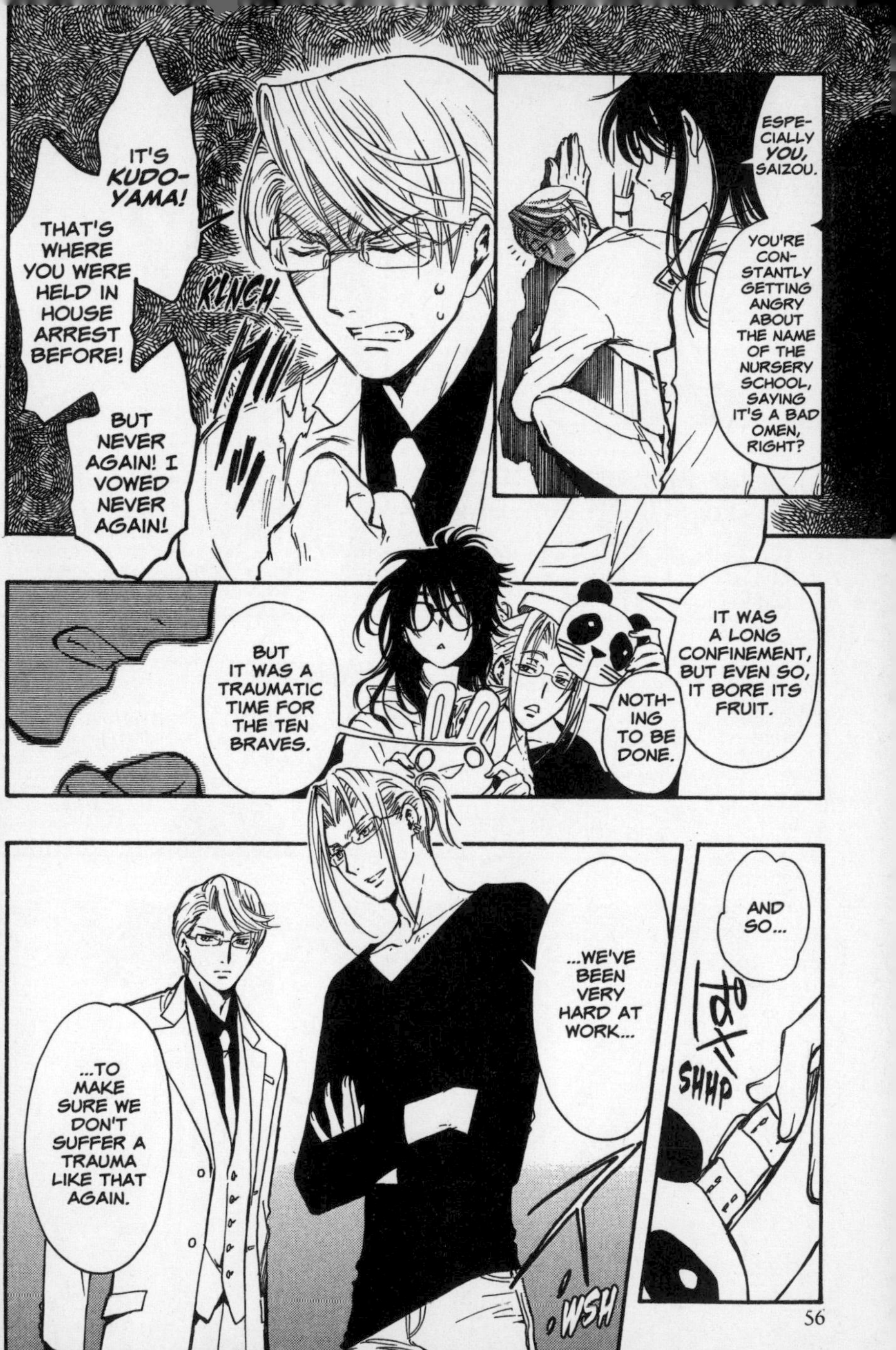
ESPE-CIALLY YOU, SAIZOU.
YOU'RE CON-STANTLY GETTING ANGRY ABOUT THE NAME OF THE NURSERY SCHOOL, SAYING IT'S A BAD OMEN, RIGHT?
IT'S KUDO-YAMA!
THAT'S WHERE YOU WERE HELD IN HOUSE ARREST BEFORE!
KLNCH
BUT NEVER AGAIN! I VOWED NEVER AGAIN!
IT WAS A LONG CONFINEMENT, BUT EVEN SO, IT BORE ITS FRUIT.
NOTH-ING TO BE DONE.
BUT IT WAS A TRAUMATIC TIME FOR THE TEN BRAVES.
AND SO...
SHHP
...WE'VE BEEN VERY HARD AT WORK...
...TO MAKE SURE WE DON'T SUFFER A TRAUMA LIKE THAT AGAIN.
WSH

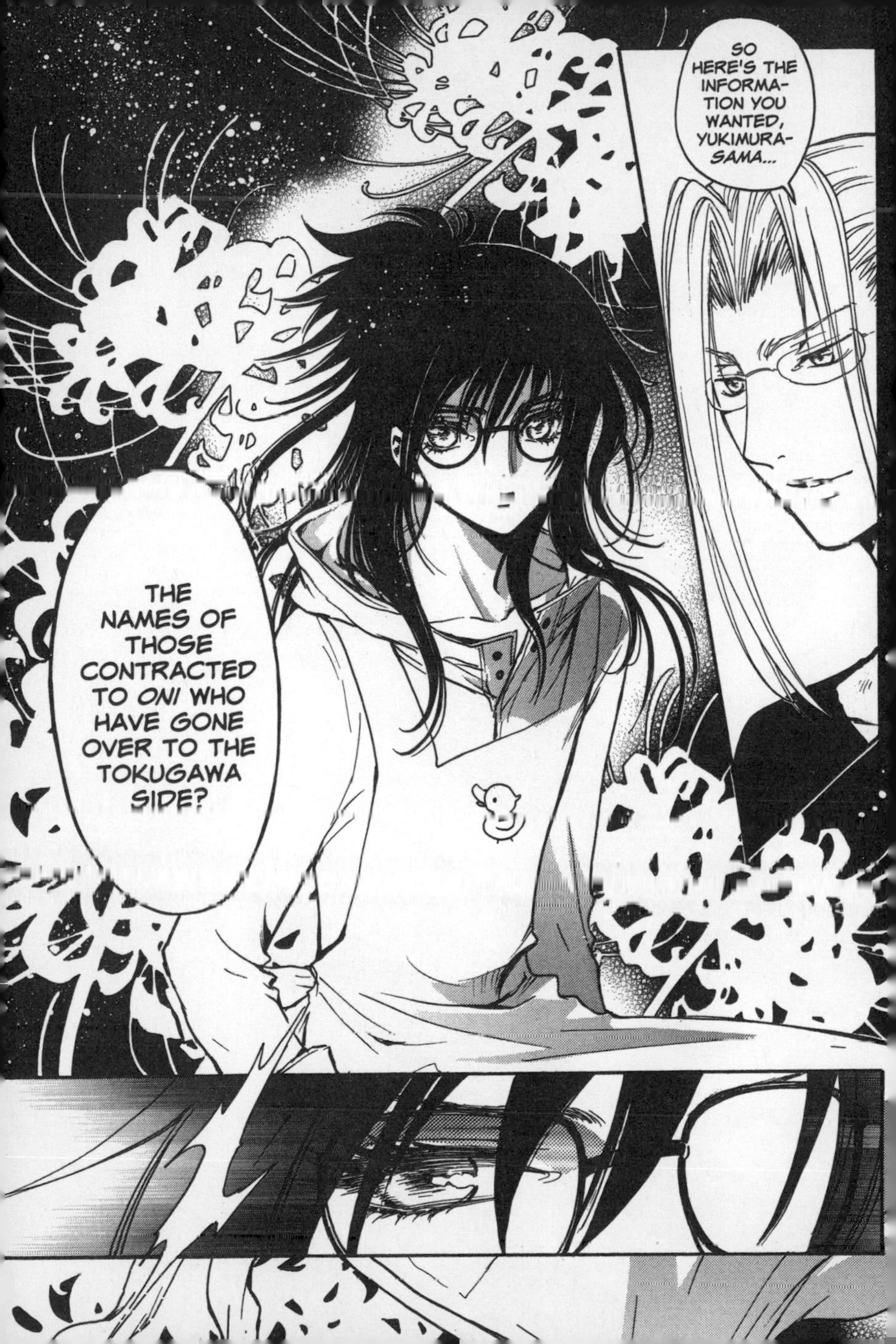
SO HERE'S THE INFORMATION YOU WANTED, YUKIMURA-SAMA...
THE NAMES OF THOSE CONTRACTED TO *ONI* WHO HAVE GONE OVER TO THE TOKUGAWA SIDE?

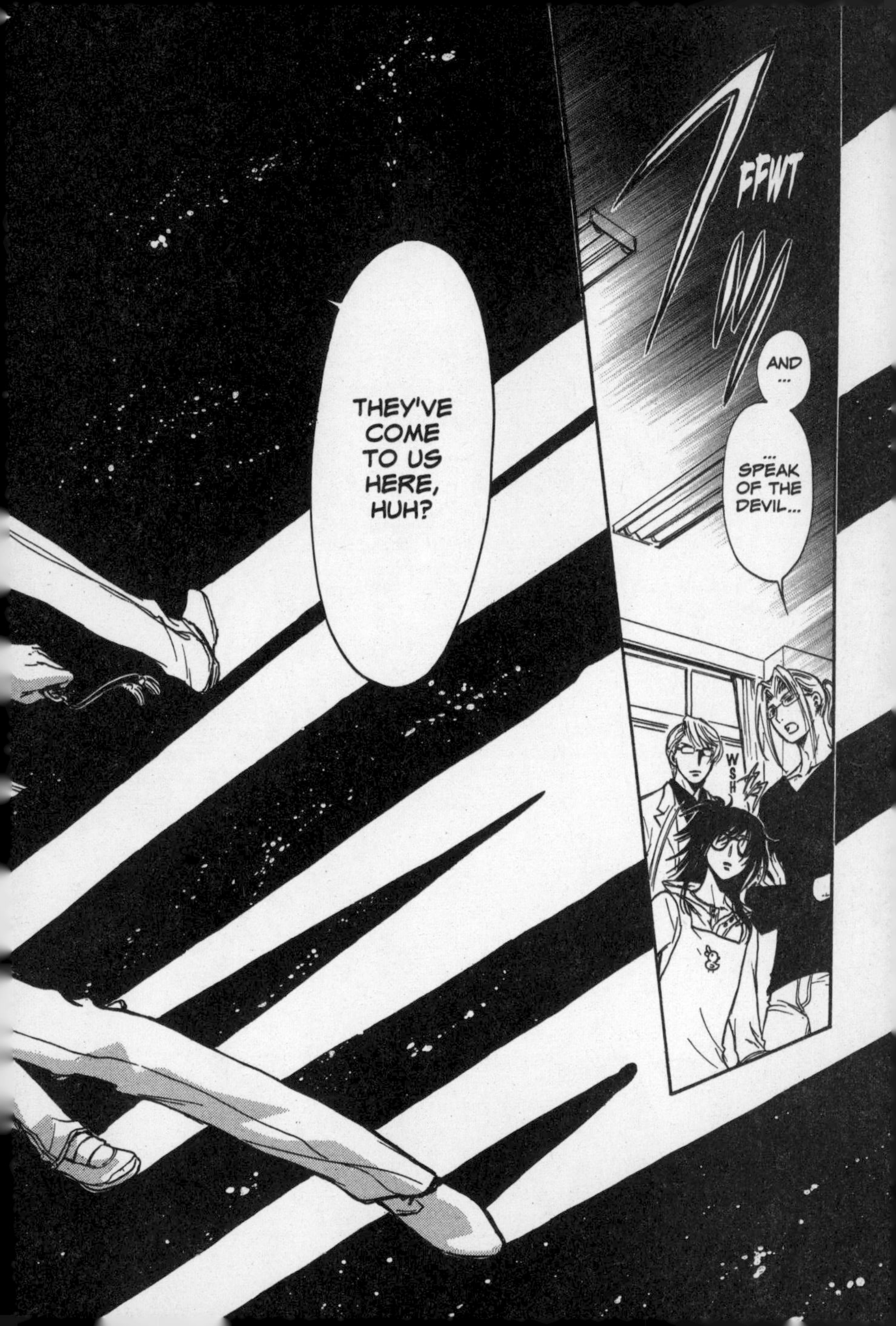

FFWT
AND ...
... SPEAK OF THE DEVIL...
WSH
THEY'VE COME TO US HERE, HUH?

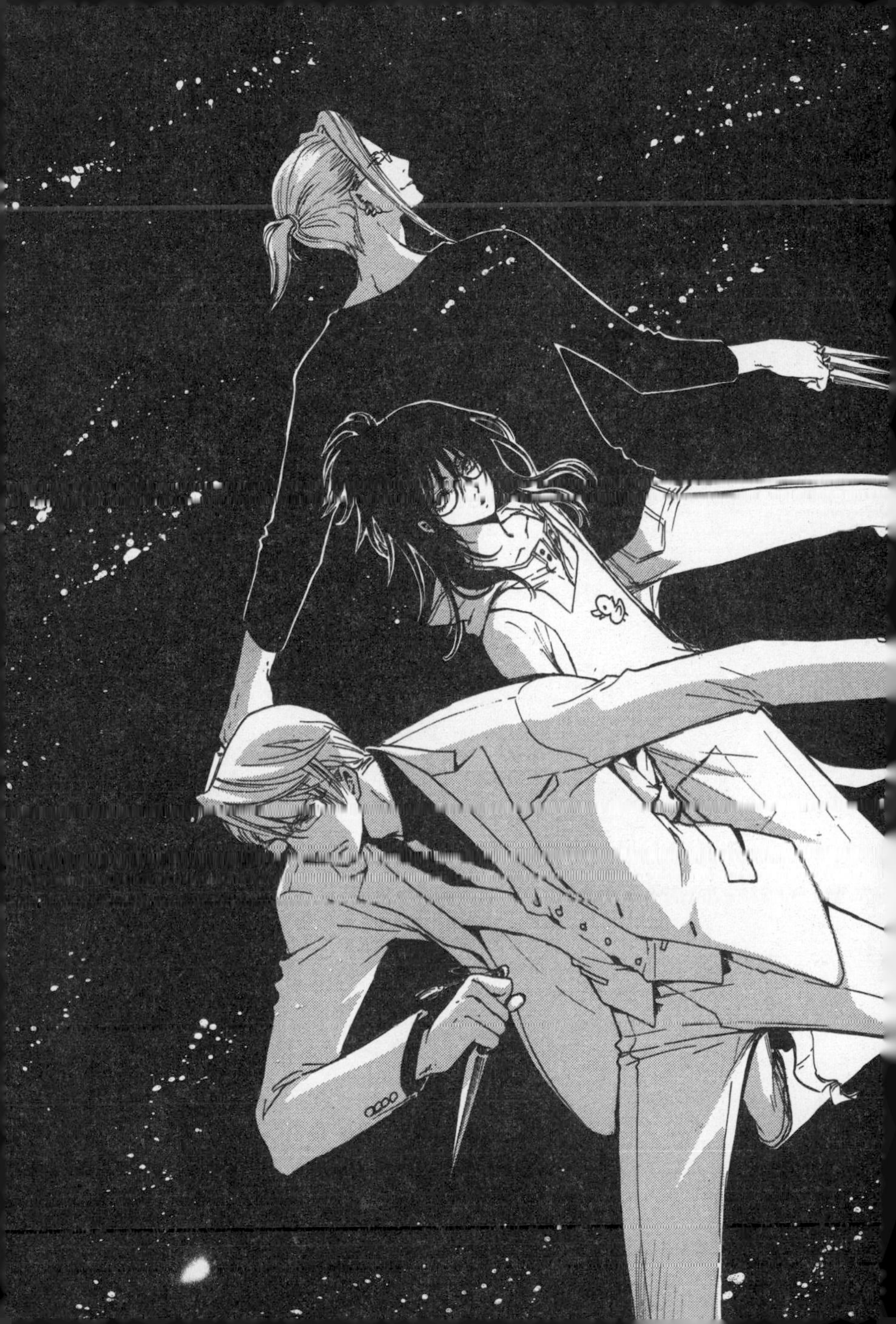

GATE 7

ゲート セブン

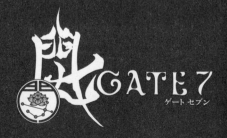

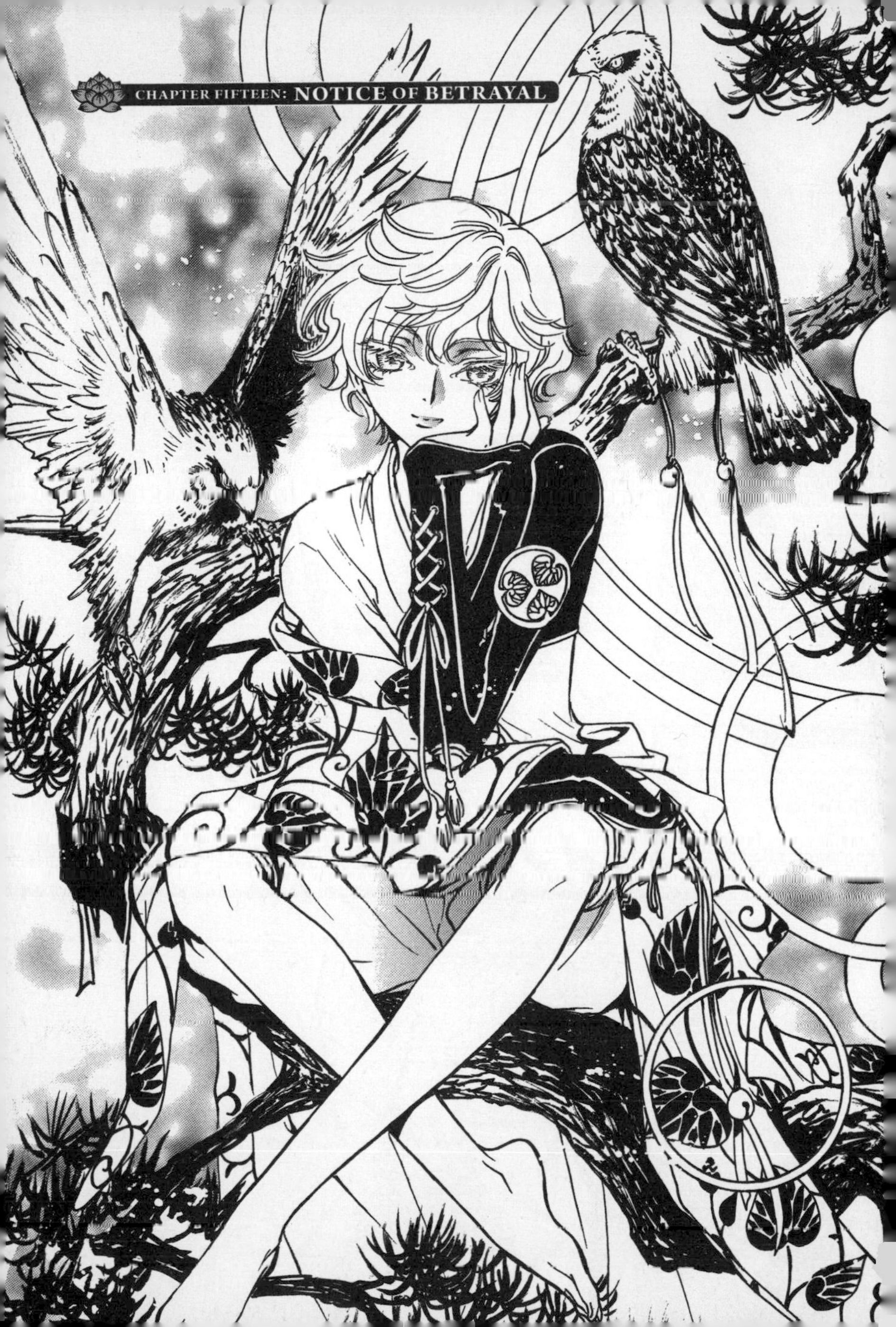
CHAPTER FIFTEEN: NOTICE OF BETRAYAL

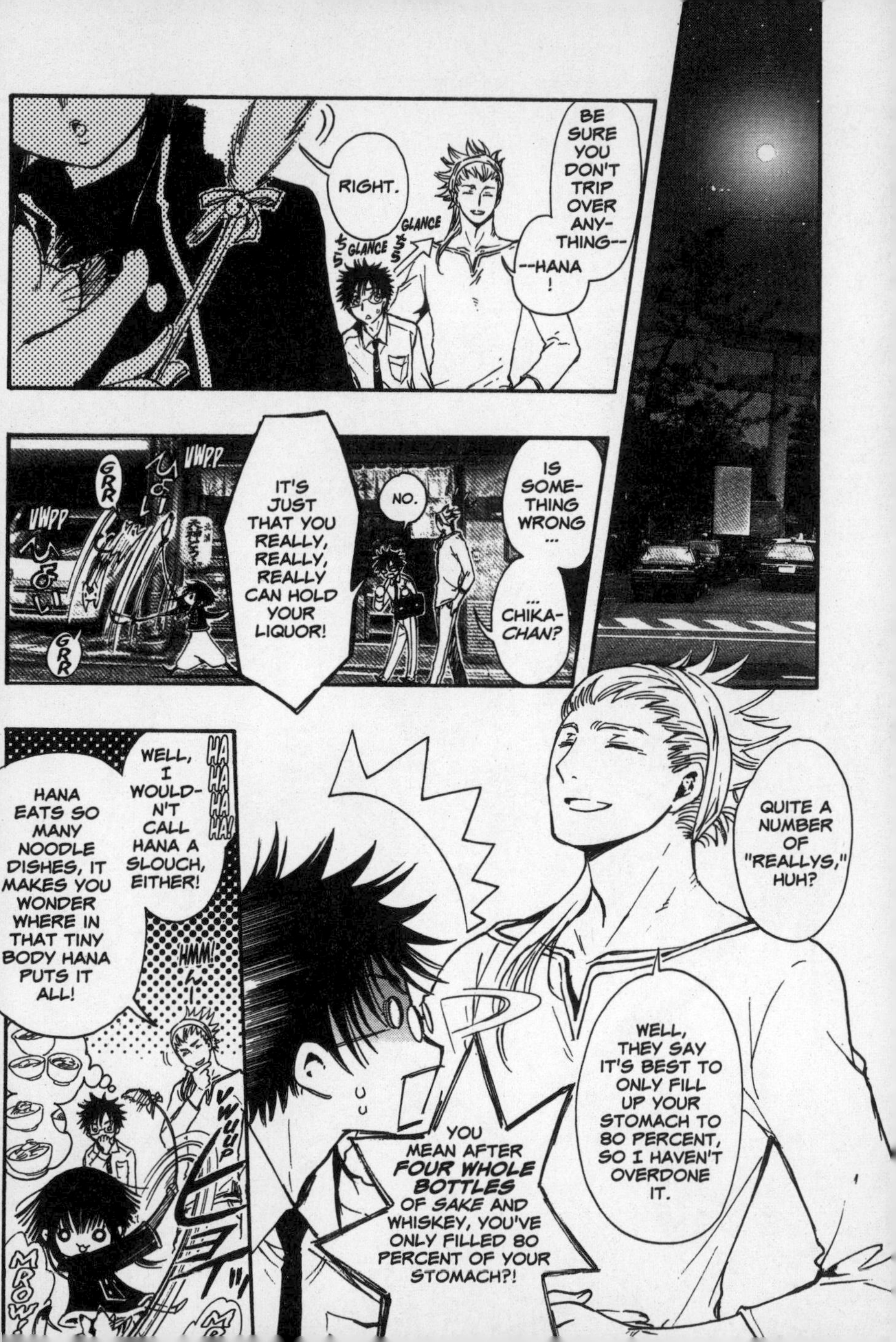
BE SURE YOU DON'T TRIP OVER ANYTHING--
--HANA!
RIGHT.
GLANCE
GLANCE
IS SOMETHING WRONG ...
...CHIKA-CHAN?
NO.
IT'S JUST THAT YOU REALLY, REALLY, REALLY CAN HOLD YOUR LIQUOR!
UWPP
UWPP
GRR
GRR
QUITE A NUMBER OF "REALLYS," HUH?
WELL, THEY SAY IT'S BEST TO ONLY FILL UP YOUR STOMACH TO 80 PERCENT, SO I HAVEN'T OVERDONE IT.
YOU MEAN AFTER **FOUR WHOLE BOTTLES** OF SAKE AND WHISKEY, YOU'VE ONLY FILLED 80 PERCENT OF YOUR STOMACH?!
HA HA HA HA!
WELL, I WOULDN'T CALL HANA A SLOUCH, EITHER!
HANA EATS SO MANY NOODLE DISHES, IT MAKES YOU WONDER WHERE IN THAT TINY BODY HANA PUTS IT ALL!
HMM!
VWUUP
MROW

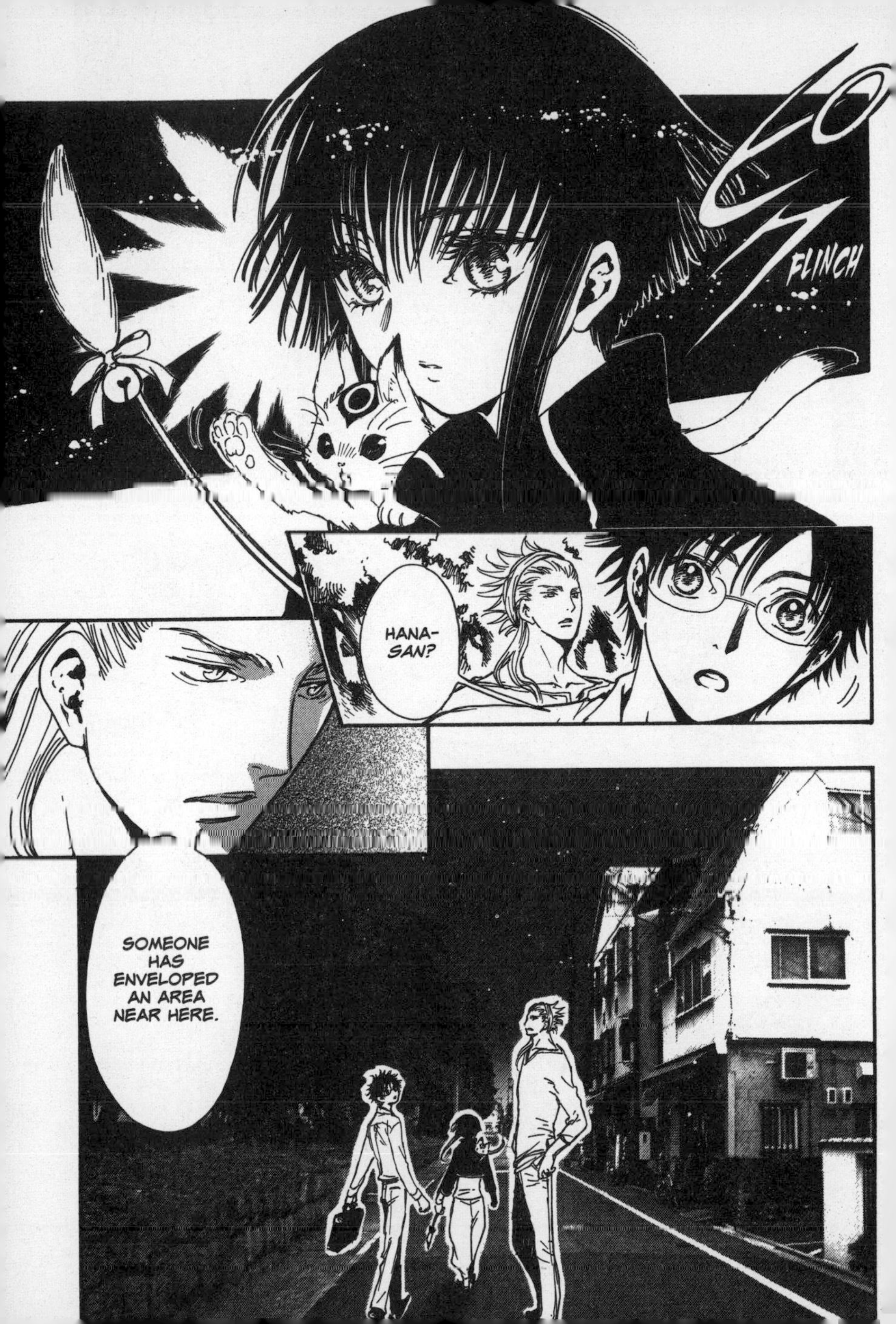
FLINCH
HANA-SAN?
SOMEONE HAS ENVELOPED AN AREA NEAR HERE.

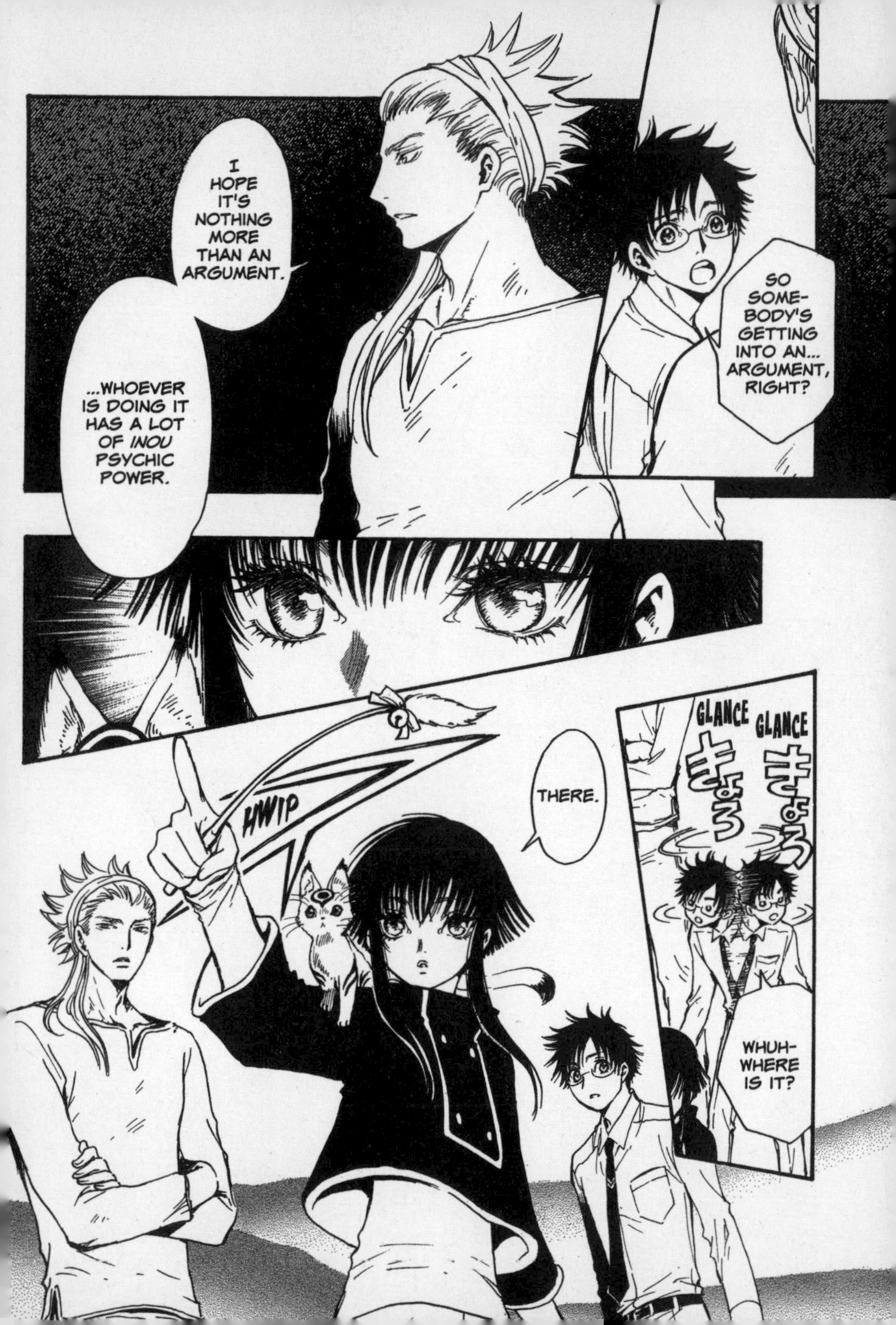
SO SOME-BODY'S GETTING INTO AN... ARGUMENT, RIGHT?
I HOPE IT'S NOTHING MORE THAN AN ARGUMENT.
...WHOEVER IS DOING IT HAS A LOT OF *INOU* PSYCHIC POWER.
GLANCE GLANCE
きょろきょろ
WHUH-WHERE IS IT?
HWIP
THERE.

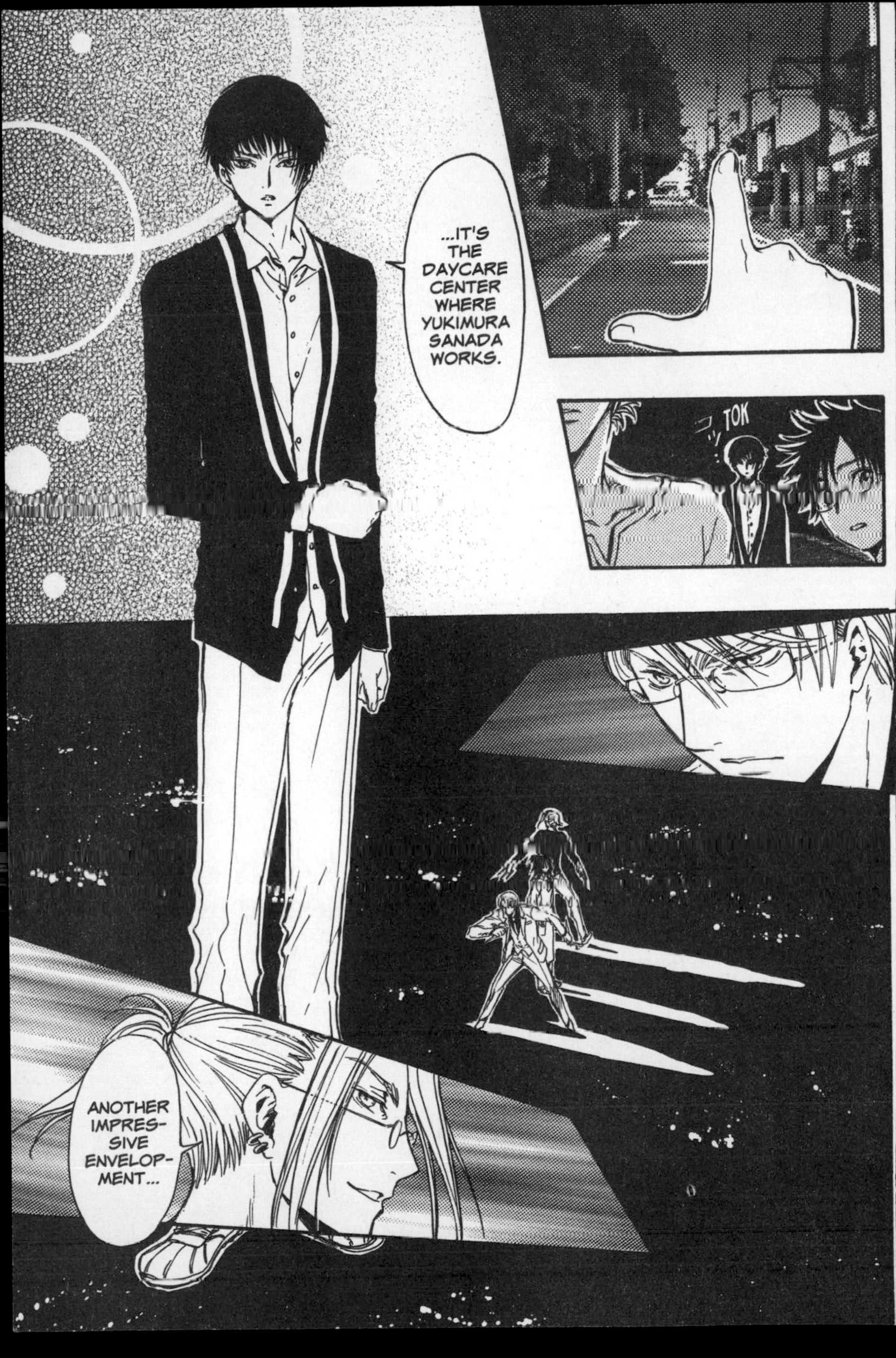
...IT'S THE DAYCARE CENTER WHERE YUKIMURA SANADA WORKS.
TOK
ANOTHER IMPRESSIVE ENVELOPMENT...

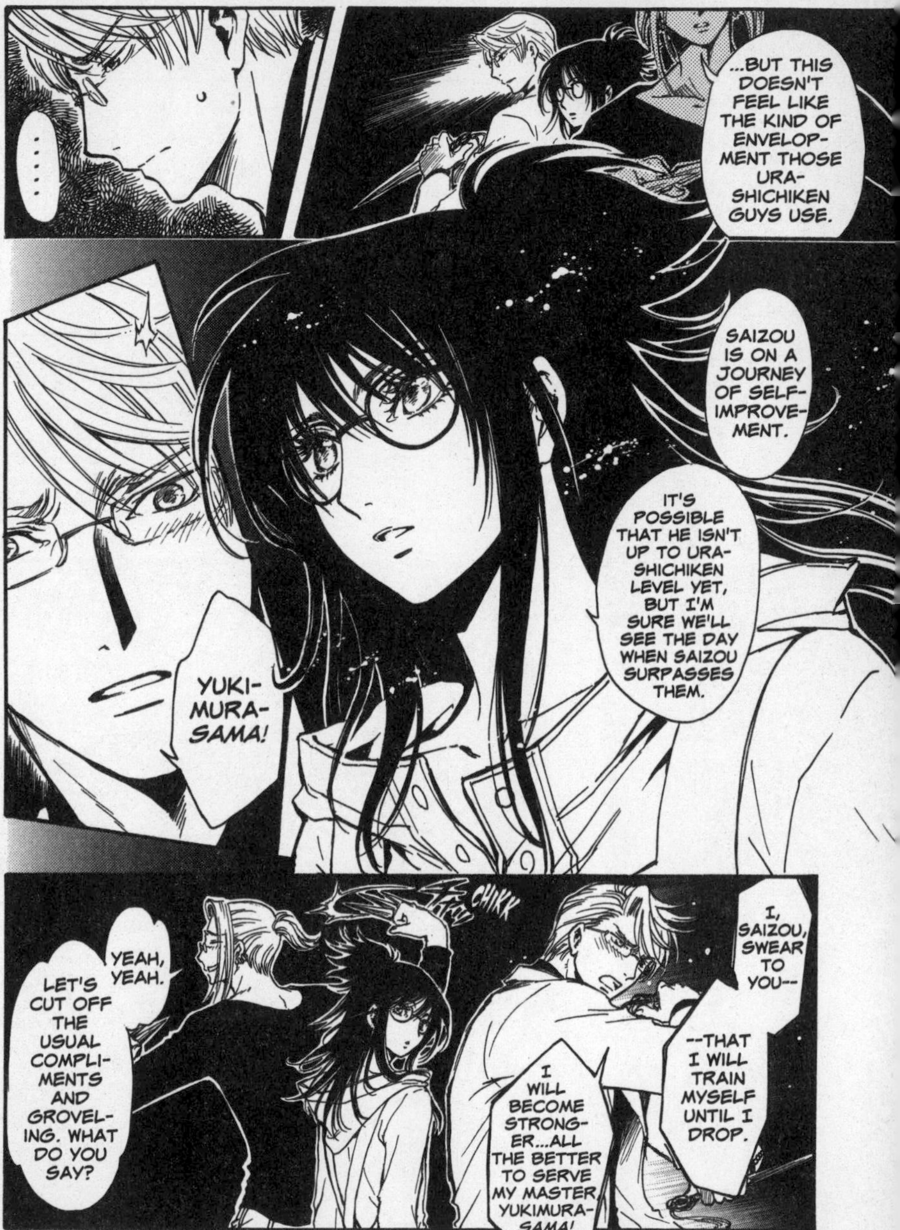
...BUT THIS DOESN'T FEEL LIKE THE KIND OF ENVELOPMENT THOSE URA-SHICHIKEN GUYS USE.
......
SAIZOU IS ON A JOURNEY OF SELF-IMPROVEMENT.
IT'S POSSIBLE THAT HE ISN'T UP TO URA-SHICHIKEN LEVEL YET, BUT I'M SURE WE'LL SEE THE DAY WHEN SAIZOU SURPASSES THEM.
YUKIMURA-SAMA!
I, SAIZOU, SWEAR TO YOU--
--THAT I WILL TRAIN MYSELF UNTIL I DROP.
I WILL BECOME STRONGER...ALL THE BETTER TO SERVE MY MASTER YUKIMURA-SAMA!
CHIKK
YEAH, YEAH.
LET'S CUT OFF THE USUAL COMPLIMENTS AND GROVELING. WHAT DO YOU SAY?

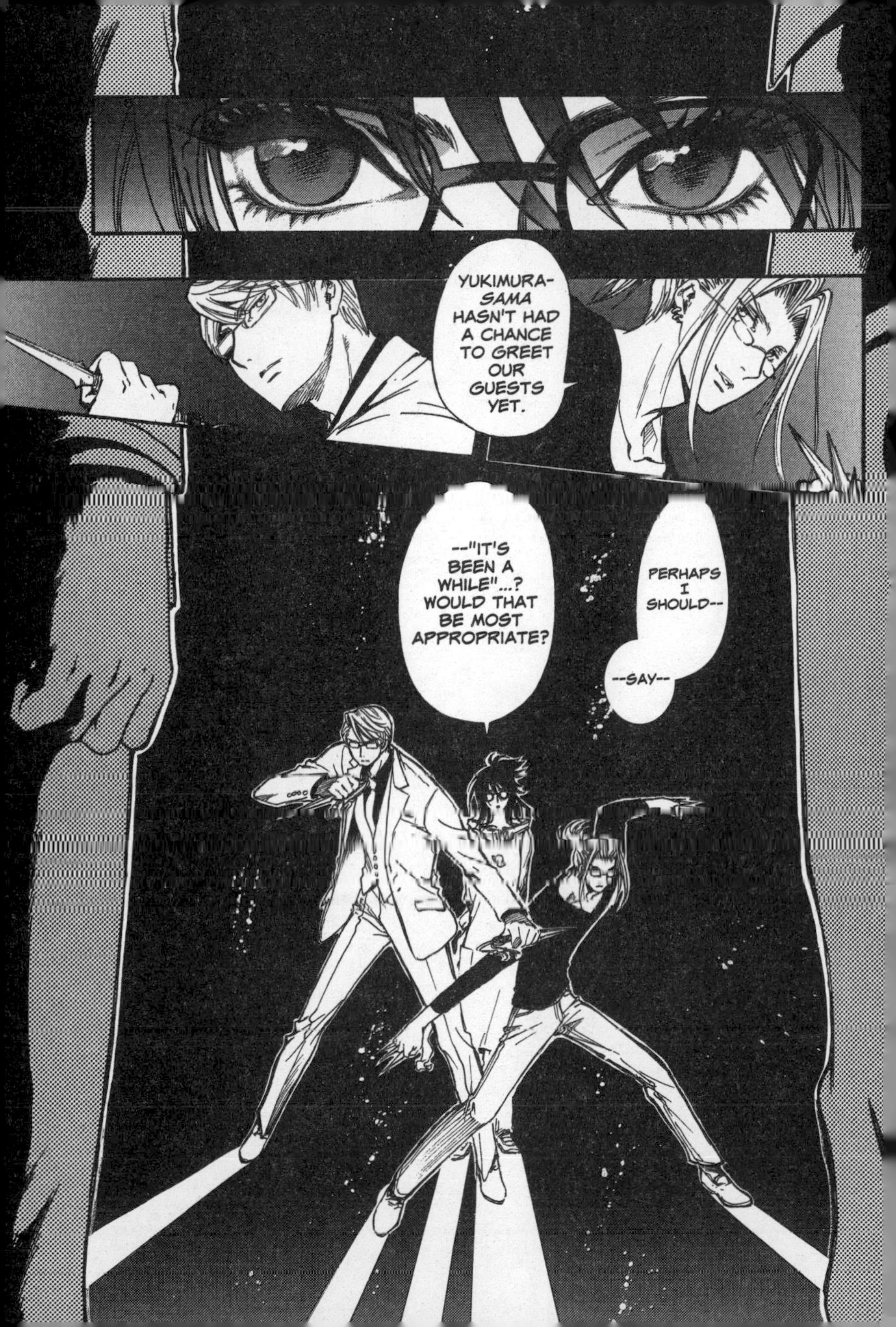
YUKIMURA-SAMA HASN'T HAD A CHANCE TO GREET OUR GUESTS YET.
PERHAPS I SHOULD--
--SAY--
--"IT'S BEEN A WHILE"...? WOULD THAT BE MOST APPROPRIATE?

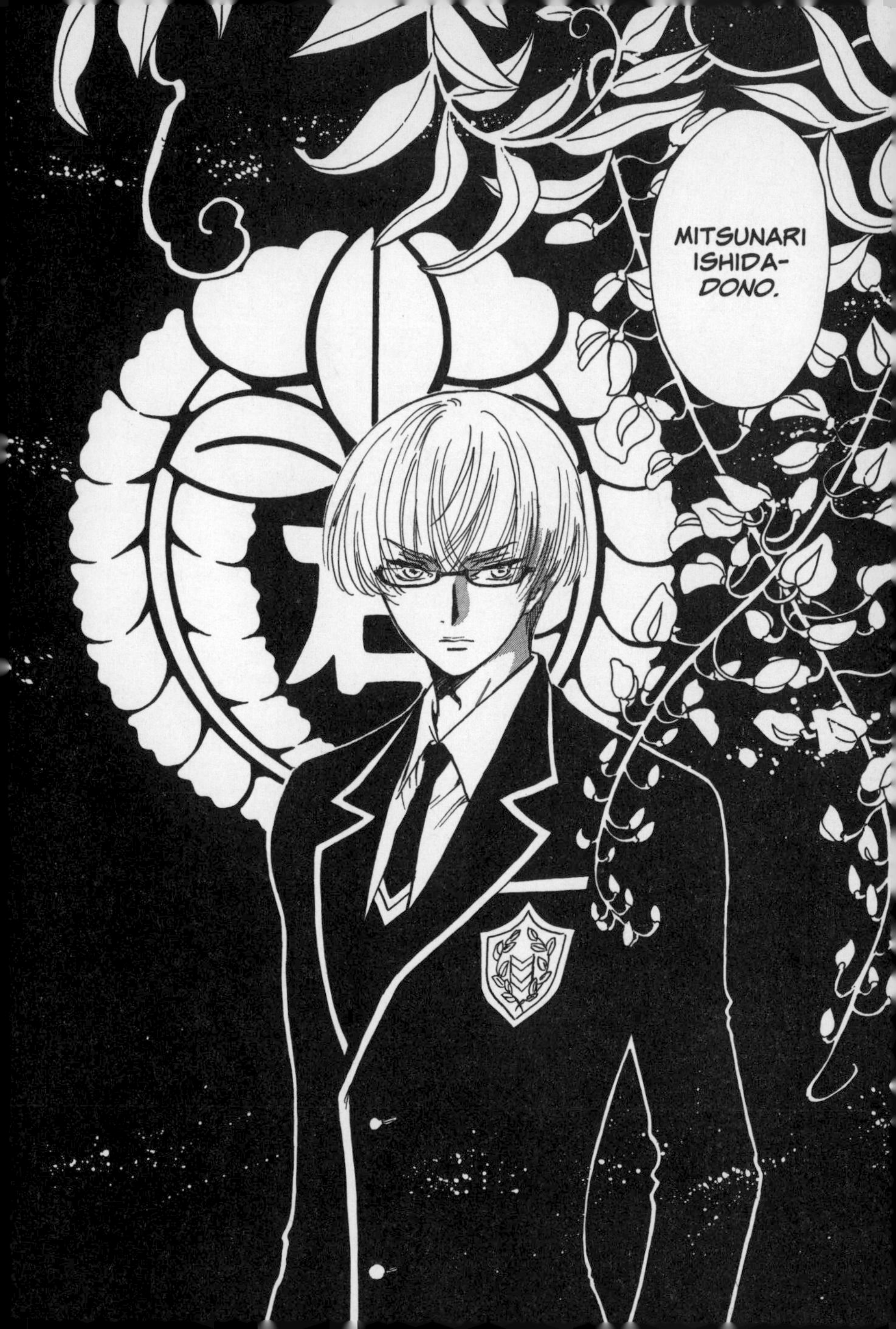
MITSUNARI ISHIDA-DONO.

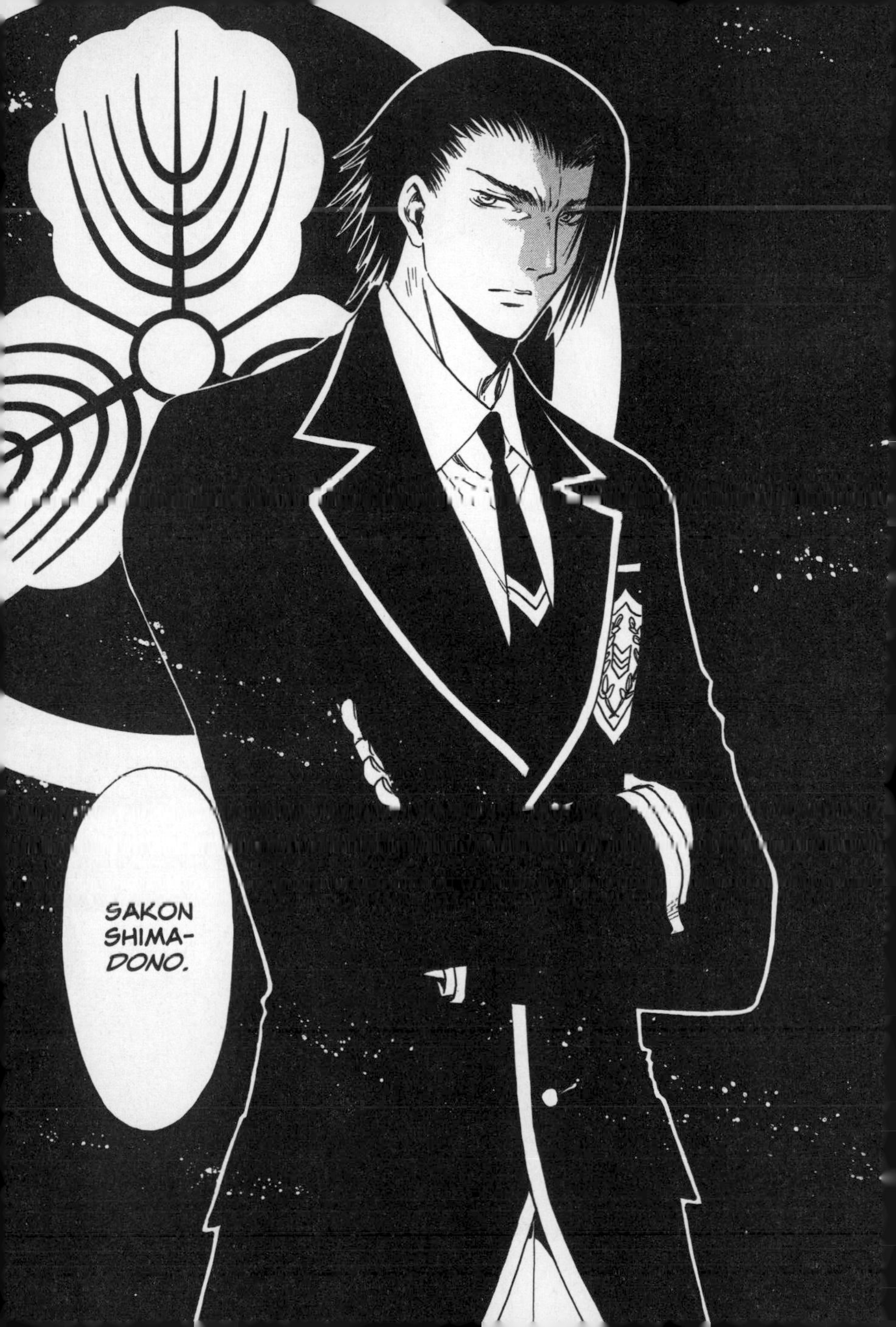
SAKON SHIMA-DONO.

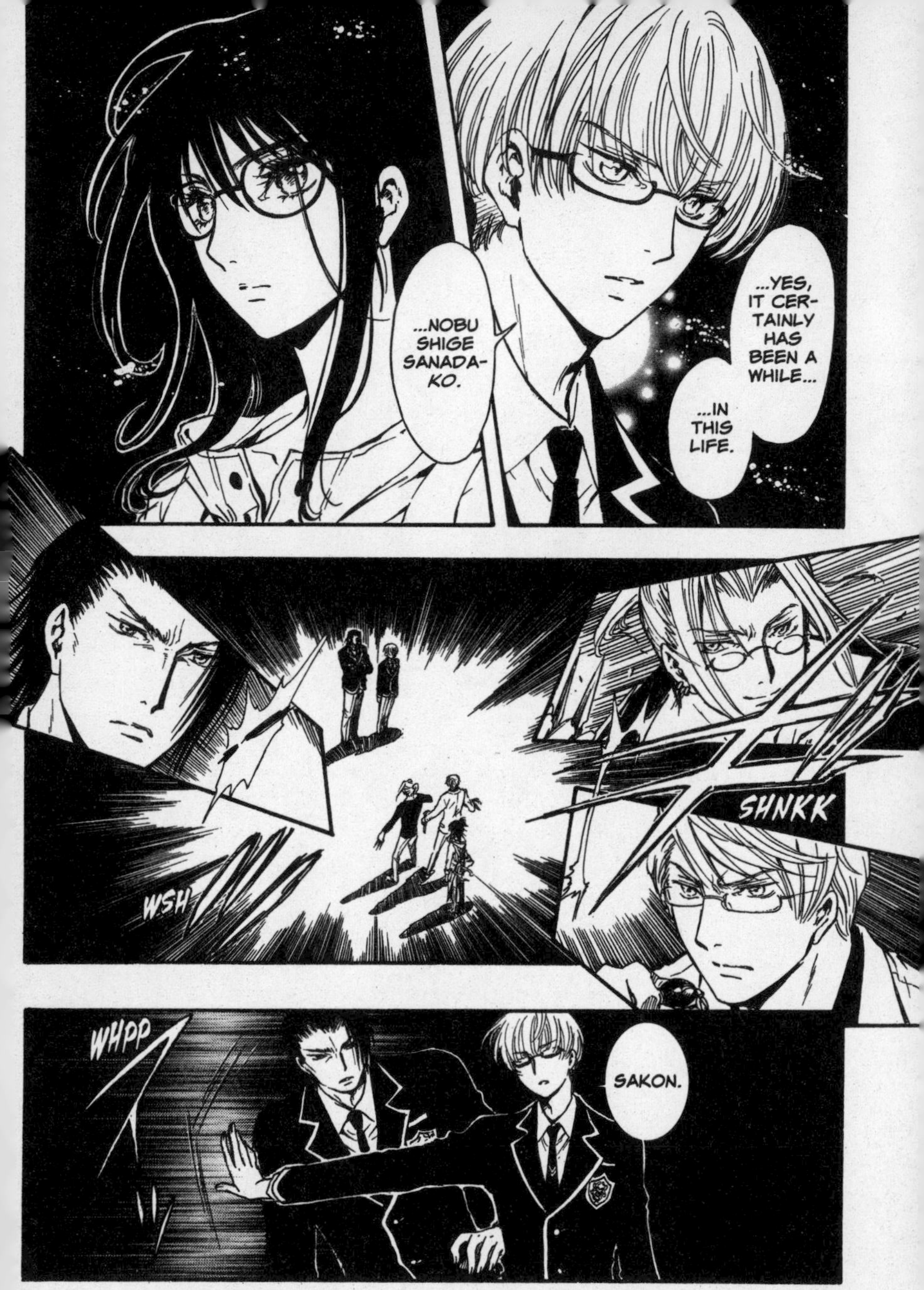
...YES, IT CER-TAINLY HAS BEEN A WHILE...
...IN THIS LIFE.
...NOBU SHIGE SANADA-KO.
SHNKK
WSH
SAKON.
WHPP

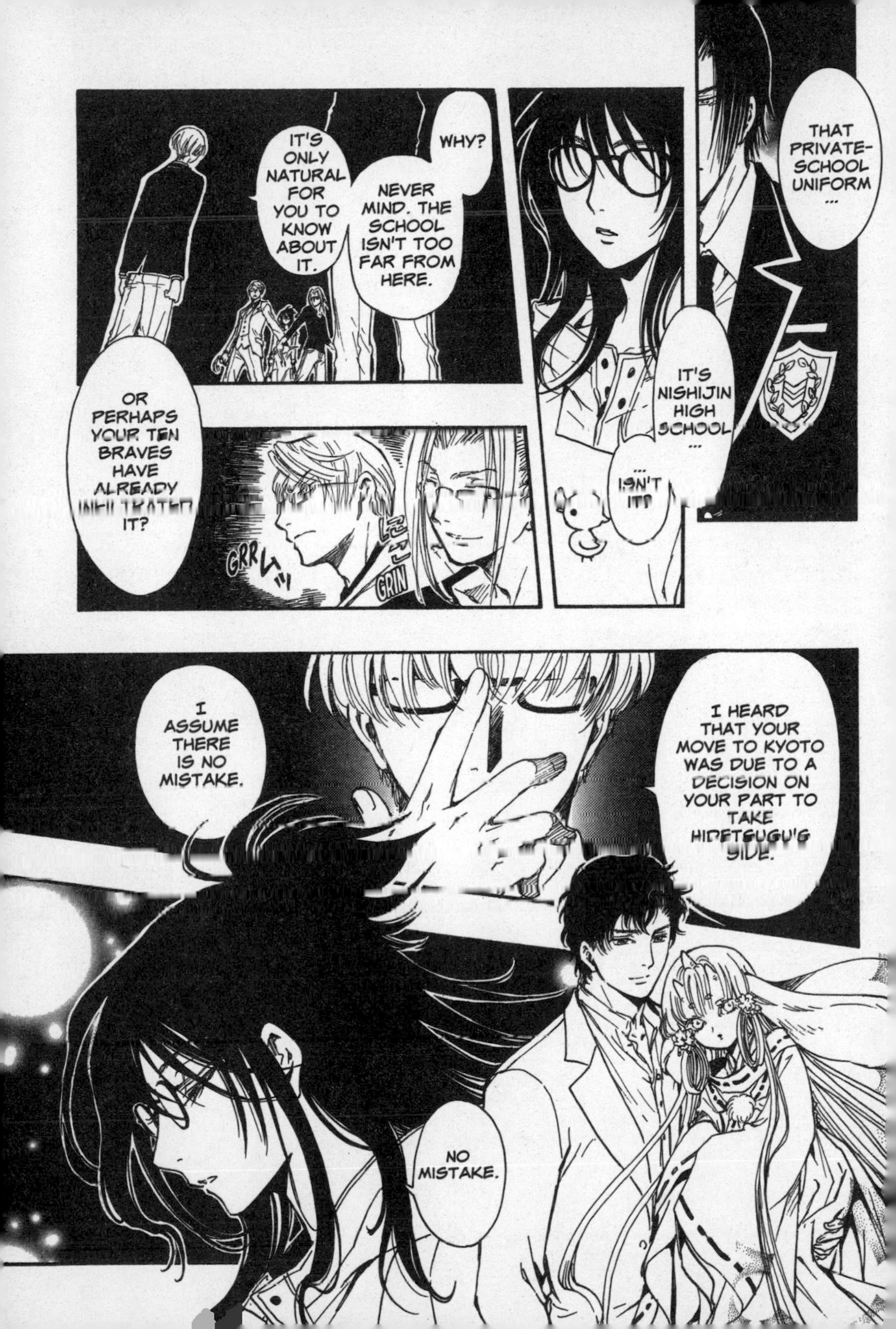
THAT PRIVATE-SCHOOL UNIFORM ...
IT'S NISHIJIN HIGH SCHOOL ...
... ISN'T IT?
WHY?
NEVER MIND. THE SCHOOL ISN'T TOO FAR FROM HERE.
IT'S ONLY NATURAL FOR YOU TO KNOW ABOUT IT.
OR PERHAPS YOUR TEN BRAVES HAVE ALREADY INFILTRATED IT?
GRIN
GRR
I HEARD THAT YOUR MOVE TO KYOTO WAS DUE TO A DECISION ON YOUR PART TO TAKE HIDETSUGU'S SIDE.
I ASSUME THERE IS NO MISTAKE.
NO MISTAKE.

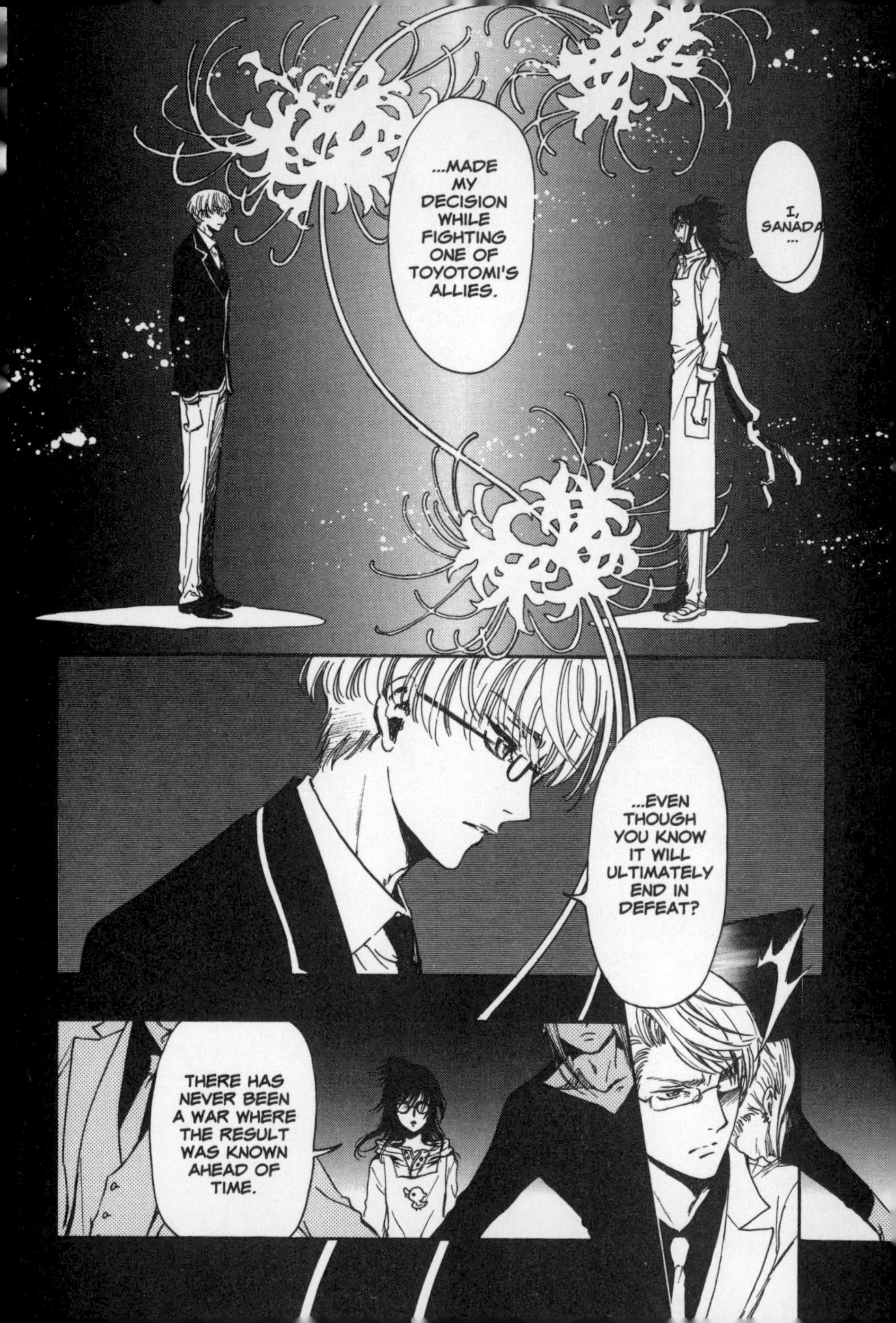
I, SANADA...
...MADE MY DECISION WHILE FIGHTING ONE OF TOYOTOMI'S ALLIES.
...EVEN THOUGH YOU KNOW IT WILL ULTIMATELY END IN DEFEAT?
THERE HAS NEVER BEEN A WAR WHERE THE RESULT WAS KNOWN AHEAD OF TIME.

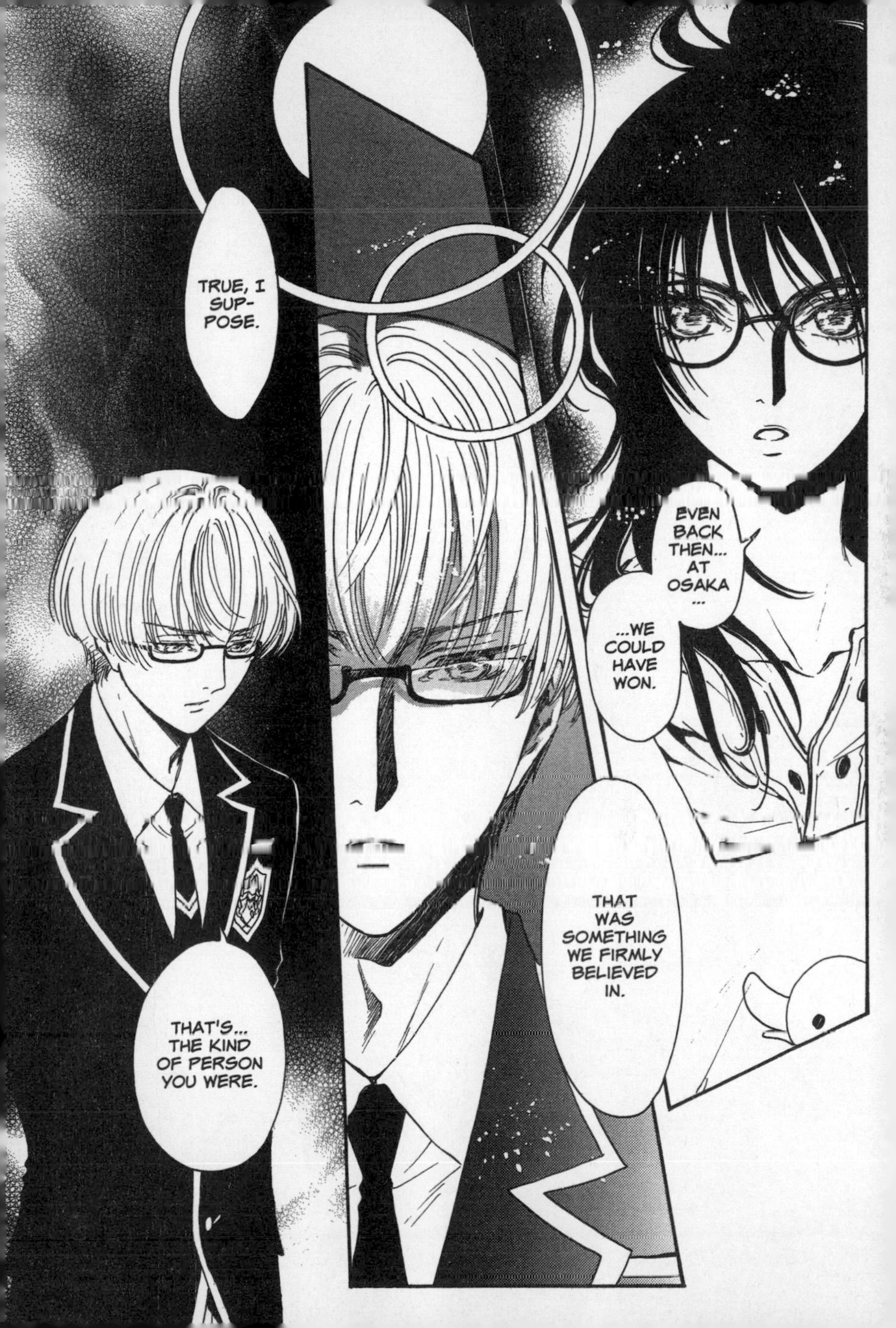
EVEN BACK THEN... AT OSAKA...
...WE COULD HAVE WON.
THAT WAS SOMETHING WE FIRMLY BELIEVED IN.
TRUE, I SUP-POSE.
THAT'S... THE KIND OF PERSON YOU WERE.

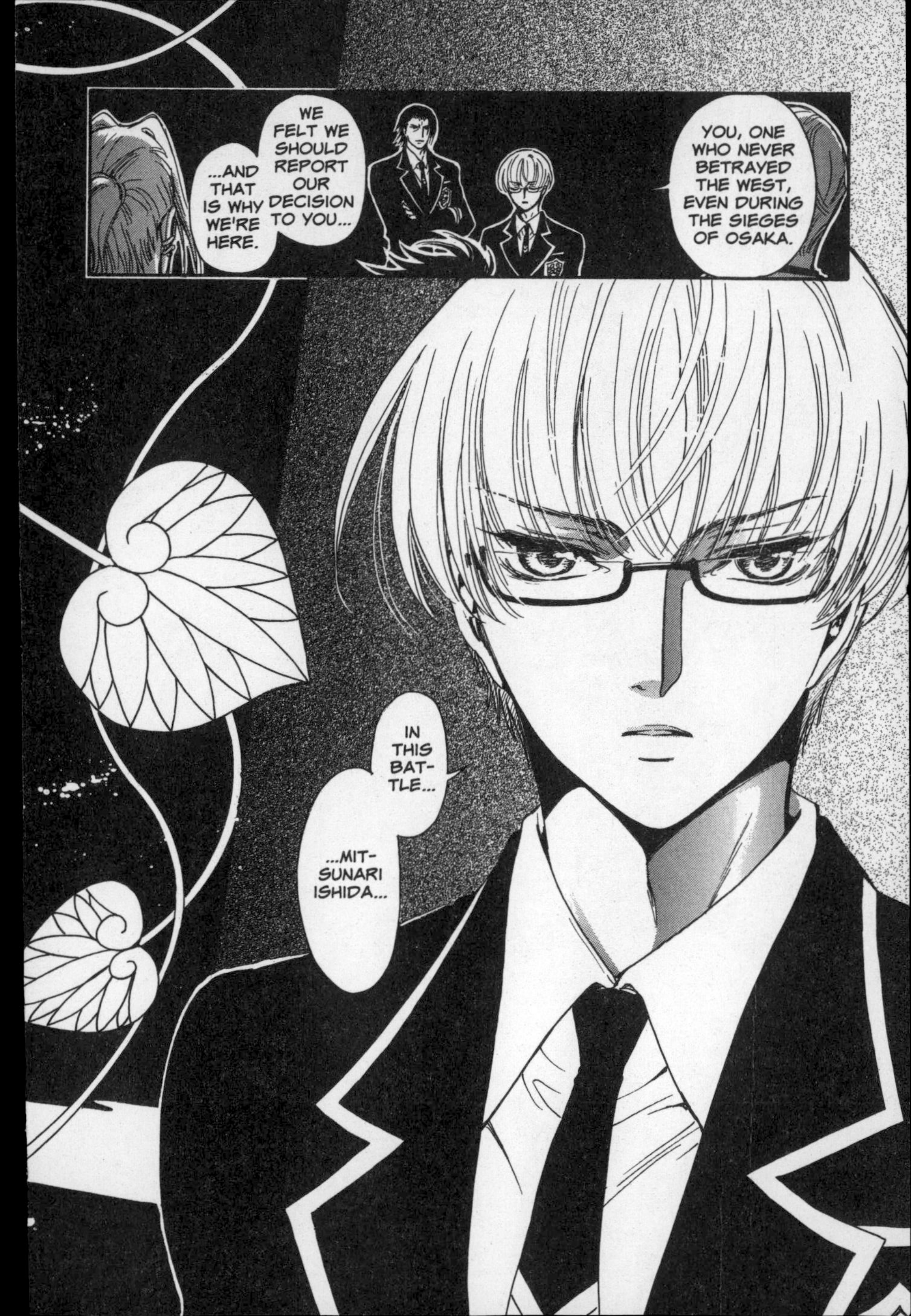
YOU, ONE WHO NEVER BETRAYED THE WEST, EVEN DURING THE SIEGES OF OSAKA.
WE FELT WE SHOULD REPORT OUR DECISION TO YOU...
...AND THAT IS WHY WE'RE HERE.
IN THIS BAT-TLE...
...MIT-SUNARI ISHIDA...

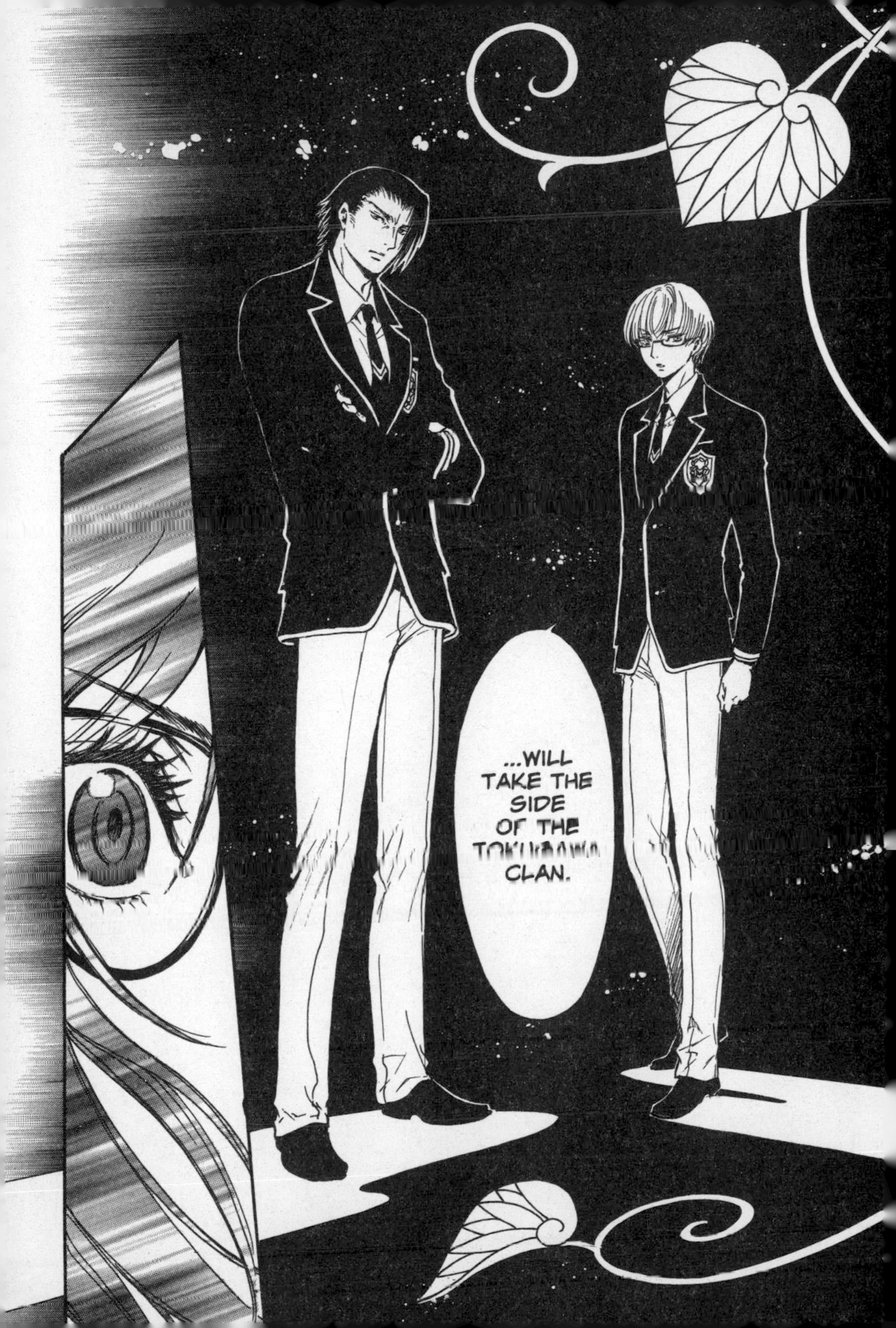
...WILL TAKE THE SIDE OF THE TOKUGAWA CLAN.

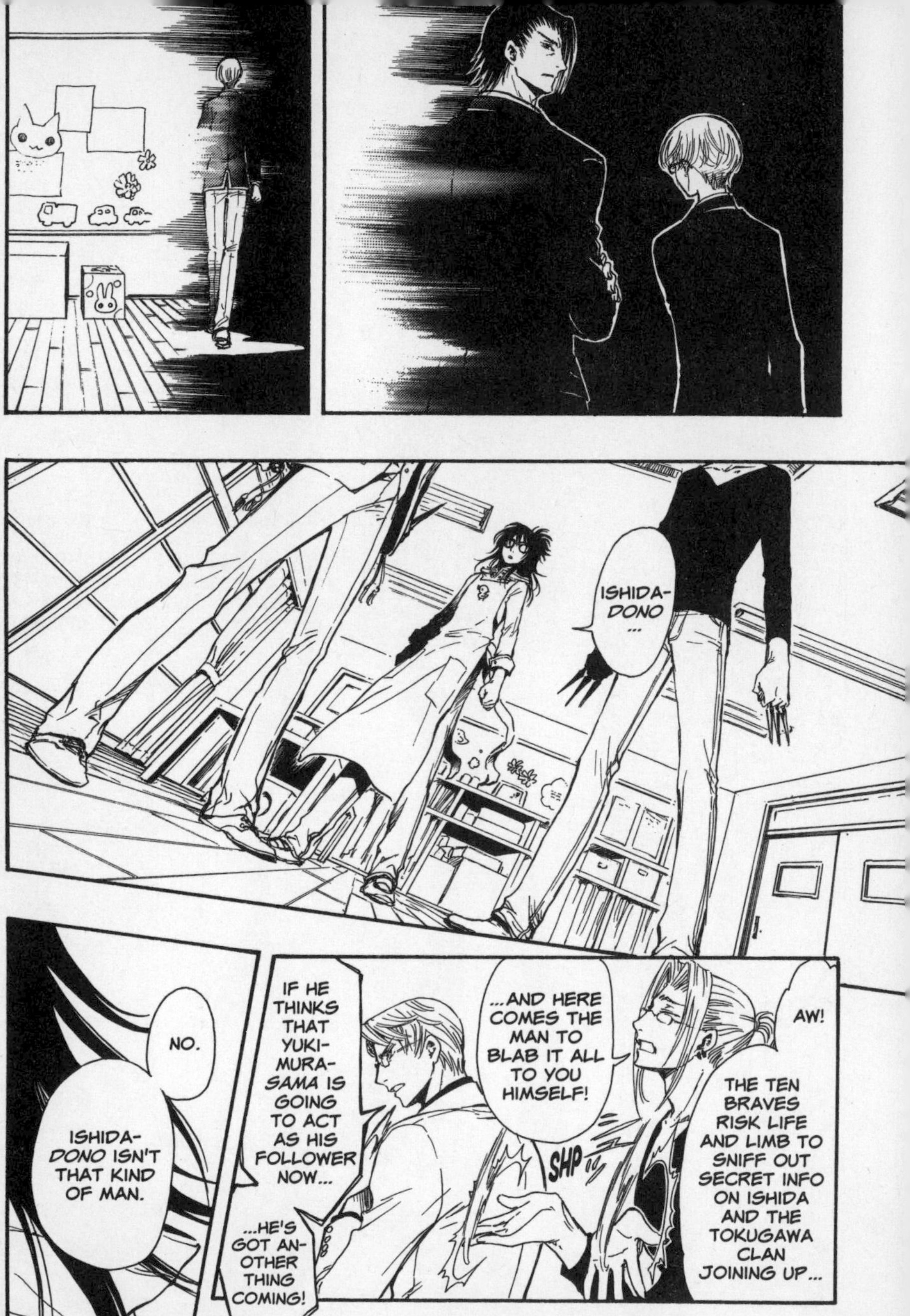
ISHIDA-DONO ...
AW!
THE TEN BRAVES RISK LIFE AND LIMB TO SNIFF OUT SECRET INFO ON ISHIDA AND THE TOKUGAWA CLAN JOINING UP...
...AND HERE COMES THE MAN TO BLAB IT ALL TO YOU HIMSELF!
SHP
IF HE THINKS THAT YUKIMURA-SAMA IS GOING TO ACT AS HIS FOLLOWER NOW...
...HE'S GOT ANOTHER THING COMING!
NO.
ISHIDA-DONO ISN'T THAT KIND OF MAN.

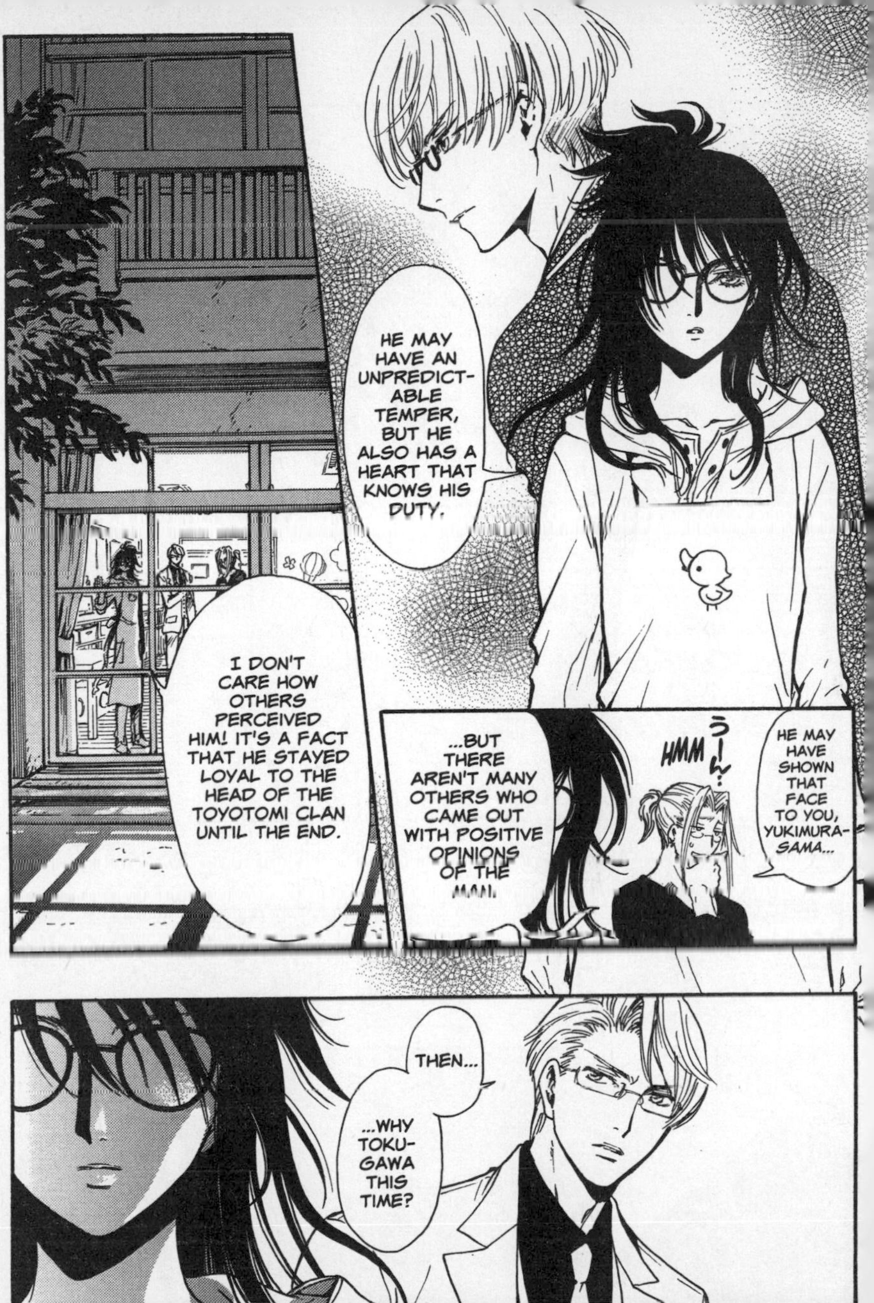
HE MAY HAVE AN UNPREDICT-ABLE TEMPER, BUT HE ALSO HAS A HEART THAT KNOWS HIS DUTY.
HE MAY HAVE SHOWN THAT FACE TO YOU, YUKIMURA-SAMA...
HMM
うーん…
...BUT THERE AREN'T MANY OTHERS WHO CAME OUT WITH POSITIVE OPINIONS OF THE MAN.
I DON'T CARE HOW OTHERS PERCEIVED HIM! IT'S A FACT THAT HE STAYED LOYAL TO THE HEAD OF THE TOYOTOMI CLAN UNTIL THE END.
THEN...
...WHY TOKU-GAWA THIS TIME?

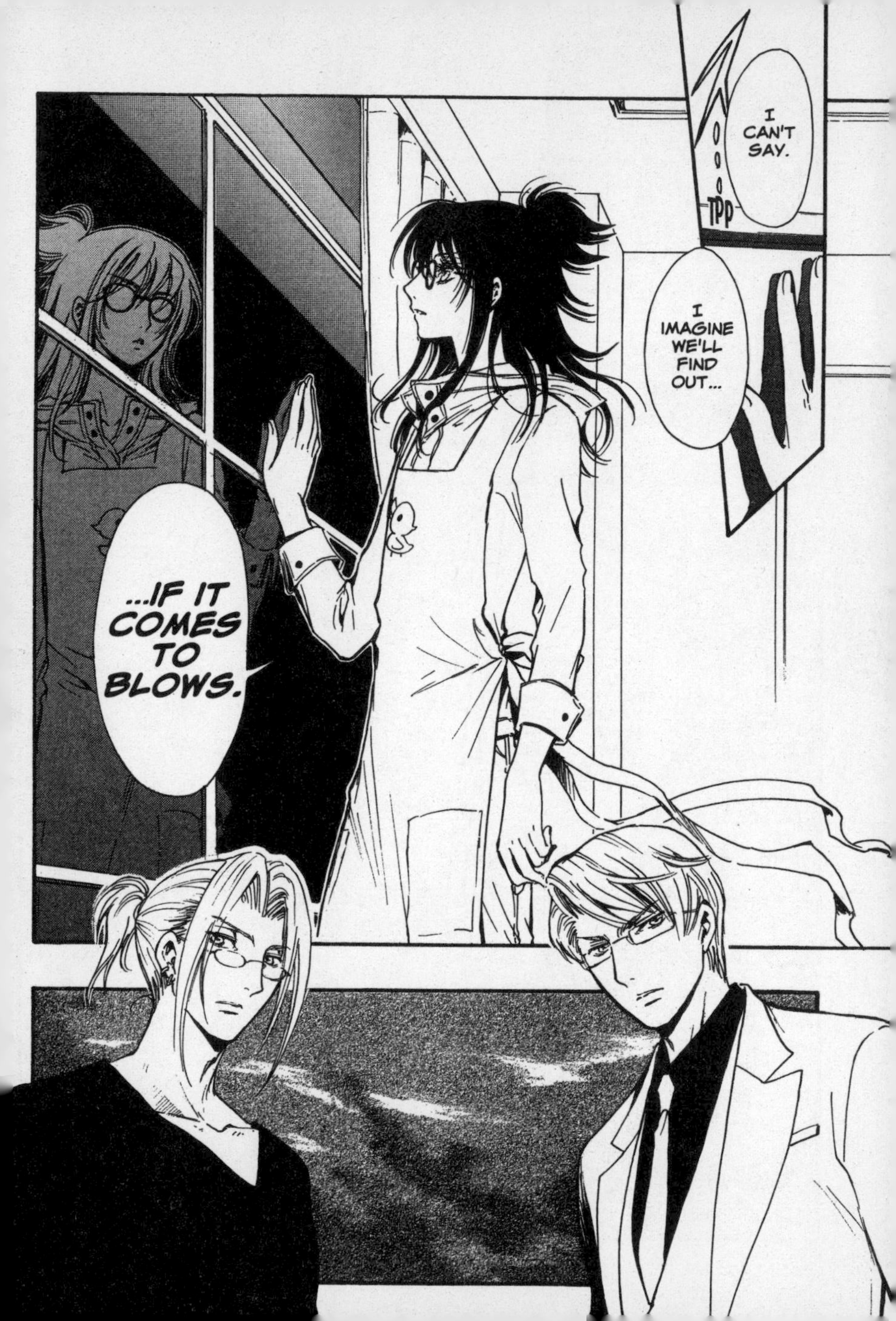
I CAN'T SAY.
TPP
I IMAGINE WE'LL FIND OUT...
...IF IT COMES TO BLOWS.

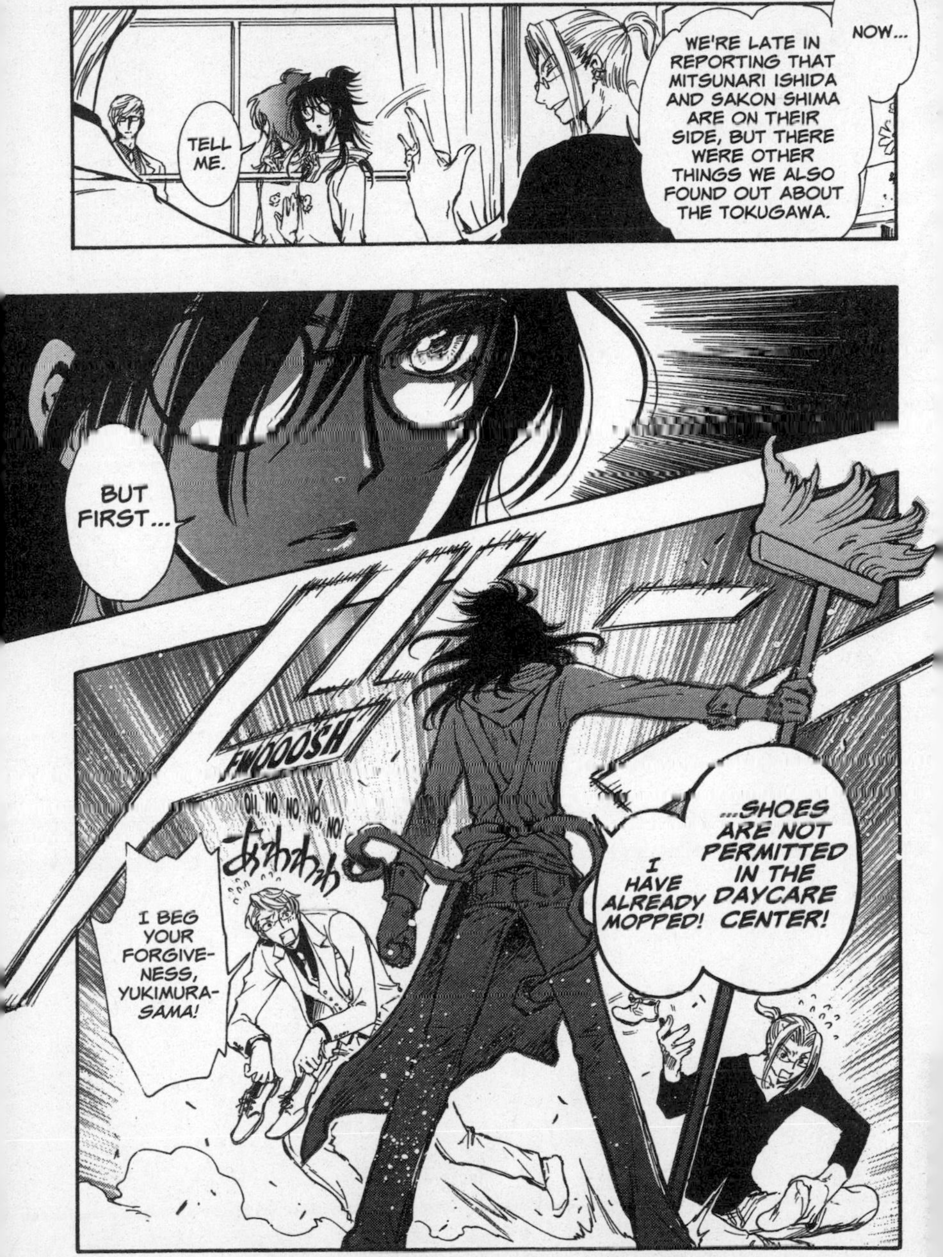
NOW...
WE'RE LATE IN REPORTING THAT MITSUNARI ISHIDA AND SAKON SHIMA ARE ON THEIR SIDE, BUT THERE WERE OTHER THINGS WE ALSO FOUND OUT ABOUT THE TOKUGAWA.
TELL ME.
BUT FIRST...
FWOOOSH
...SHOES ARE NOT PERMITTED IN THE DAYCARE CENTER!
I HAVE ALREADY MOPPED!
OH, NO, NO, NO, NO!
I BEG YOUR FORGIVENESS, YUKIMURA-SAMA!

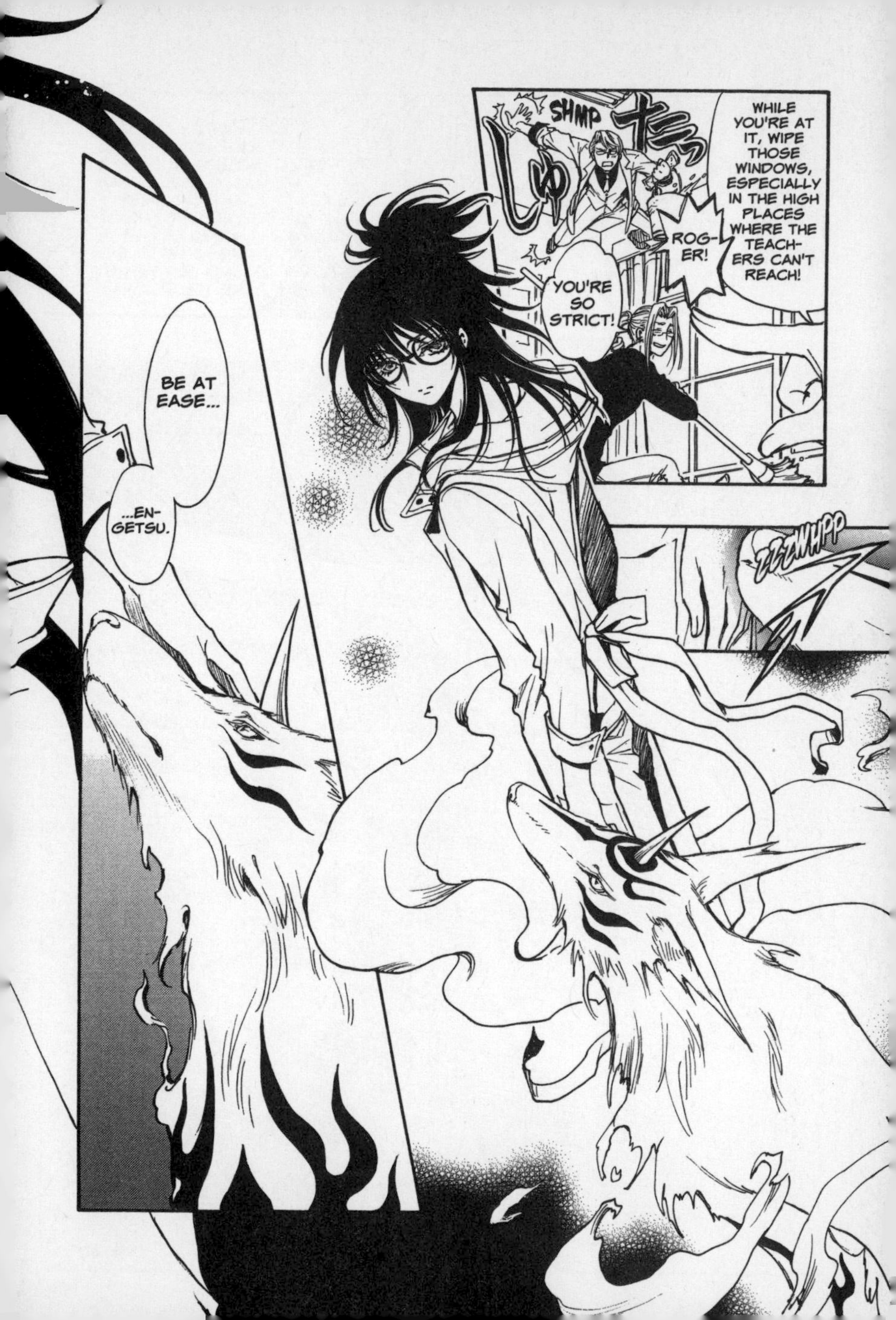
WHILE YOU'RE AT IT, WIPE THOSE WINDOWS, ESPECIALLY IN THE HIGH PLACES WHERE THE TEACHERS CAN'T REACH!
SHMP
ROG-ER!
YOU'RE SO STRICT!
ZZZWHPP
BE AT EASE...
...EN-GETSU.

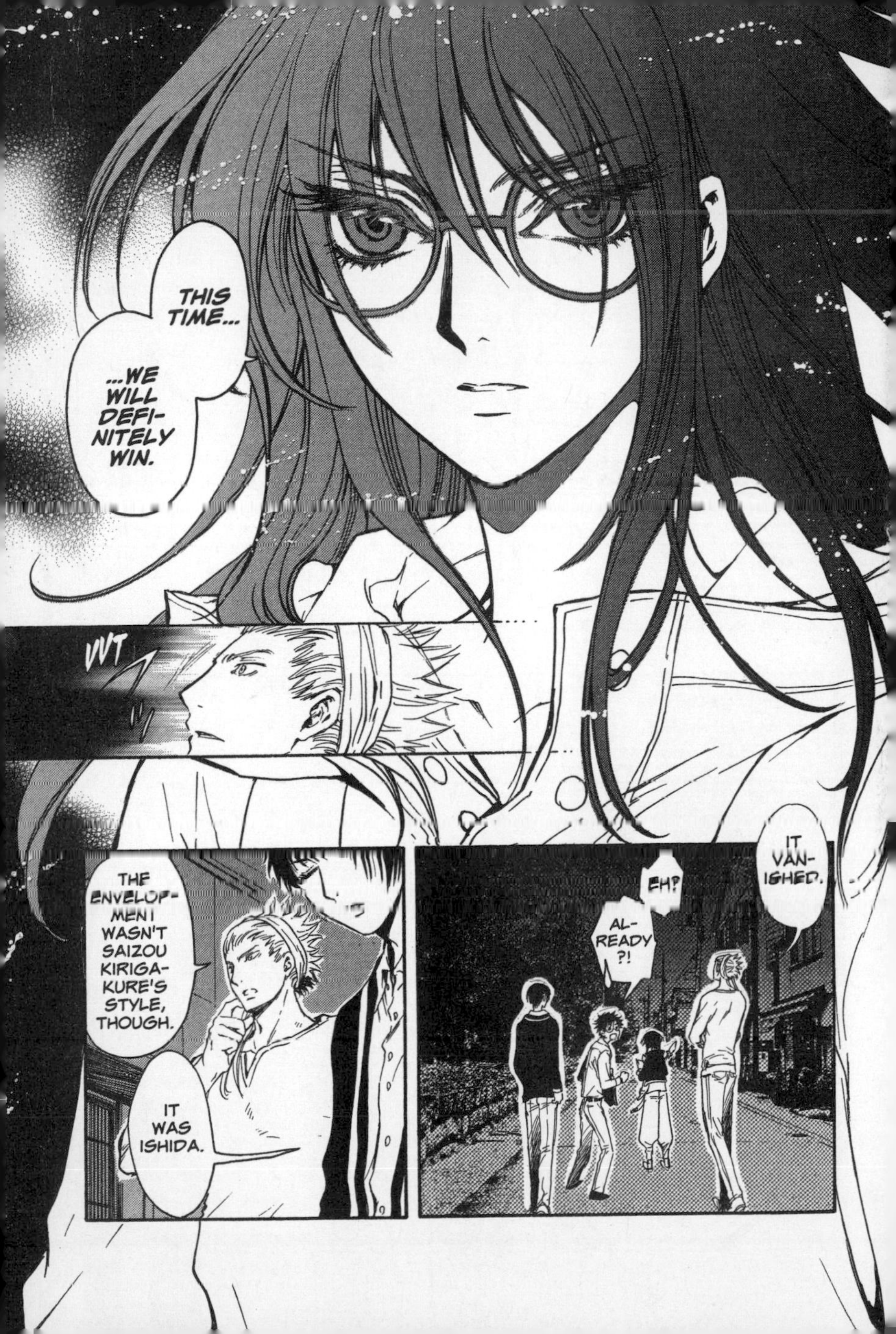
THIS TIME...
...WE WILL DEFINITELY WIN.
VVT
IT VANISHED.
EH?
ALREADY?!
THE ENVELOPMENT WASN'T SAIZOU KIRIGAKURE'S STYLE, THOUGH.
IT WAS ISHIDA.

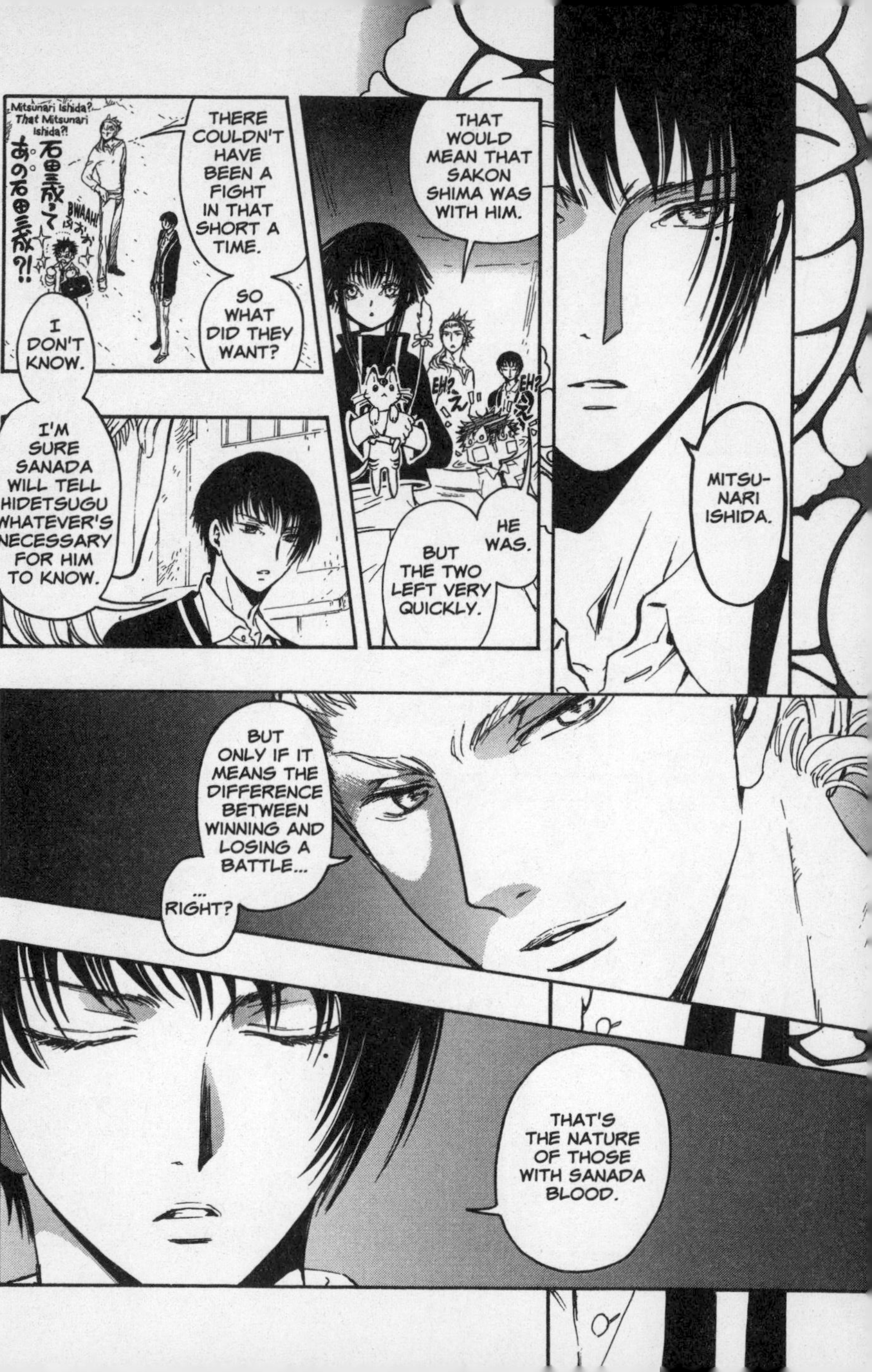
MITSU-NARI ISHIDA.
THAT WOULD MEAN THAT SAKON SHIMA WAS WITH HIM.
EH? え
EH? え
HE WAS.
BUT THE TWO LEFT VERY QUICKLY.
Mitsunari Ishida?! That Mitsunari Ishida?!
石田三成って あの石田三成?!
BWAAH!
THERE COULDN'T HAVE BEEN A FIGHT IN THAT SHORT A TIME.
SO WHAT DID THEY WANT?
I DON'T KNOW.
I'M SURE SANADA WILL TELL HIDETSUGU WHATEVER'S NECESSARY FOR HIM TO KNOW.
BUT ONLY IF IT MEANS THE DIFFERENCE BETWEEN WINNING AND LOSING A BATTLE...
...RIGHT?
THAT'S THE NATURE OF THOSE WITH SANADA BLOOD.

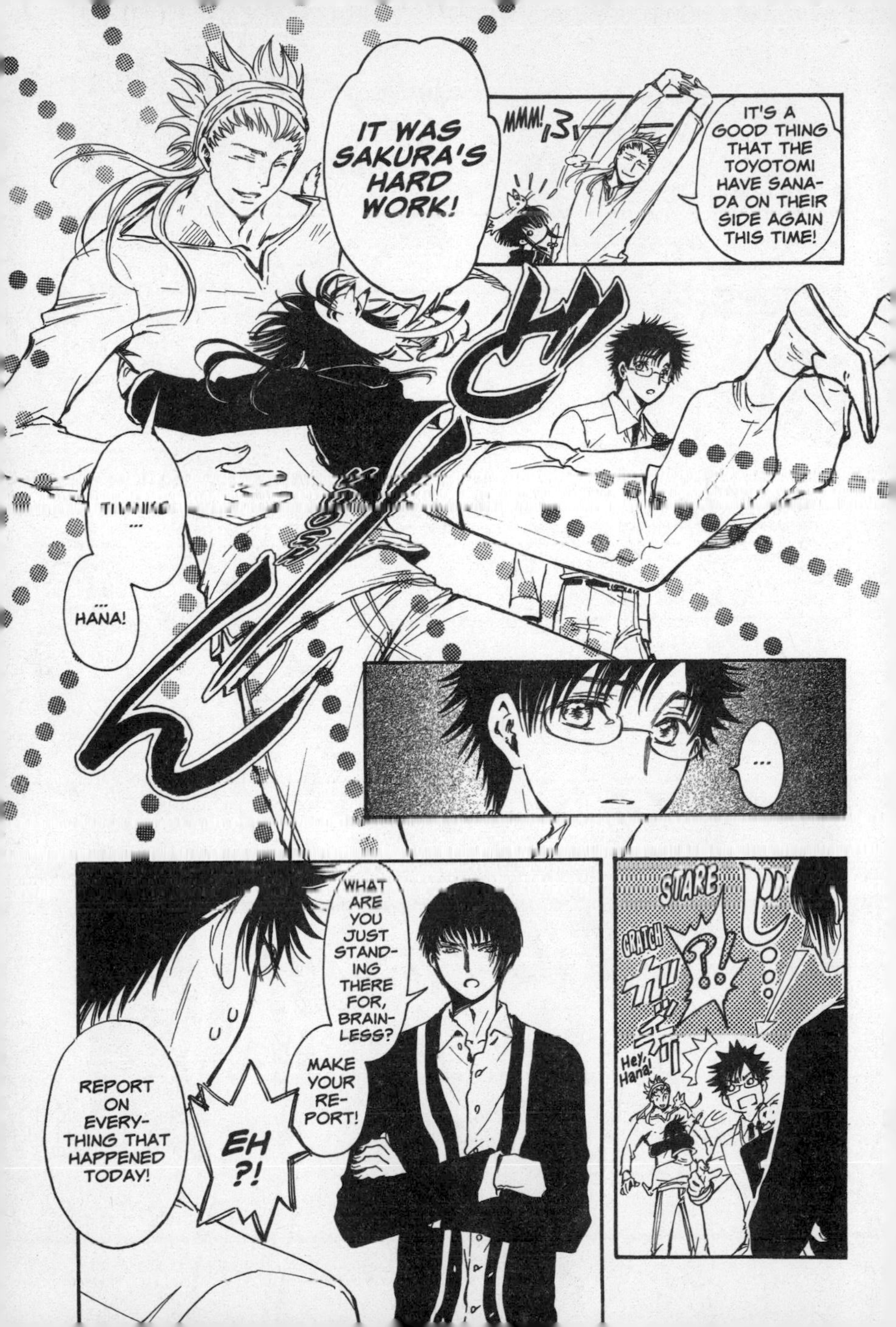
MMM!
IT'S A GOOD THING THAT THE TOYOTOMI HAVE SANADA ON THEIR SIDE AGAIN THIS TIME!
IT WAS SAKURA'S HARD WORK!
...
... HANA!
...
STARE
GRATCH
Hey, Hana!
WHAT ARE YOU JUST STANDING THERE FOR, BRAINLESS?
MAKE YOUR REPORT!
EH ?!
REPORT ON EVERYTHING THAT HAPPENED TODAY!

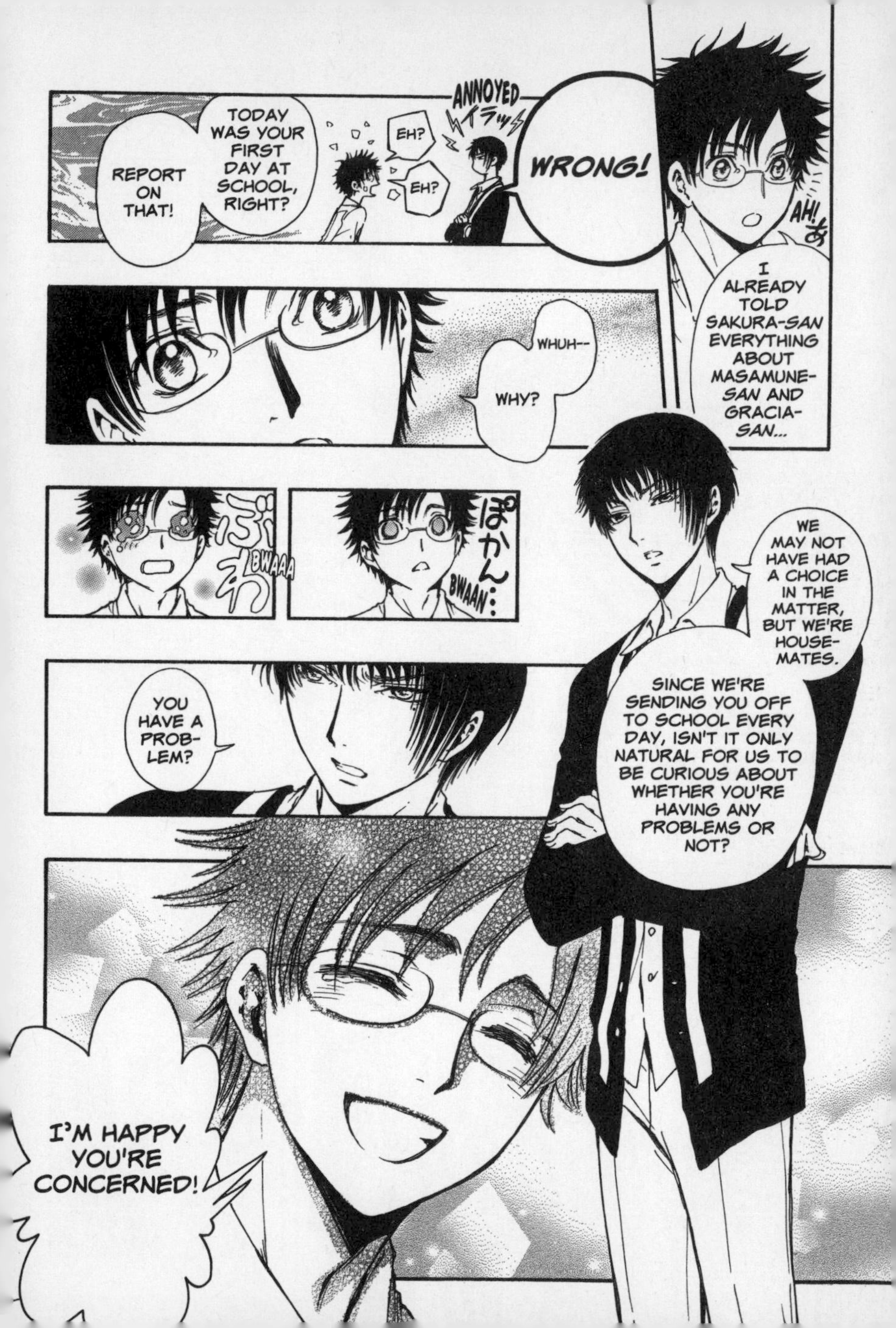
AH! あ
I ALREADY TOLD SAKURA-SAN EVERYTHING ABOUT MASAMUNE-SAN AND GRACIA-SAN...
WRONG!
ANNOYED イラッ
EH?
EH?
TODAY WAS YOUR FIRST DAY AT SCHOOL, RIGHT?
REPORT ON THAT!
WHUH--
WHY?
ぽかん BWAAN
ぶわ BWAAA
WE MAY NOT HAVE HAD A CHOICE IN THE MATTER, BUT WE'RE HOUSE-MATES.
SINCE WE'RE SENDING YOU OFF TO SCHOOL EVERY DAY, ISN'T IT ONLY NATURAL FOR US TO BE CURIOUS ABOUT WHETHER YOU'RE HAVING ANY PROBLEMS OR NOT?
YOU HAVE A PROB-LEM?
I'M HAPPY YOU'RE CONCERNED!

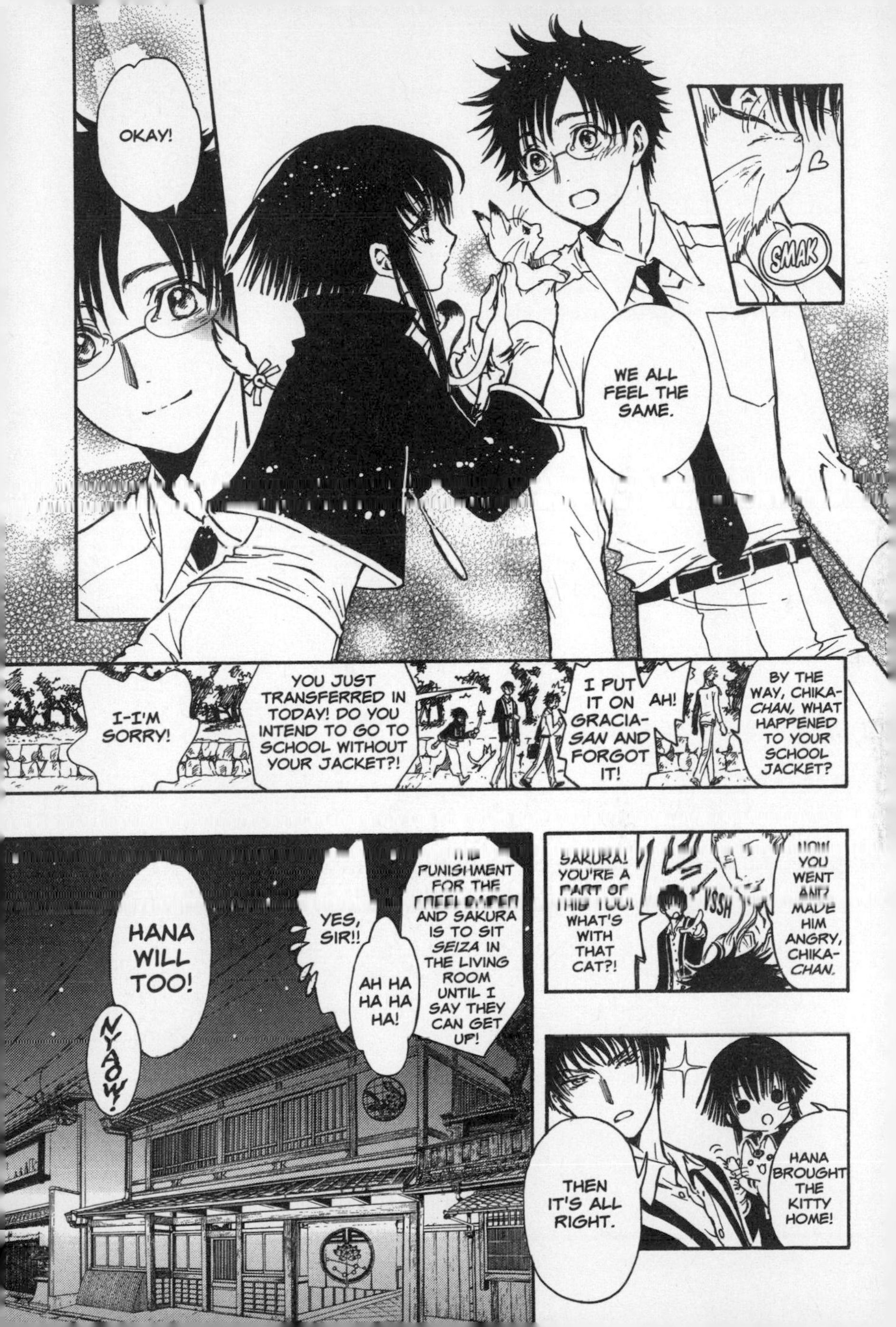
SMAK
WE ALL FEEL THE SAME.
OKAY!
BY THE WAY, CHIKA-CHAN, WHAT HAPPENED TO YOUR SCHOOL JACKET?
AH!
I PUT IT ON GRACIA-SAN AND FORGOT IT!
YOU JUST TRANSFERRED IN TODAY! DO YOU INTEND TO GO TO SCHOOL WITHOUT YOUR JACKET?!
I-I'M SORRY!
NOW YOU WENT AND MADE HIM ANGRY, CHIKA-CHAN.
VSSH
SAKURA! YOU'RE A PART OF THIS TOO! WHAT'S WITH THAT CAT?!
HANA BROUGHT THE KITTY HOME!
THEN IT'S ALL RIGHT.
THE PUNISHMENT FOR THE FREELOADER AND SAKURA IS TO SIT SEIZA IN THE LIVING ROOM UNTIL I SAY THEY CAN GET UP!
YES, SIR!!
AH HA HA HA HA!
HANA WILL TOO!
NYAOW!

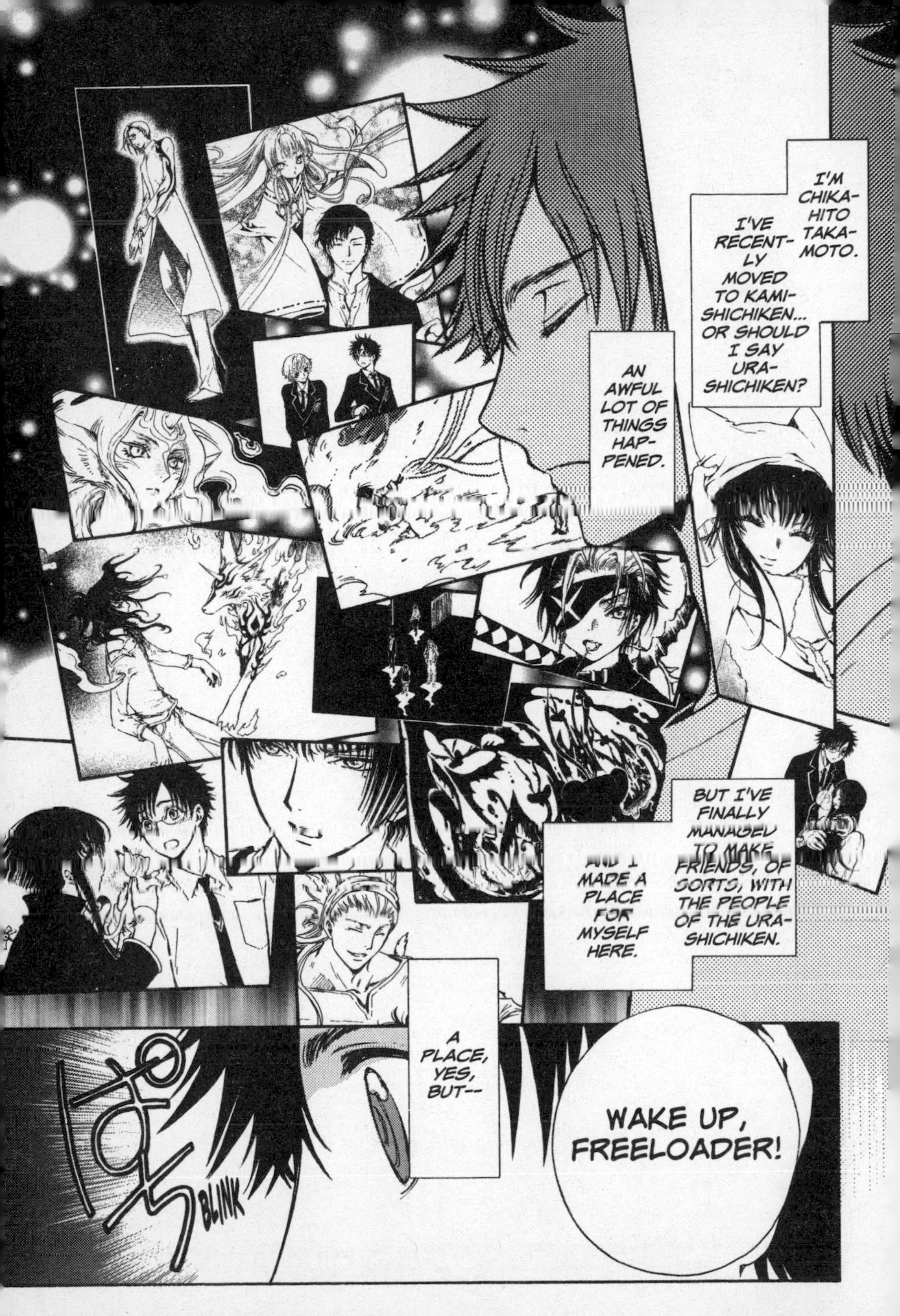
I'M CHIKA-HITO TAKA-MOTO.
I'VE RECENT-LY MOVED TO KAMI-SHICHIKEN... OR SHOULD I SAY URA-SHICHIKEN?
AN AWFUL LOT OF THINGS HAP-PENED.
BUT I'VE FINALLY MANAGED TO MAKE FRIENDS, OF SORTS, WITH THE PEOPLE OF THE URA-SHICHIKEN.
AND I MADE A PLACE FOR MYSELF HERE.
A PLACE, YES, BUT--
WAKE UP, FREELOADER!
BLINK

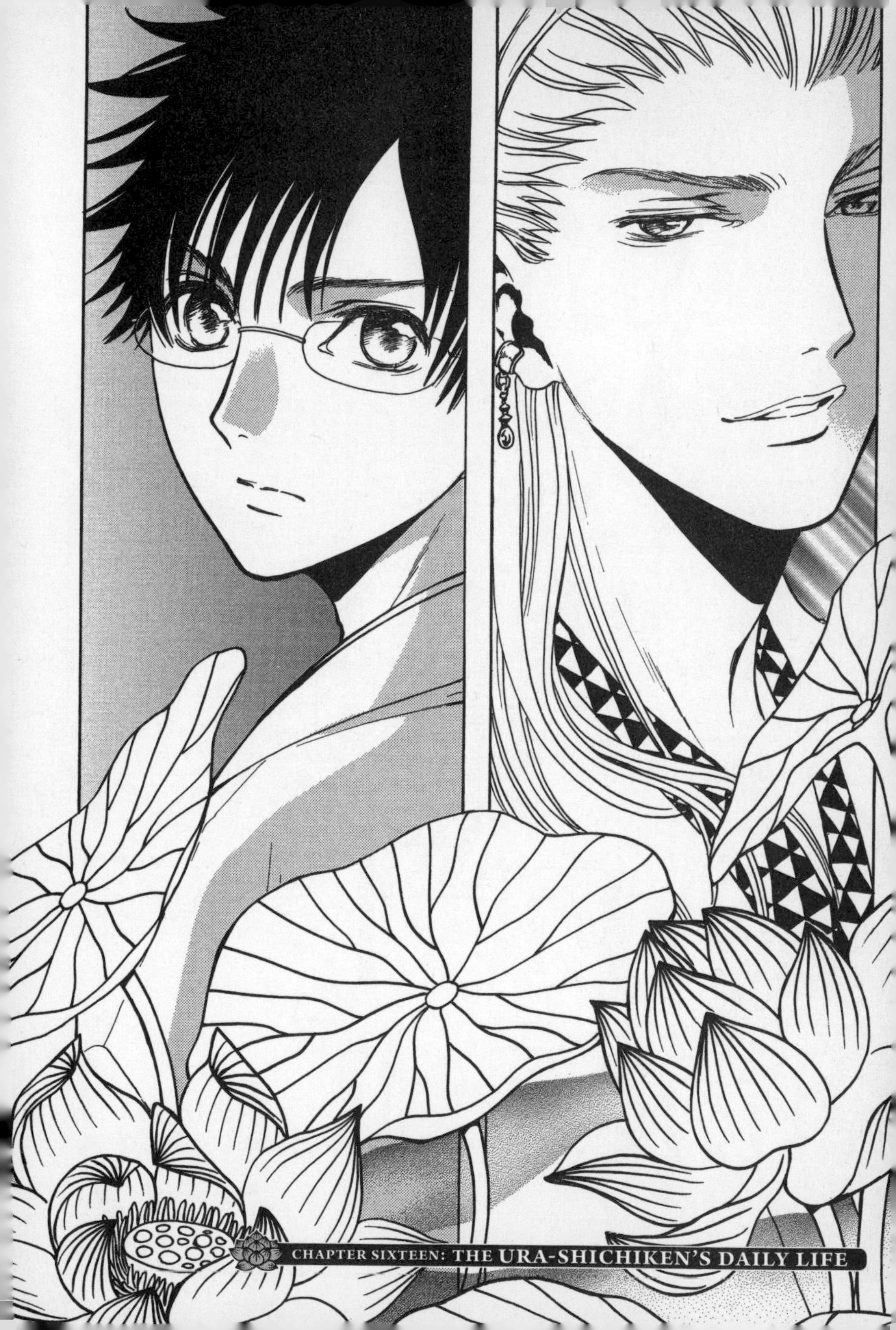
CHAPTER SIXTEEN: THE URA-SHICHIKEN'S DAILY LIFE

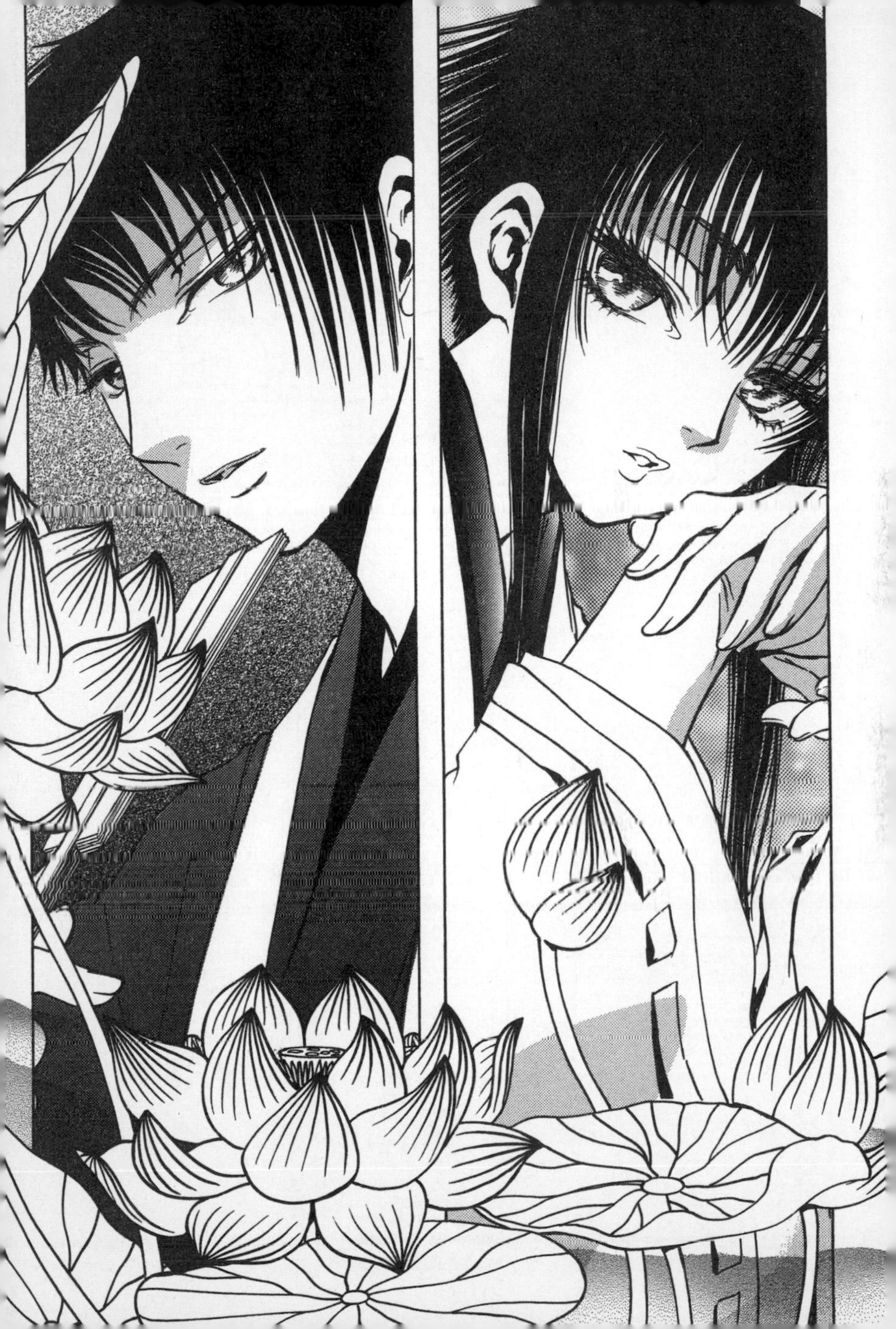

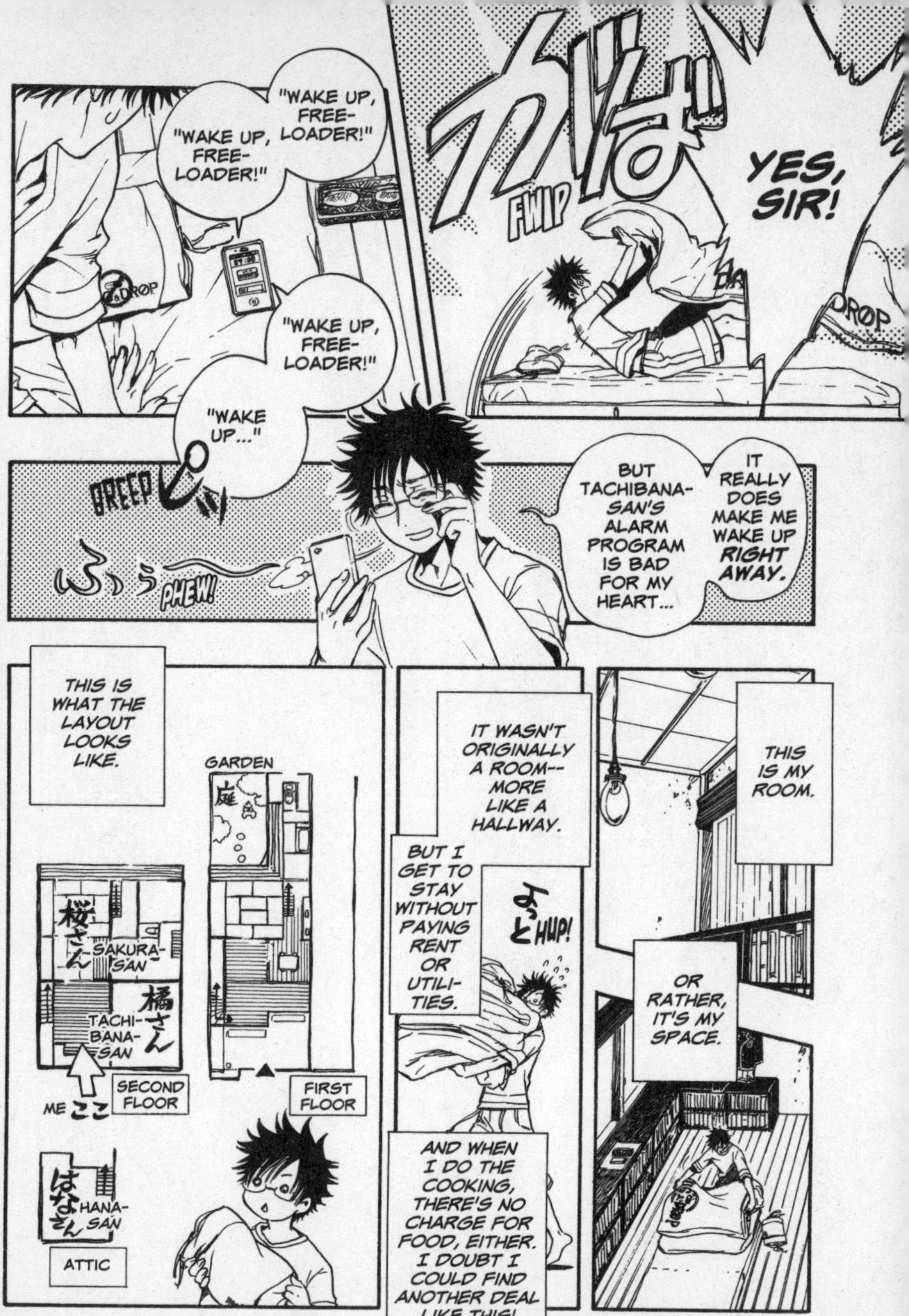
FWIP
YES, SIR!
"WAKE UP, FREE-LOADER!"
"WAKE UP, FREE-LOADER!"
"WAKE UP, FREE-LOADER!"
"WAKE UP..."
BREEP
PHEW!
IT REALLY DOES MAKE ME WAKE UP RIGHT AWAY.
BUT TACHIBANA-SAN'S ALARM PROGRAM IS BAD FOR MY HEART...
THIS IS MY ROOM.
OR RATHER, IT'S MY SPACE.
IT WASN'T ORIGINALLY A ROOM-- MORE LIKE A HALLWAY.
BUT I GET TO STAY WITHOUT PAYING RENT OR UTILI-TIES.
よっと HUP!
AND WHEN I DO THE COOKING, THERE'S NO CHARGE FOR FOOD, EITHER. I DOUBT I COULD FIND ANOTHER DEAL LIKE THIS!
THIS IS WHAT THE LAYOUT LOOKS LIKE.
GARDEN
庭
桜さん SAKURA-SAN
橘さん TACHIBANA-SAN
ME ここ
SECOND FLOOR
FIRST FLOOR
はなさん HANA-SAN
ATTIC

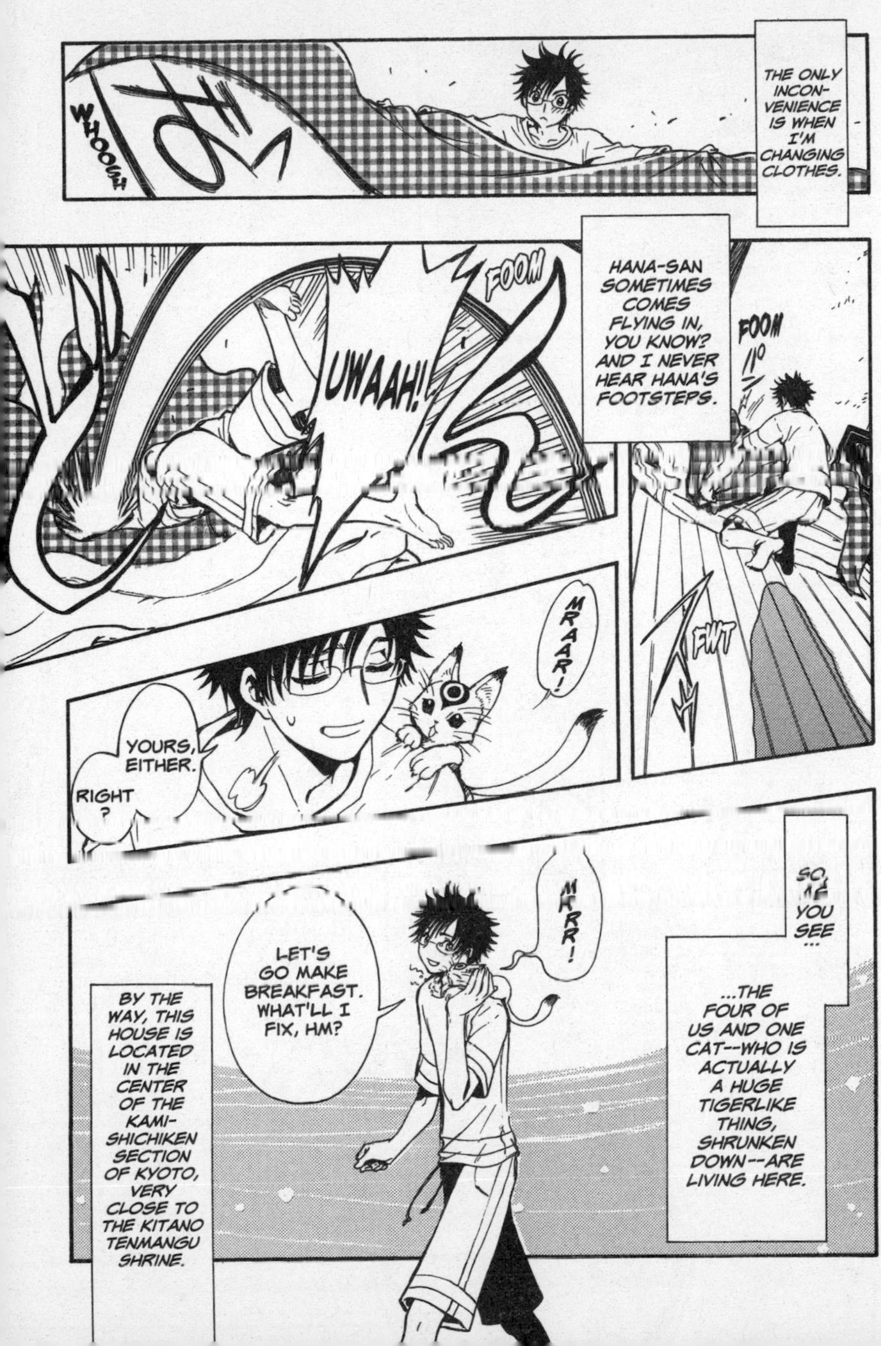

THE ONLY INCONVENIENCE IS WHEN I'M CHANGING CLOTHES.
WHOOSH
HANA-SAN SOMETIMES COMES FLYING IN, YOU KNOW? AND I NEVER HEAR HANA'S FOOTSTEPS.
FOOM
FWT
FOOM
UWAAH!
MRAAR!
YOURS, EITHER.
RIGHT?
SO, YOU SEE...
...THE FOUR OF US AND ONE CAT--WHO IS ACTUALLY A HUGE TIGERLIKE THING, SHRUNKEN DOWN--ARE LIVING HERE.
MHRR!
LET'S GO MAKE BREAKFAST. WHAT'LL I FIX, HM?
BY THE WAY, THIS HOUSE IS LOCATED IN THE CENTER OF THE KAMI-SHICHIKEN SECTION OF KYOTO, VERY CLOSE TO THE KITANO TENMANGU SHRINE.

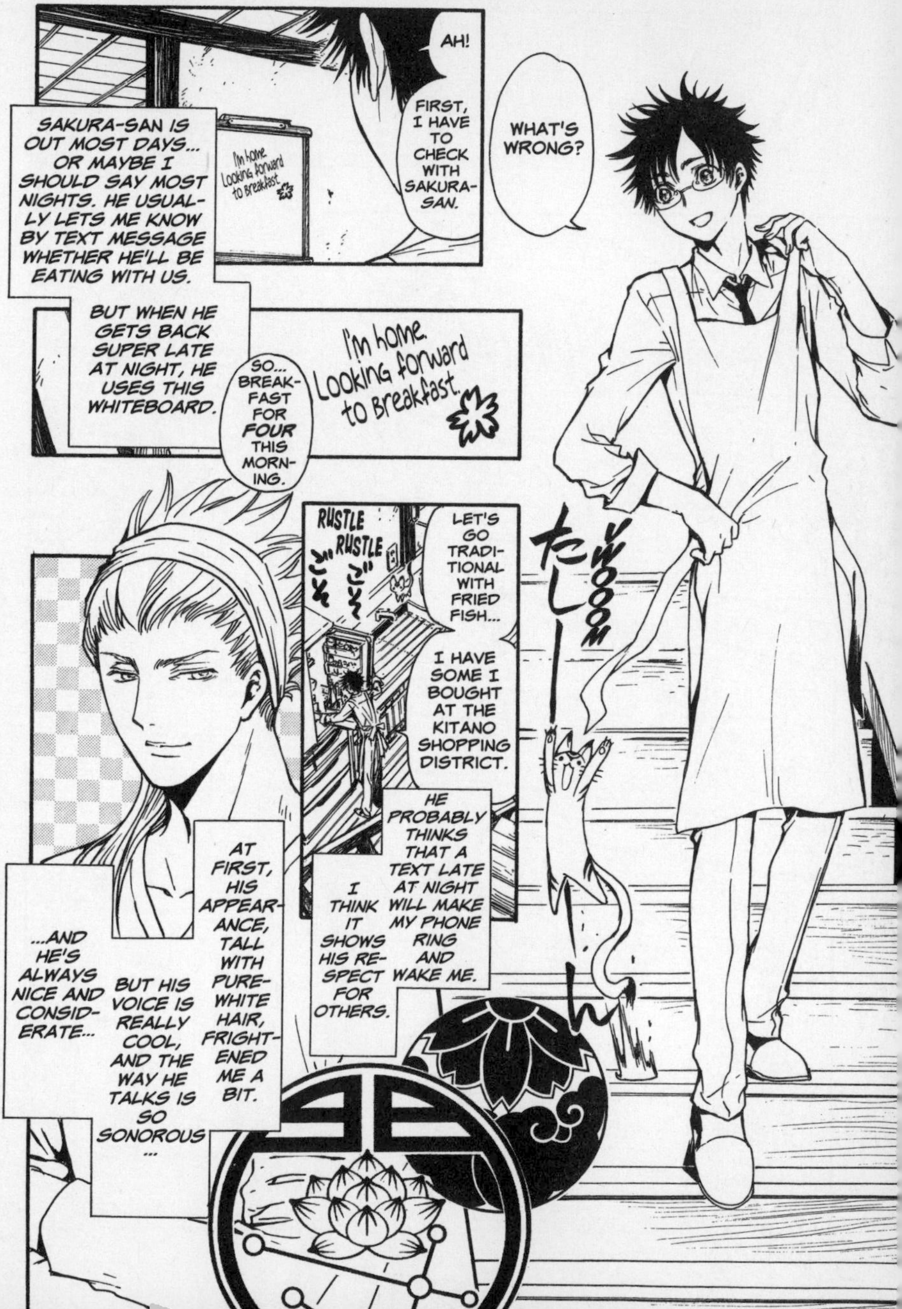
WHAT'S WRONG?
たしーん
WOOOOM
AH!
FIRST, I HAVE TO CHECK WITH SAKURA-SAN.
SAKURA-SAN IS OUT MOST DAYS... OR MAYBE I SHOULD SAY MOST NIGHTS. HE USUALLY LETS ME KNOW BY TEXT MESSAGE WHETHER HE'LL BE EATING WITH US.
I'm home Looking forward to Breakfast
BUT WHEN HE GETS BACK SUPER LATE AT NIGHT, HE USES THIS WHITEBOARD.
I'm home. Looking forward to Breakfast.
SO... BREAKFAST FOR FOUR THIS MORNING.
RUSTLE RUSTLE
ごそ ごそ
LET'S GO TRADITIONAL WITH FRIED FISH...
I HAVE SOME I BOUGHT AT THE KITANO SHOPPING DISTRICT.
HE PROBABLY THINKS THAT A TEXT LATE AT NIGHT WILL MAKE MY PHONE RING AND WAKE ME.
I THINK IT SHOWS HIS RESPECT FOR OTHERS.
AT FIRST, HIS APPEARANCE, TALL WITH PURE-WHITE HAIR, FRIGHTENED ME A BIT.
BUT HIS VOICE IS REALLY COOL, AND THE WAY HE TALKS IS SO SONOROUS...
...AND HE'S ALWAYS NICE AND CONSIDERATE...

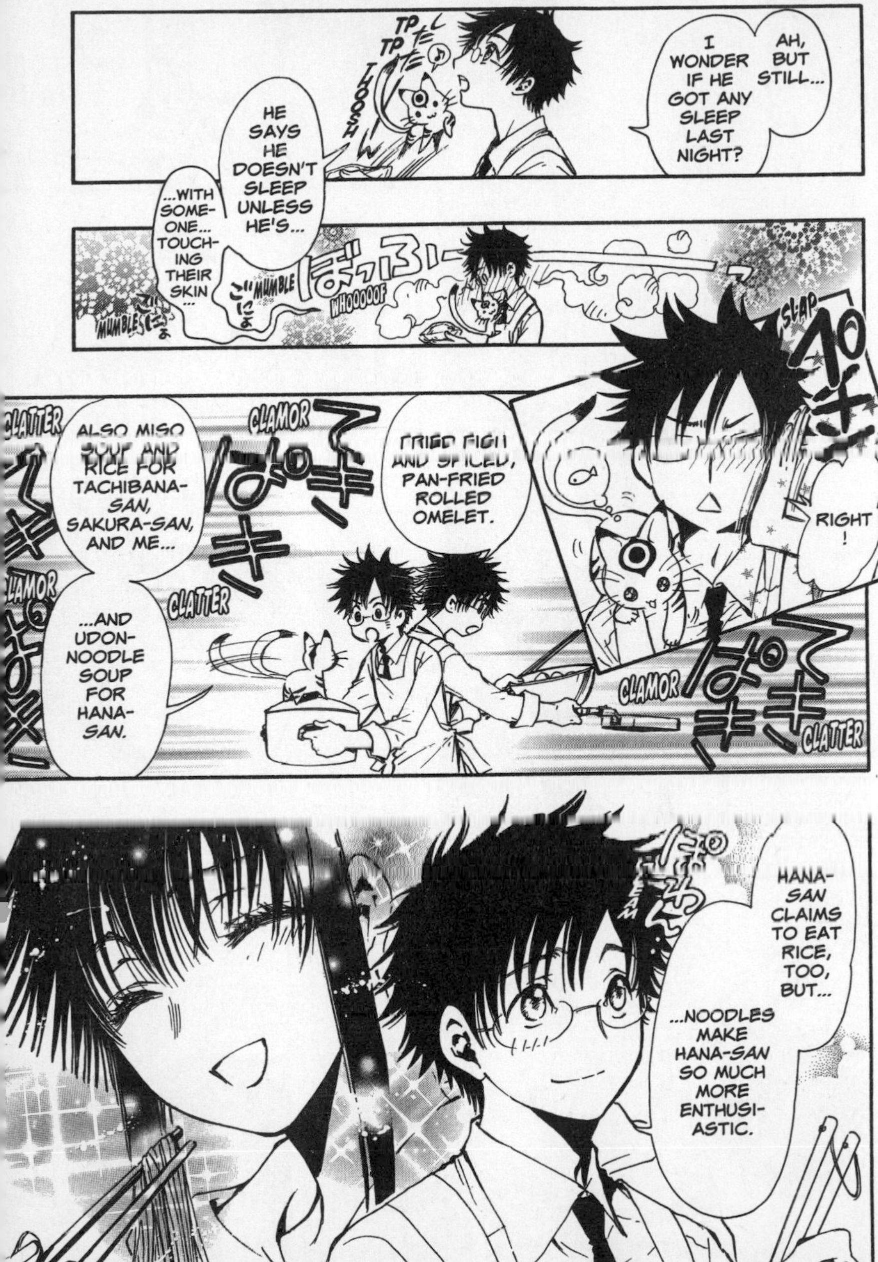
AH, BUT STILL...
I WONDER IF HE GOT ANY SLEEP LAST NIGHT?
TP TP
THOOSH
HE SAYS HE DOESN'T SLEEP UNLESS HE'S...
...WITH SOME-ONE... TOUCH-ING THEIR SKIN...
WHOOOOOF
MUMBLE
MUMBLE
SLAP
RIGHT!
FRIED FISH AND SPICED, PAN-FRIED ROLLED OMELET.
CLAMOR
CLATTER
ALSO MISO SOUP AND RICE FOR TACHIBANA-SAN, SAKURA-SAN, AND ME...
...AND UDON-NOODLE SOUP FOR HANA-SAN.
CLAMOR
CLATTER
CLATTER
CLAMOR
BEAM
HANA-SAN CLAIMS TO EAT RICE, TOO, BUT...
...NOODLES MAKE HANA-SAN SO MUCH MORE ENTHUSI-ASTIC.

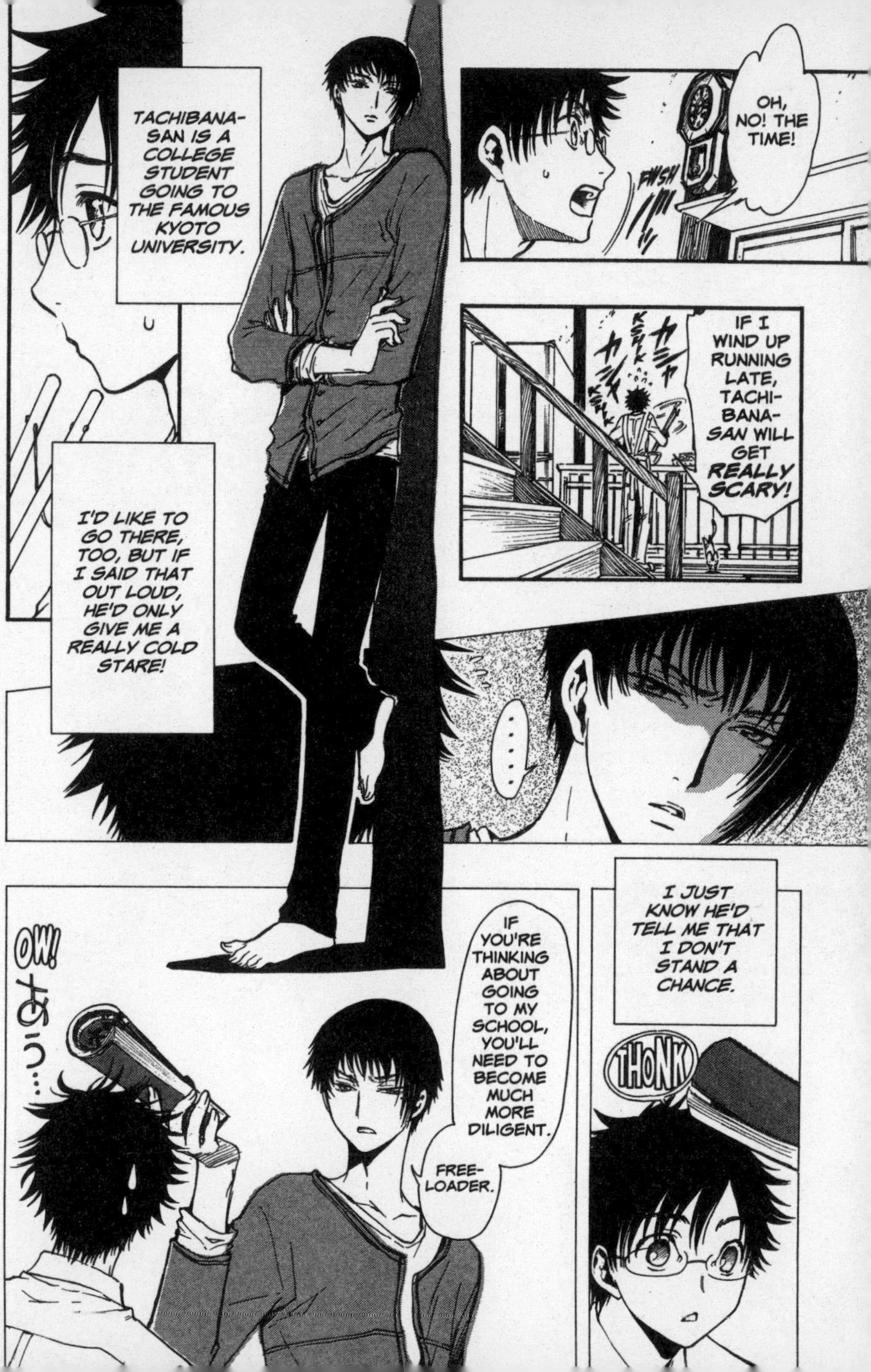

OH, NO! THE TIME!
FWSH
IF I WIND UP RUNNING LATE, TACHIBANA-SAN WILL GET REALLY SCARY!
......
TACHIBANA-SAN IS A COLLEGE STUDENT GOING TO THE FAMOUS KYOTO UNIVERSITY.
I'D LIKE TO GO THERE, TOO, BUT IF I SAID THAT OUT LOUD, HE'D ONLY GIVE ME A REALLY COLD STARE!
I JUST KNOW HE'D TELL ME THAT I DON'T STAND A CHANCE.
THONK
IF YOU'RE THINKING ABOUT GOING TO MY SCHOOL, YOU'LL NEED TO BECOME MUCH MORE DILIGENT.
FREE-LOADER.
OW!
あう…

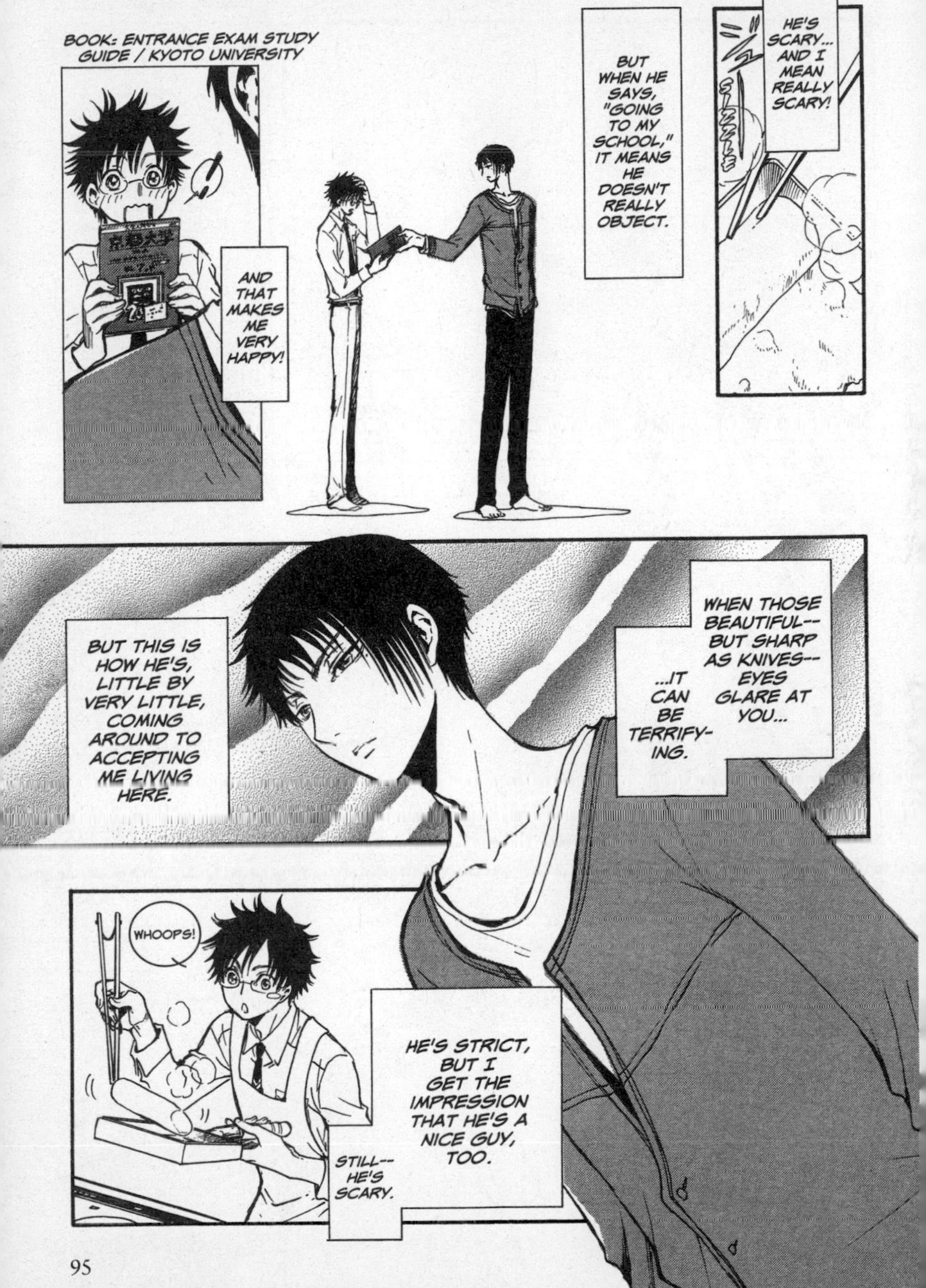

HE'S SCARY... AND I MEAN REALLY SCARY!
BUT WHEN HE SAYS, "GOING TO MY SCHOOL," IT MEANS HE DOESN'T REALLY OBJECT.
BOOK: ENTRANCE EXAM STUDY GUIDE / KYOTO UNIVERSITY
AND THAT MAKES ME VERY HAPPY!
WHEN THOSE BEAUTIFUL-- BUT SHARP AS KNIVES-- EYES GLARE AT YOU...
...IT CAN BE TERRIFYING.
BUT THIS IS HOW HE'S, LITTLE BY VERY LITTLE, COMING AROUND TO ACCEPTING ME LIVING HERE.
HE'S STRICT, BUT I GET THE IMPRESSION THAT HE'S A NICE GUY, TOO.
WHOOPS!
STILL-- HE'S SCARY.

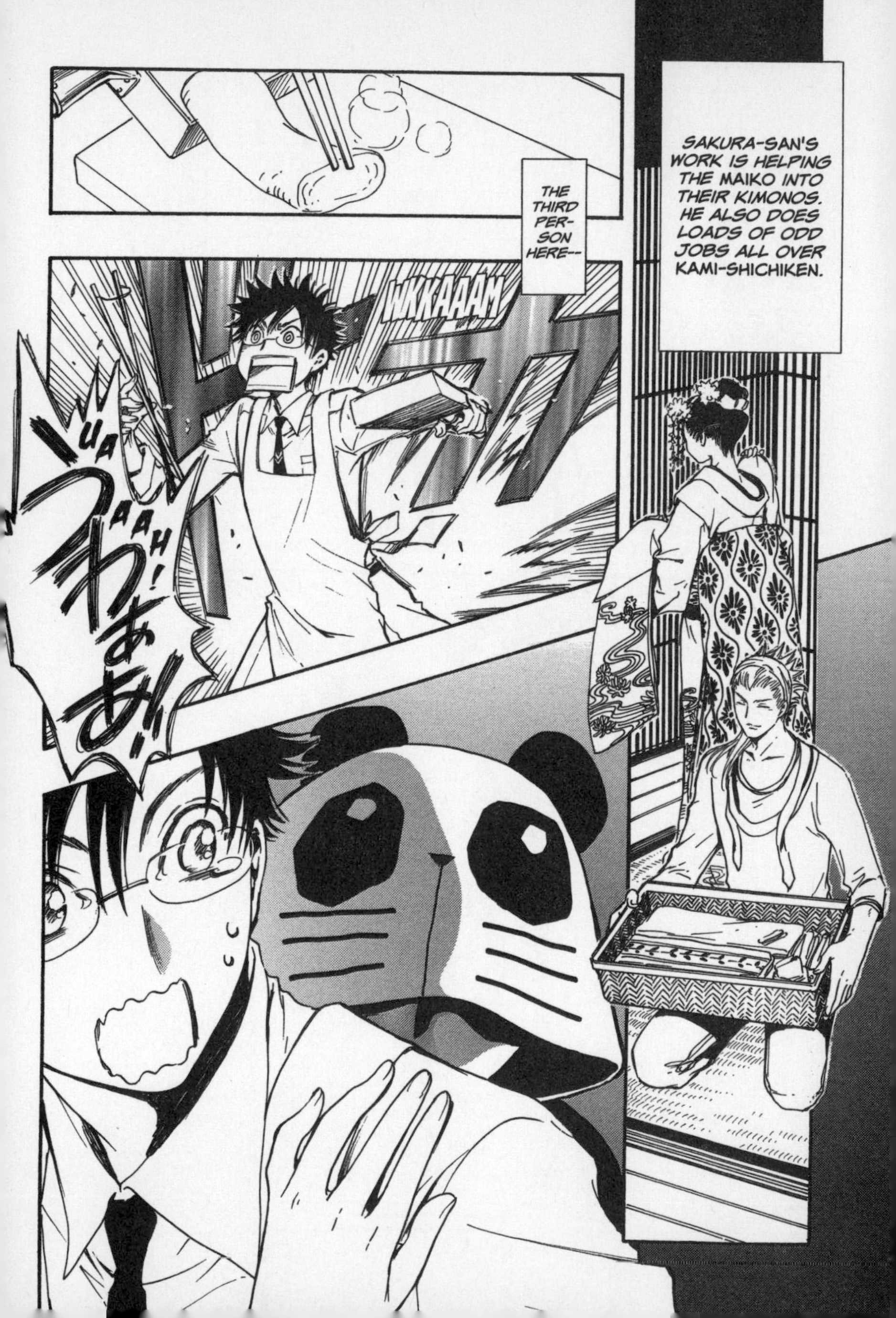
SAKURA-SAN'S WORK IS HELPING THE MAIKO INTO THEIR KIMONOS. HE ALSO DOES LOADS OF ODD JOBS ALL OVER KAMI-SHICHIKEN.
THE THIRD PERSON HERE--
WKKAAAM
UAAAH!
うわああ!!

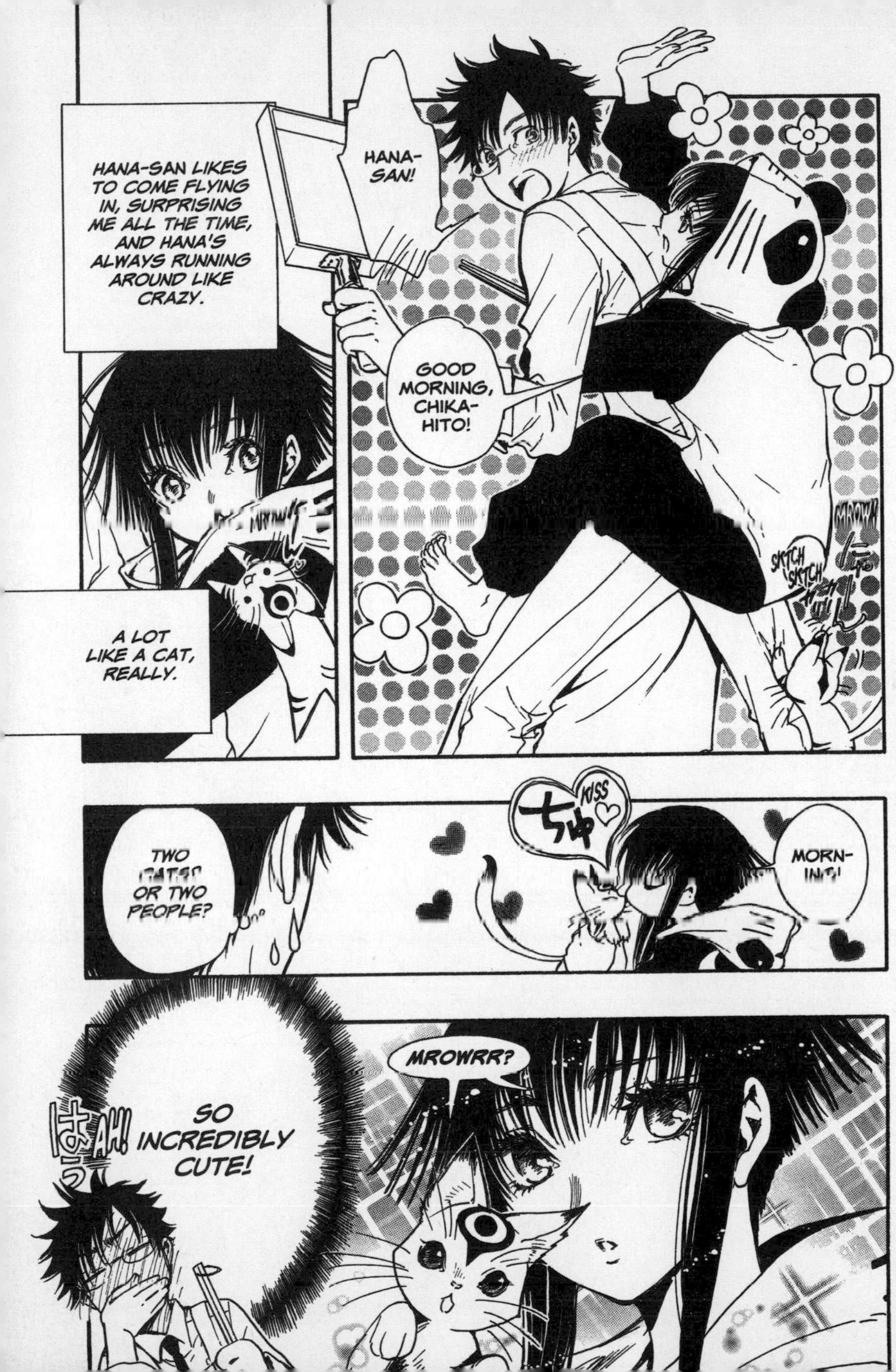
HANA-SAN!
GOOD MORNING, CHIKA-HITO!
MROW!
SKTCH SKTCH
HANA-SAN LIKES TO COME FLYING IN, SURPRISING ME ALL THE TIME, AND HANA'S ALWAYS RUNNING AROUND LIKE CRAZY.
A LOT LIKE A CAT, REALLY.
MORN-
KISS
TWO
OR TWO PEOPLE?
MROWRR?
AH!
SO INCREDIBLY CUTE!

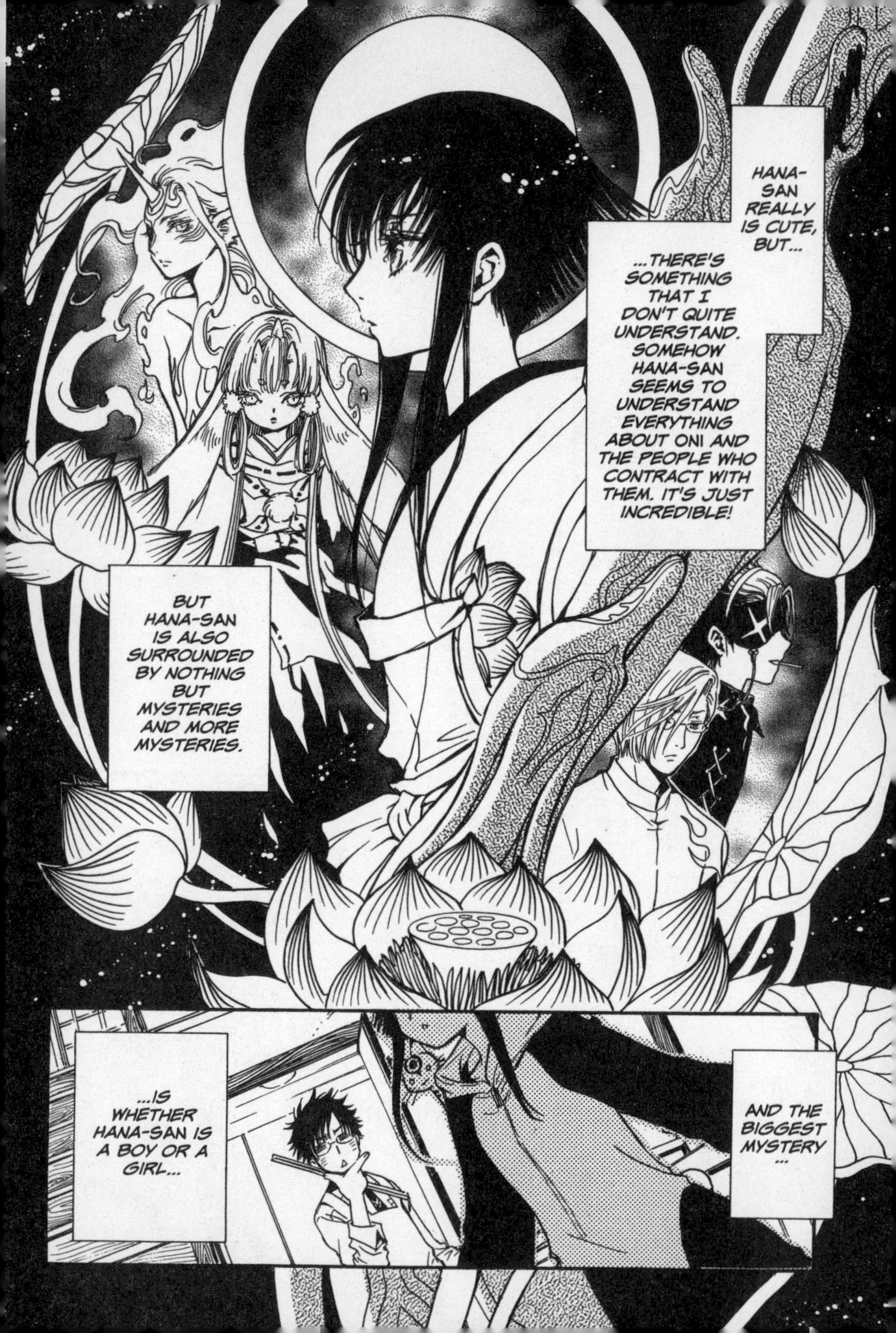
HANA-SAN REALLY IS CUTE, BUT...
...THERE'S SOMETHING THAT I DON'T QUITE UNDERSTAND. SOMEHOW HANA-SAN SEEMS TO UNDERSTAND EVERYTHING ABOUT ONI AND THE PEOPLE WHO CONTRACT WITH THEM. IT'S JUST INCREDIBLE!
BUT HANA-SAN IS ALSO SURROUNDED BY NOTHING BUT MYSTERIES AND MORE MYSTERIES.
AND THE BIGGEST MYSTERY...
...IS WHETHER HANA-SAN IS A BOY OR A GIRL...

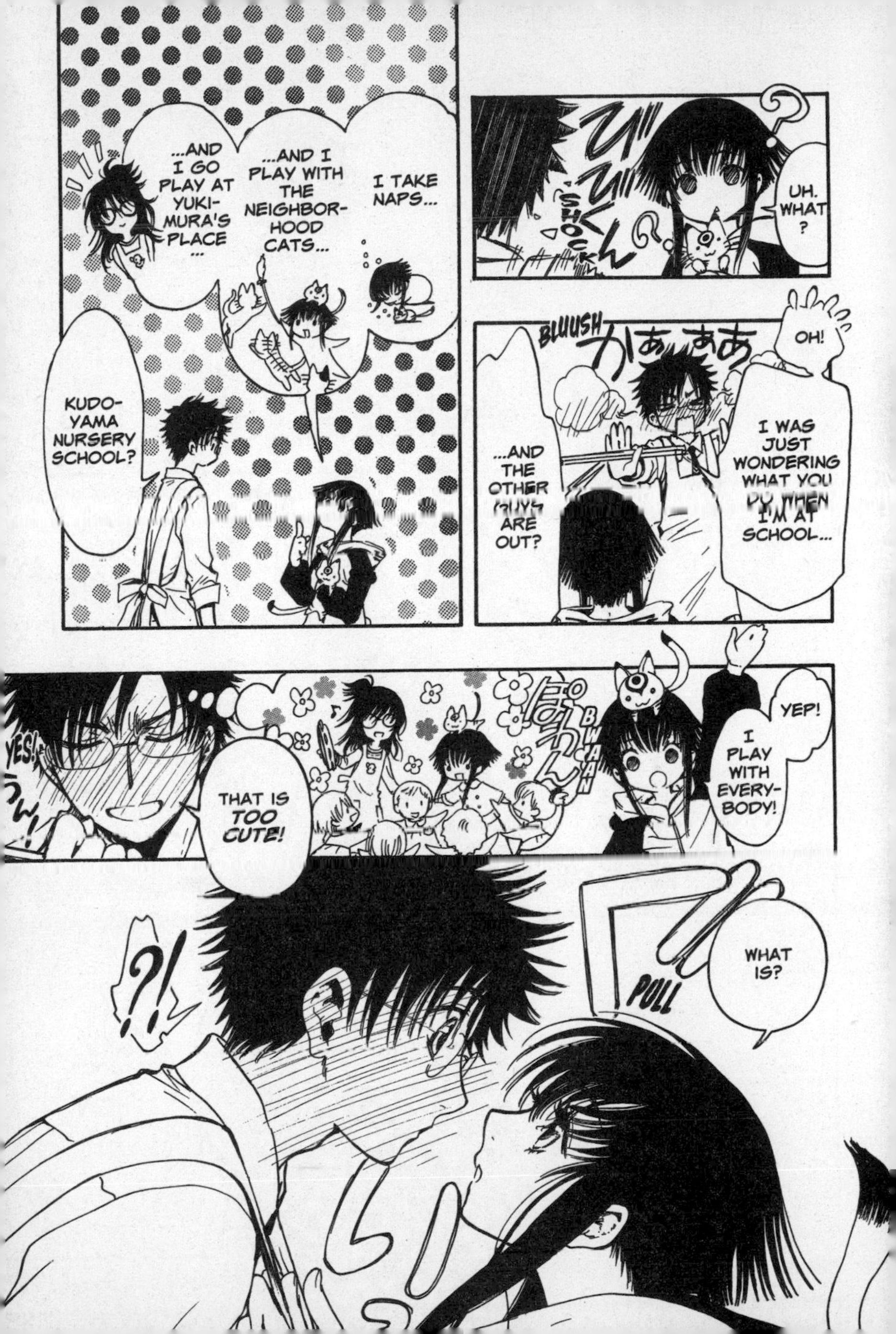

UH. WHAT?
SHOCK
OH!
BLUUSH
かあああ
I WAS JUST WONDERING WHAT YOU DO WHEN I'M AT SCHOOL...
...AND THE OTHER GUYS ARE OUT?
I TAKE NAPS...
...AND I PLAY WITH THE NEIGHBOR-HOOD CATS...
...AND I GO PLAY AT YUKI-MURA'S PLACE ...
KUDO-YAMA NURSERY SCHOOL?
YEP! I PLAY WITH EVERY-BODY!
BWAAN
THAT IS TOO CUTE!
YES!
WHAT IS?
PULL
?!

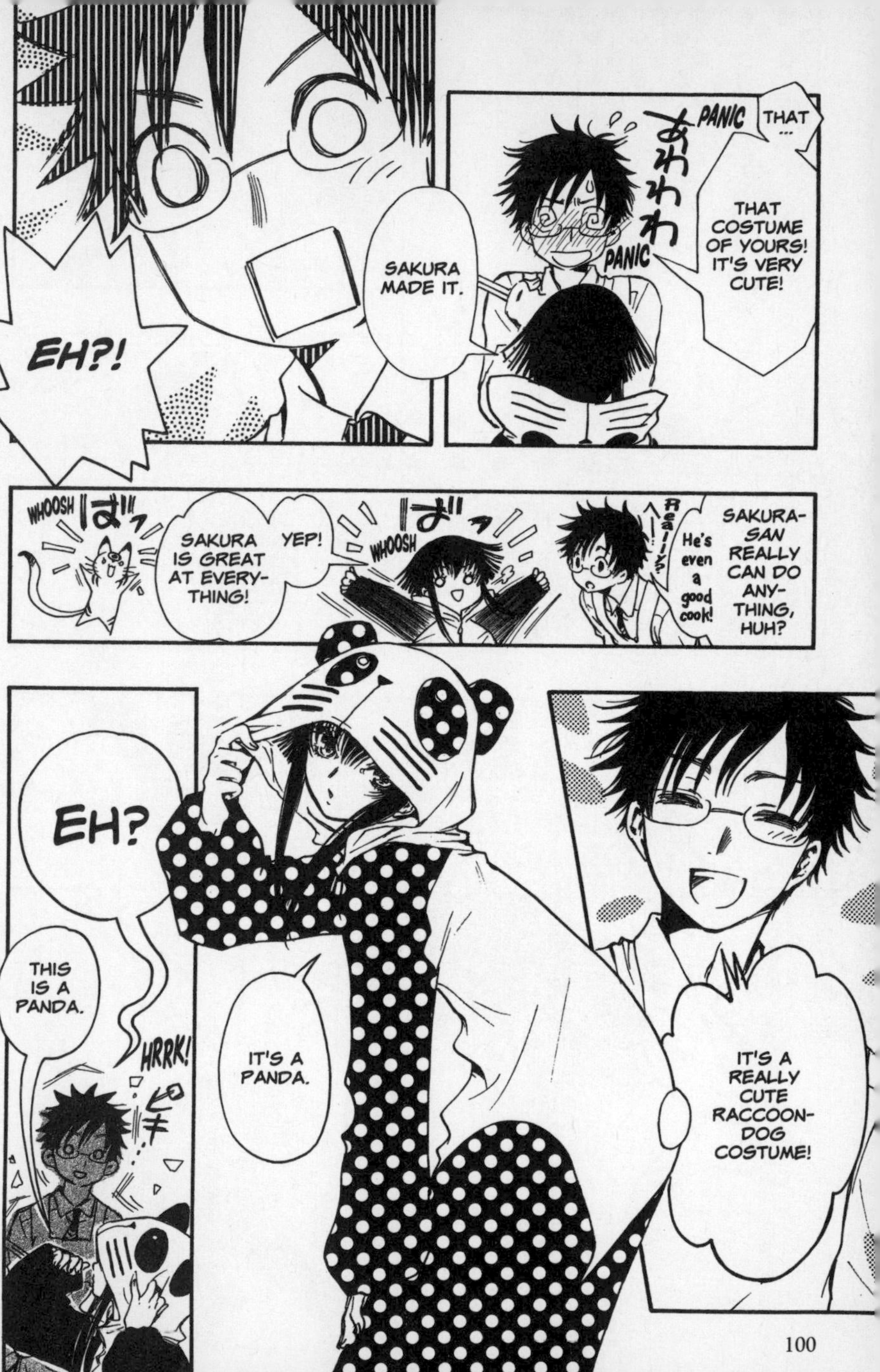
THAT ...
THAT COSTUME OF YOURS! IT'S VERY CUTE!
PANIC
あわわわ
PANIC
SAKURA MADE IT.
EH?!
SAKURA-SAN REALLY CAN DO ANY-THING, HUH?
Rea~lly?
He's even a good cook!
WHOOSH
ばっ
YEP!
SAKURA IS GREAT AT EVERY-THING!
WHOOSH
ばっ
IT'S A REALLY CUTE RACCOON-DOG COSTUME!
IT'S A PANDA.
EH?
THIS IS A PANDA.
HRRK!
ピキ

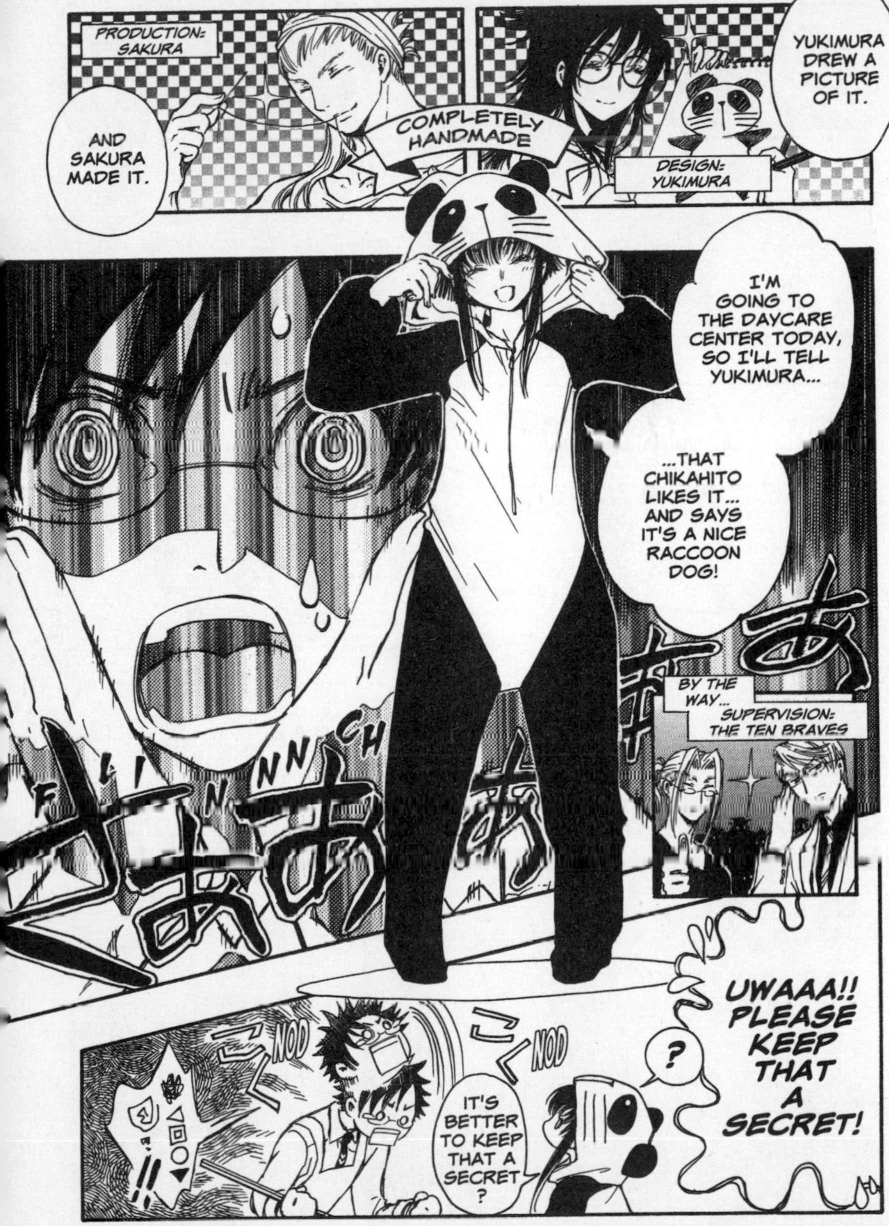
YUKIMURA DREW A PICTURE OF IT.
DESIGN: YUKIMURA
COMPLETELY HANDMADE
PRODUCTION: SAKURA
AND SAKURA MADE IT.
I'M GOING TO THE DAYCARE CENTER TODAY, SO I'LL TELL YUKIMURA...
...THAT CHIKAHITO LIKES IT... AND SAYS IT'S A NICE RACCOON DOG!
BY THE WAY... SUPERVISION: THE TEN BRAVES
FLINNNCH
UWAAA!! PLEASE KEEP THAT A SECRET!
?
IT'S BETTER TO KEEP THAT A SECRET?
NOD
NOD

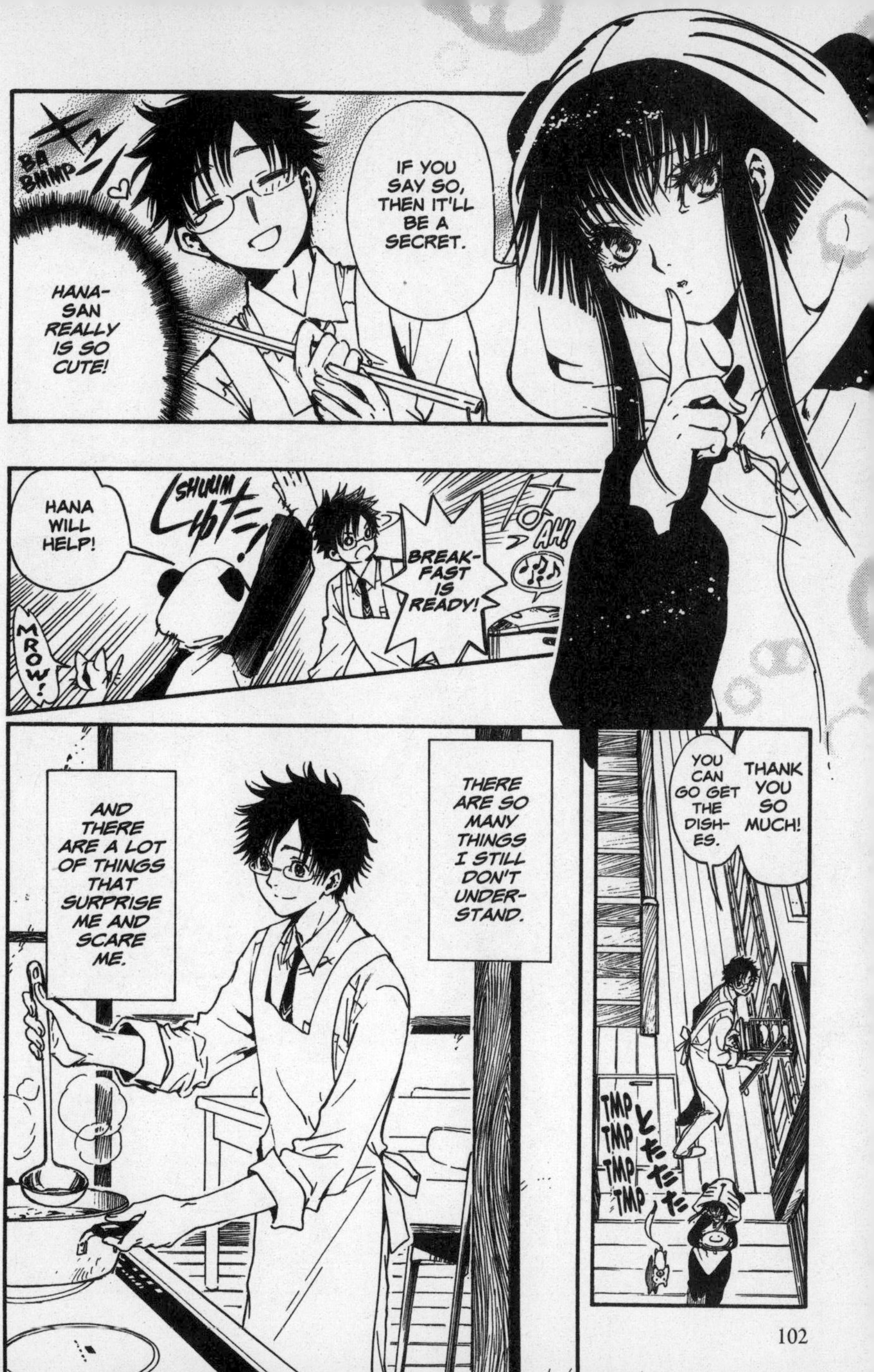
IF YOU SAY SO, THEN IT'LL BE A SECRET.
BA BMMP
HANA-SAN REALLY IS SO CUTE!
AH!
BREAK-FAST IS READY!
SHUUM
HANA WILL HELP!
MROW!
THANK YOU SO MUCH!
YOU CAN GO GET THE DISH-ES.
TMP TMP TMP TMP
THERE ARE SO MANY THINGS I STILL DON'T UNDER-STAND.
AND THERE ARE A LOT OF THINGS THAT SURPRISE ME AND SCARE ME.

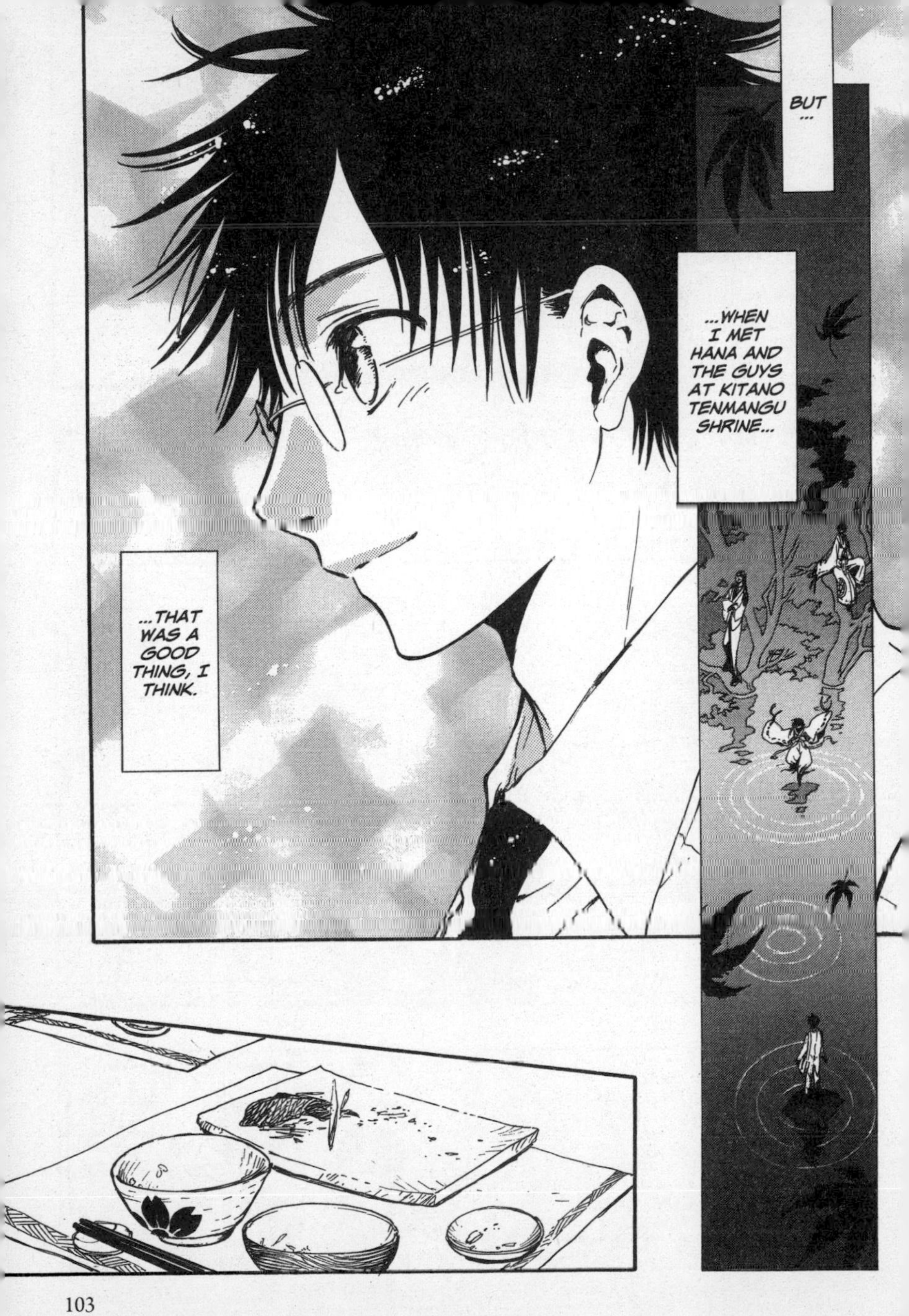
BUT ...
...WHEN I MET HANA AND THE GUYS AT KITANO TENMANGU SHRINE...
...THAT WAS A GOOD THING, I THINK.

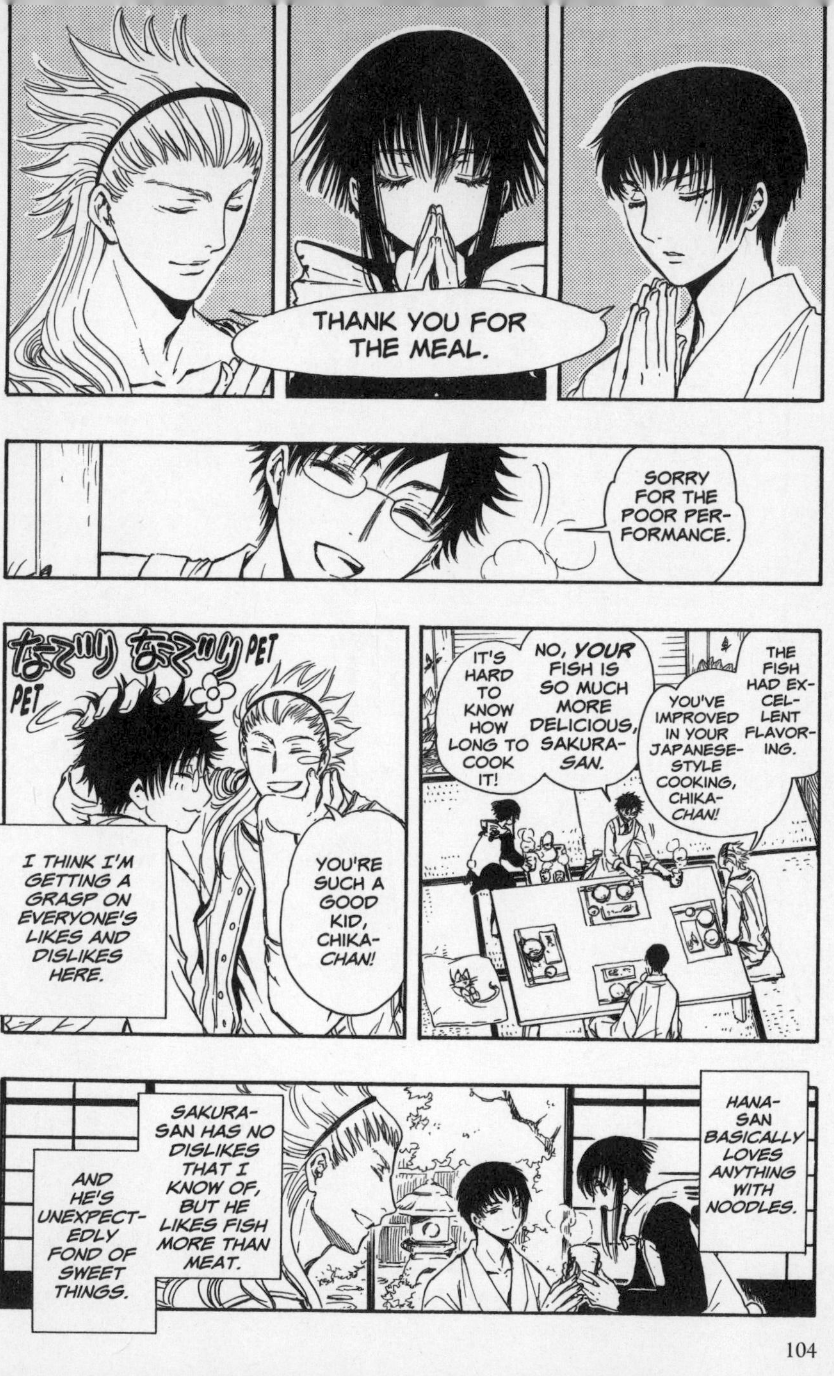
THANK YOU FOR THE MEAL.
SORRY FOR THE POOR PERFORMANCE.
THE FISH HAD EXCELLENT FLAVORING.
YOU'VE IMPROVED IN YOUR JAPANESE-STYLE COOKING, CHIKA-CHAN!
NO, *YOUR* FISH IS SO MUCH MORE DELICIOUS, SAKURA-SAN.
IT'S HARD TO KNOW HOW LONG TO COOK IT!
なでり なでり PET PET
YOU'RE SUCH A GOOD KID, CHIKA-CHAN!
I THINK I'M GETTING A GRASP ON EVERYONE'S LIKES AND DISLIKES HERE.
HANA-SAN BASICALLY LOVES ANYTHING WITH NOODLES.
SAKURA-SAN HAS NO DISLIKES THAT I KNOW OF, BUT HE LIKES FISH MORE THAN MEAT.
AND HE'S UNEXPECTEDLY FOND OF SWEET THINGS.

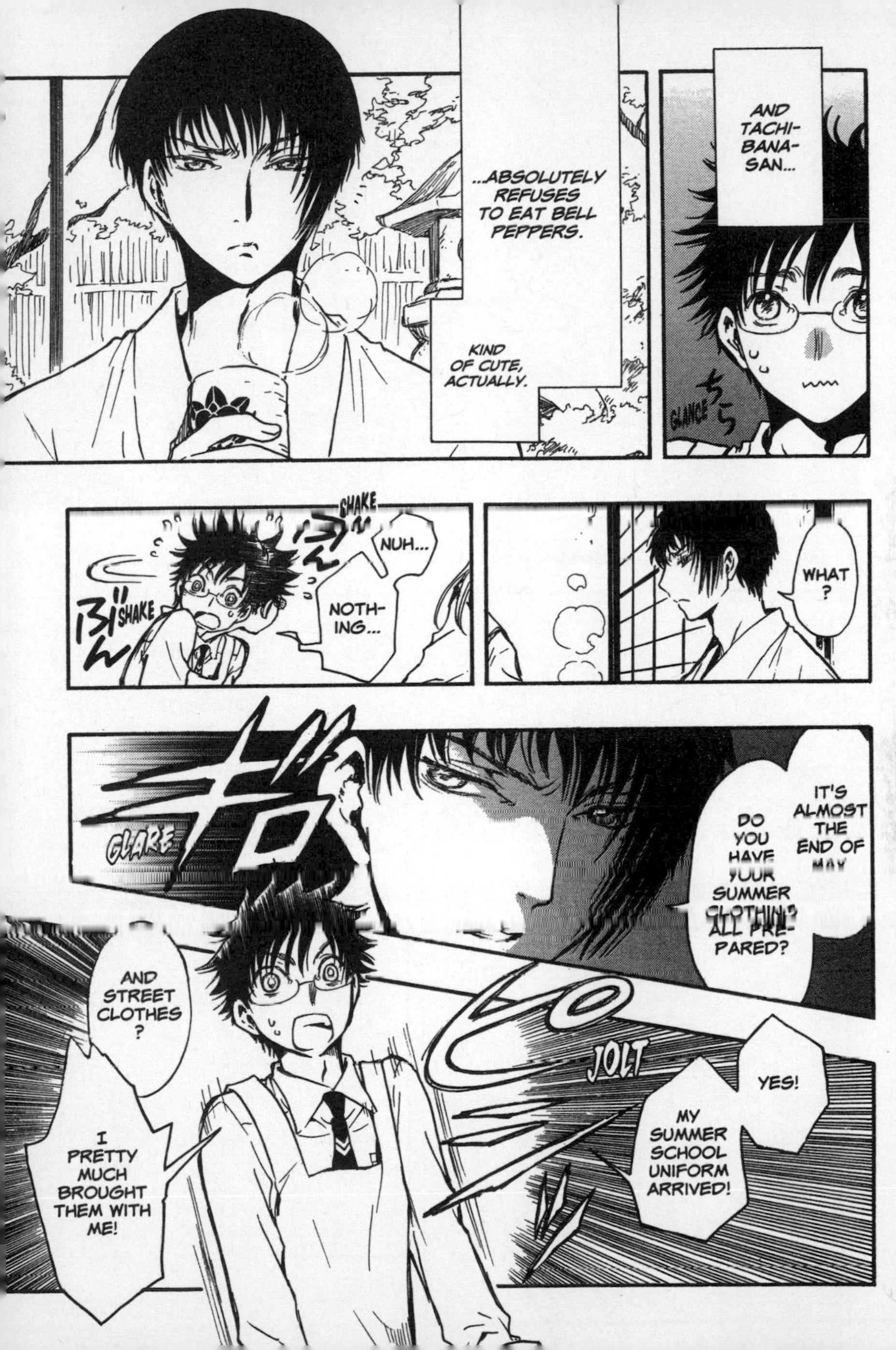
AND TACHIBANA-SAN...
GLANCE
...ABSOLUTELY REFUSES TO EAT BELL PEPPERS.
KIND OF CUTE, ACTUALLY.
WHAT?
SHAKE
NUH...
NOTHING...
SHAKE
IT'S ALMOST THE END OF MAY.
DO YOU HAVE YOUR SUMMER CLOTHING ALL PREPARED?
GLARE
JOLT
YES!
MY SUMMER SCHOOL UNIFORM ARRIVED!
AND STREET CLOTHES?
I PRETTY MUCH BROUGHT THEM WITH ME!

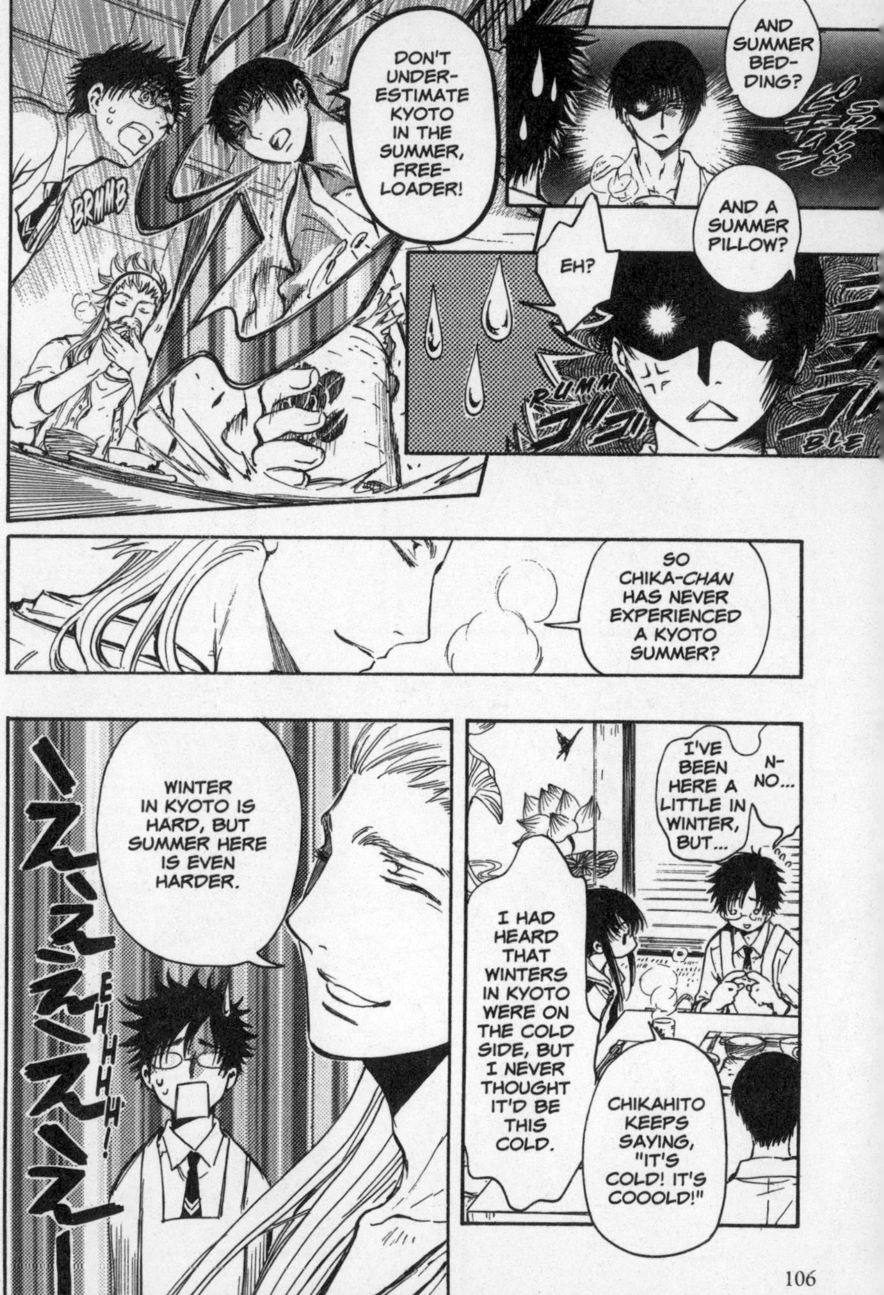
AND SUMMER BEDDING?
AND A SUMMER PILLOW?
EH?
RUMM
BLE
DON'T UNDER-ESTIMATE KYOTO IN THE SUMMER, FREE-LOADER!
BRMMB
SO CHIKA-*CHAN* HAS NEVER EXPERIENCED A KYOTO SUMMER?
N-NO...
I'VE BEEN HERE A LITTLE IN WINTER, BUT...
I HAD HEARD THAT WINTERS IN KYOTO WERE ON THE COLD SIDE, BUT I NEVER THOUGHT IT'D BE THIS COLD.
CHIKAHITO KEEPS SAYING, "IT'S COLD! IT'S COOOLD!"
WINTER IN KYOTO IS HARD, BUT SUMMER HERE IS EVEN HARDER.
EHHHH!

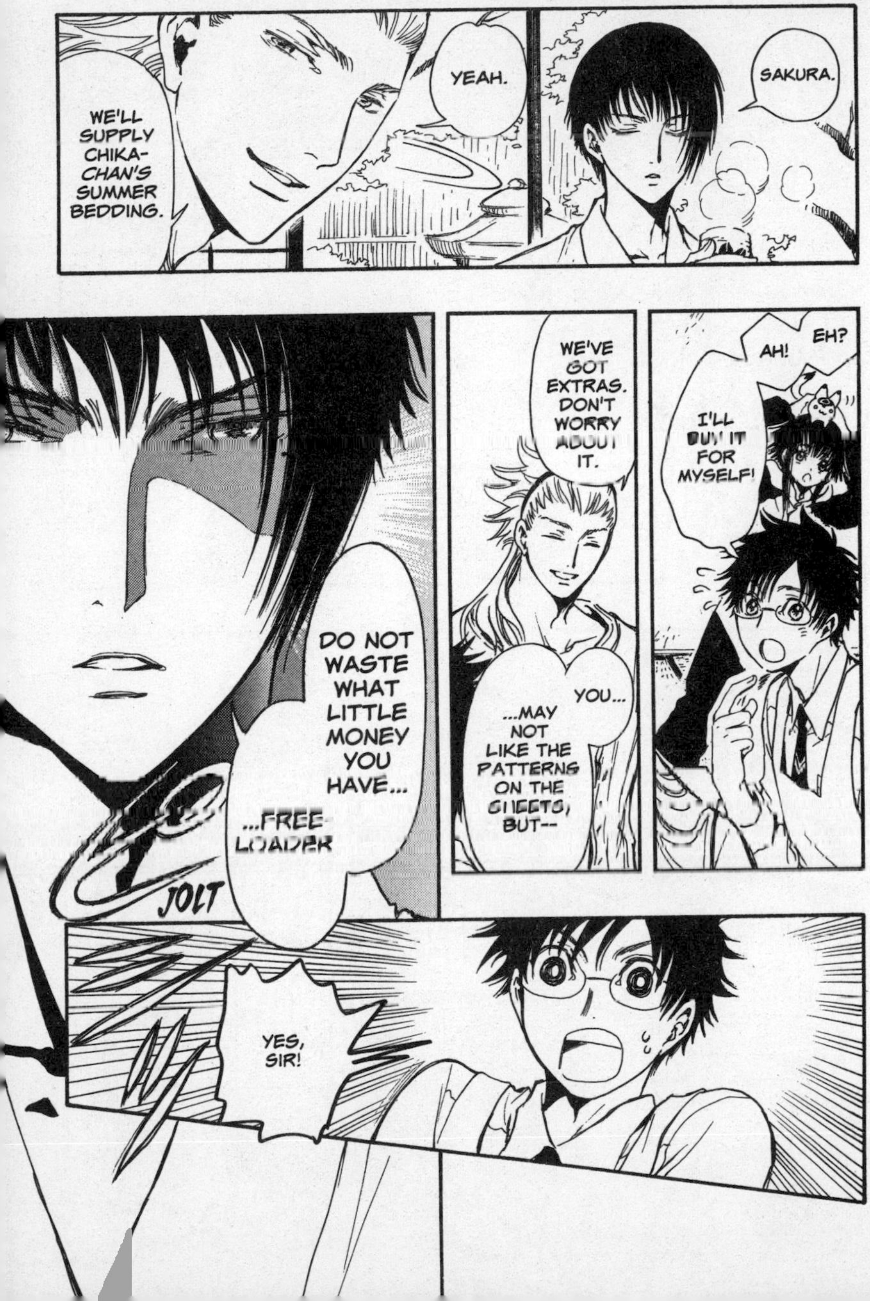
SAKURA.
YEAH.
WE'LL SUPPLY CHIKA-CHAN'S SUMMER BEDDING.
EH?
AH!
I'LL BUY IT FOR MYSELF!
WE'VE GOT EXTRAS. DON'T WORRY ABOUT IT.
YOU...
...MAY NOT LIKE THE PATTERNS ON THE SHEETS, BUT--
DO NOT WASTE WHAT LITTLE MONEY YOU HAVE...
...FREE-LOADER
JOLT
YES, SIR!

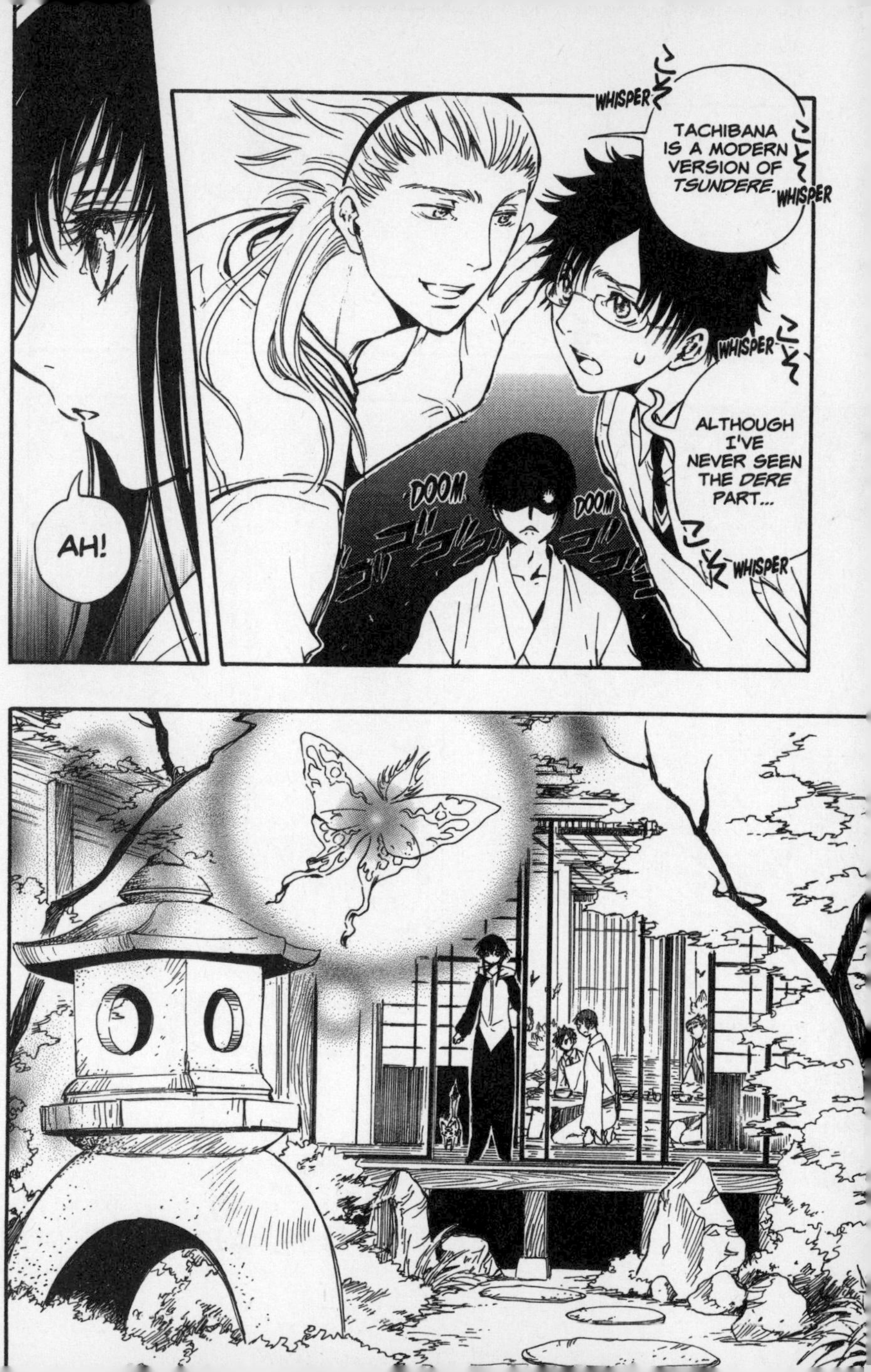
WHISPER
TACHIBANA IS A MODERN VERSION OF TSUNDERE.
WHISPER
WHISPER
ALTHOUGH I'VE NEVER SEEN THE DERE PART...
WHISPER
DOOM
DOOM
AH!

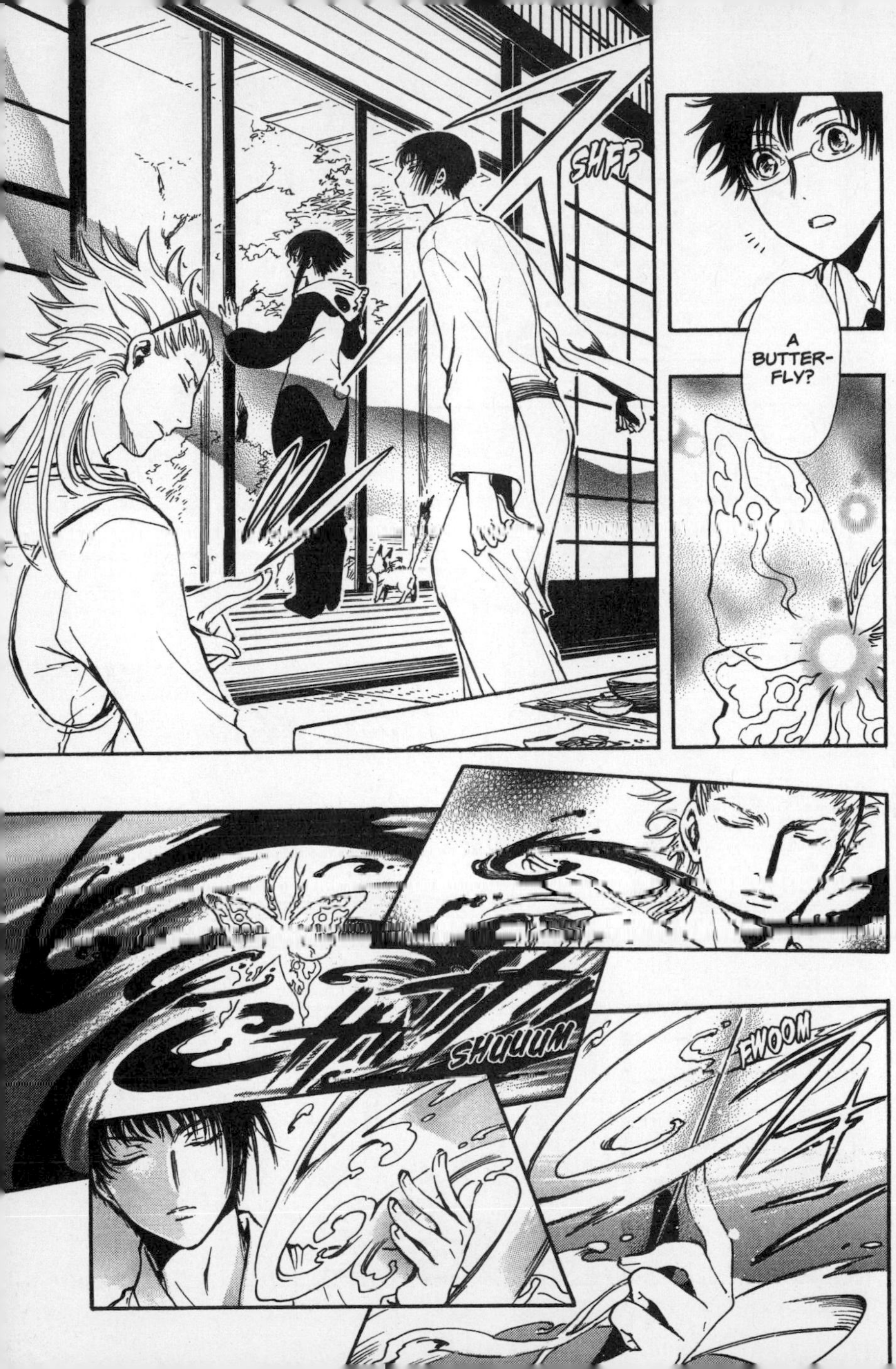
SHFF
A BUTTER-FLY?
SHUUUM
FWOOM

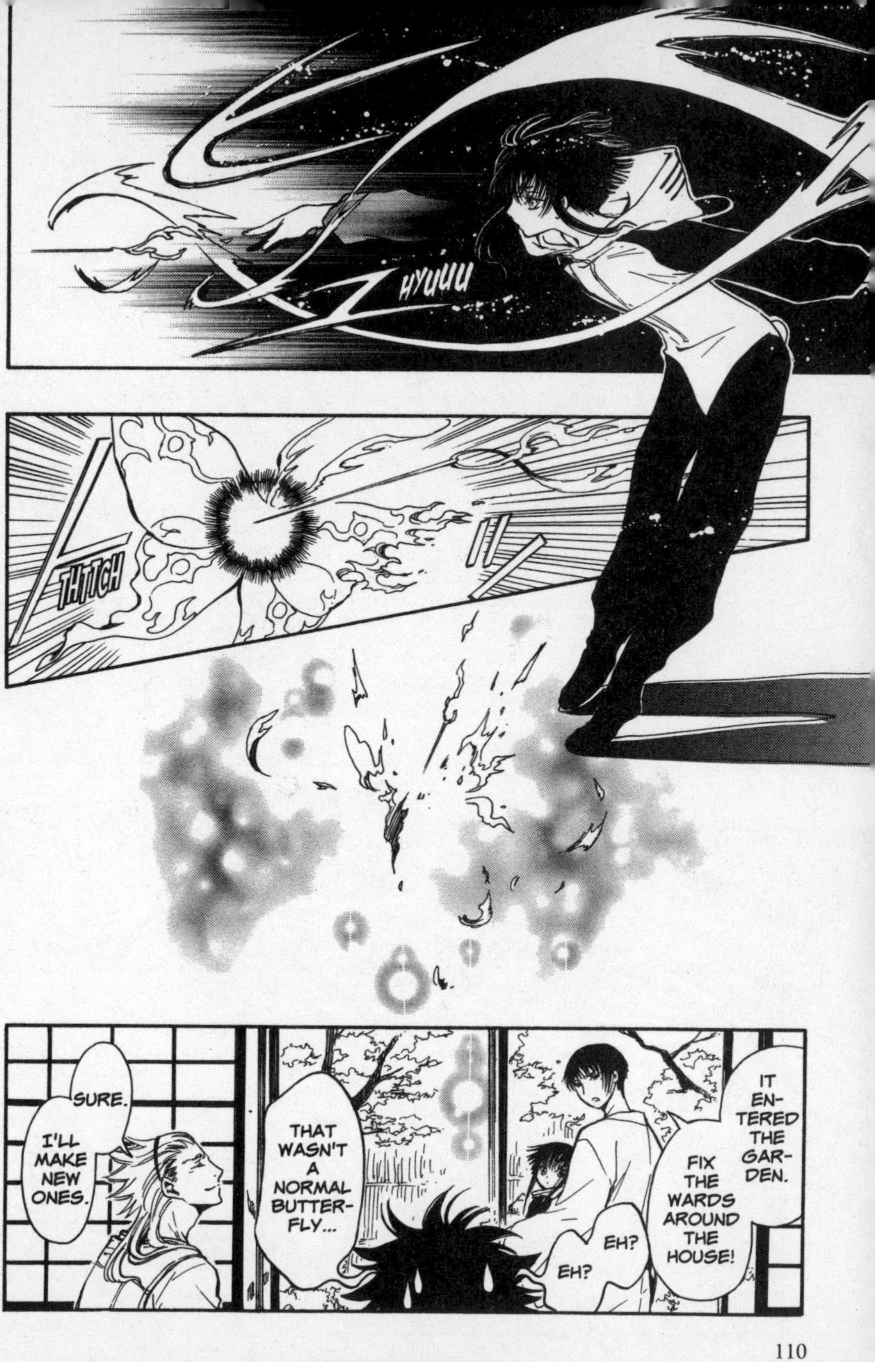
HYUUU
THTTCH
IT ENTERED THE GARDEN.
FIX THE WARDS AROUND THE HOUSE!
EH?
EH?
THAT WASN'T A NORMAL BUTTERFLY...
SURE.
I'LL MAKE NEW ONES.

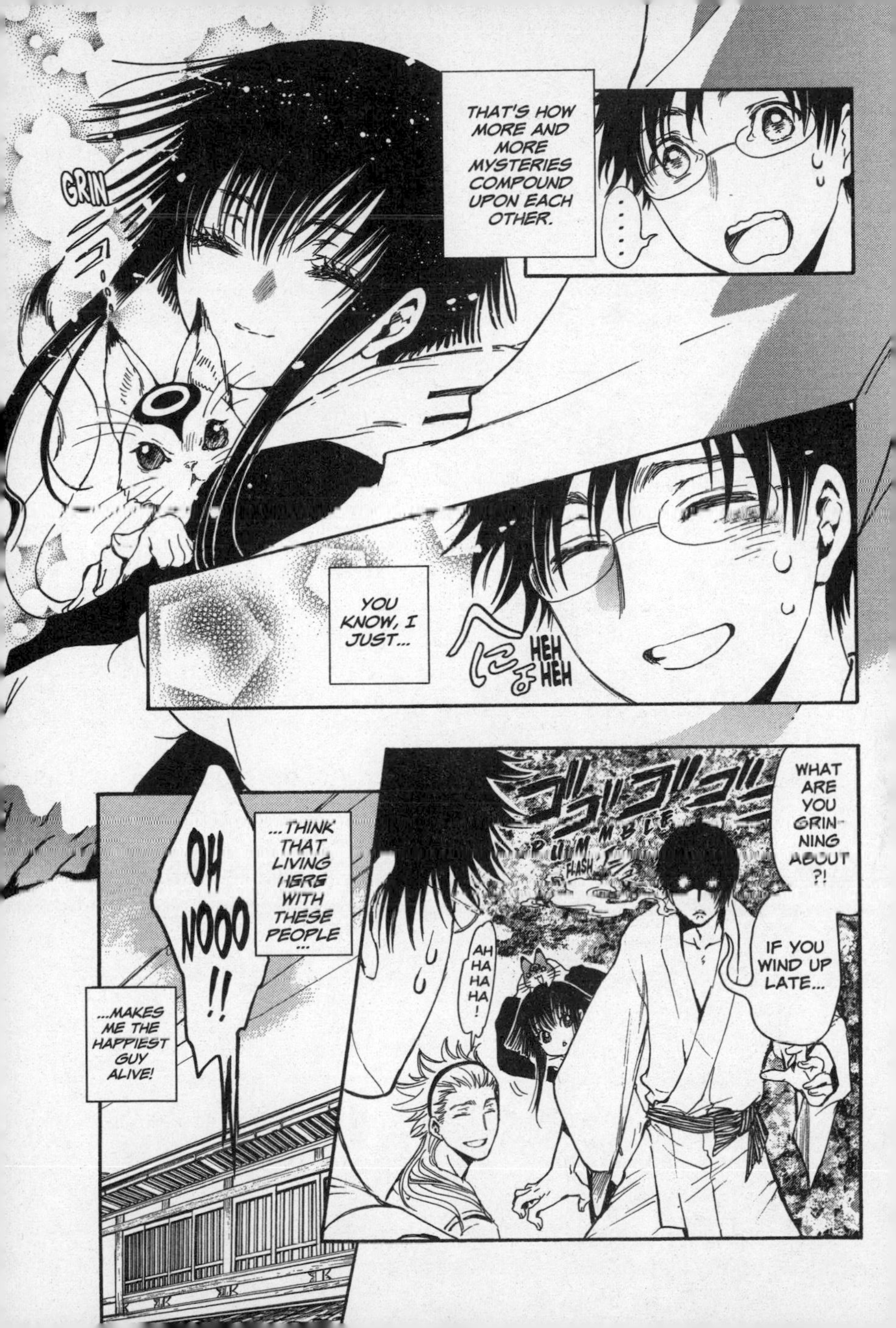
THAT'S HOW MORE AND MORE MYSTERIES COMPOUND UPON EACH OTHER.
.....
GRIN
YOU KNOW, I JUST...
HEH HEH
RUMBLE
FLASH
WHAT ARE YOU GRINNING ABOUT?!
IF YOU WIND UP LATE...
AH HA HA HA!
...THINK THAT LIVING HERE WITH THESE PEOPLE...
OH NOOO!!
...MAKES ME THE HAPPIEST GUY ALIVE!

GATE 7
ゲート セブン

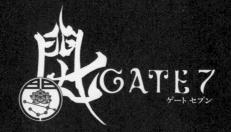

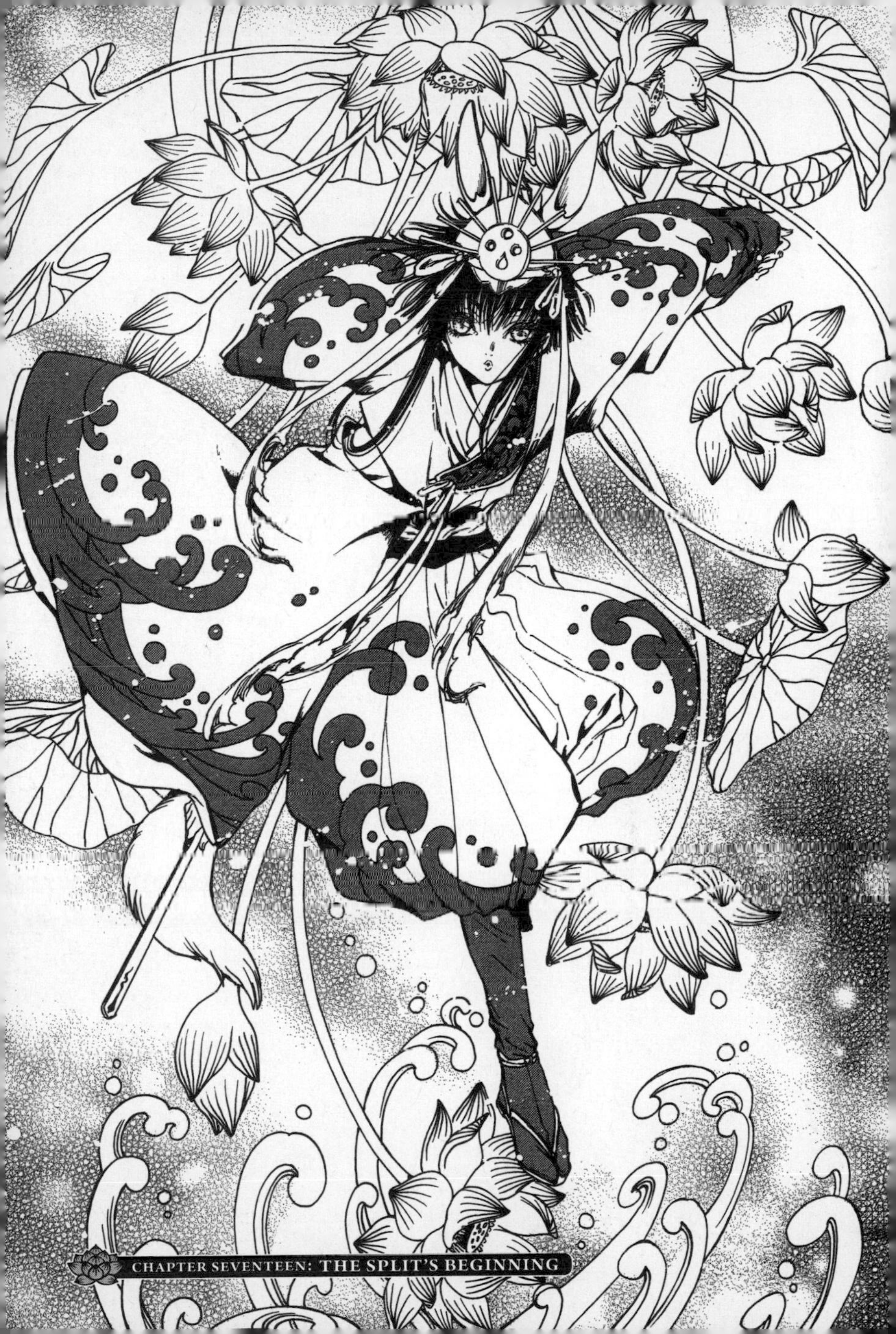
CHAPTER SEVENTEEN: THE SPLIT'S BEGINNING

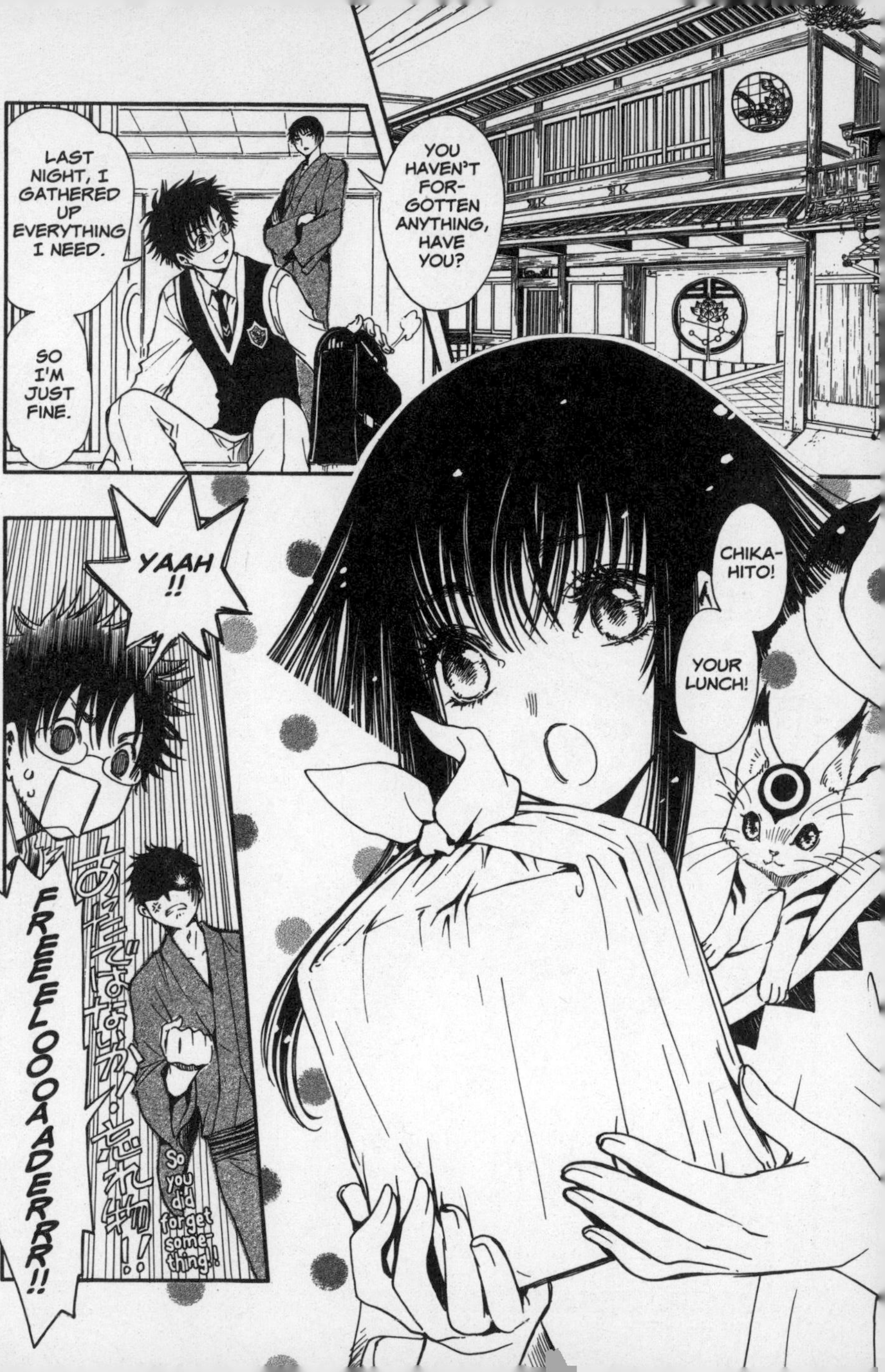
YOU HAVEN'T FOR-GOTTEN ANYTHING, HAVE YOU?
LAST NIGHT, I GATHERED UP EVERYTHING I NEED.
SO I'M JUST FINE.
CHIKA-HITO!
YOUR LUNCH!
YAAH!!
FREEELOOOAADERRR!!
So you did forget some-thing!!

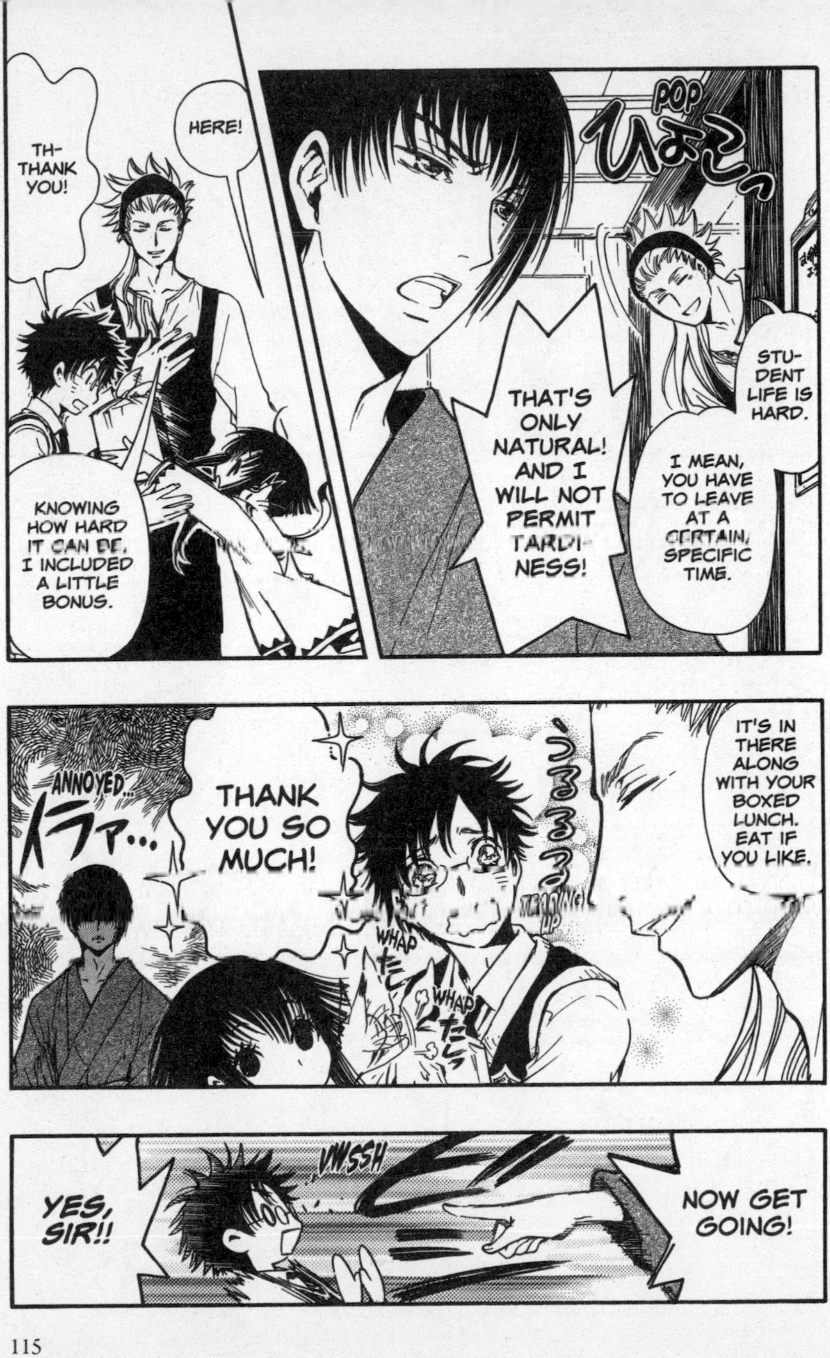
POP
ひょこっ
STU-DENT LIFE IS HARD.
I MEAN, YOU HAVE TO LEAVE AT A CERTAIN, SPECIFIC TIME.
THAT'S ONLY NATURAL! AND I WILL NOT PERMIT TARDI-NESS!
HERE!
TH-THANK YOU!
KNOWING HOW HARD IT CAN BE, I INCLUDED A LITTLE BONUS.
IT'S IN THERE ALONG WITH YOUR BOXED LUNCH. EAT IF YOU LIKE.
うるるっ
THANK YOU SO MUCH!
WHAP
たしっ
WHAP
たしっ
ANNOYED...
イラァ...
NOW GET GOING!
VWSSH
YES, SIR!!

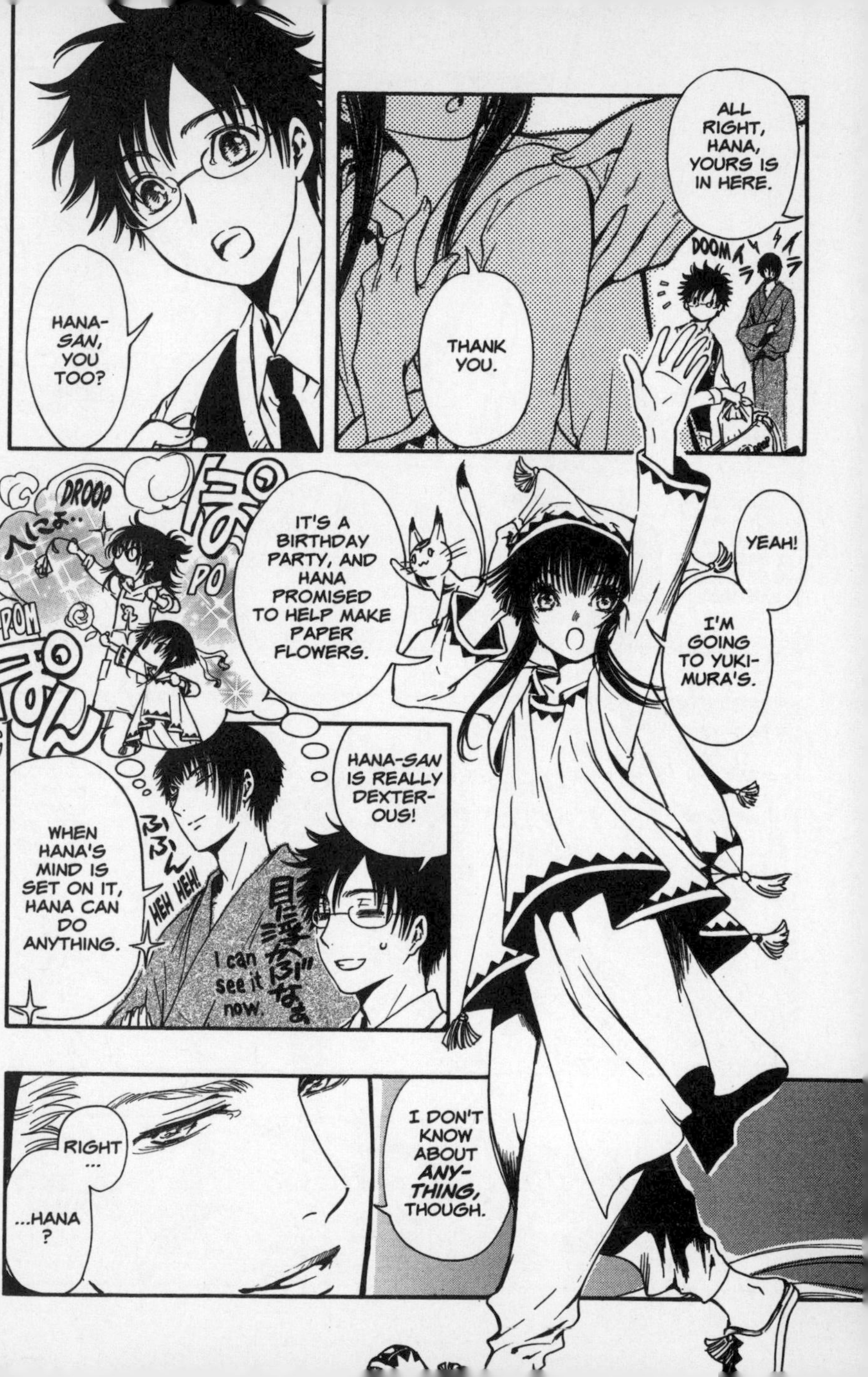
ALL RIGHT, HANA, YOURS IS IN HERE.
DOOM
THANK YOU.
HANA-SAN, YOU TOO?
YEAH!
I'M GOING TO YUKIMURA'S.
IT'S A BIRTHDAY PARTY, AND HANA PROMISED TO HELP MAKE PAPER FLOWERS.
DROOP
PO
POM
HANA-SAN IS REALLY DEXTEROUS!
WHEN HANA'S MIND IS SET ON IT, HANA CAN DO ANYTHING.
HEH HEH!
I can see it now.
I DON'T KNOW ABOUT *ANYTHING*, THOUGH.
RIGHT...
...HANA?

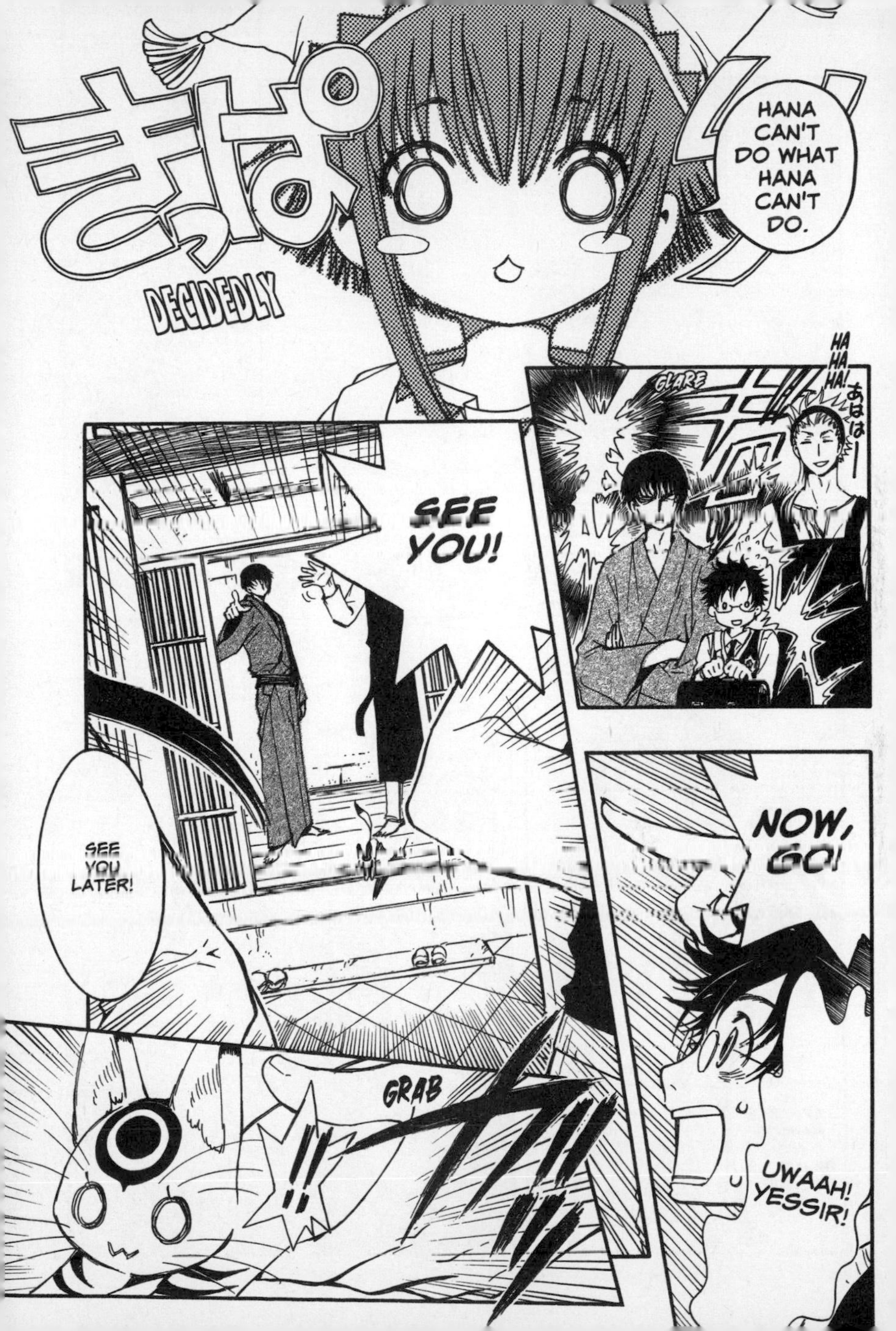
きっぱ
DECIDEDLY
HANA CAN'T DO WHAT HANA CAN'T DO.
GLARE
HA HA HA!
あははー
SEE YOU!
SEE YOU LATER!
NOW, GO!
UWAAH! YESSIR!
GRAB

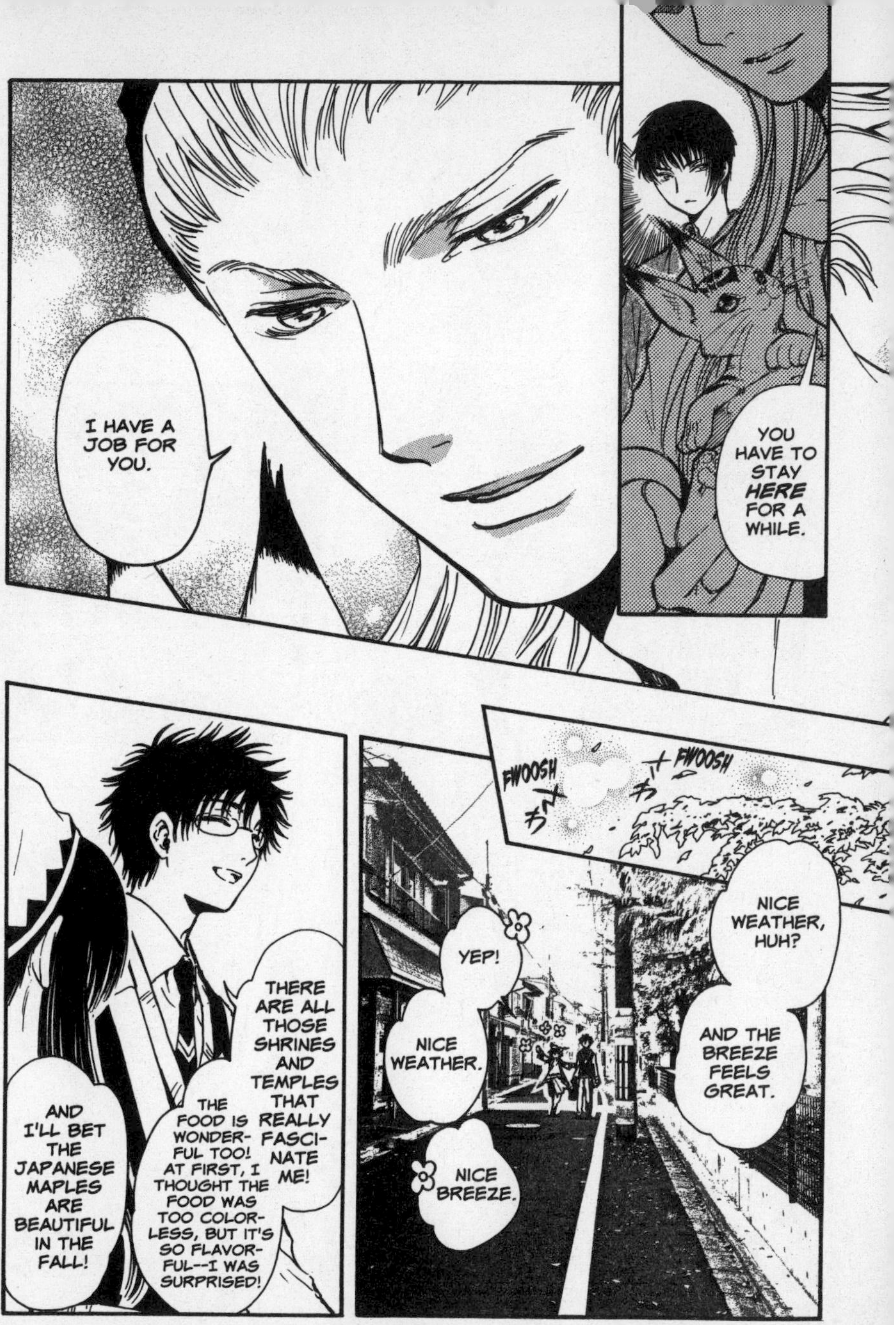
YOU HAVE TO STAY *HERE* FOR A WHILE.
I HAVE A JOB FOR YOU.
FWOOSH
FWOOSH
NICE WEATHER, HUH?
AND THE BREEZE FEELS GREAT.
YEP!
NICE WEATHER.
NICE BREEZE.
THERE ARE ALL THOSE SHRINES AND TEMPLES THAT REALLY FASCINATE ME!
THE FOOD IS WONDERFUL TOO! AT FIRST, I THOUGHT THE FOOD WAS TOO COLORLESS, BUT IT'S SO FLAVORFUL--I WAS SURPRISED!
AND I'LL BET THE JAPANESE MAPLES ARE BEAUTIFUL IN THE FALL!

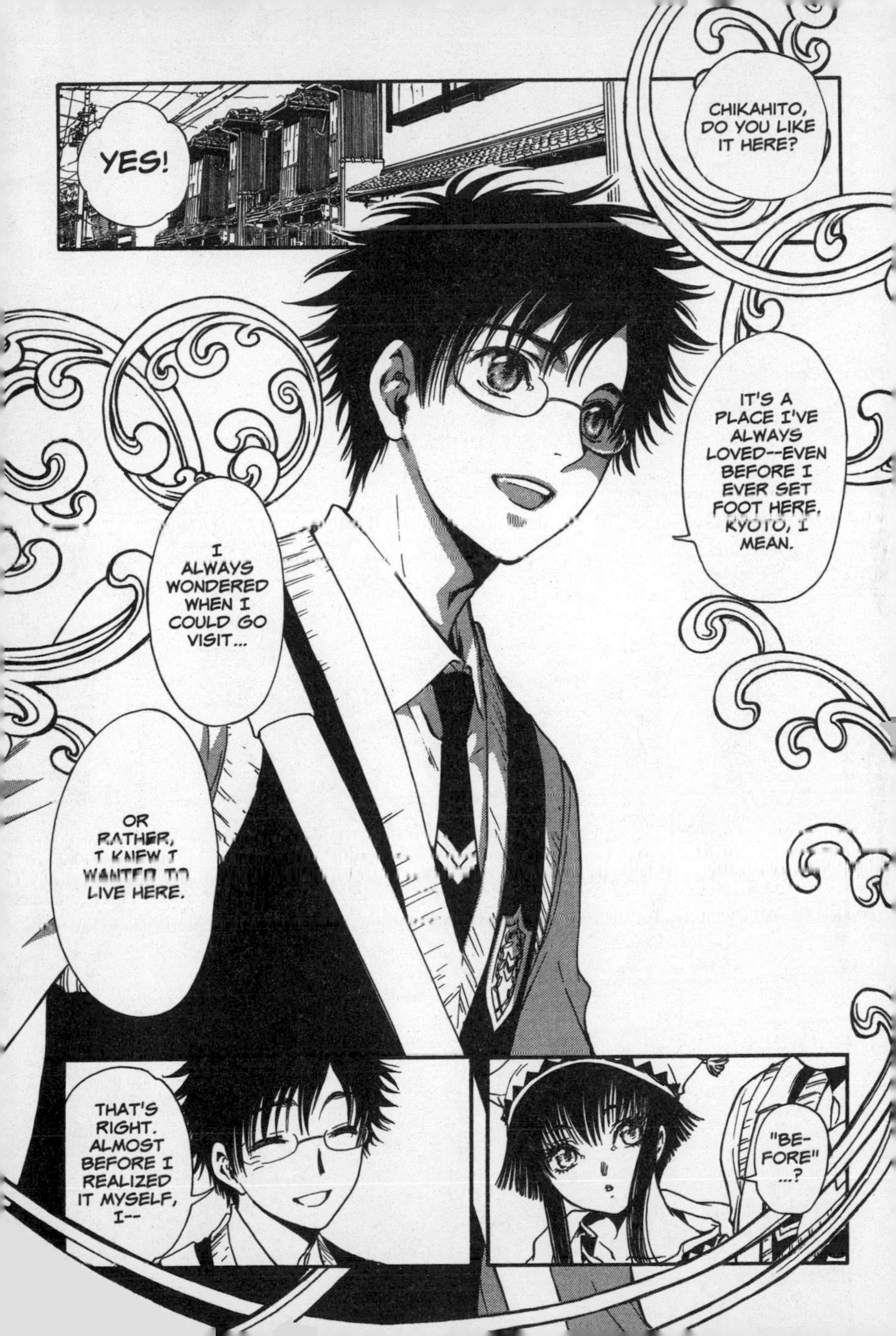
CHIKAHITO, DO YOU LIKE IT HERE?
YES!
IT'S A PLACE I'VE ALWAYS LOVED--EVEN BEFORE I EVER SET FOOT HERE. KYOTO, I MEAN.
I ALWAYS WONDERED WHEN I COULD GO VISIT...
OR RATHER, I KNEW I WANTED TO LIVE HERE.
"BE-FORE"...?
THAT'S RIGHT. ALMOST BEFORE I REALIZED IT MYSELF, I--

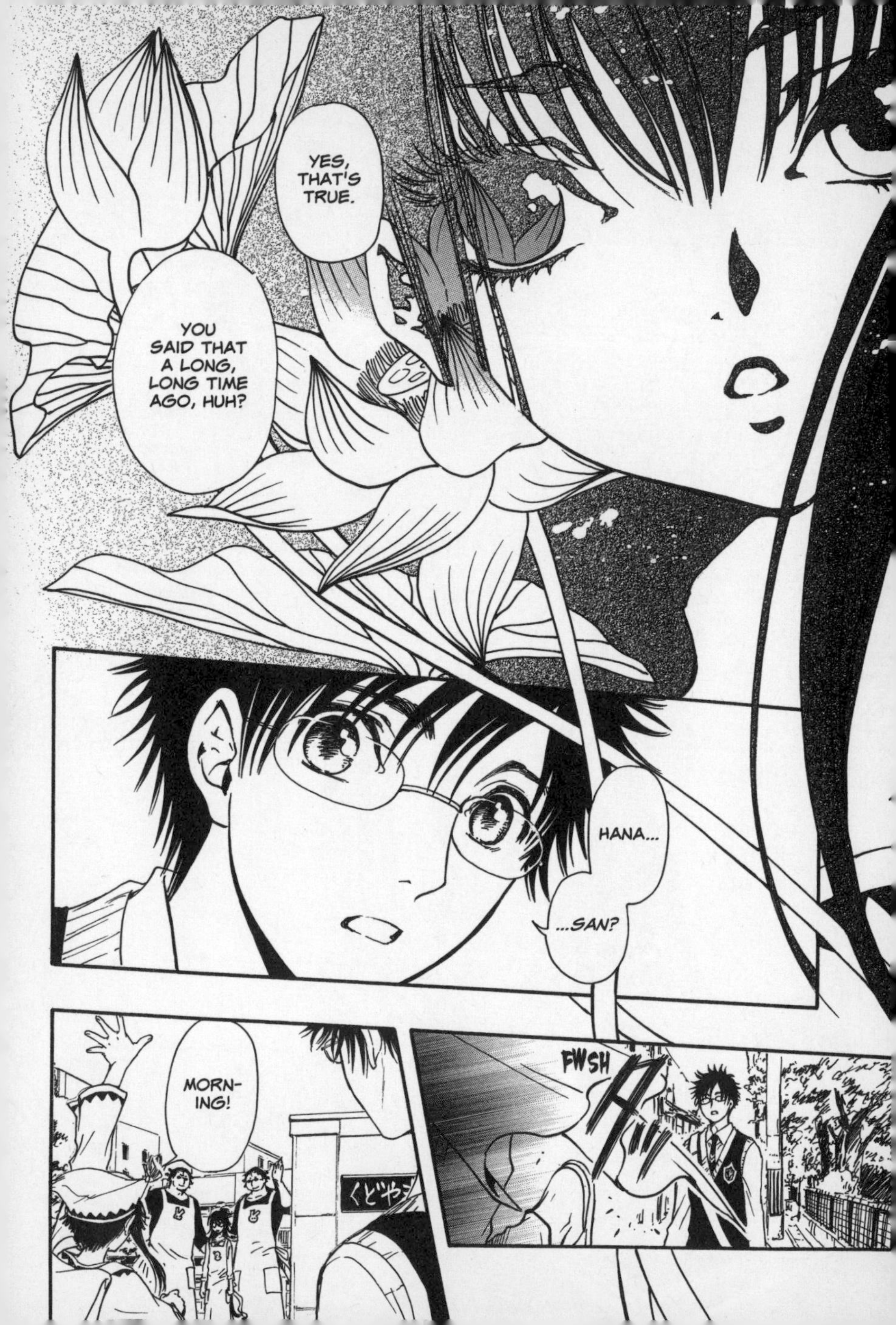
YES, THAT'S TRUE.
YOU SAID THAT A LONG, LONG TIME AGO, HUH?
HANA...
...SAN?
FWSH
MORNING!

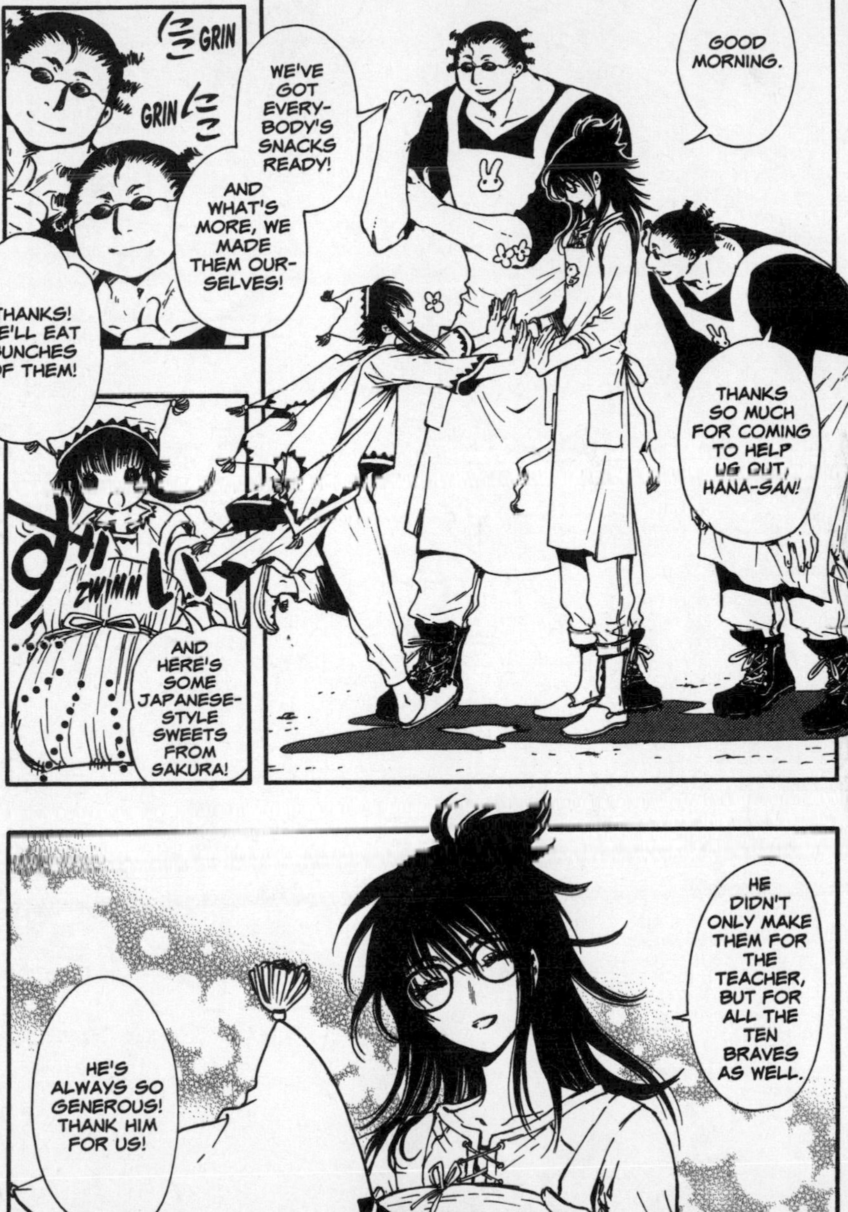
GOOD MORNING.
THANKS SO MUCH FOR COMING TO HELP US OUT, HANA-SAN!
GRIN
GRIN
WE'VE GOT EVERY-BODY'S SNACKS READY!
AND WHAT'S MORE, WE MADE THEM OUR-SELVES!
THANKS! WE'LL EAT BUNCHES OF THEM!
ZWIMM
AND HERE'S SOME JAPANESE-STYLE SWEETS FROM SAKURA!
HE DIDN'T ONLY MAKE THEM FOR THE TEACHER, BUT FOR ALL THE TEN BRAVES AS WELL.
HE'S ALWAYS SO GENEROUS! THANK HIM FOR US!

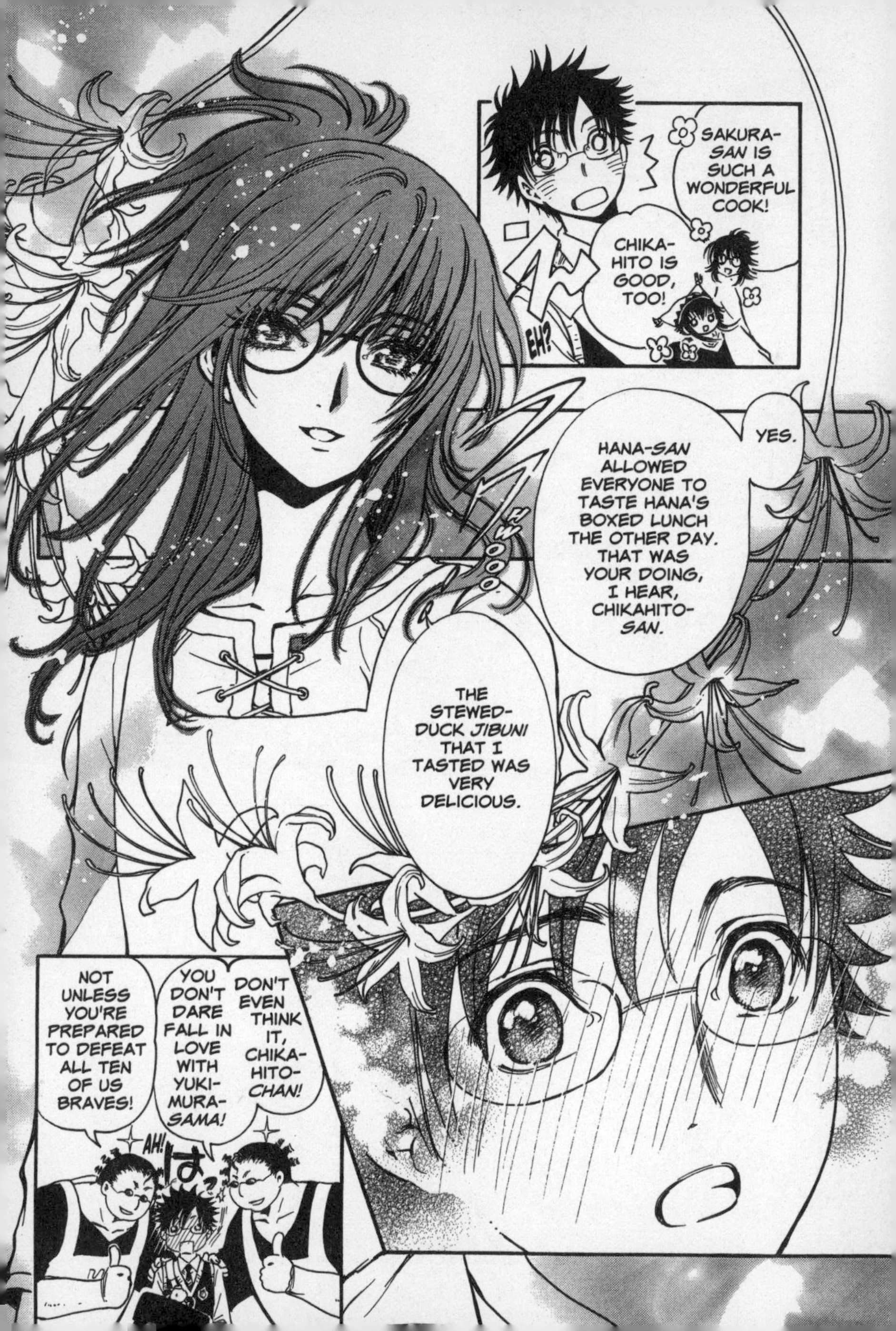
SAKURA-SAN IS SUCH A WONDERFUL COOK!
CHIKAHITO IS GOOD, TOO!
EH?
YES.
HANA-SAN ALLOWED EVERYONE TO TASTE HANA'S BOXED LUNCH THE OTHER DAY. THAT WAS YOUR DOING, I HEAR, CHIKAHITO-SAN.
THE STEWED-DUCK *JIBUNI* THAT I TASTED WAS VERY DELICIOUS.
DON'T EVEN THINK IT, CHIKAHITO-*CHAN*!
YOU DON'T DARE FALL IN LOVE WITH YUKIMURA-*SAMA*!
NOT UNLESS YOU'RE PREPARED TO DEFEAT ALL TEN OF US BRAVES!
AH!

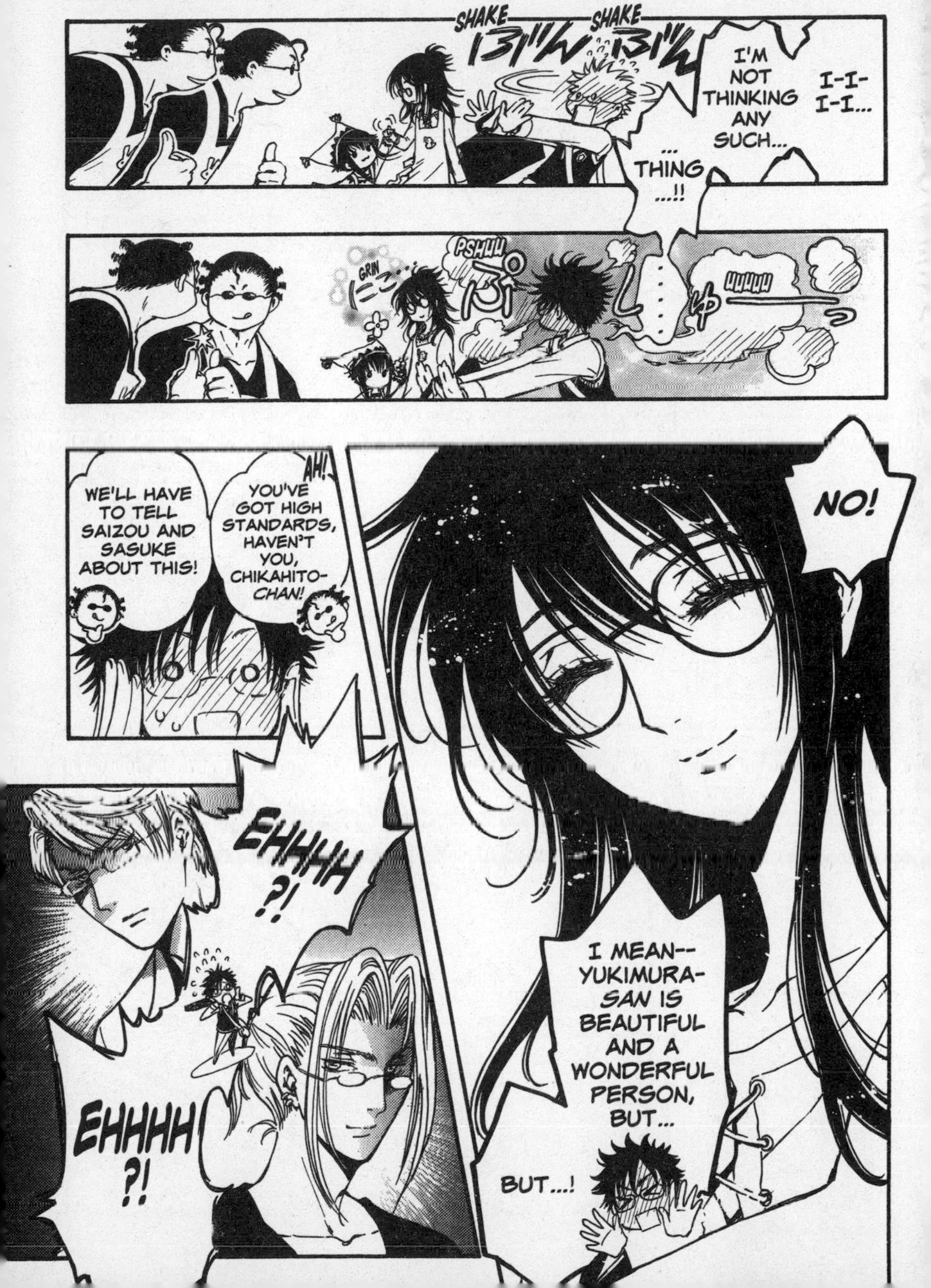
I-I-I-I...
I'M NOT THINKING ANY SUCH...
... THING ...!!
SHAKE
SHAKE
PSHUU
GRIN
NO!
I MEAN-- YUKIMURA-SAN IS BEAUTIFUL AND A WONDERFUL PERSON, BUT...
BUT...!
AH!
YOU'VE GOT HIGH STANDARDS, HAVEN'T YOU, CHIKAHITO-CHAN!
WE'LL HAVE TO TELL SAIZOU AND SASUKE ABOUT THIS!
EHHHH ?!
EHHHH ?!

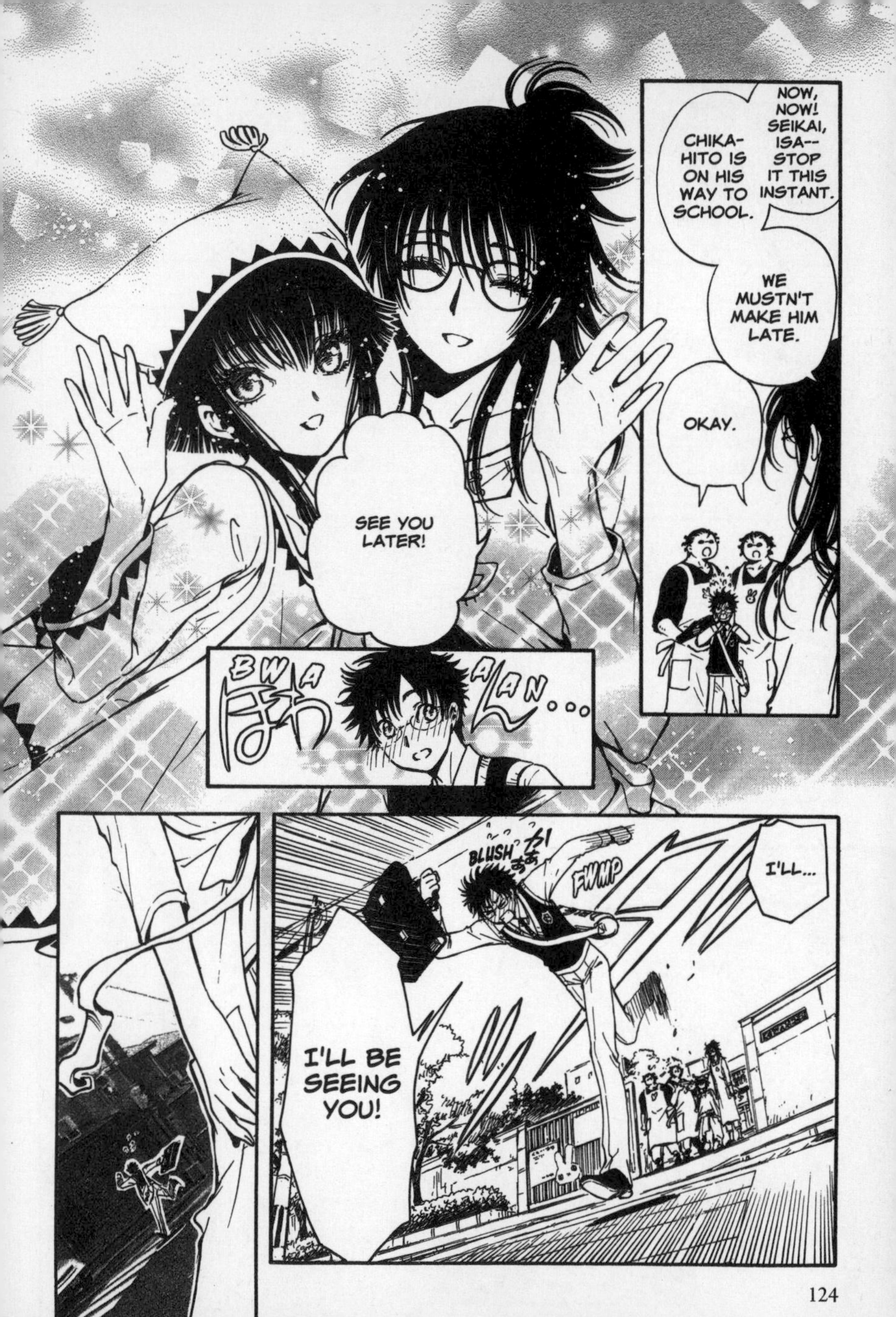
NOW, NOW! SEIKAI, ISA-- STOP IT THIS INSTANT.
CHIKA-HITO IS ON HIS WAY TO SCHOOL.
WE MUSTN'T MAKE HIM LATE.
OKAY.
SEE YOU LATER!
BWAAAN...
I'LL...
FWMP
BLUSH
I'LL BE SEEING YOU!

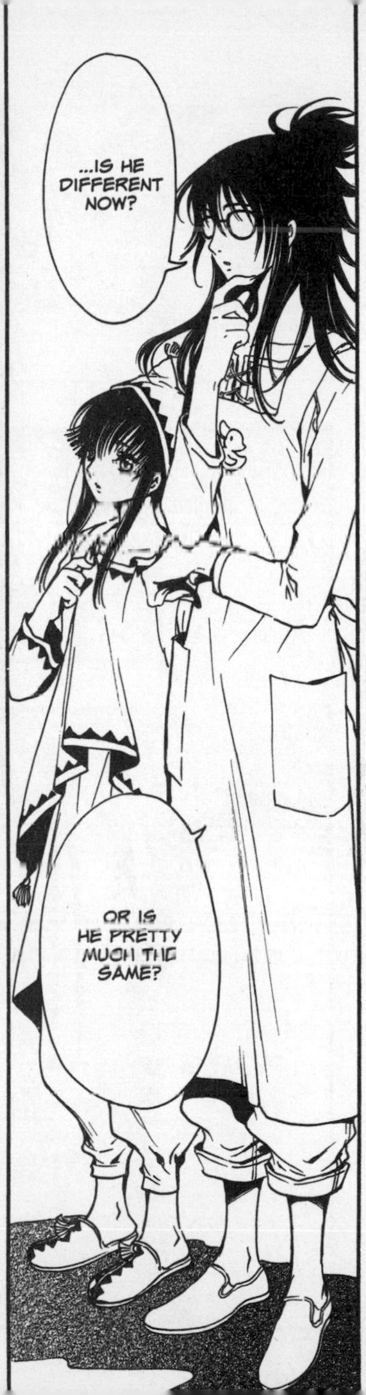
...IS HE DIFFERENT NOW?
OR IS HE PRETTY MUCH THE SAME?

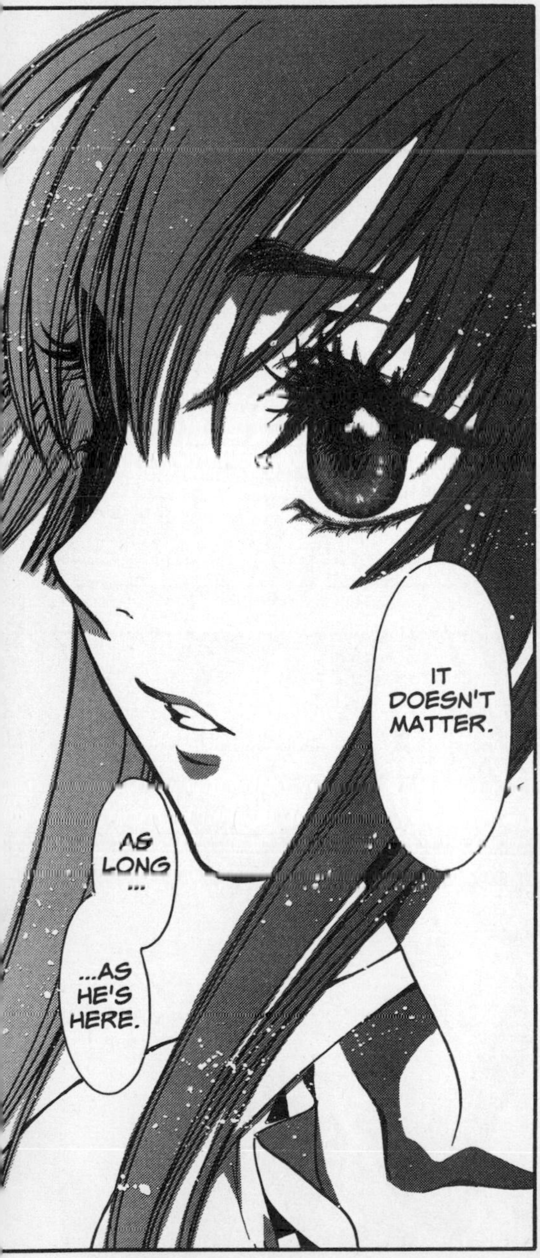
IT DOESN'T MATTER.
AS LONG ...
...AS HE'S HERE.

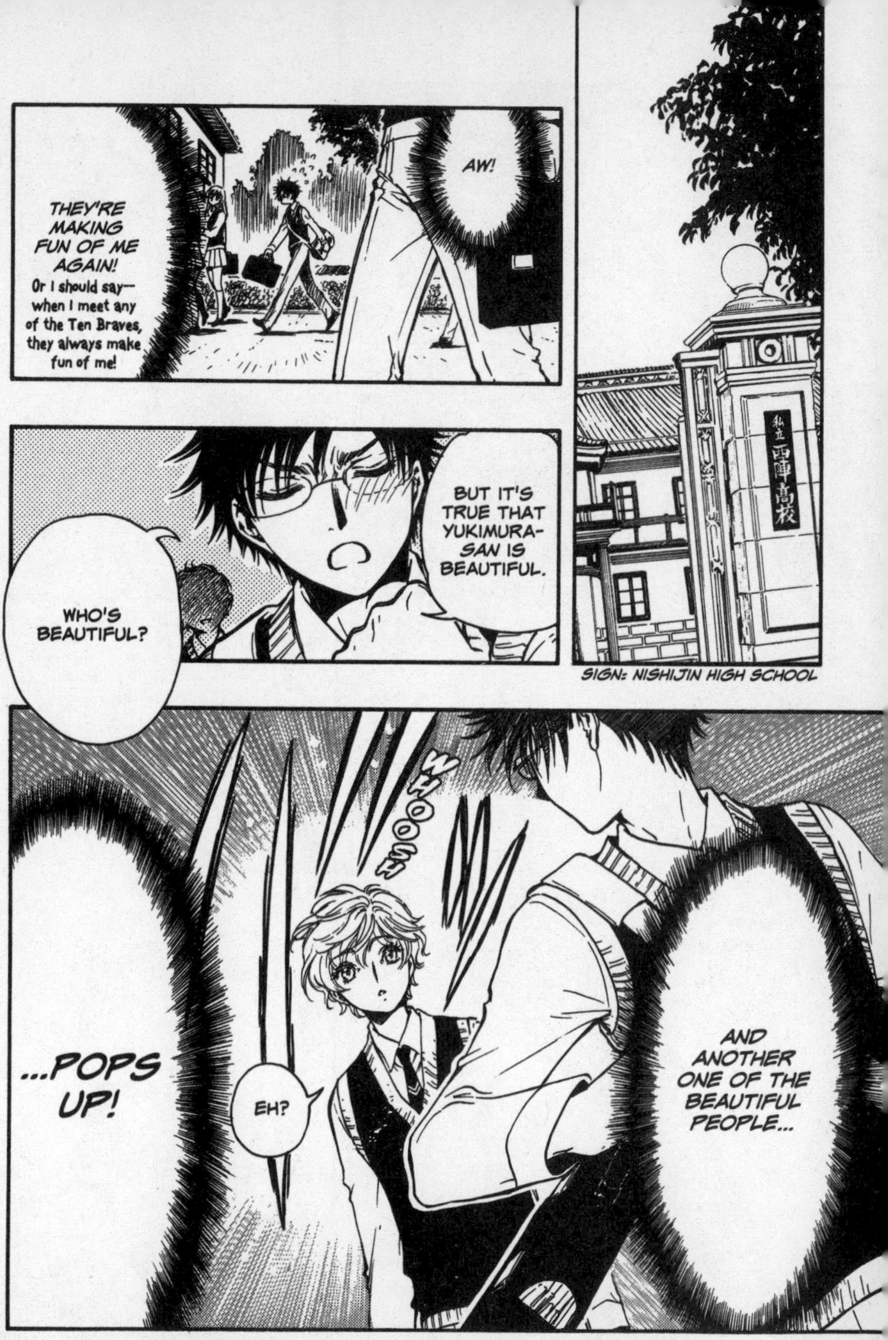
私立
西陣高校
SIGN: NISHIJIN HIGH SCHOOL
AW!
THEY'RE MAKING FUN OF ME AGAIN!
Or I should say— when I meet any of the Ten Braves, they always make fun of me!
BUT IT'S TRUE THAT YUKIMURA-SAN IS BEAUTIFUL.
WHO'S BEAUTIFUL?
WHOOOSH
AND ANOTHER ONE OF THE BEAUTIFUL PEOPLE...
EH?
...POPS UP!

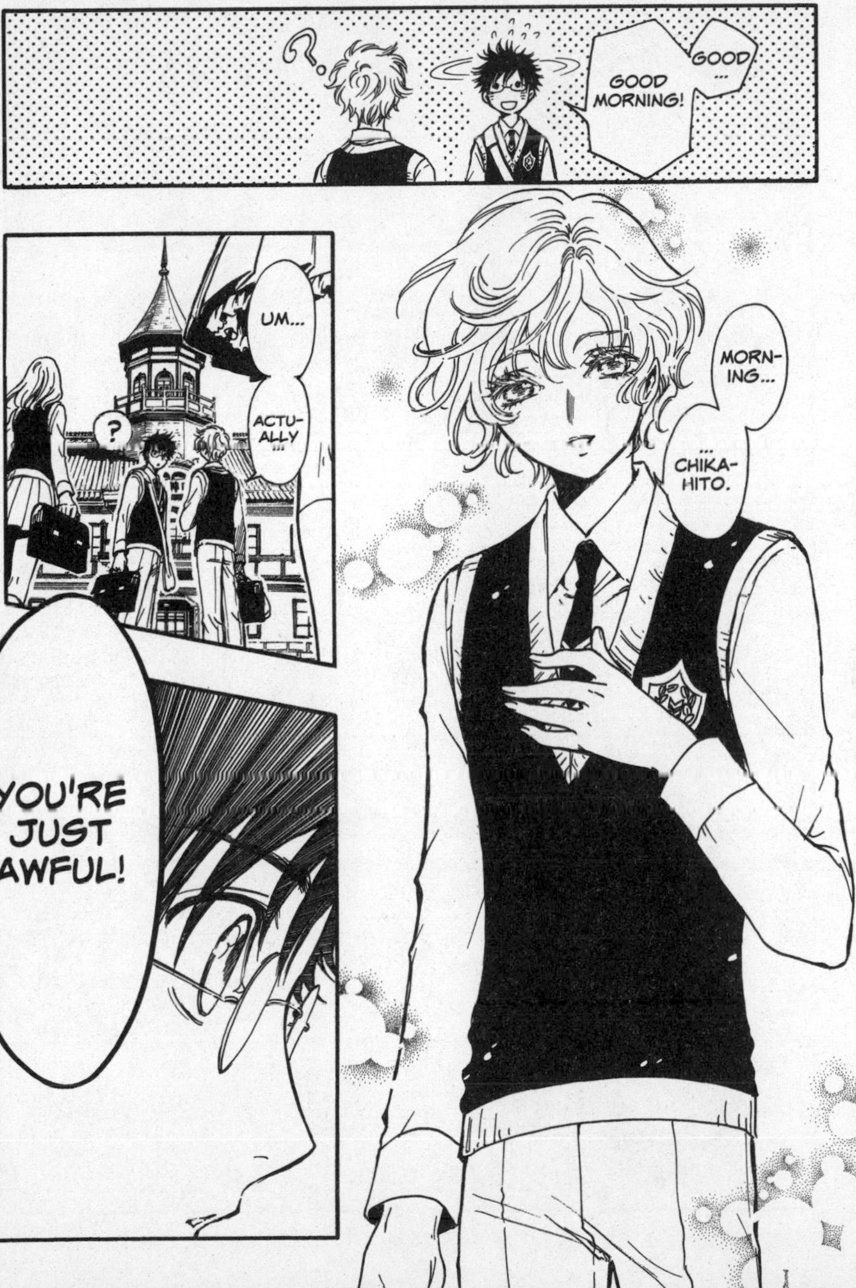
?
GOOD...
GOOD MORNING!
MORNING...
...CHIKAHITO.
UM...
ACTUALLY...
?
YOU'RE JUST AWFUL!

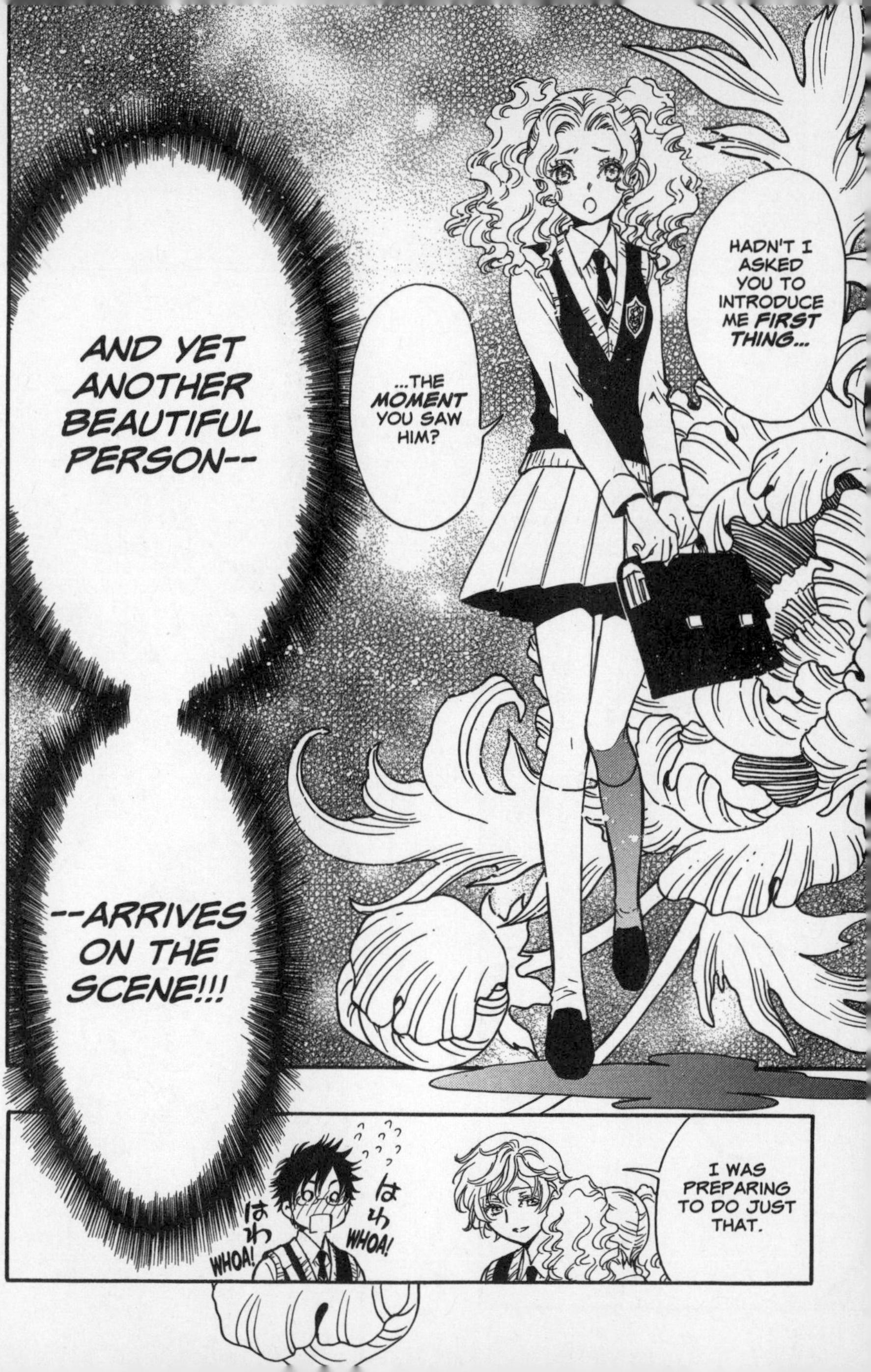
HADN'T I ASKED YOU TO INTRODUCE ME FIRST THING...
...THE MOMENT YOU SAW HIM?
AND YET ANOTHER BEAUTIFUL PERSON--
--ARRIVES ON THE SCENE!!!
I WAS PREPARING TO DO JUST THAT.
はわ
WHOA!
はわ
WHOA!

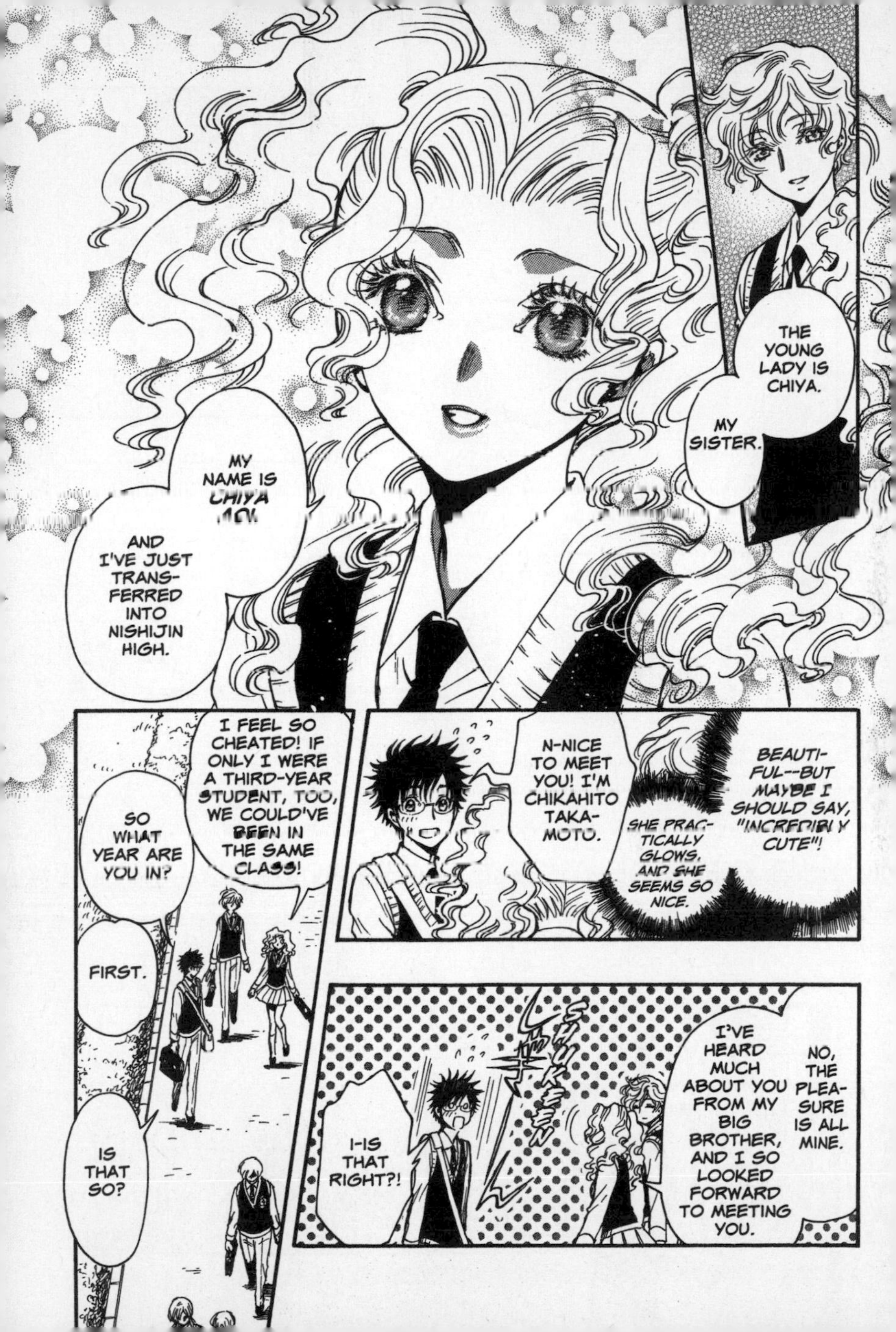
THE YOUNG LADY IS CHIYA.
MY SISTER.
MY NAME IS CHIYA AOI
AND I'VE JUST TRANSFERRED INTO NISHIJIN HIGH.
BEAUTIFUL--BUT MAYBE I SHOULD SAY, "INCREDIBLY CUTE"!
N-NICE TO MEET YOU! I'M CHIKAHITO TAKAMOTO.
SHE PRACTICALLY GLOWS, AND SHE SEEMS SO NICE.
NO, THE PLEASURE IS ALL MINE.
I'VE HEARD MUCH ABOUT YOU FROM MY BIG BROTHER, AND I SO LOOKED FORWARD TO MEETING YOU.
I-IS THAT RIGHT?!
I FEEL SO CHEATED! IF ONLY I WERE A THIRD-YEAR STUDENT, TOO, WE COULD'VE BEEN IN THE SAME CLASS!
SO WHAT YEAR ARE YOU IN?
FIRST.
IS THAT SO?

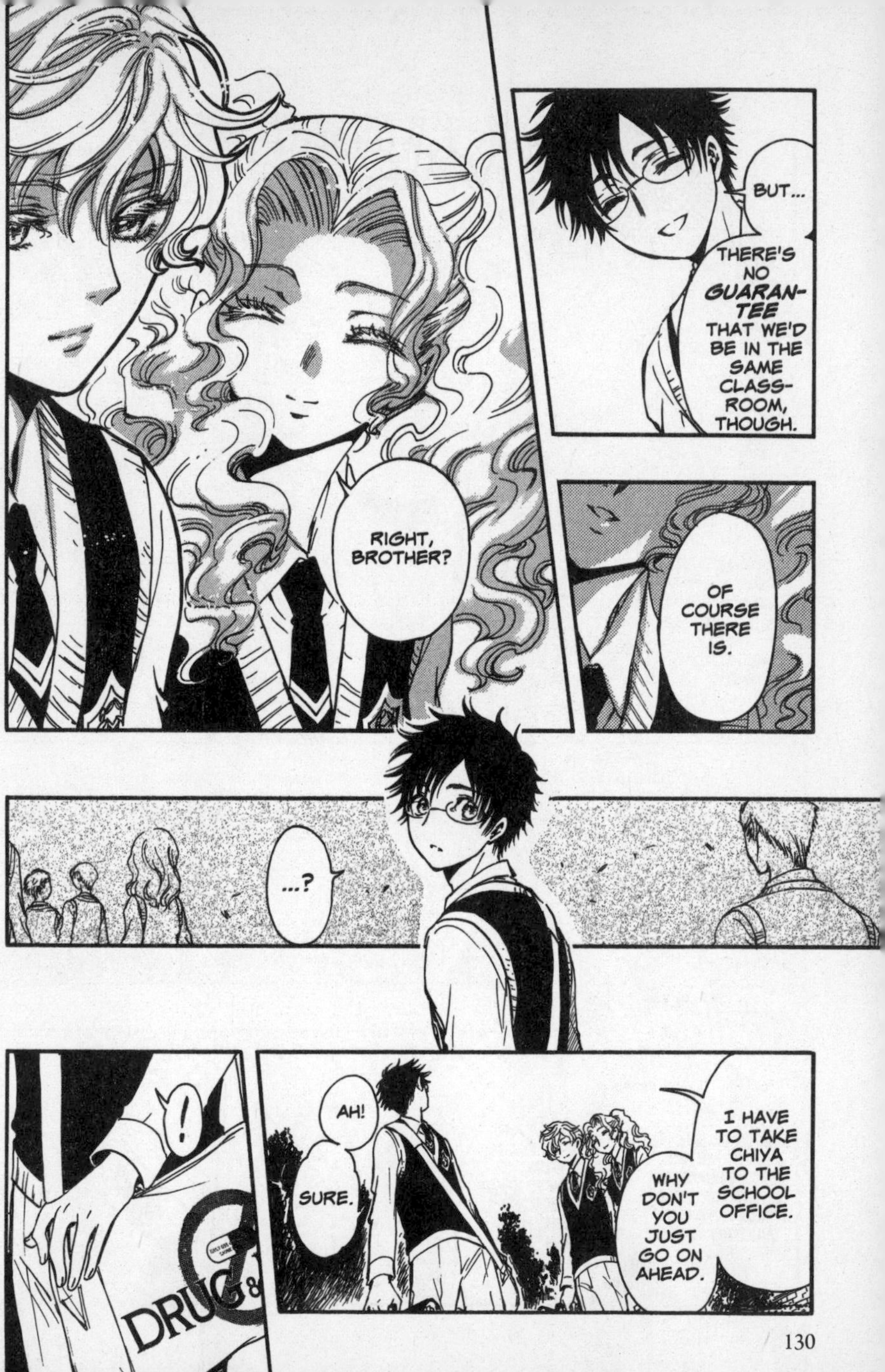
BUT...
THERE'S NO *GUARANTEE* THAT WE'D BE IN THE SAME CLASSROOM, THOUGH.
OF COURSE THERE IS.
RIGHT, BROTHER?
...?
I HAVE TO TAKE CHIYA TO THE SCHOOL OFFICE.
WHY DON'T YOU JUST GO ON AHEAD.
AH!
SURE.
!
DRUG 8

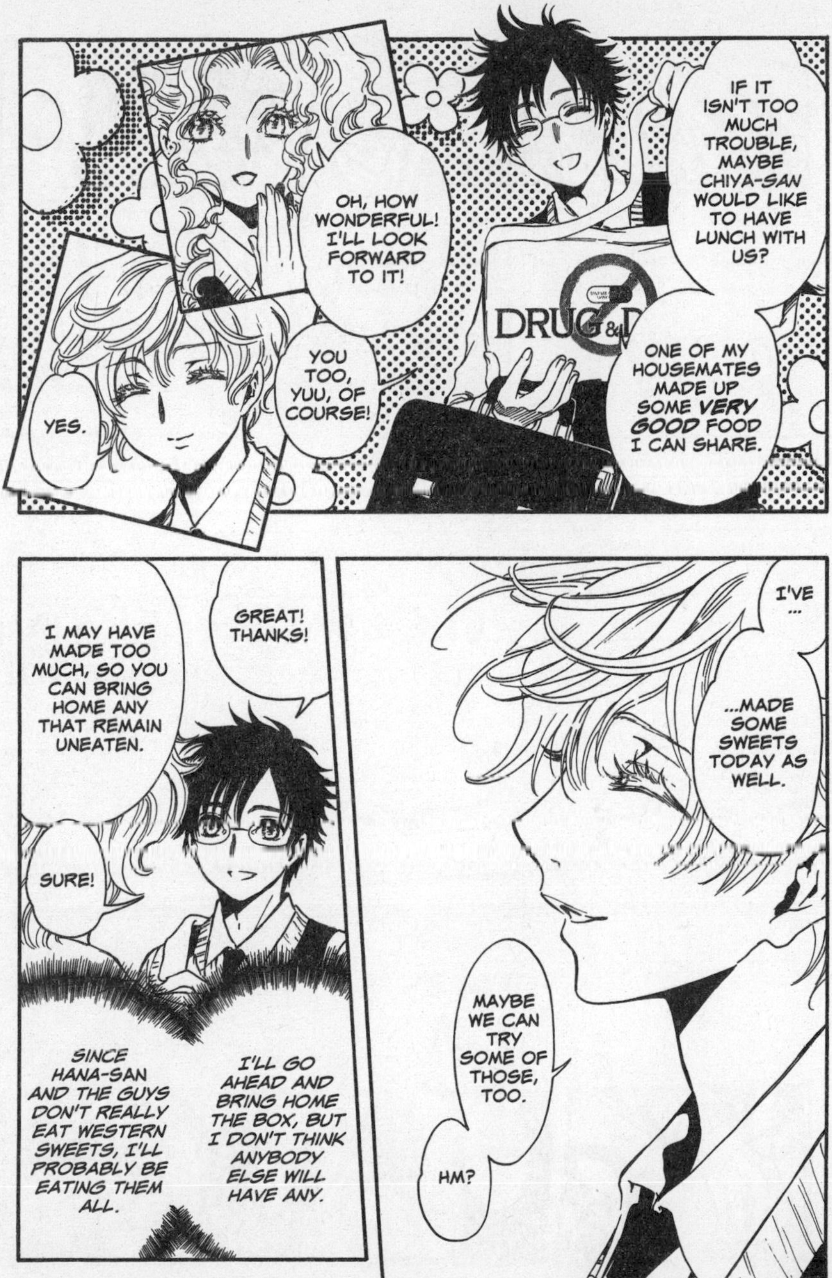

IF IT ISN'T TOO MUCH TROUBLE, MAYBE CHIYA-SAN WOULD LIKE TO HAVE LUNCH WITH US?
ONE OF MY HOUSEMATES MADE UP SOME *VERY GOOD* FOOD I CAN SHARE.
DRUG&D
OH, HOW WONDERFUL! I'LL LOOK FORWARD TO IT!
YOU TOO, YUU, OF COURSE!
YES.
I'VE ...
...MADE SOME SWEETS TODAY AS WELL.
MAYBE WE CAN TRY SOME OF THOSE, TOO.
HM?
GREAT! THANKS!
I MAY HAVE MADE TOO MUCH, SO YOU CAN BRING HOME ANY THAT REMAIN UNEATEN.
SURE!
I'LL GO AHEAD AND BRING HOME THE BOX, BUT I DON'T THINK ANYBODY ELSE WILL HAVE ANY.
SINCE HANA-SAN AND THE GUYS DON'T REALLY EAT WESTERN SWEETS, I'LL PROBABLY BE EATING THEM ALL.

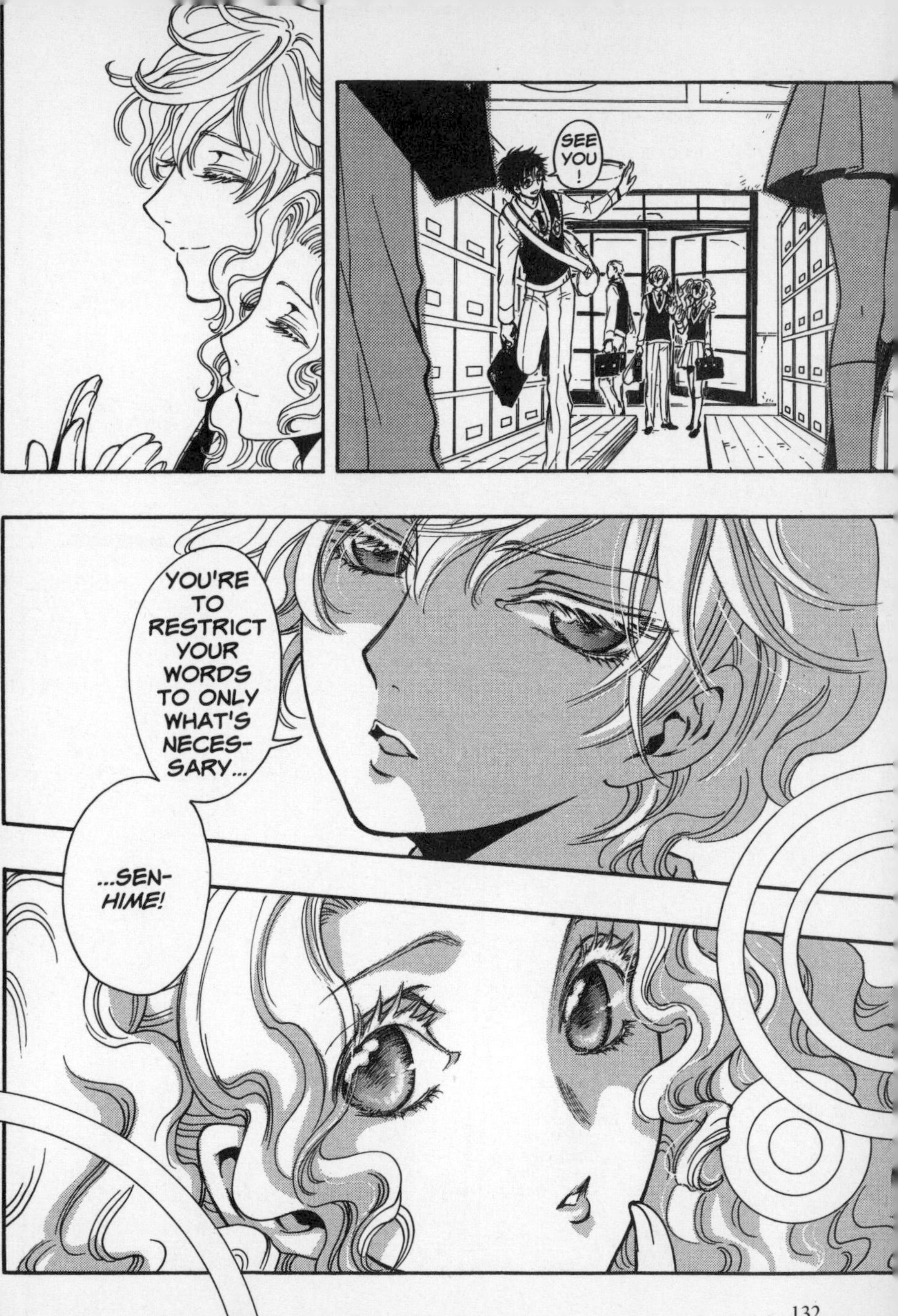
SEE YOU!
YOU'RE TO RESTRICT YOUR WORDS TO ONLY WHAT'S NECES-SARY...
...SEN-HIME!

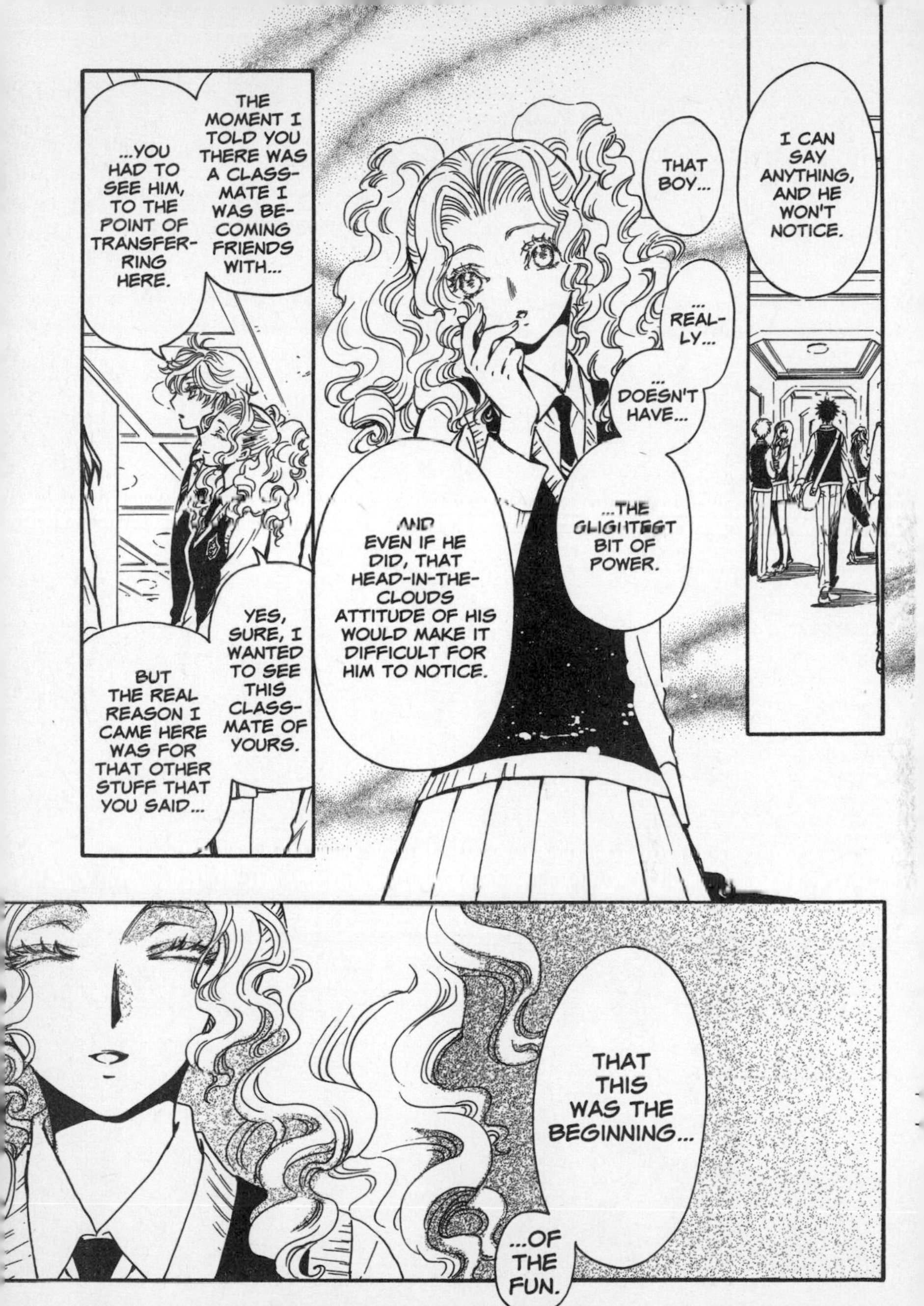
I CAN SAY ANYTHING, AND HE WON'T NOTICE.
THAT BOY...
...REALLY...
...DOESN'T HAVE...
...THE SLIGHTEST BIT OF POWER.
AND EVEN IF HE DID, THAT HEAD-IN-THE-CLOUDS ATTITUDE OF HIS WOULD MAKE IT DIFFICULT FOR HIM TO NOTICE.
THE MOMENT I TOLD YOU THERE WAS A CLASSMATE I WAS BECOMING FRIENDS WITH...
...YOU HAD TO SEE HIM, TO THE POINT OF TRANSFERRING HERE.
YES, SURE, I WANTED TO SEE THIS CLASSMATE OF YOURS.
BUT THE REAL REASON I CAME HERE WAS FOR THAT OTHER STUFF THAT YOU SAID...
THAT THIS WAS THE BEGINNING...
...OF THE FUN.

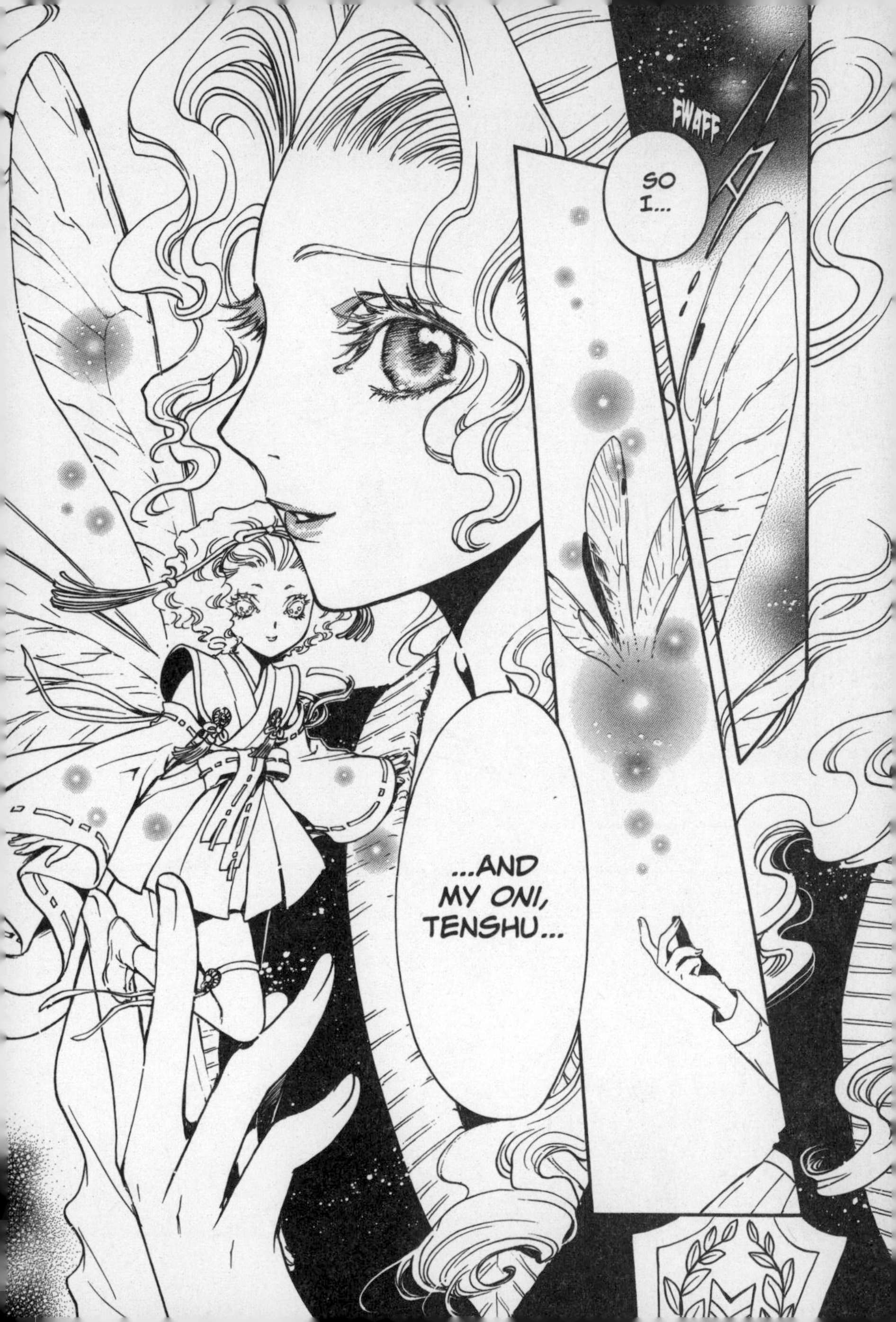
FWAFF
SO I...
...AND MY ONI, TENSHU...

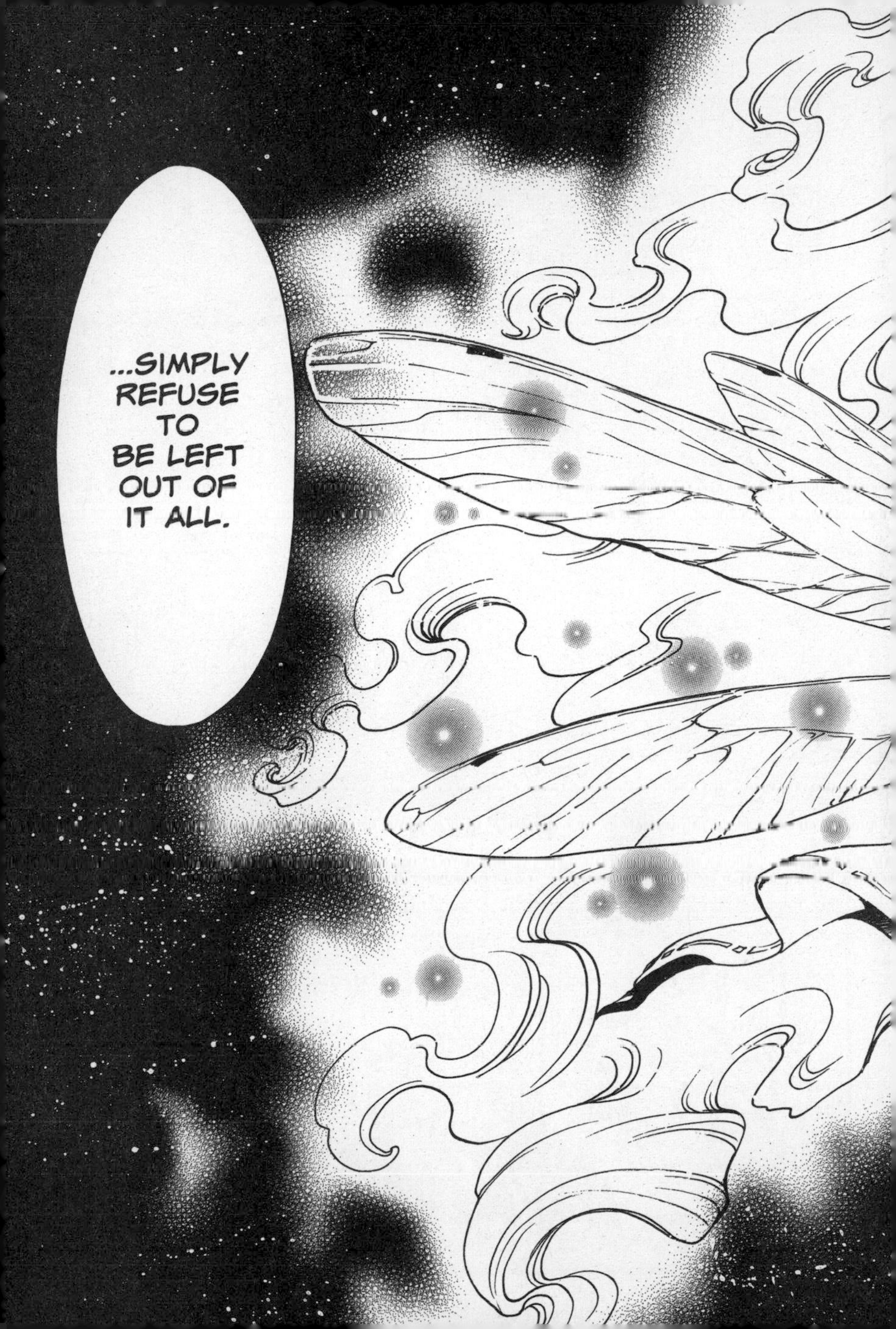
...SIMPLY REFUSE TO BE LEFT OUT OF IT ALL.

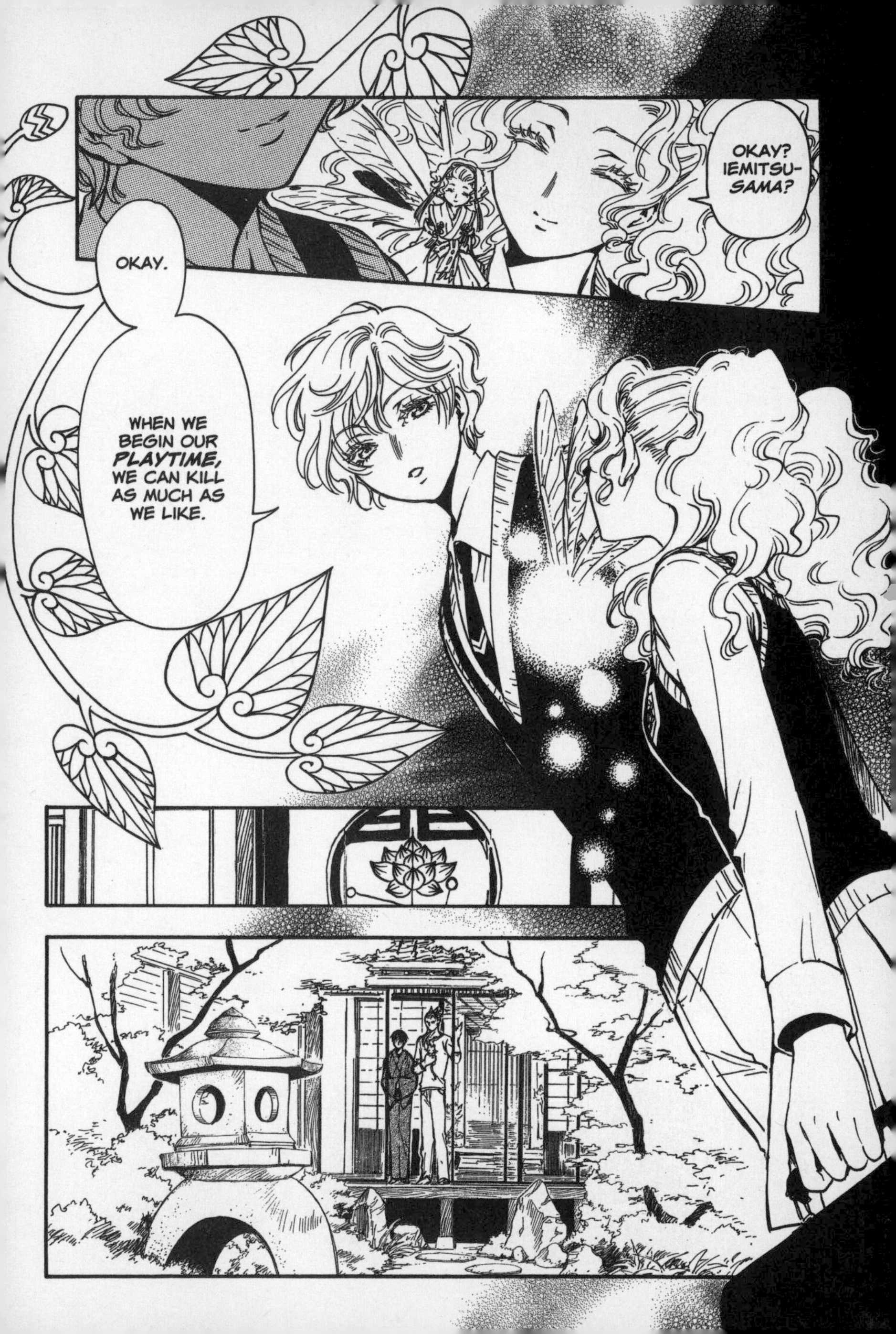
OKAY? IEMITSU-SAMA?
OKAY.
WHEN WE BEGIN OUR *PLAYTIME,* WE CAN KILL AS MUCH AS WE LIKE.

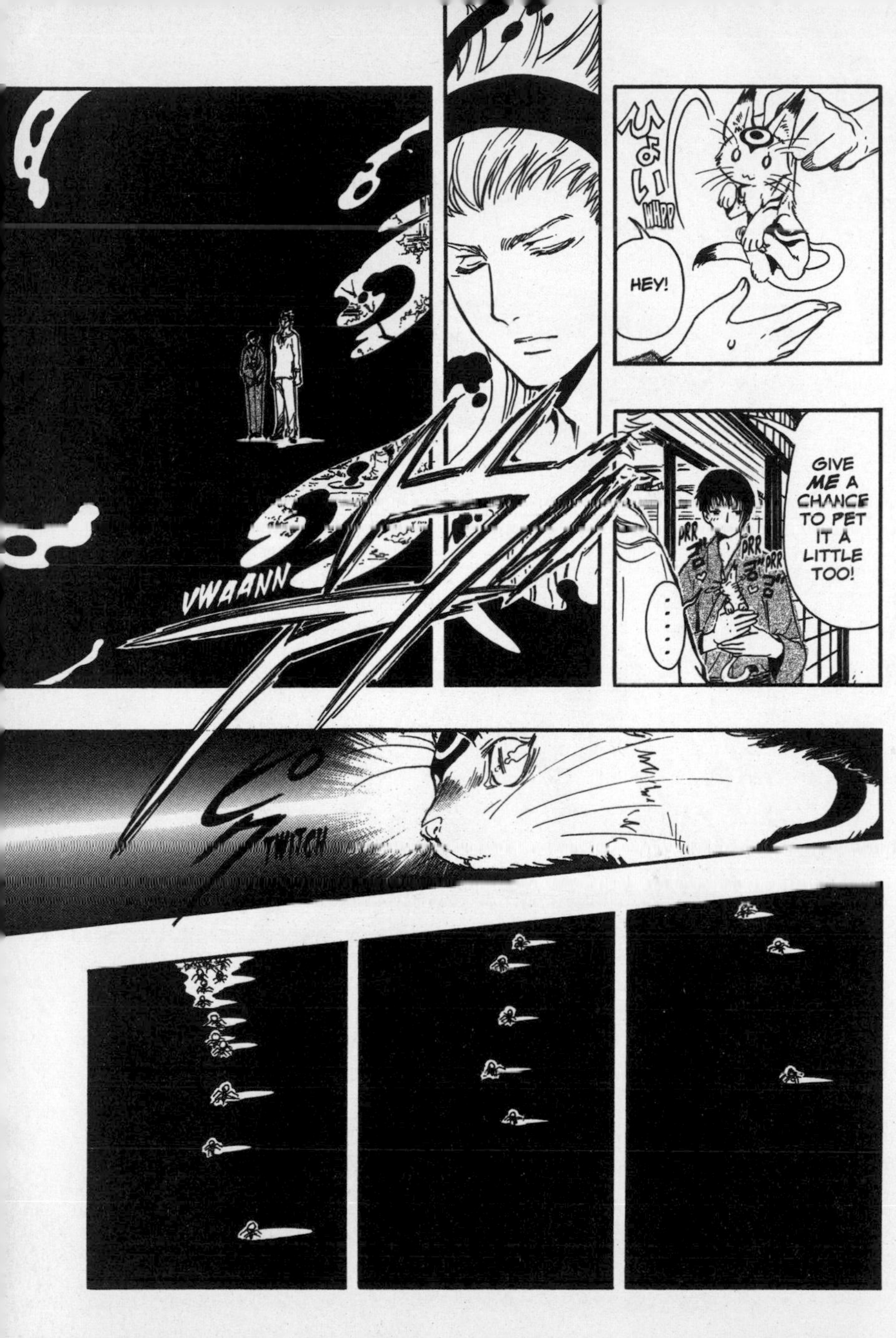
ひょい
WHPP
HEY!
GIVE ME A CHANCE TO PET IT A LITTLE TOO!
PRR PRR PRR
...
VWAANN
TWITCH

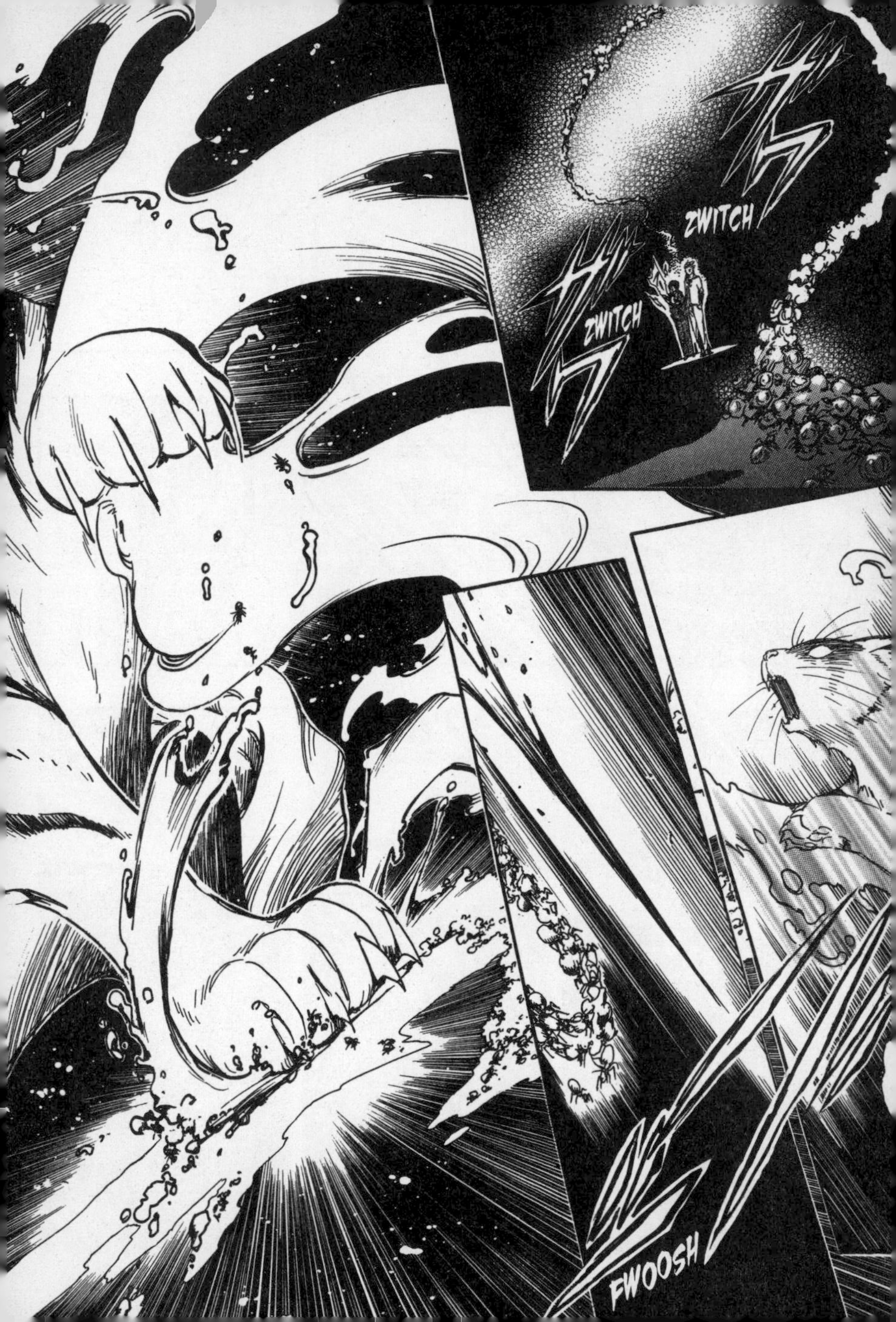
ZWITCH
ZWITCH
FWOOSH

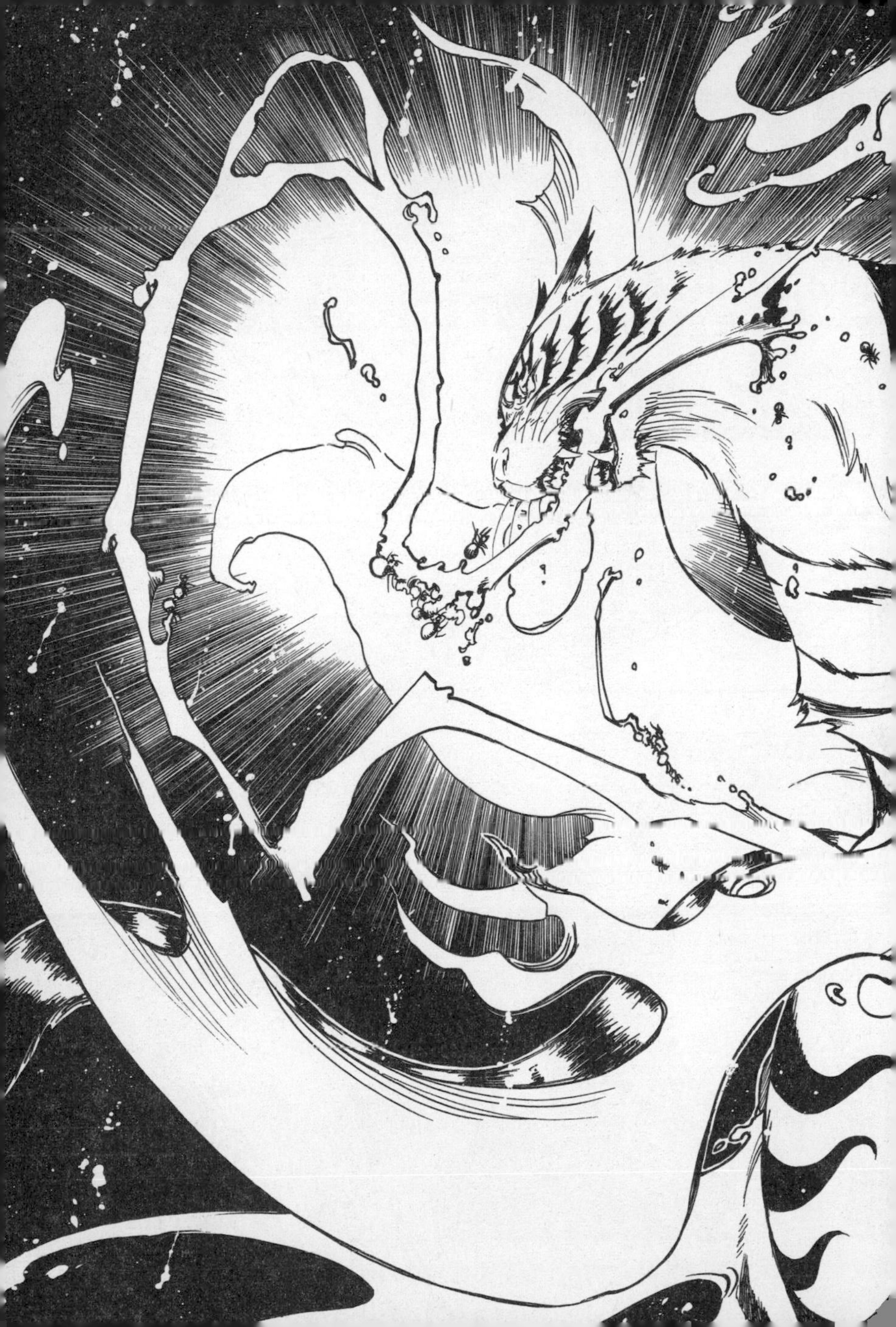

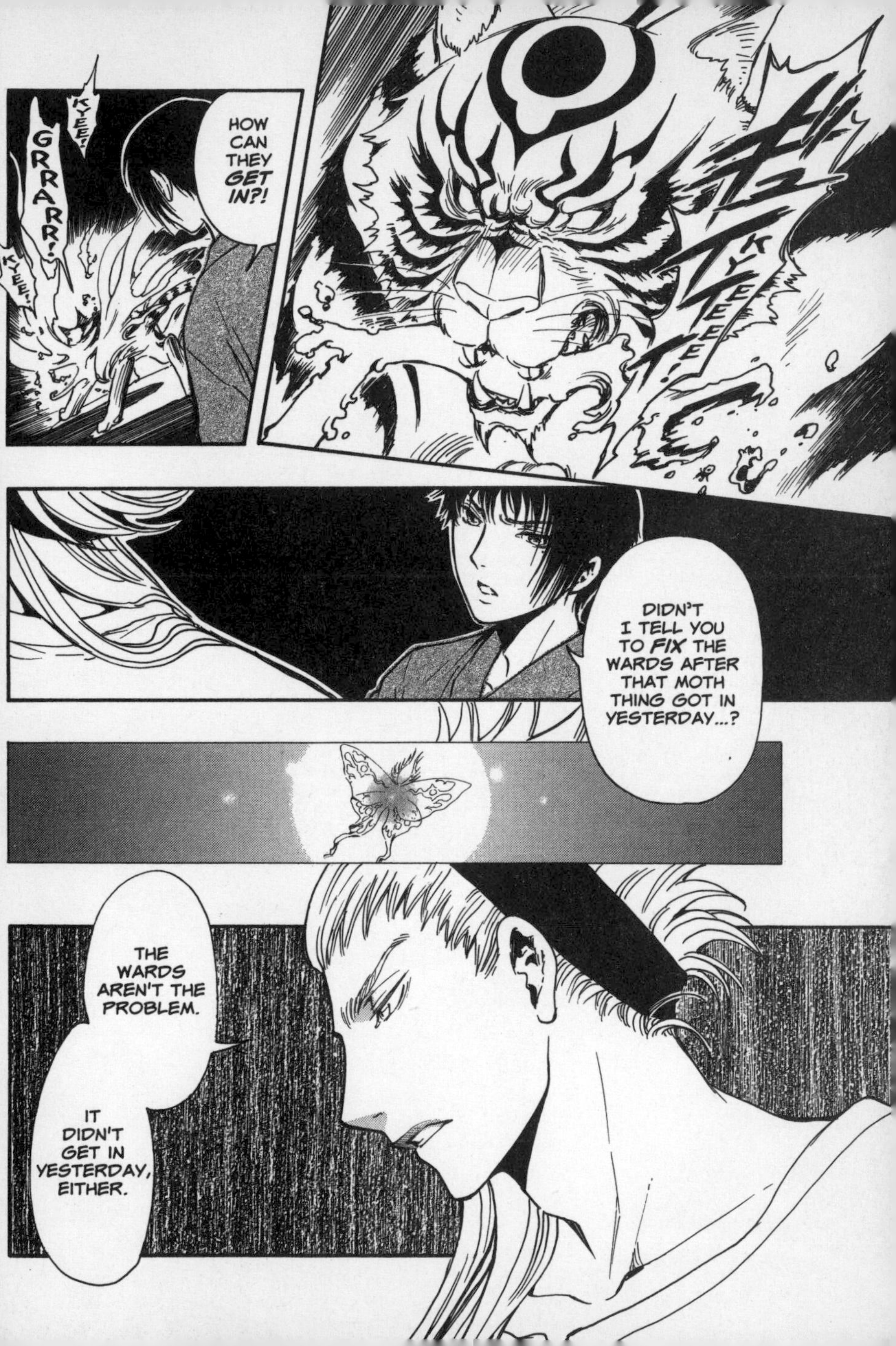
KYEEEE!!
HOW CAN THEY GET IN?!
KYEE!!
GRRARR!!
KYEE!!
DIDN'T I TELL YOU TO FIX THE WARDS AFTER THAT MOTH THING GOT IN YESTERDAY...?
THE WARDS AREN'T THE PROBLEM.
IT DIDN'T GET IN YESTERDAY, EITHER.

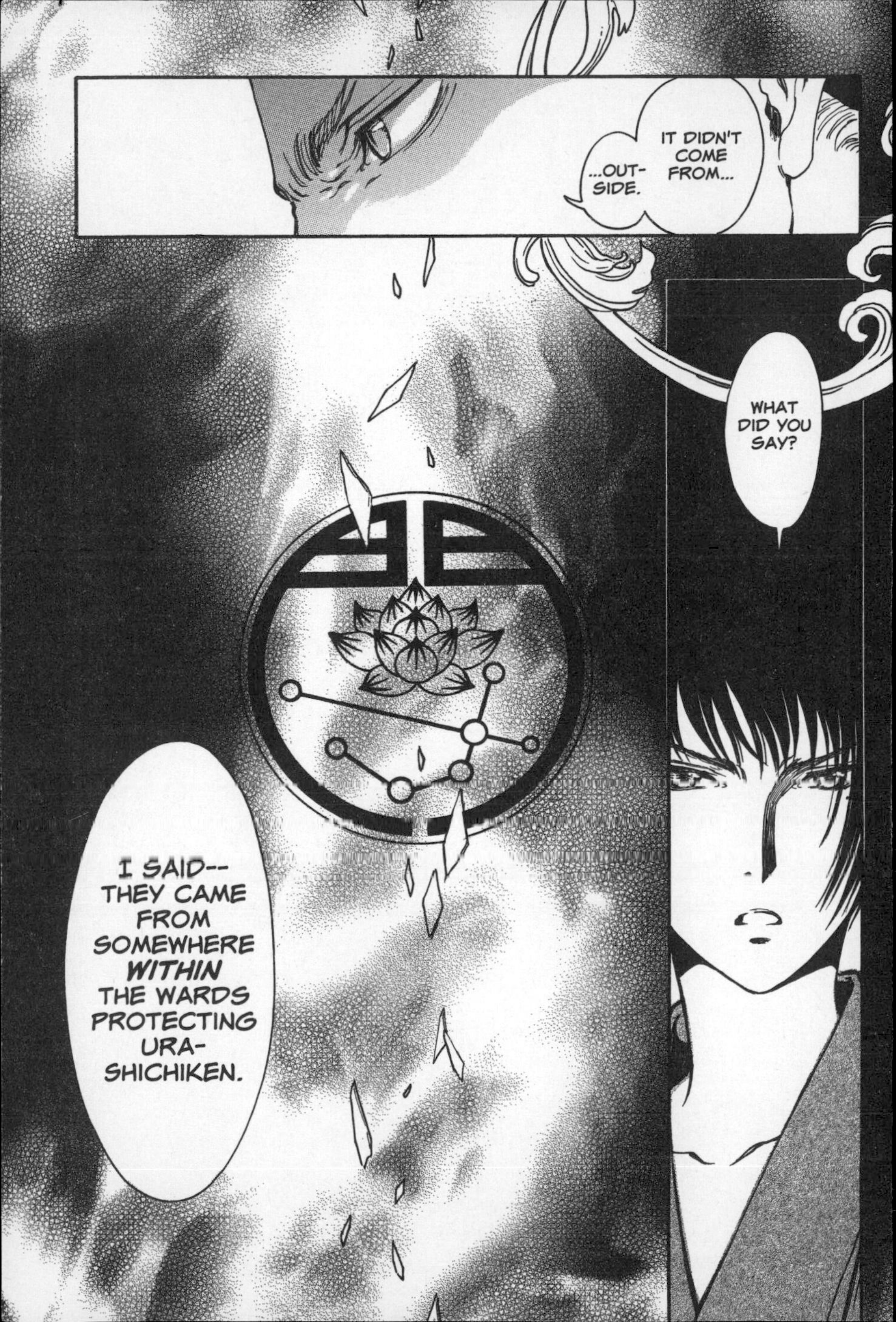
IT DIDN'T COME FROM...
...OUT-SIDE.
WHAT DID YOU SAY?
I SAID-- THEY CAME FROM SOMEWHERE *WITHIN* THE WARDS PROTECTING URA-SHICHIKEN.

GATE 7
ゲートセブン

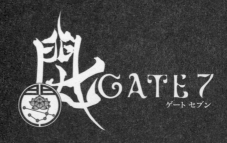

CHAPTER EIGHTEEN: THE ENCROACHING ENVELOPMENT

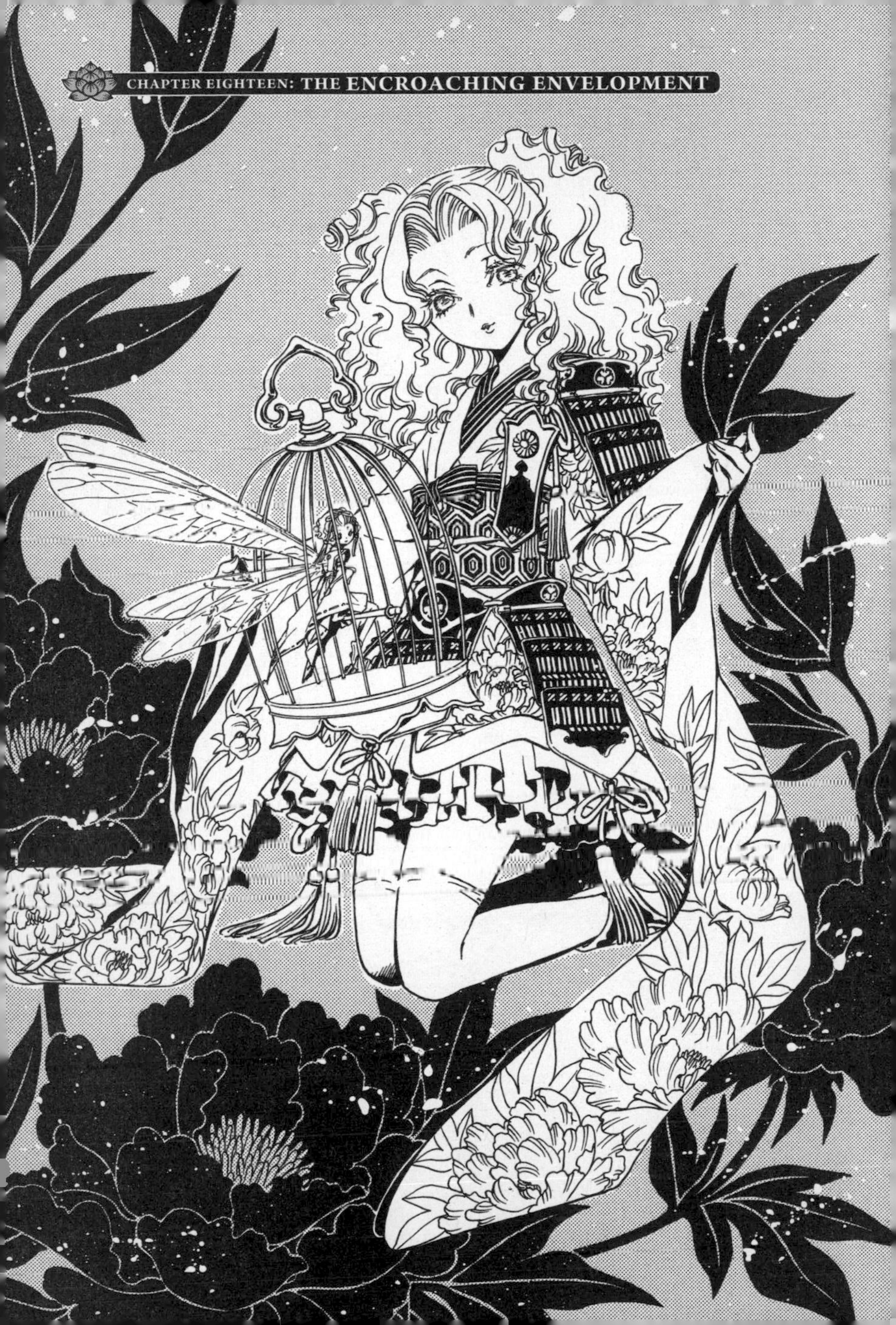

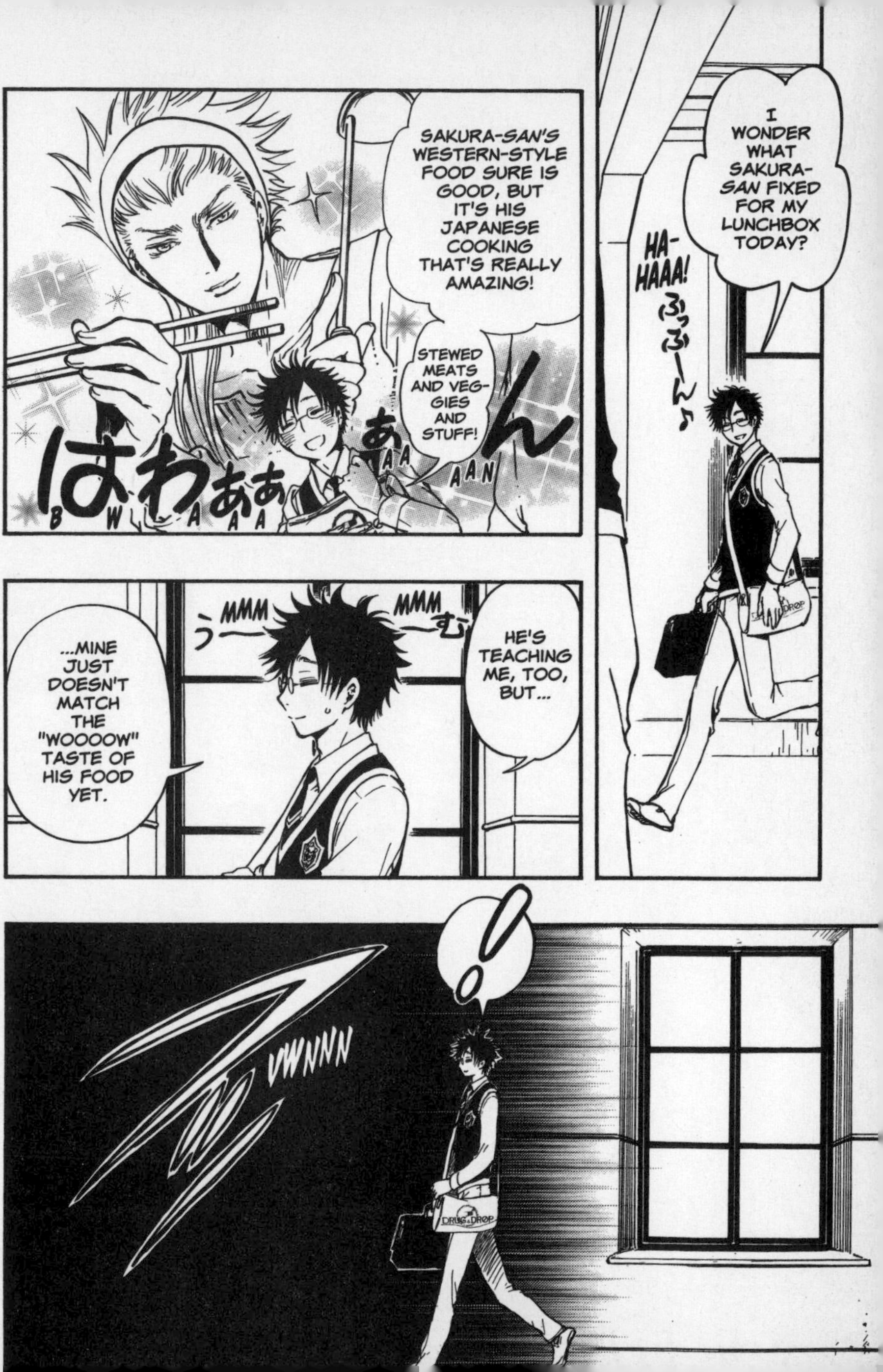
I WONDER WHAT SAKURA-SAN FIXED FOR MY LUNCHBOX TODAY?
HA-HAAA! ふっふ〜ん♪
SAKURA-SAN'S WESTERN-STYLE FOOD SURE IS GOOD, BUT IT'S HIS JAPANESE COOKING THAT'S REALLY AMAZING!
STEWED MEATS AND VEGGIES AND STUFF!
あ AAAAN ん
はわあああ BWAAAA
HE'S TEACHING ME, TOO, BUT...
...MINE JUST DOESN'T MATCH THE "WOOOOW" TASTE OF HIS FOOD YET.
う〜 MMM MMM〜む
!
VWNNN
DRUG&DROP

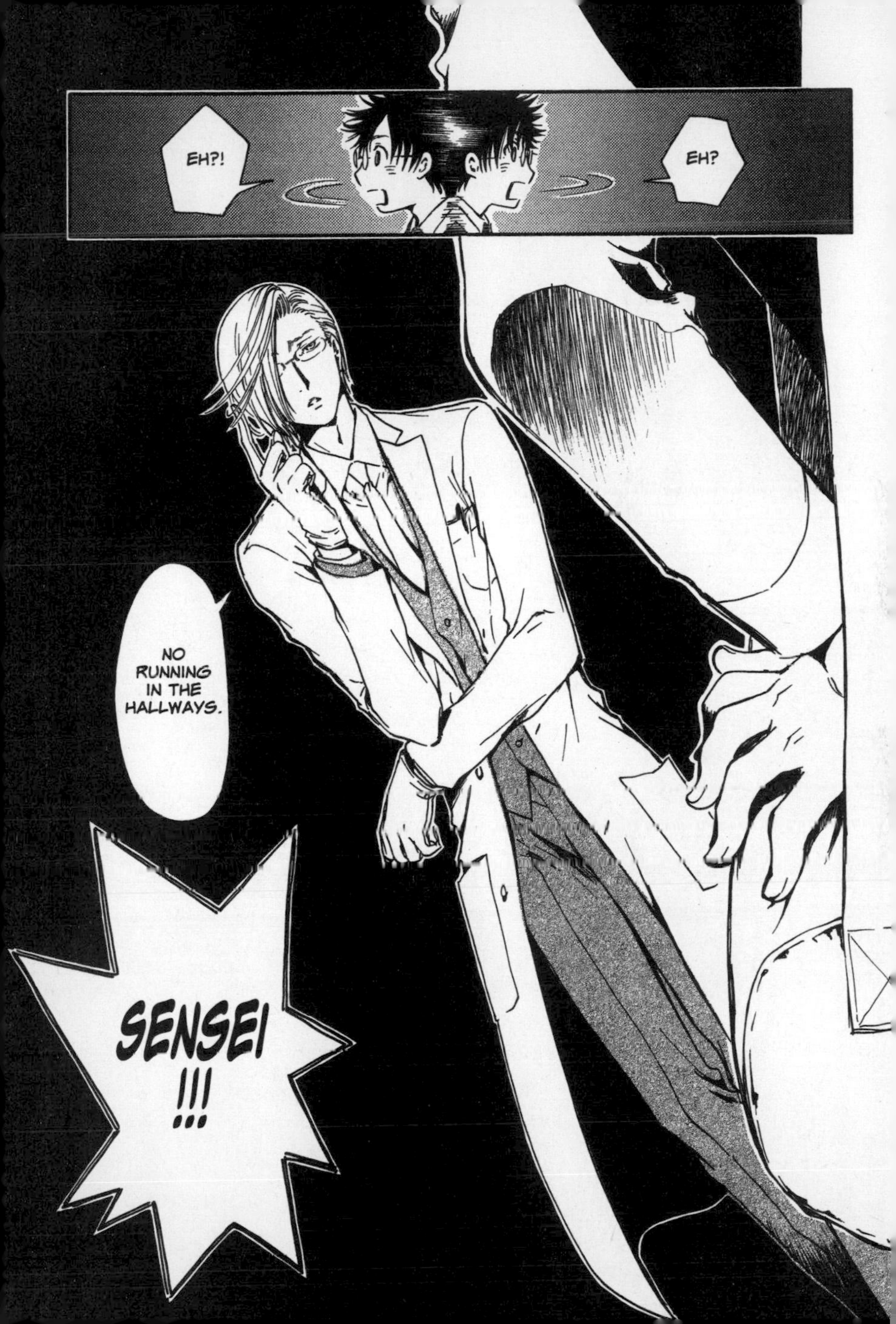
EH?
EH?!
NO RUNNING IN THE HALLWAYS.
SENSEI !!!

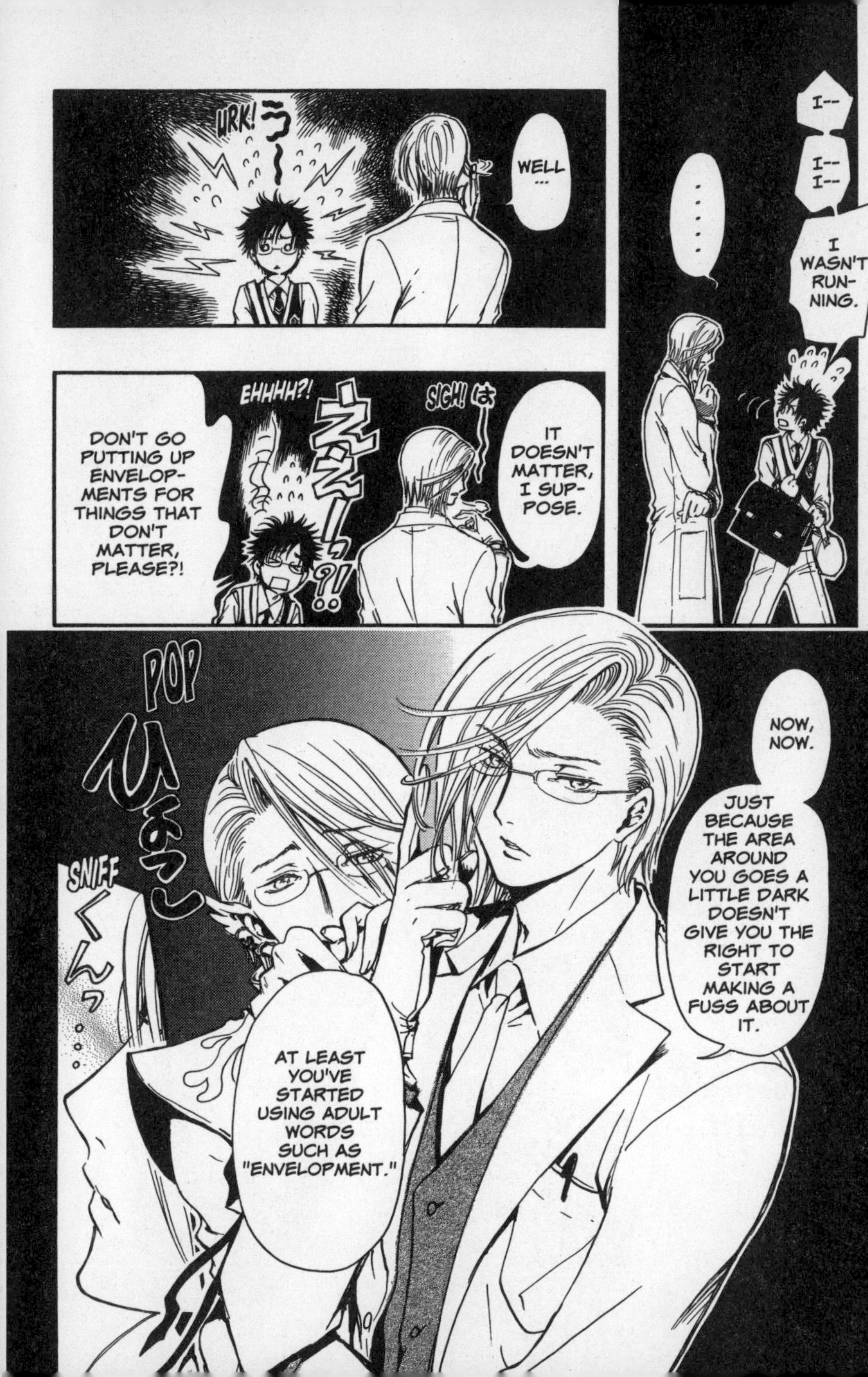
I--
I-- I--
I WASN'T RUN-NING.
.....
URK!
WELL ...
SIGH!
IT DOESN'T MATTER, I SUP-POSE.
EHHHH?!
DON'T GO PUTTING UP ENVELOP-MENTS FOR THINGS THAT DON'T MATTER, PLEASE?!
NOW, NOW.
JUST BECAUSE THE AREA AROUND YOU GOES A LITTLE DARK DOESN'T GIVE YOU THE RIGHT TO START MAKING A FUSS ABOUT IT.
POP
SNIFF
AT LEAST YOU'VE STARTED USING ADULT WORDS SUCH AS "ENVELOPMENT."

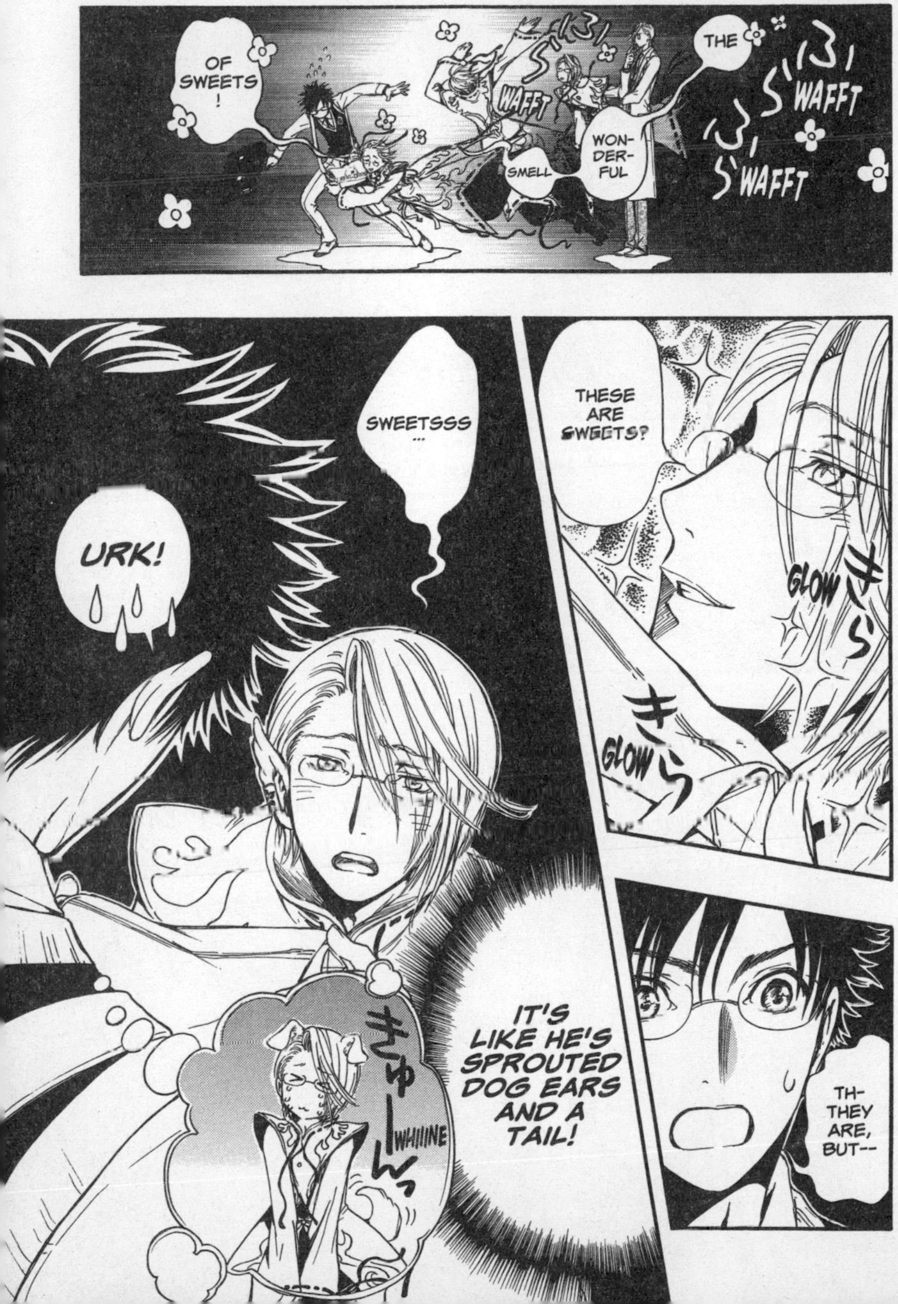
THE
WONDERFUL
SMELL
OF SWEETS!
ふわ WAFFT
ふわ WAFFT
WAFFT
THESE ARE SWEETS?
GLOW きら
GLOW きら
TH-THEY ARE, BUT--
SWEETSSS...
URK!
IT'S LIKE HE'S SPROUTED DOG EARS AND A TAIL!
WHIIINE

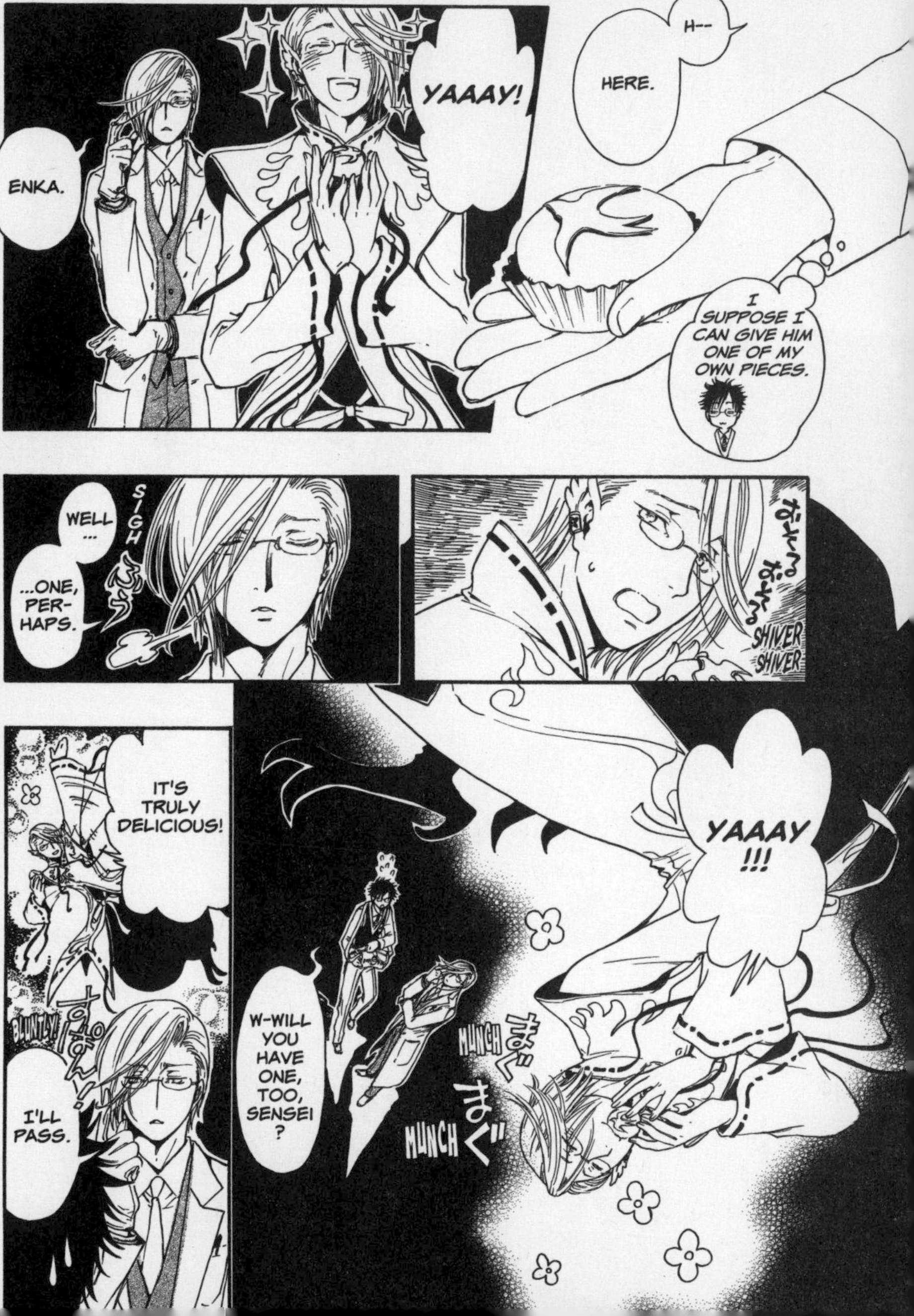
H--
HERE.
I SUPPOSE I CAN GIVE HIM ONE OF MY OWN PIECES.
YAAAY!
ENKA.
SHIVER SHIVER
SIGH
WELL ...
...ONE, PER-HAPS.
YAAAY !!!
MUNCH まぐ
MUNCH まぐ
W-WILL YOU HAVE ONE, TOO, SENSEI ?
IT'S TRULY DELICIOUS!
BLUNTLY!
I'LL PASS.

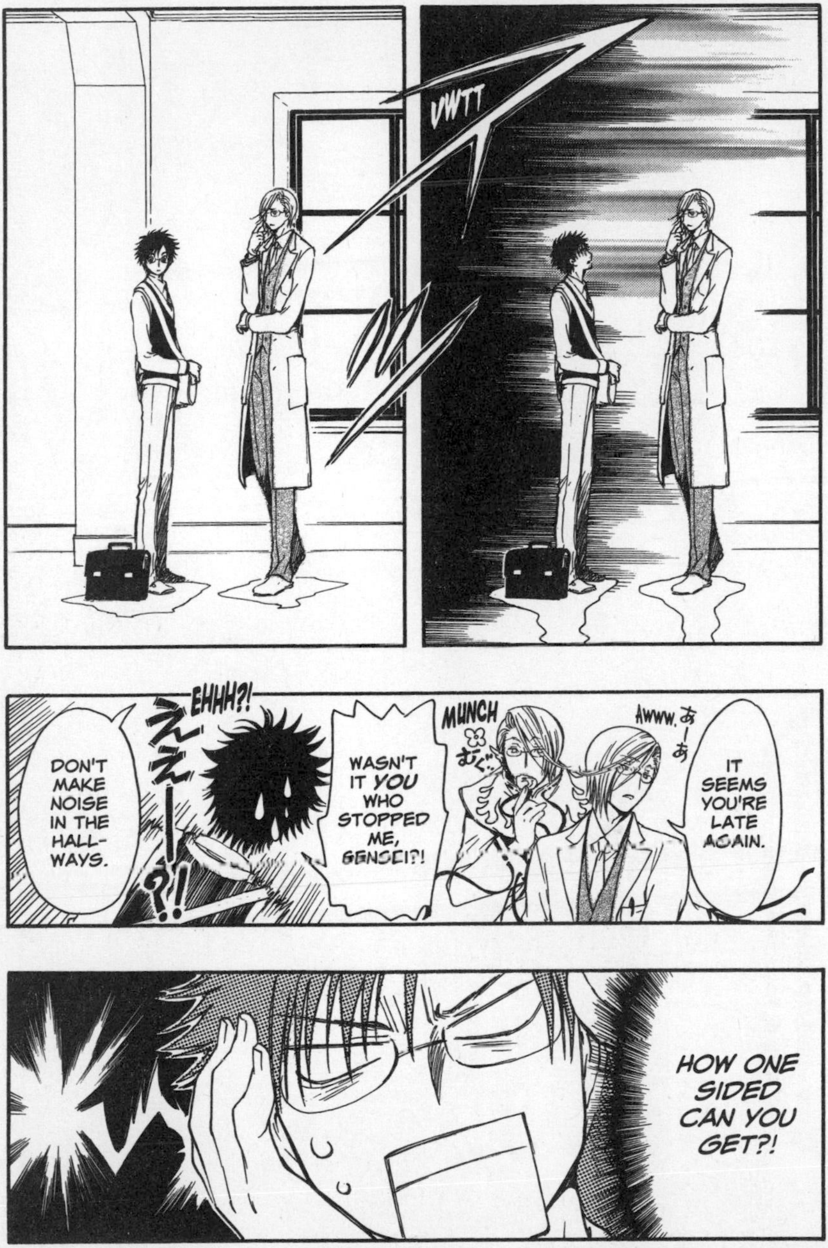
VWTT
AWWW. あーあ
IT SEEMS YOU'RE LATE AGAIN.
MUNCH
むぐ
WASN'T IT YOU WHO STOPPED ME, SENSEI?!
EHHH?!
DON'T MAKE NOISE IN THE HALL-WAYS.
HOW ONE SIDED CAN YOU GET?!

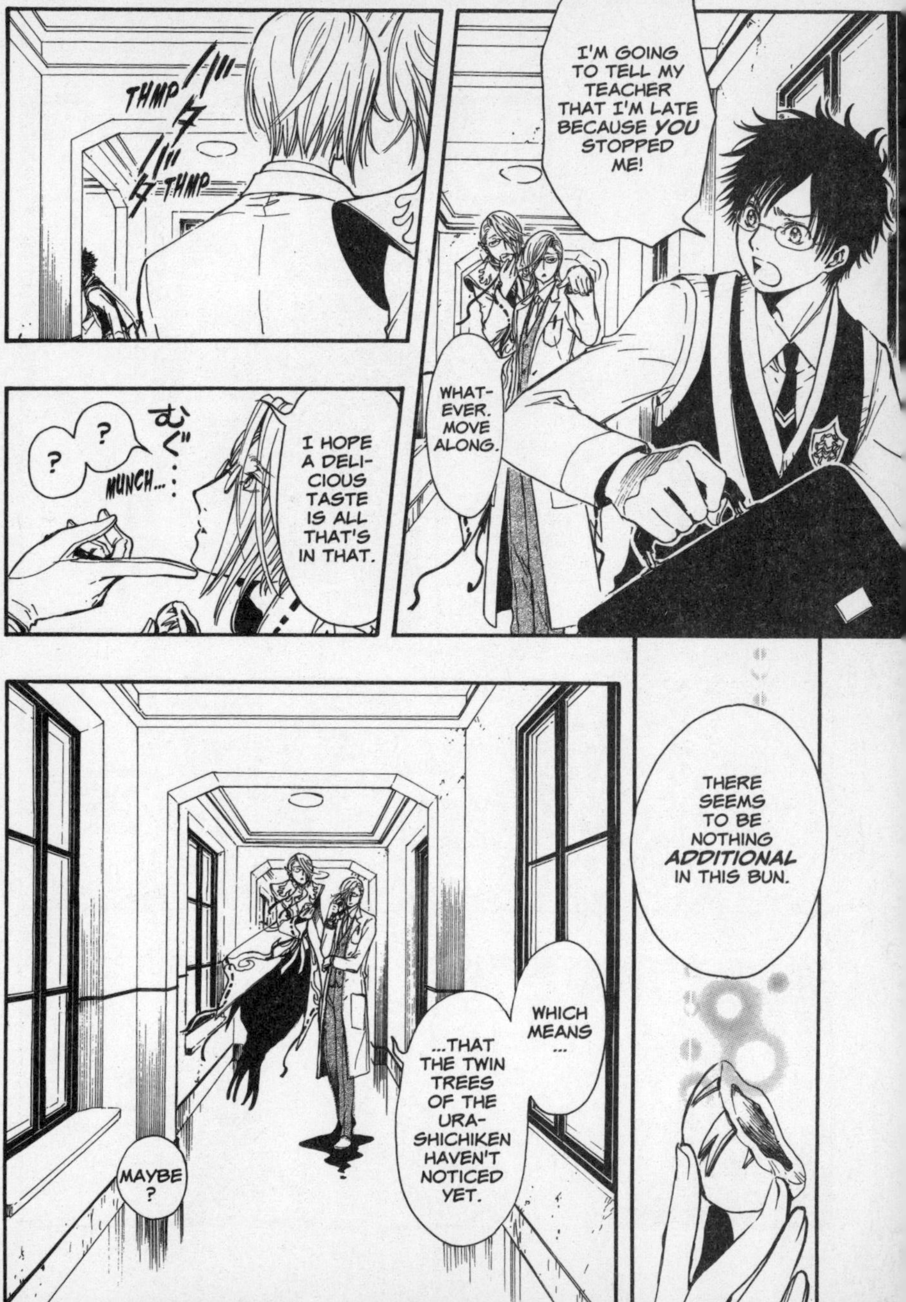
I'M GOING TO TELL MY TEACHER THAT I'M LATE BECAUSE *YOU* STOPPED ME!
WHAT-EVER. MOVE ALONG.
THMP
THMP
I HOPE A DELICIOUS TASTE IS ALL THAT'S IN THAT.
むぐ
MUNCH...
? ?
THERE SEEMS TO BE NOTHING *ADDITIONAL* IN THIS BUN.
WHICH MEANS ...
...THAT THE TWIN TREES OF THE URA-SHICHIKEN HAVEN'T NOTICED YET.
MAYBE?

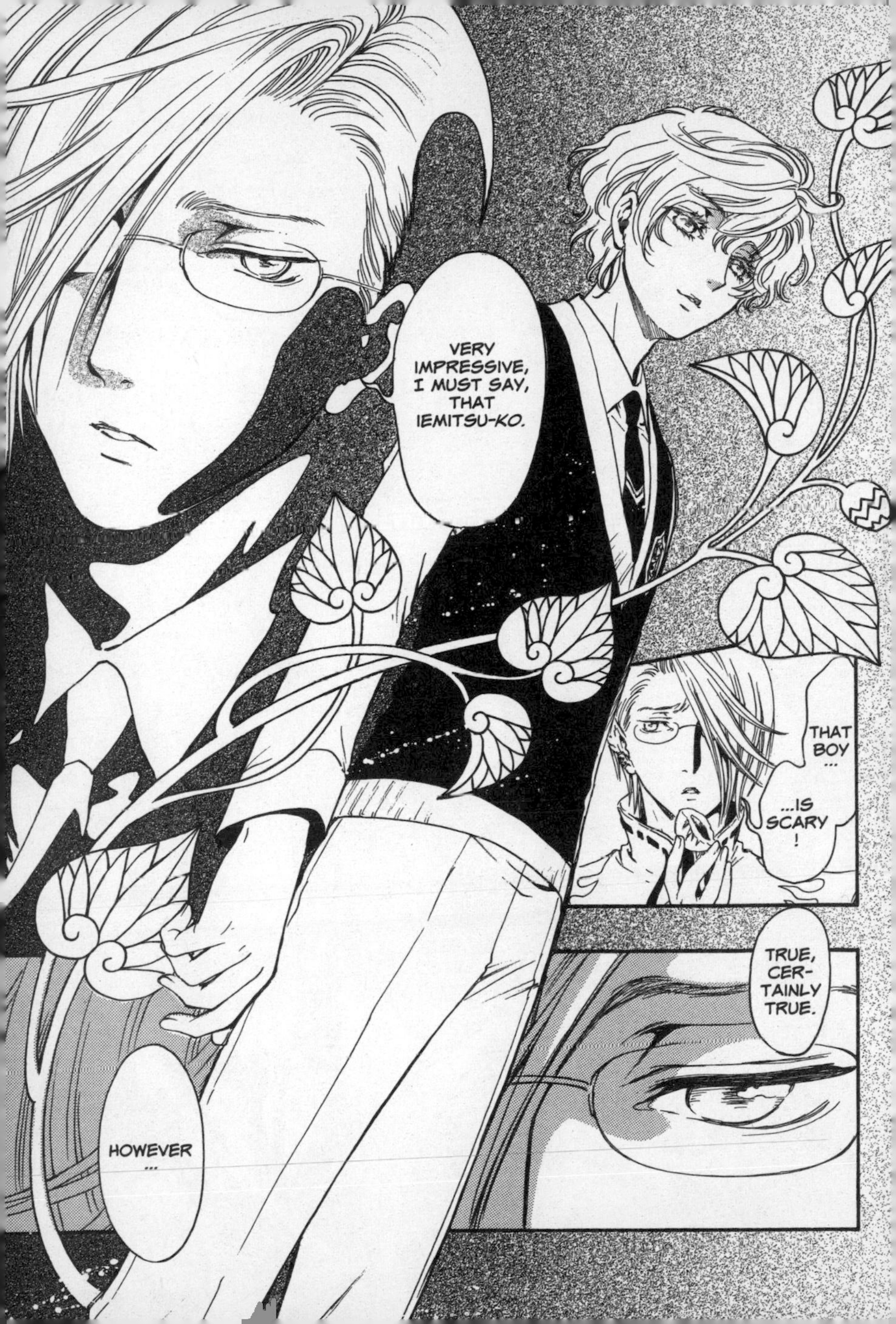
VERY IMPRESSIVE, I MUST SAY, THAT IEMITSU-KO.
THAT BOY ...
...IS SCARY !
TRUE, CER-TAINLY TRUE.
HOWEVER ...

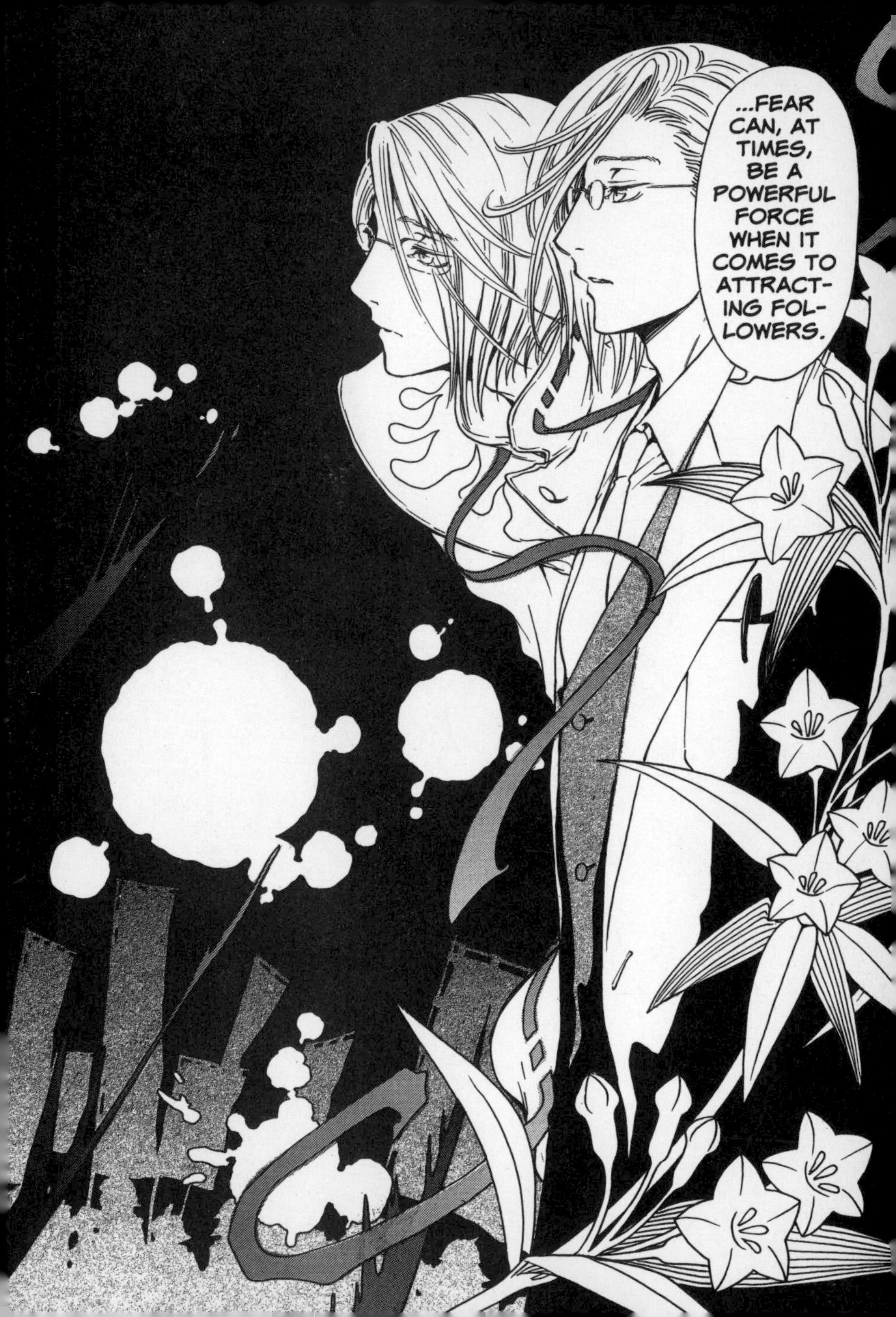
...FEAR CAN, AT TIMES, BE A POWERFUL FORCE WHEN IT COMES TO ATTRACTING FOLLOWERS.

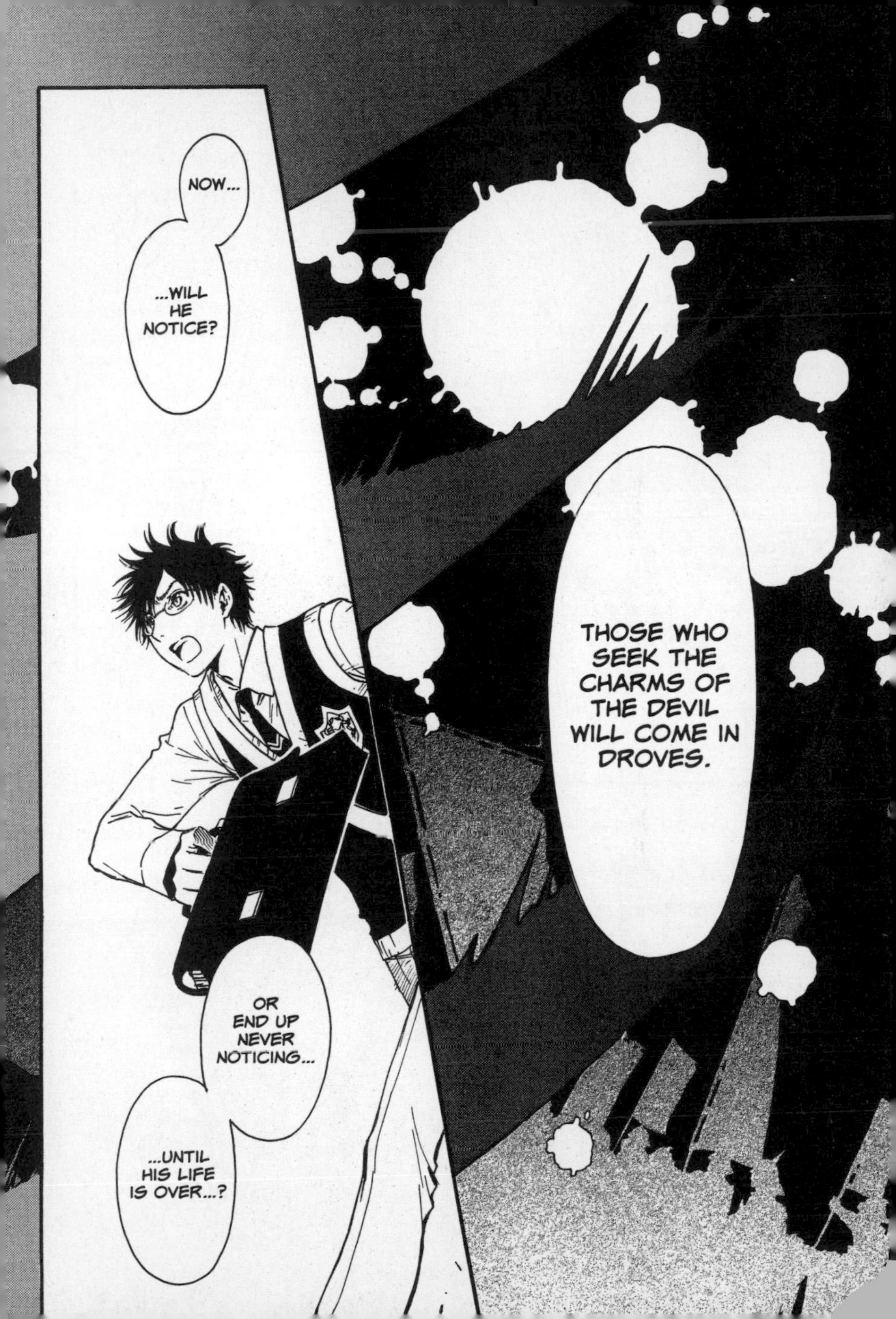
THOSE WHO SEEK THE CHARMS OF THE DEVIL WILL COME IN DROVES.
NOW...
...WILL HE NOTICE?
OR END UP NEVER NOTICING...
...UNTIL HIS LIFE IS OVER...?

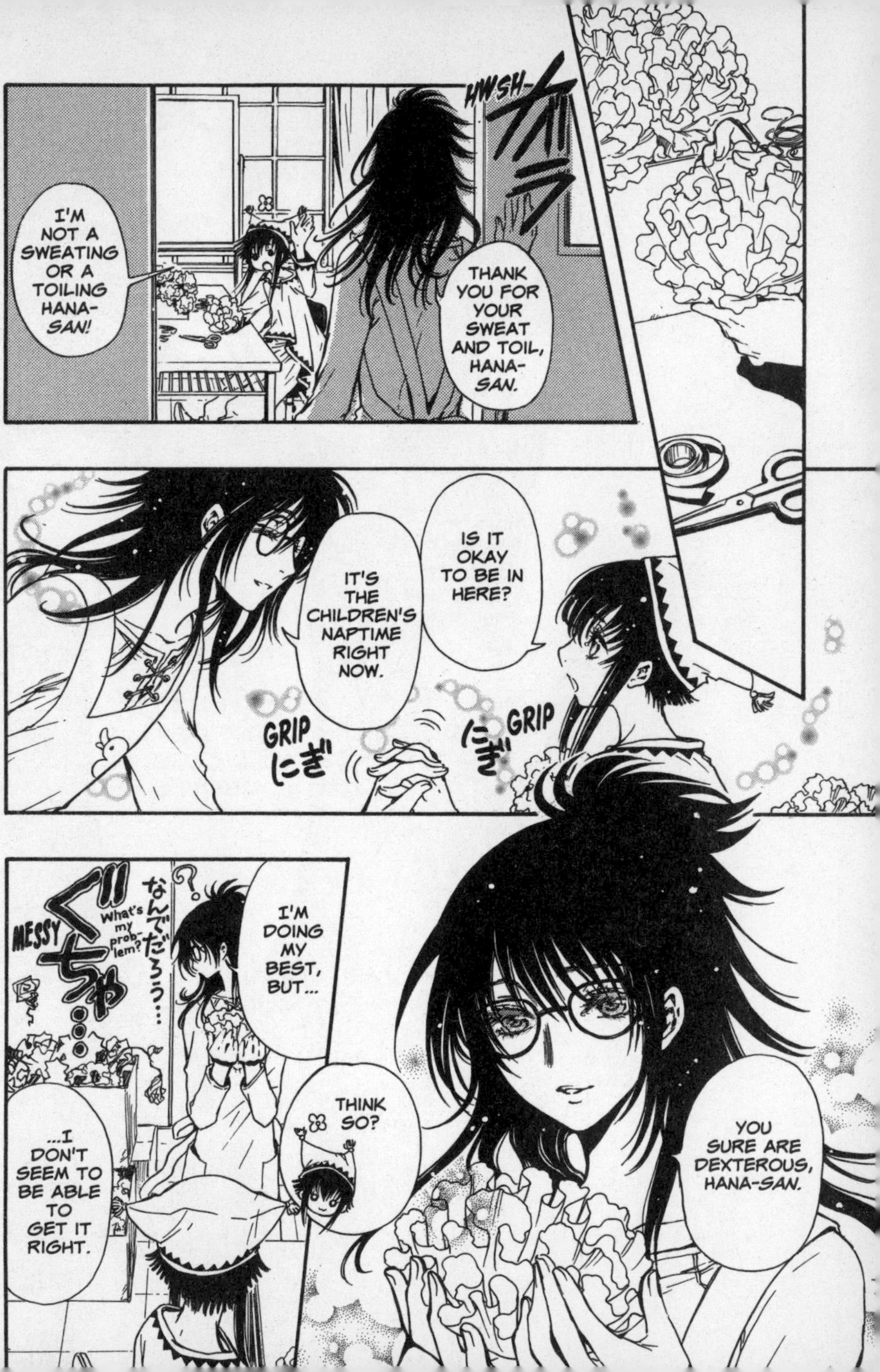
HWSH-
THANK YOU FOR YOUR SWEAT AND TOIL, HANA-SAN.
I'M NOT A SWEATING OR A TOILING HANA-SAN!
IS IT OKAY TO BE IN HERE?
IT'S THE CHILDREN'S NAPTIME RIGHT NOW.
GRIP にぎ
GRIP にぎ
YOU SURE ARE DEXTEROUS, HANA-SAN.
THINK SO?
I'M DOING MY BEST, BUT...
なんでだろう…
What's my prob-lem?
MESSY ぐちゃ
...I DON'T SEEM TO BE ABLE TO GET IT RIGHT.

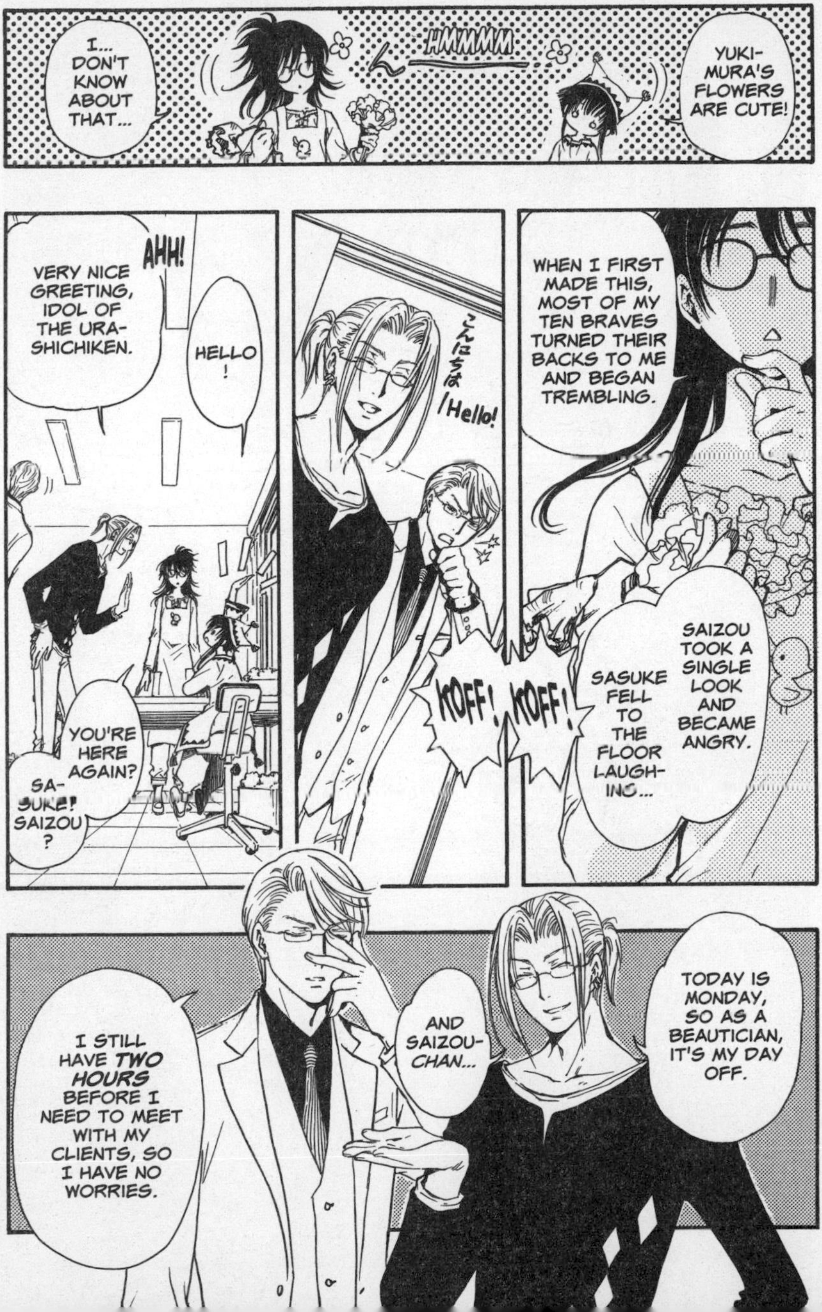
YUKI-MURA'S FLOWERS ARE CUTE!
HMMMM
I... DON'T KNOW ABOUT THAT...
WHEN I FIRST MADE THIS, MOST OF MY TEN BRAVES TURNED THEIR BACKS TO ME AND BEGAN TREMBLING.
SAIZOU TOOK A SINGLE LOOK AND BECAME ANGRY.
SASUKE FELL TO THE FLOOR LAUGHING...
KOFF! KOFF!
こんにちは/Hello!
HELLO!
AHH!
VERY NICE GREETING, IDOL OF THE URA-SHICHIKEN.
YOU'RE HERE AGAIN?
SA-SUKE! SAIZOU?
TODAY IS MONDAY, SO AS A BEAUTICIAN, IT'S MY DAY OFF.
AND SAIZOU-CHAN...
I STILL HAVE TWO HOURS BEFORE I NEED TO MEET WITH MY CLIENTS, SO I HAVE NO WORRIES.

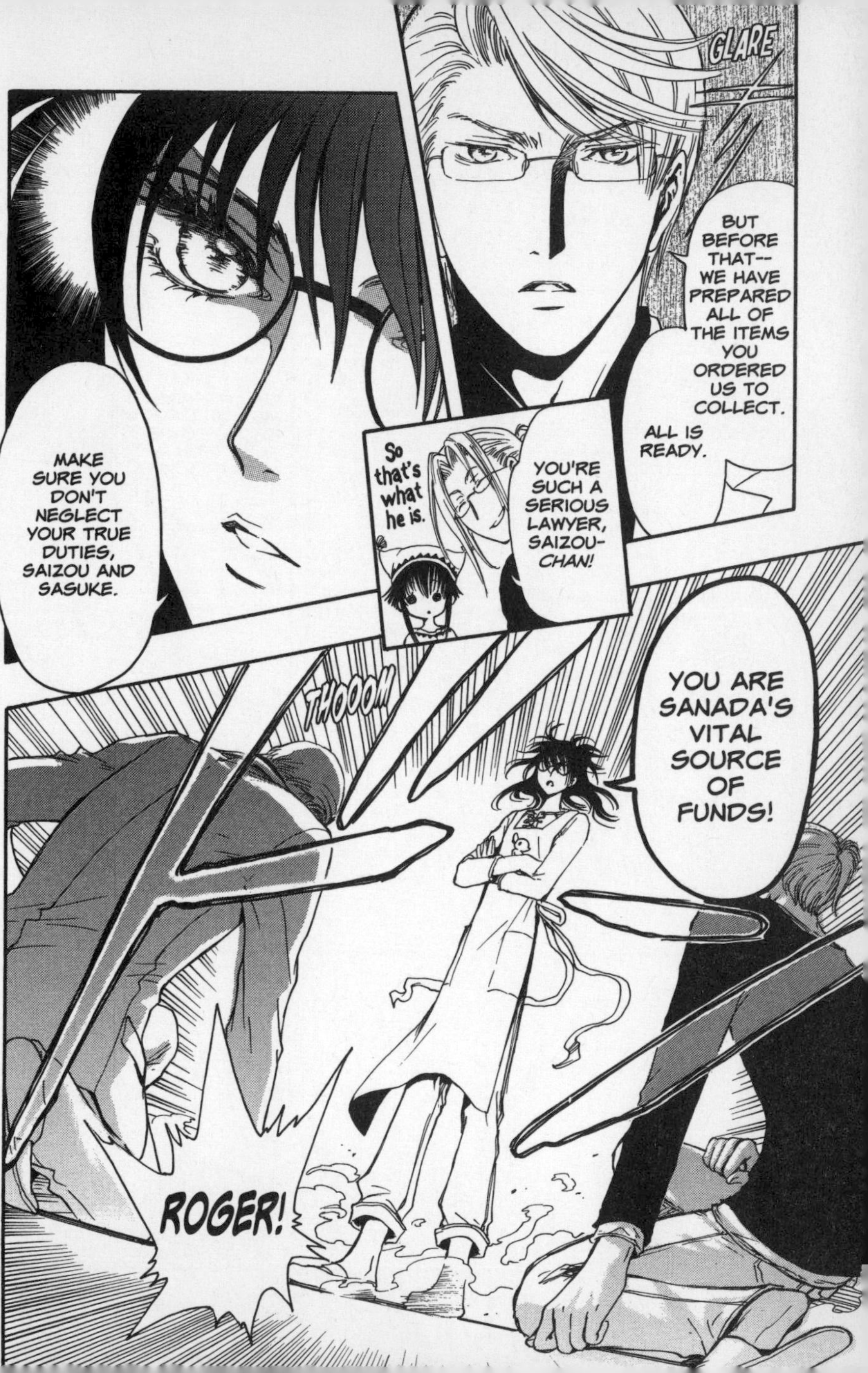
GLARE
BUT BEFORE THAT-- WE HAVE PREPARED ALL OF THE ITEMS YOU ORDERED US TO COLLECT.
ALL IS READY.
YOU'RE SUCH A SERIOUS LAWYER, SAIZOU-CHAN!
So that's what he is.
MAKE SURE YOU DON'T NEGLECT YOUR TRUE DUTIES, SAIZOU AND SASUKE.
YOU ARE SANADA'S VITAL SOURCE OF FUNDS!
THOOOM
ROGER!

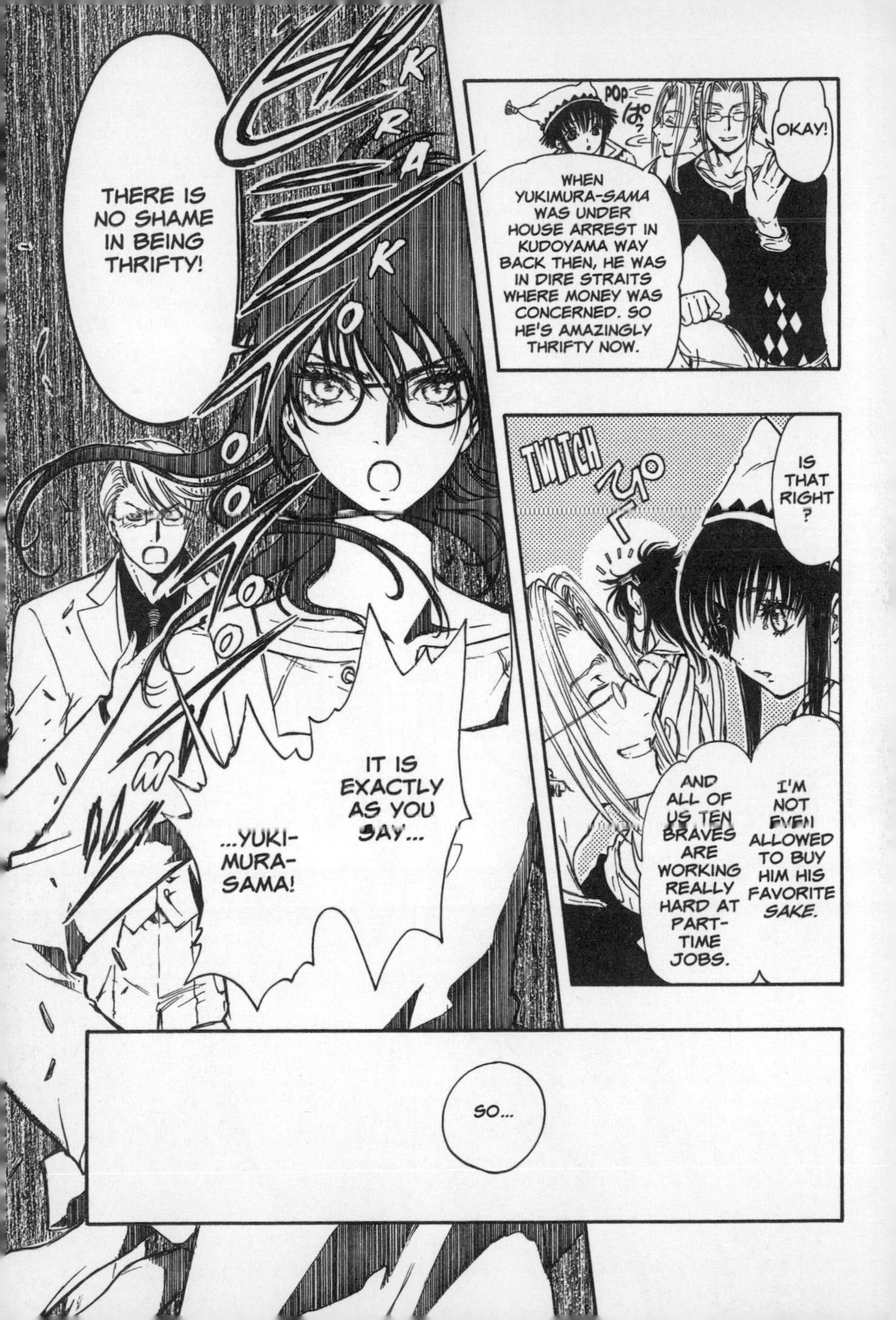
OKAY!
POP
WHEN YUKIMURA-SAMA WAS UNDER HOUSE ARREST IN KUDOYAMA WAY BACK THEN, HE WAS IN DIRE STRAITS WHERE MONEY WAS CONCERNED. SO HE'S AMAZINGLY THRIFTY NOW.
TWITCH
IS THAT RIGHT?
I'M NOT EVEN ALLOWED TO BUY HIM HIS FAVORITE SAKE.
AND ALL OF US TEN BRAVES ARE WORKING REALLY HARD AT PART-TIME JOBS.
KRAKOOOOOOM
THERE IS NO SHAME IN BEING THRIFTY!
IT IS EXACTLY AS YOU SAY...
...YUKI-MURA-SAMA!
SO...

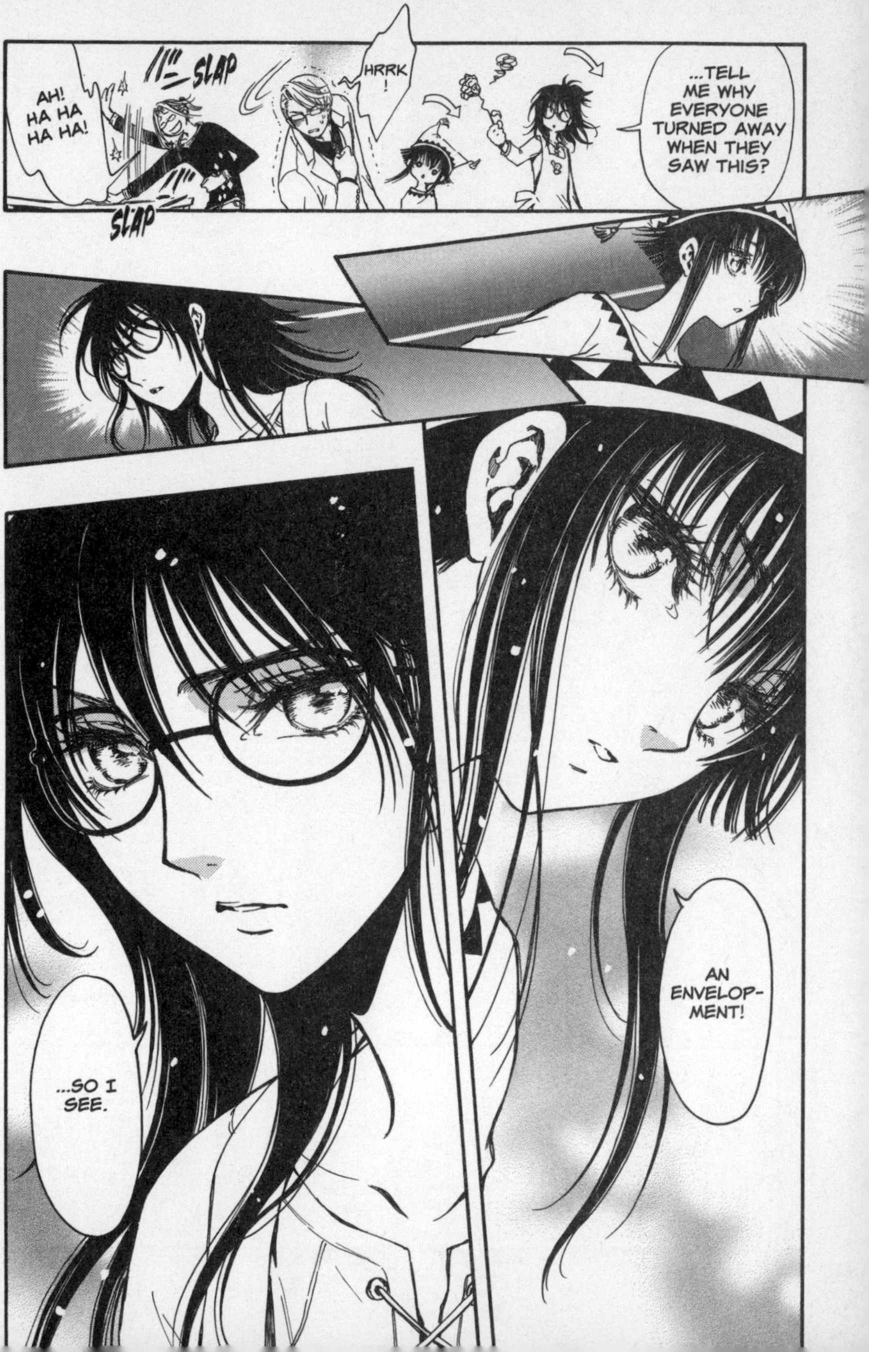
...TELL ME WHY EVERYONE TURNED AWAY WHEN THEY SAW THIS?
HRRK!
SLAP
AH! HA HA HA HA!
SLAP
AN ENVELOPMENT!
...SO I SEE.

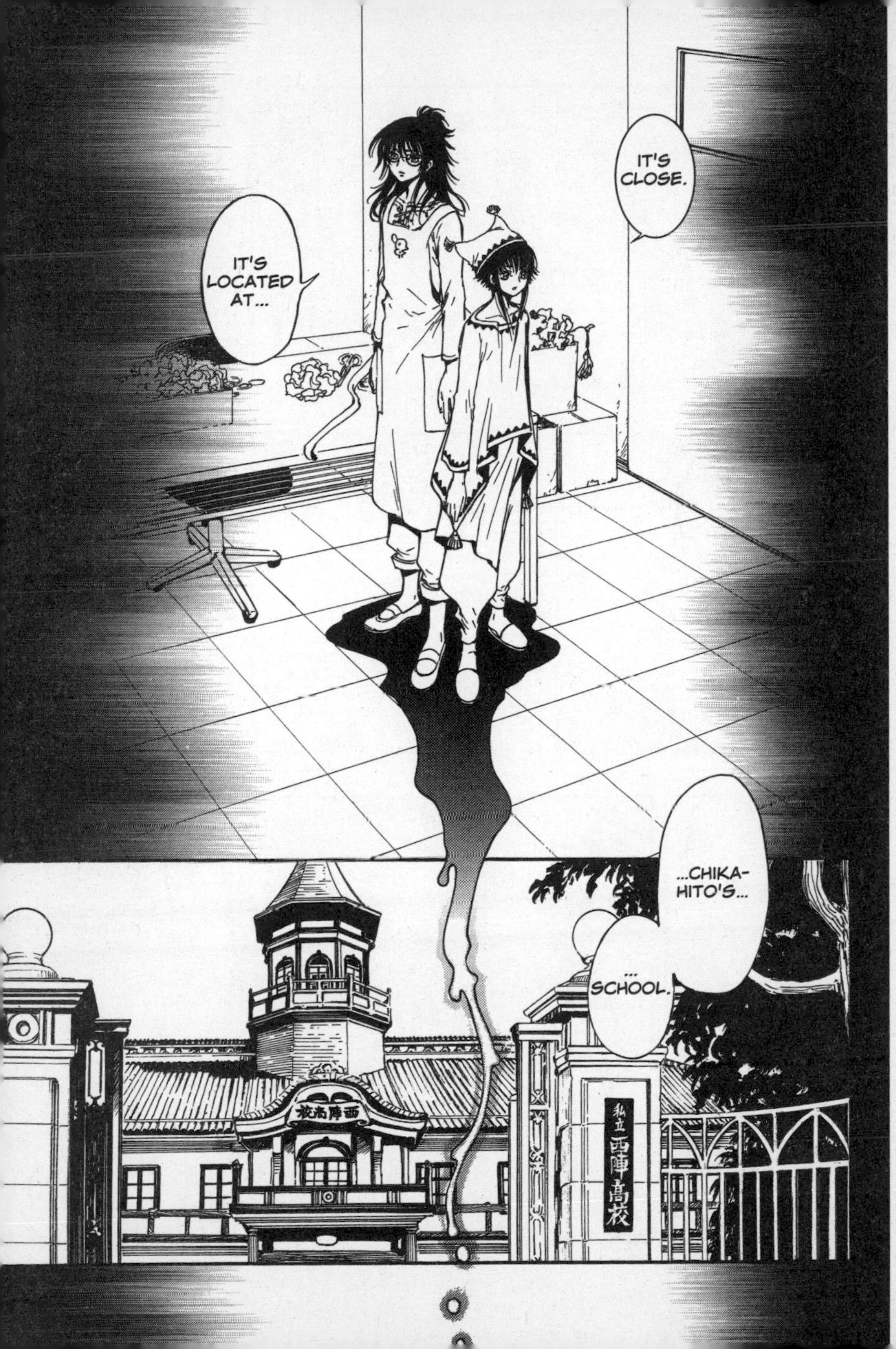
IT'S CLOSE.
IT'S LOCATED AT...
...CHIKA-HITO'S...
...SCHOOL.
西陣高校
私立 西陣高校

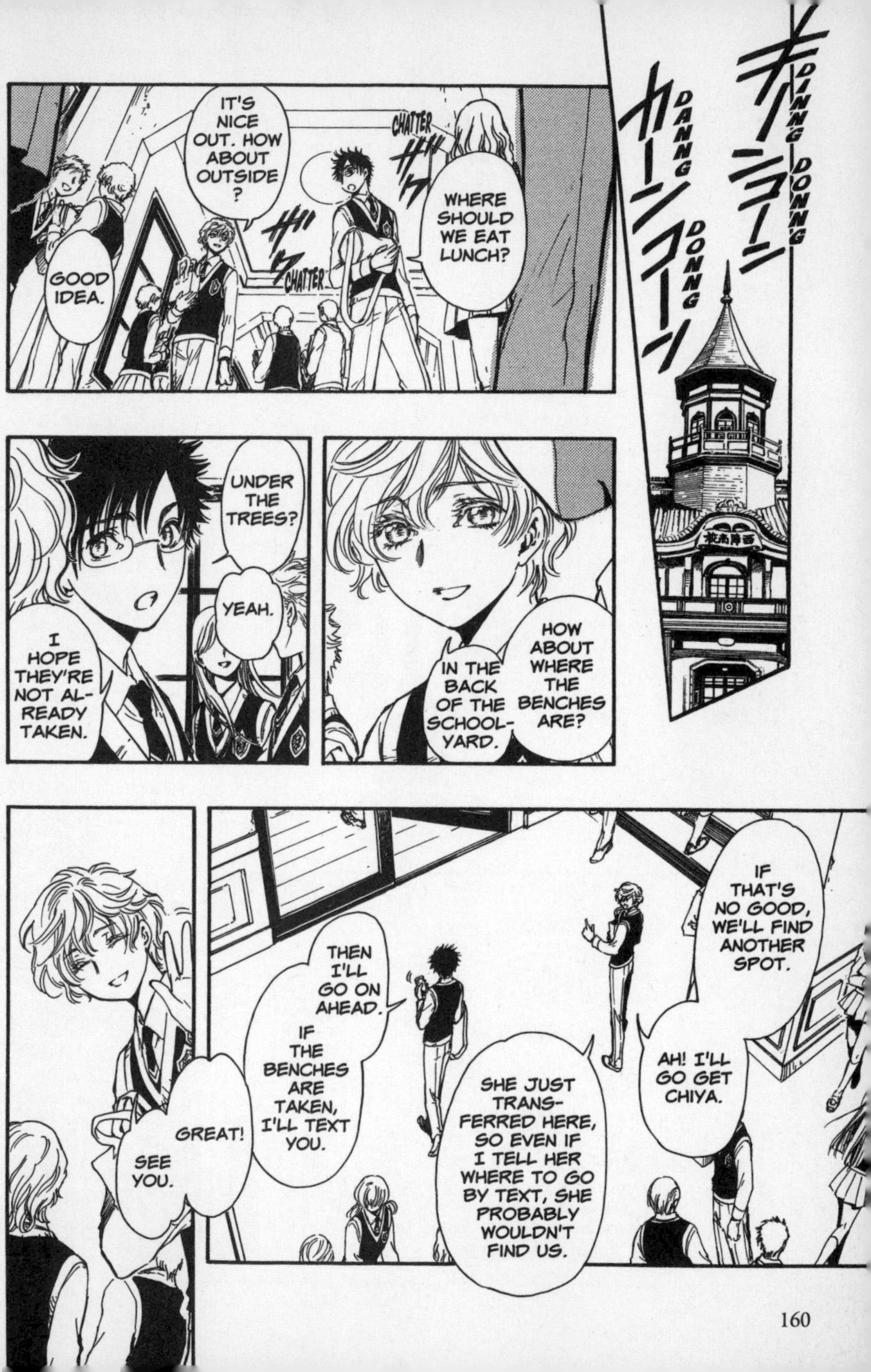
DINNG DONNG
DANNG DONNG
WHERE SHOULD WE EAT LUNCH?
CHATTER
CHATTER
IT'S NICE OUT. HOW ABOUT OUTSIDE?
GOOD IDEA.
HOW ABOUT WHERE THE BENCHES ARE?
IN THE BACK OF THE SCHOOL-YARD.
UNDER THE TREES?
YEAH.
I HOPE THEY'RE NOT AL-READY TAKEN.
IF THAT'S NO GOOD, WE'LL FIND ANOTHER SPOT.
AH! I'LL GO GET CHIYA.
SHE JUST TRANS-FERRED HERE, SO EVEN IF I TELL HER WHERE TO GO BY TEXT, SHE PROBABLY WOULDN'T FIND US.
THEN I'LL GO ON AHEAD.
IF THE BENCHES ARE TAKEN, I'LL TEXT YOU.
GREAT!
SEE YOU.

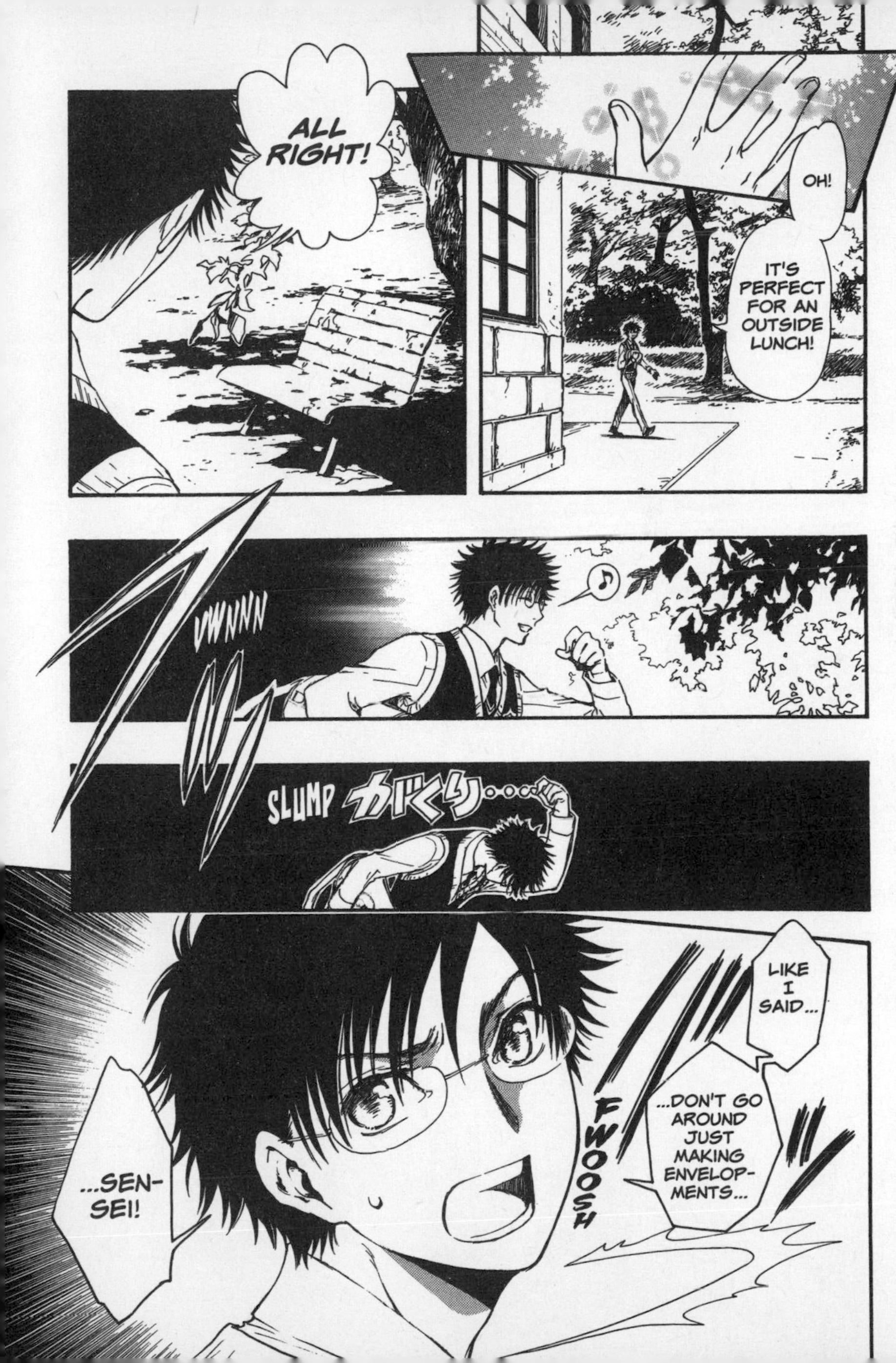
OH!
IT'S PERFECT FOR AN OUTSIDE LUNCH!
ALL RIGHT!
VWNNN
SLUMP がくり
LIKE I SAID...
...DON'T GO AROUND JUST MAKING ENVELOPMENTS...
FWOOSH
...SEN-SEI!

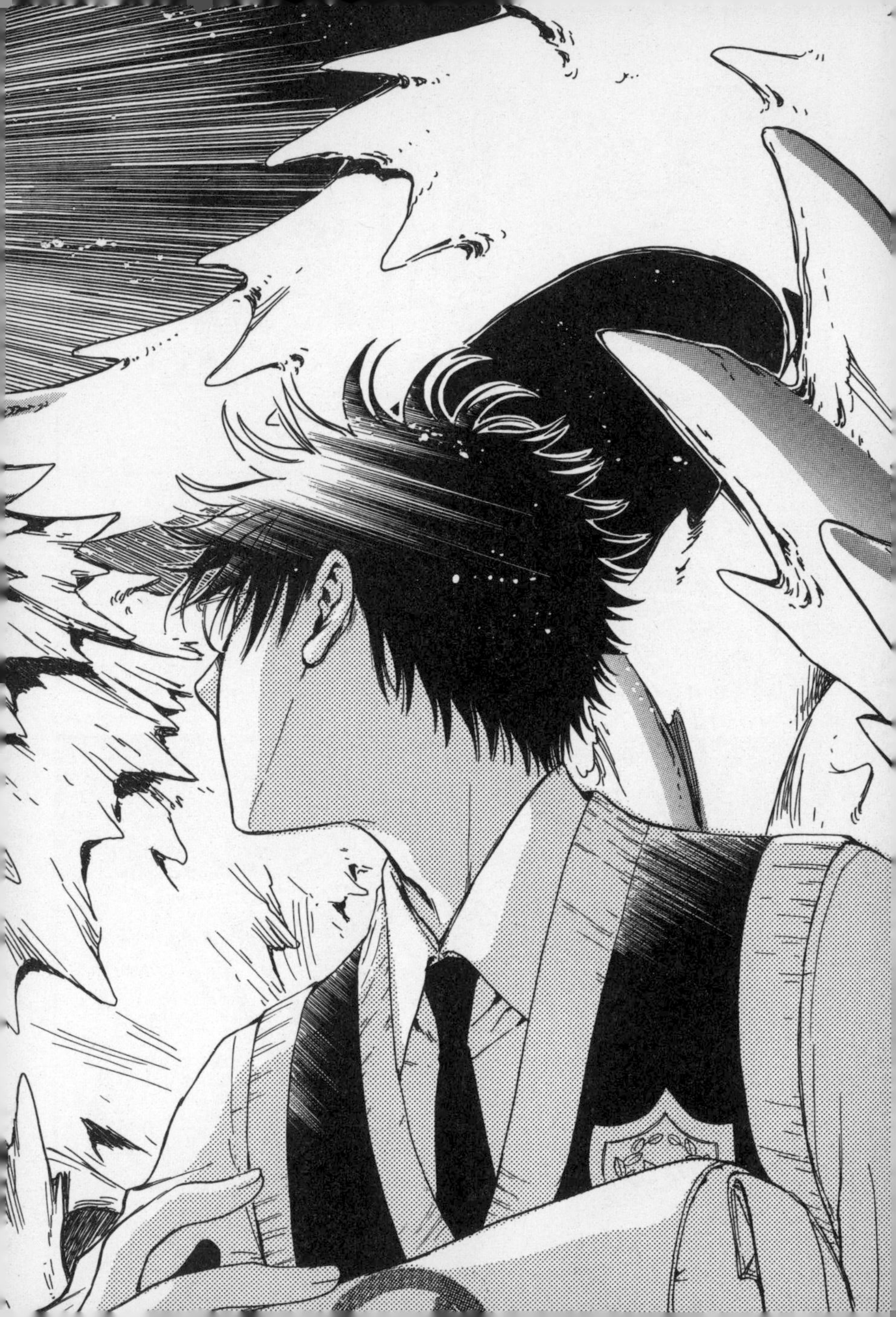

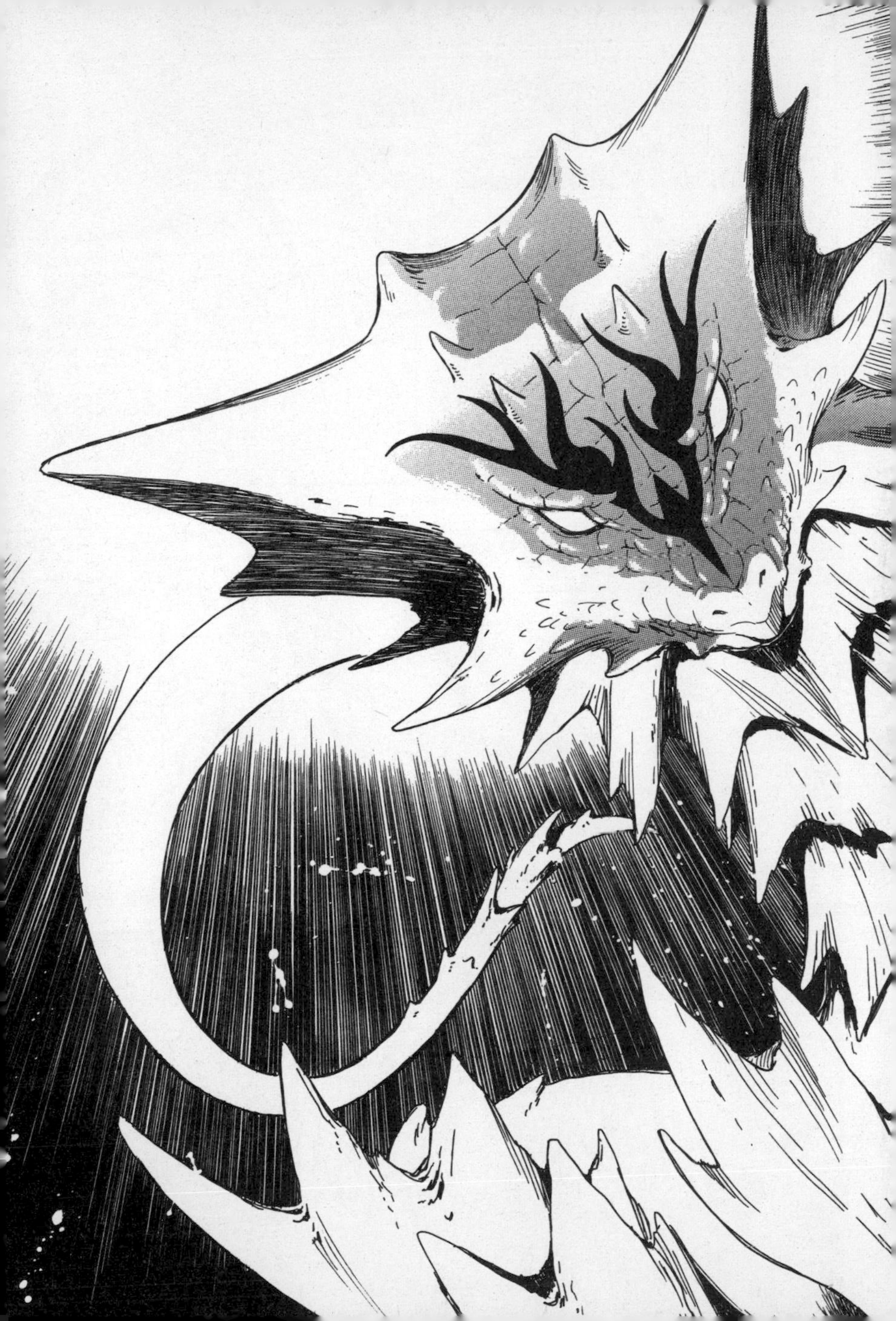

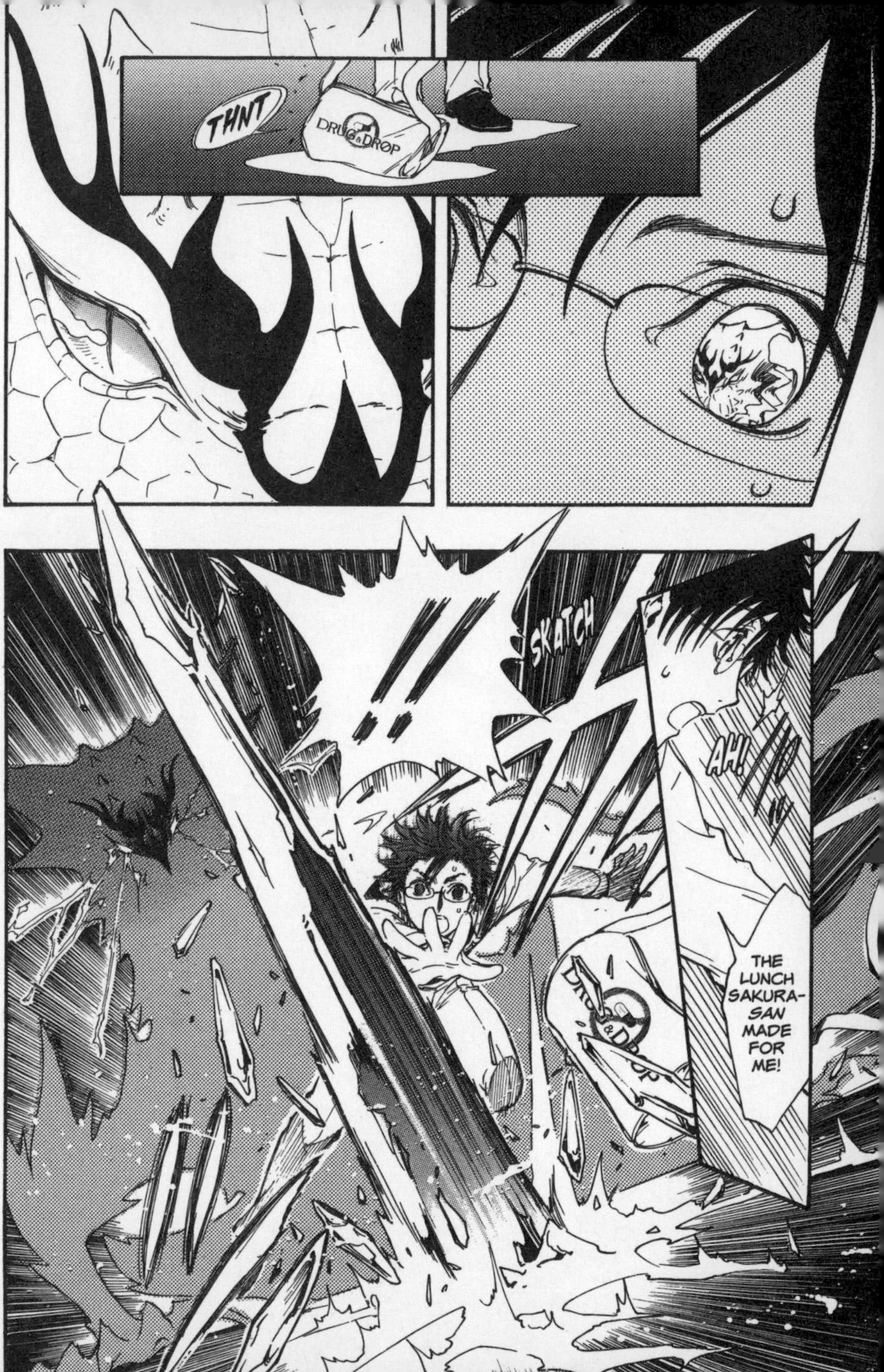
THNT
DRUG & DROP
SKATCH
AH!
THE LUNCH SAKURA-SAN MADE FOR ME!

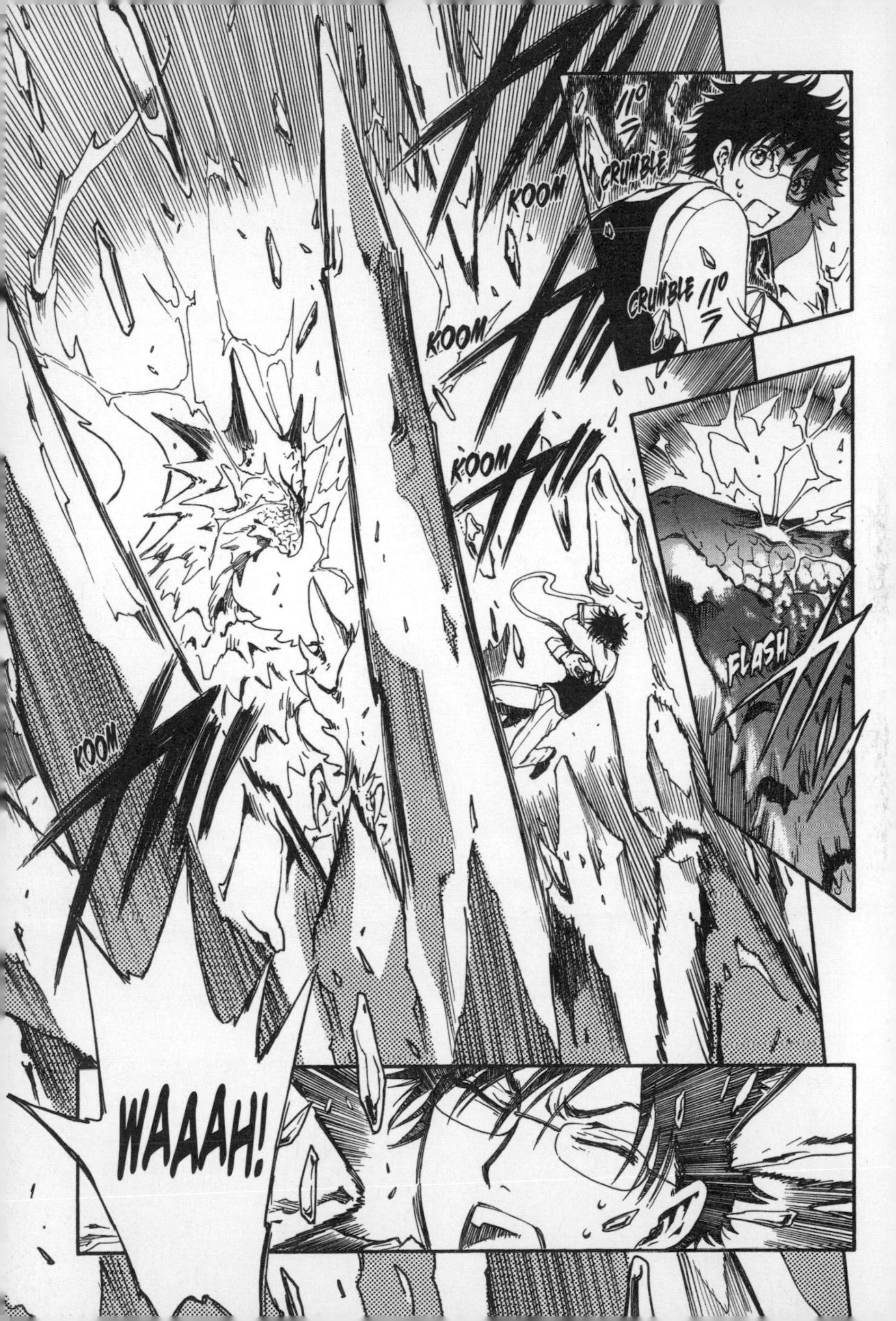

パラ
CRUMBLE
KOOM
CRUMBLE
パラ
KOOM
KOOM
FLASH
KOOM
WAAAH!

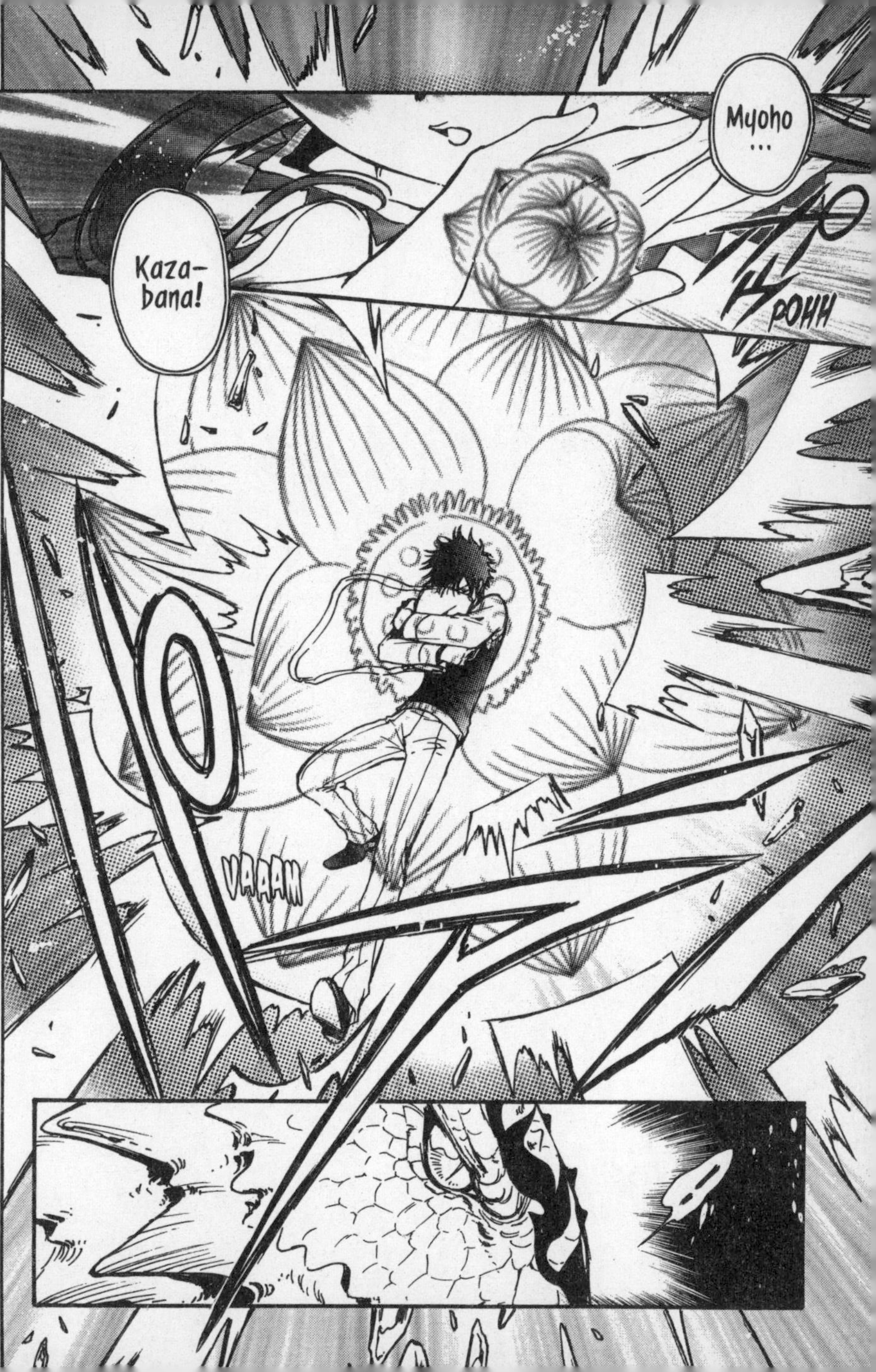
Myoho ...
Kaza-bana!
POHH
VAAAM

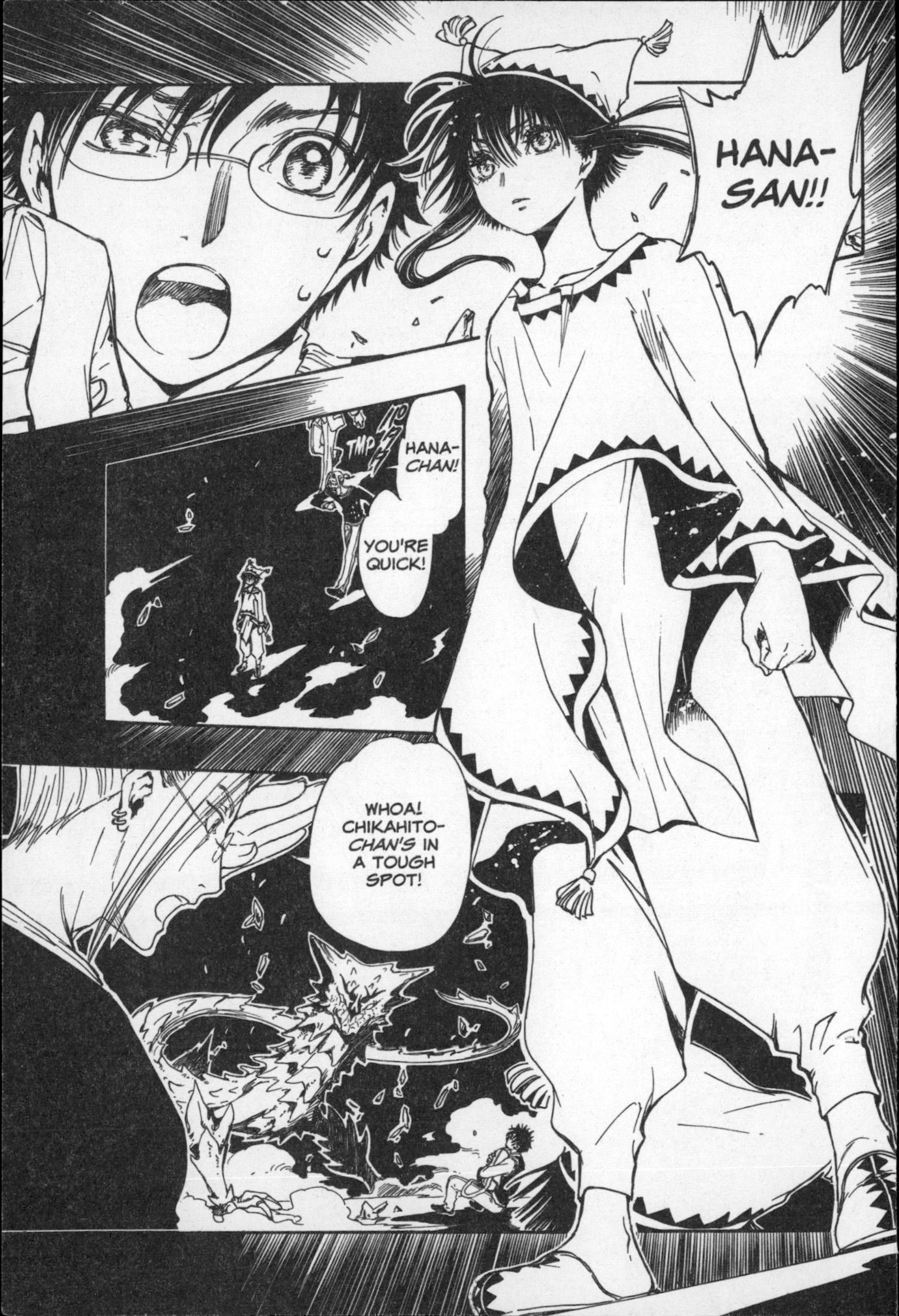
HANA-SAN!!
TMP
HANA-CHAN!
YOU'RE QUICK!
WHOA! CHIKAHITO-CHAN'S IN A TOUGH SPOT!

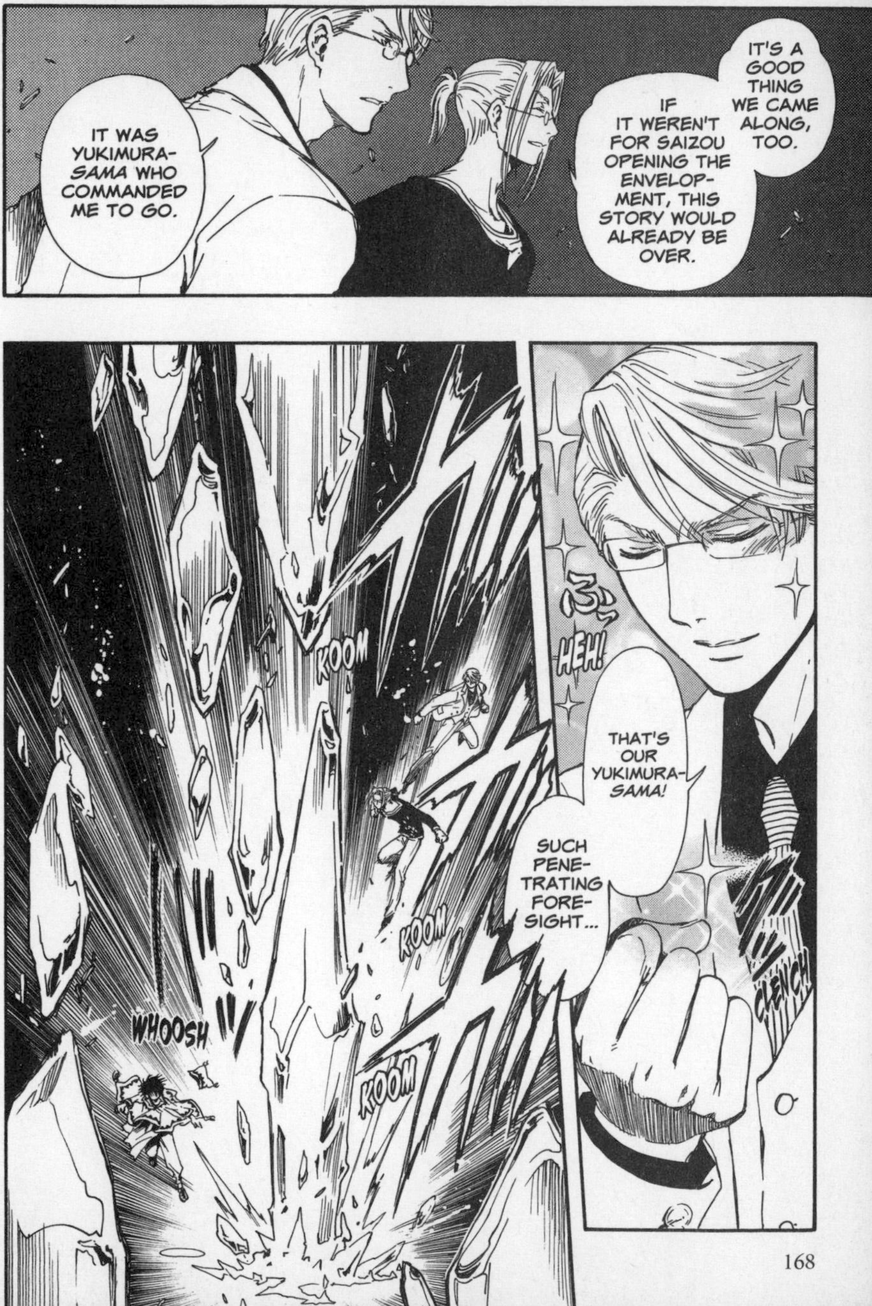
IT'S A GOOD THING WE CAME ALONG, TOO.
IF IT WEREN'T FOR SAIZOU OPENING THE ENVELOP-MENT, THIS STORY WOULD ALREADY BE OVER.
IT WAS YUKIMURA-SAMA WHO COMMANDED ME TO GO.
ふっ
HEH!
THAT'S OUR YUKIMURA-SAMA!
SUCH PENE-TRATING FORE-SIGHT...
CLENCH
KOOM
KOOM
KOOM
WHOOSH

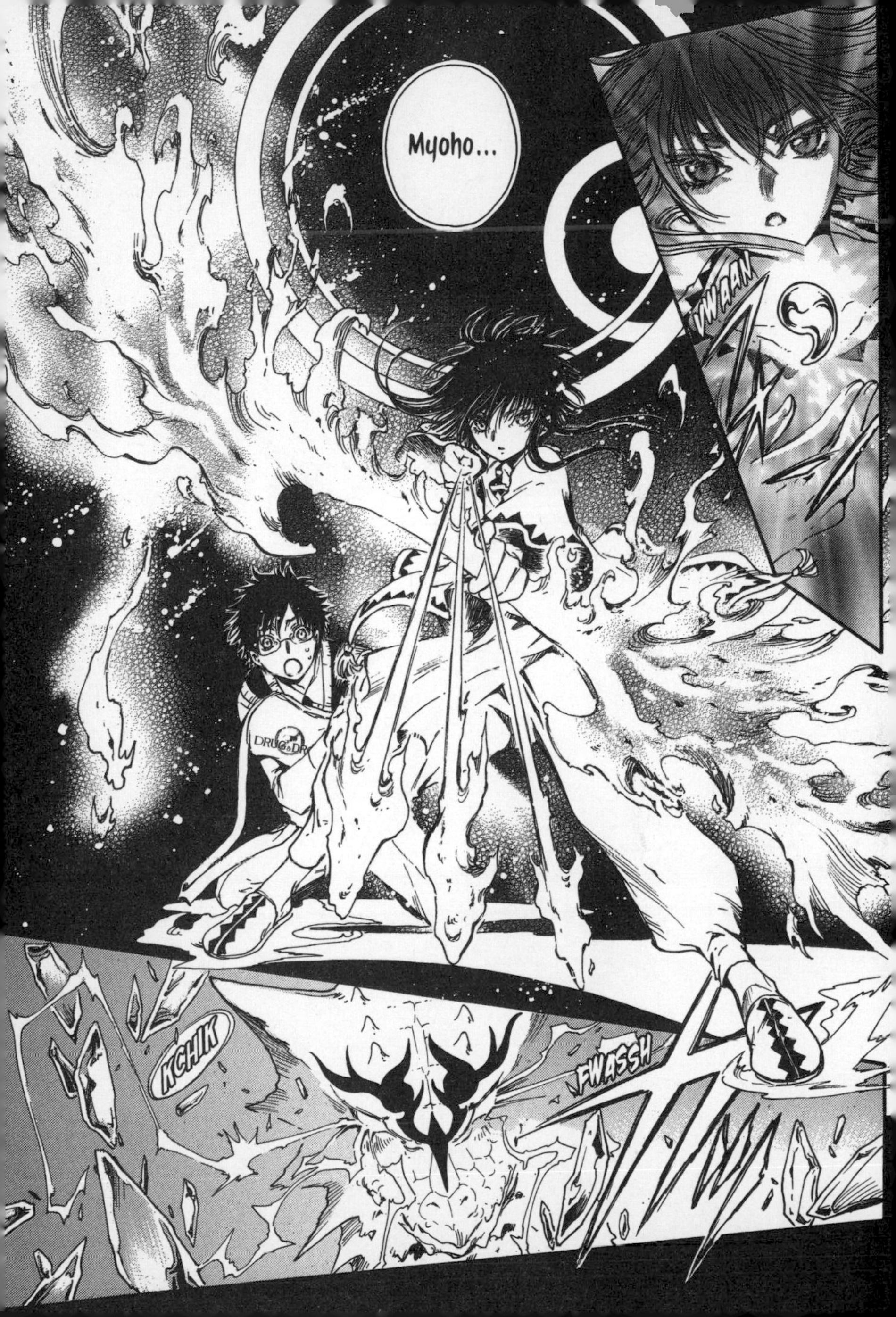
VWAAN
Myoho...
FWASSH
KCHIK

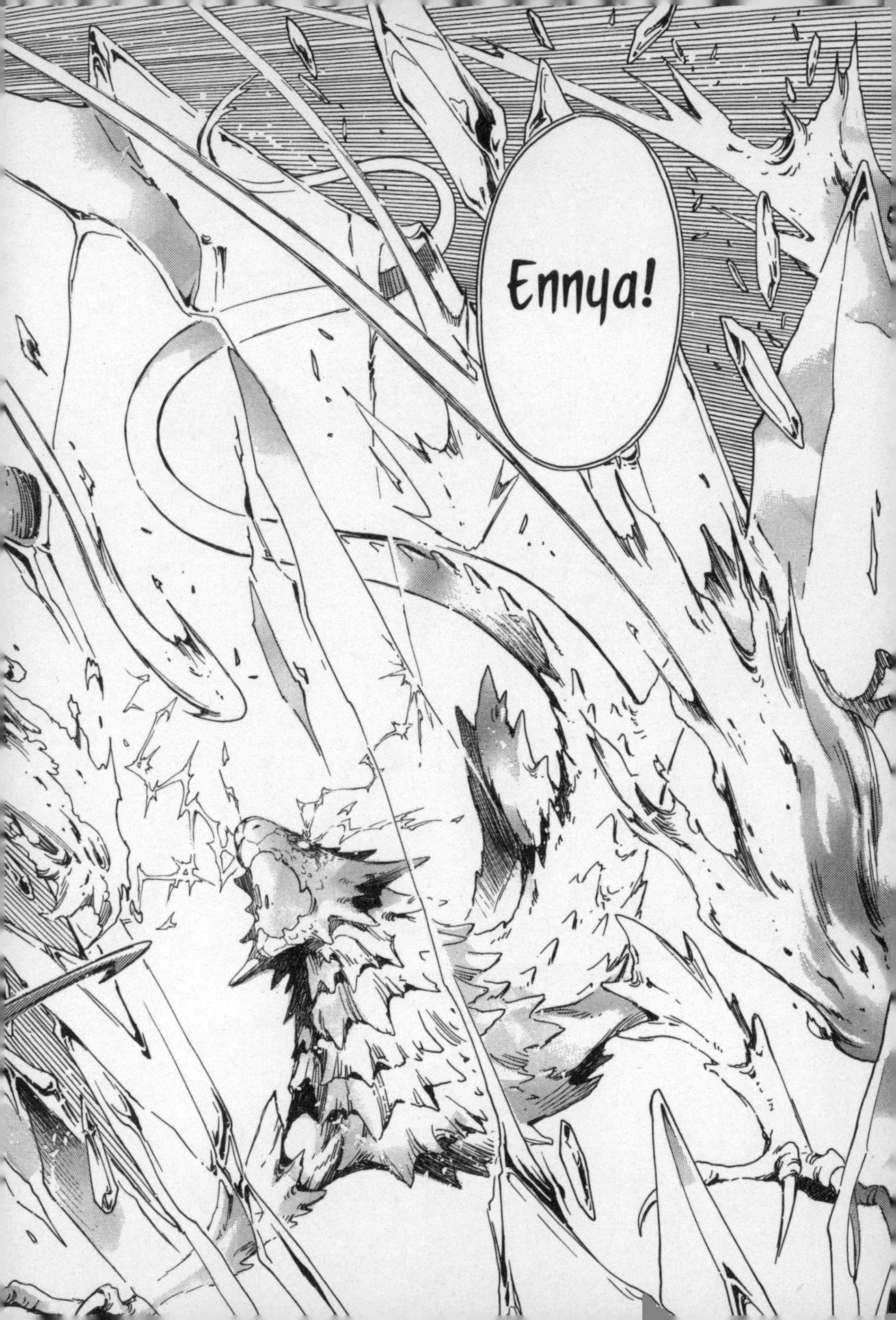
Ennya!

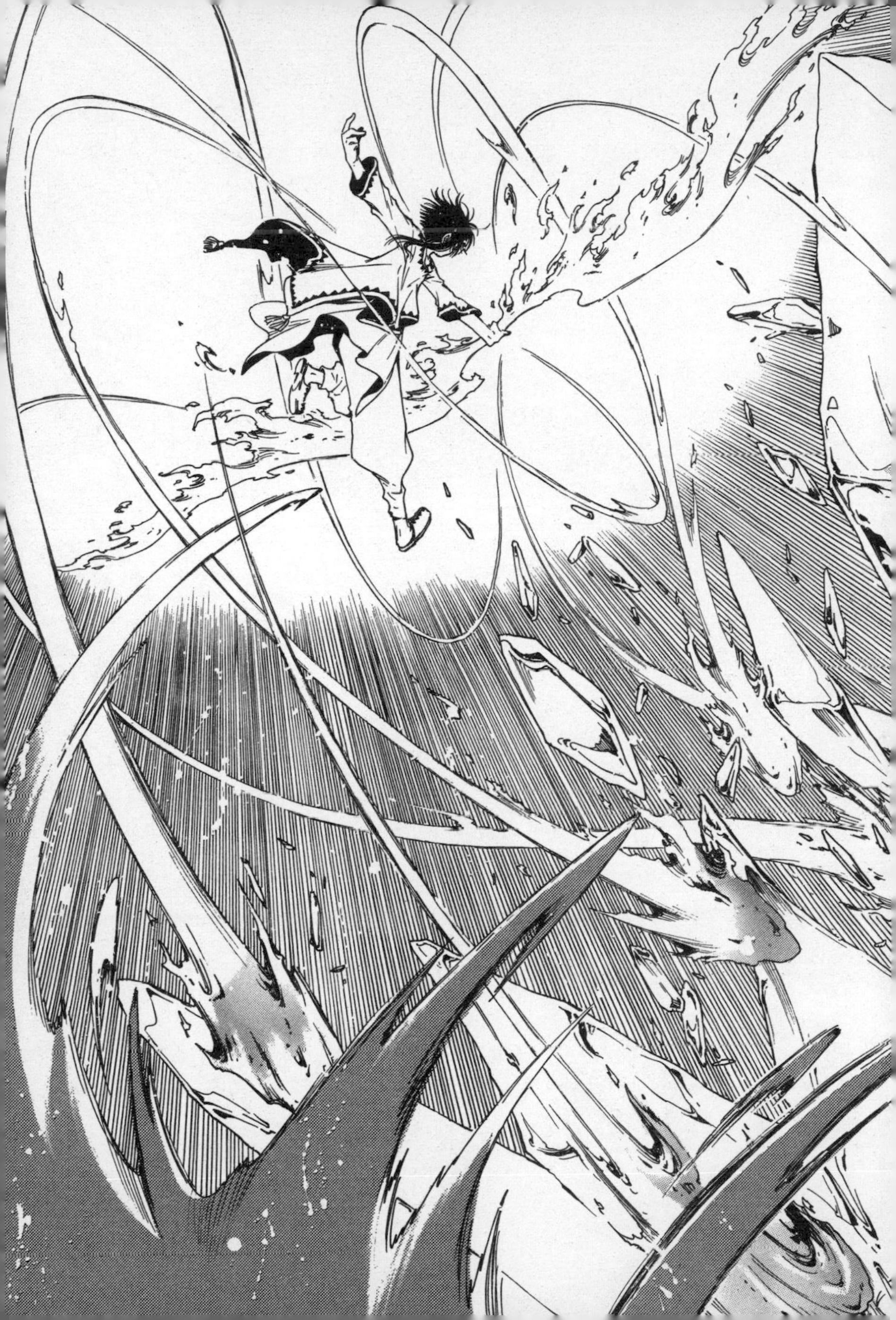

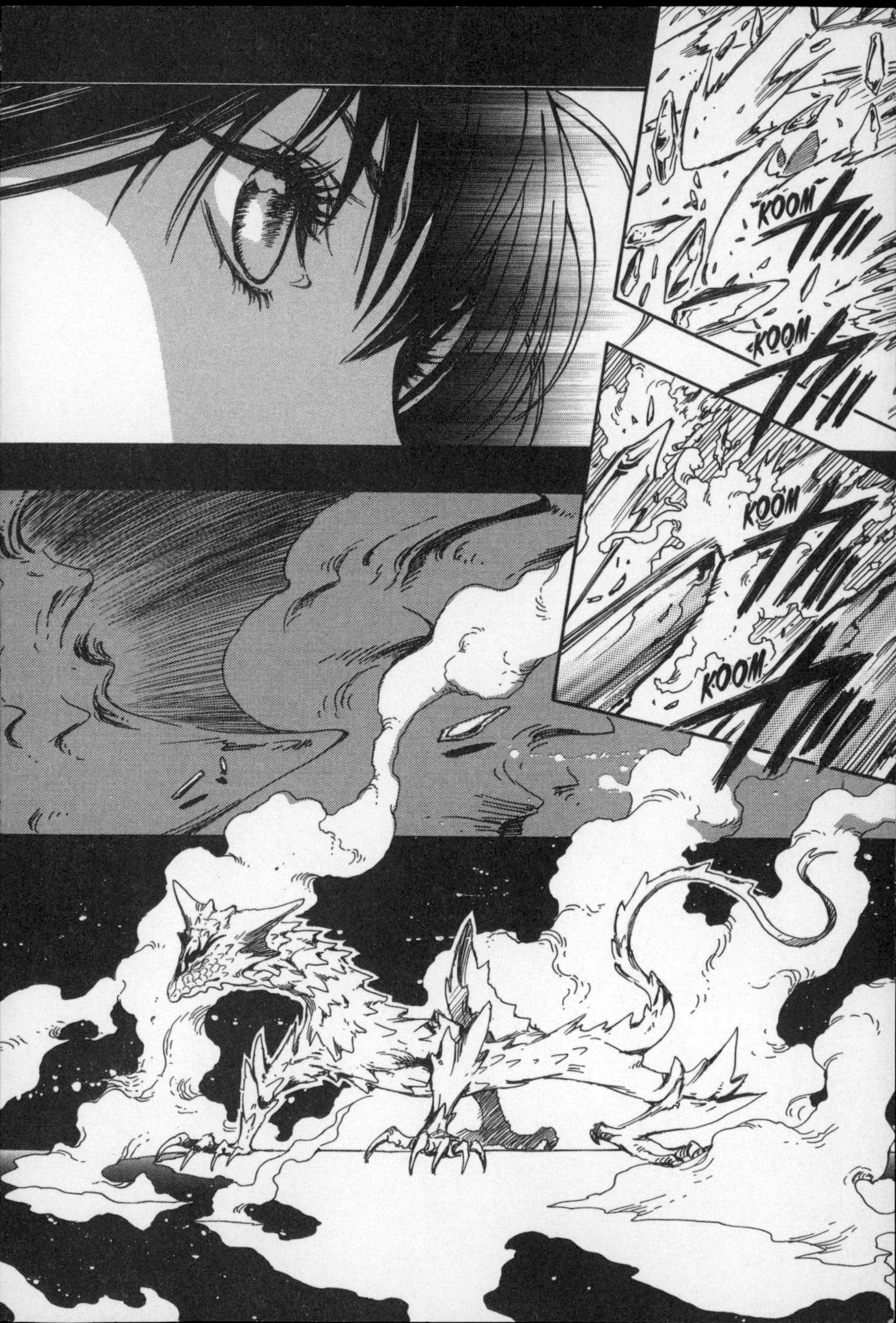
KOOM
KOOM
KOOM
KOOM

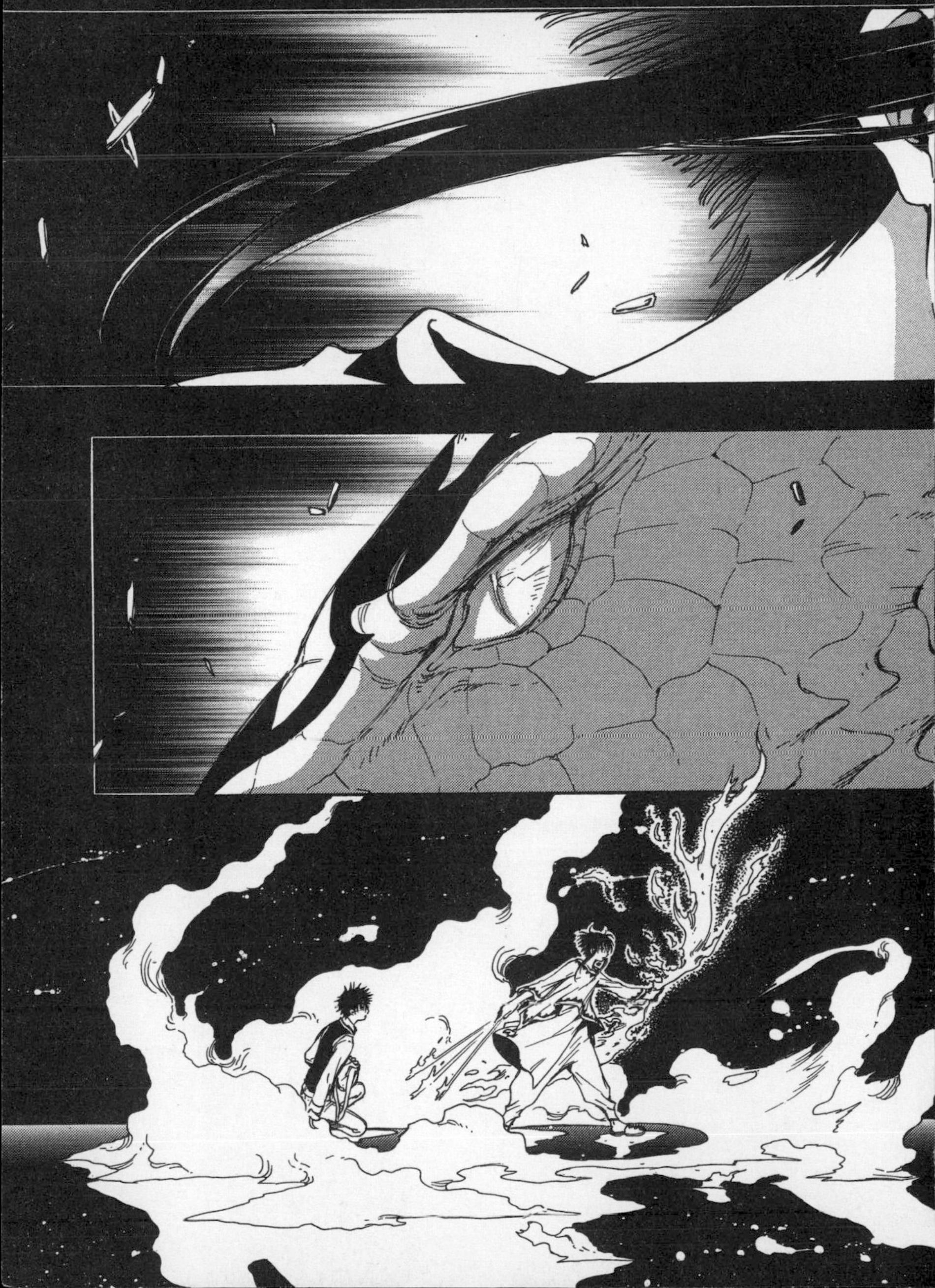

GATE 7
ゲートセブン

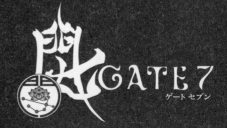

GATE 7 VOLUME 4   TRANSLATION NOTES

COMPILED BY **WILLIAM FLANAGAN**

General notes on Kyoto: *Kyoto was one of the few large Japanese population centers to escape the extremely destructive American firebombing of World War II that burned historical sites in nearly every other Japanese city close to Kyoto's size. The determination not to bomb Kyoto was a conscious decision by American civilian and military leadership in deference to Kyoto's many historical buildings and landmarks. Although some other historical sites in more rural locations—such as Ise or Izumo—were also spared, cities that were formerly rich in history (such as Tokyo, Yokohama, Nagoya, Osaka, and Kobe—not to mention Hiroshima and Nagasaki) have all had to rebuild replicas of their ancient historic landmarks. Kyoto is the one large Japanese city where history is still very much in evidence.*

Page 14, *suika*: *Suika* is a combination of two kanji; the first is *sui*, which means "water," and the second is *ka*, which means "flower." *Fuuka*: As mentioned in the notes for volume 1, the name for Hana's *myoho* technique is made up of kanji for "wind" and "flower."

Page 17, chi: Pronounced *ki* in Japanese, this is the concept in Chinese medicine of energy that can affect one's personal well-being, as well as many other aspects of humanity and the world. It is a central concept in many traditional Chinese disciplines, such as feng shui and martial arts.

Page 29: *Shin ramen* (also spelled *shin ramyun*) is a Korean hot and spicy ramen. An instant version of the dish has become a Korean export and is even available on Internet sites such as Amazon. Yawata-ya is a Kyoto restaurant founded in 1910 that features dishes skewered on wooden sticks.

Page 38: *Juufu* is made up of two *kanji*, the first meaning "curse" and the second meaning "garment."

Page 40, castle town: Administration in Japan's feudal era was conducted in a series of castles located throughout the country. Since these castles were cultural centers, the roads leading to them and the area surrounding their main gates became thriving communities of homes, shops, and other establishments. Some castle towns are preserved as tourist destinations in Japan.

Page 47: Udon is a thick wheat-flour noodle that is usually served hot in a soup along with meats, vegetables, and seafood in many different combinations.

Page 48: *Shochu* is not actually *sake*, but a different type of distilled Japanese traditional spirit. *Sake* is a rice wine, and while *shochu* can be distilled from rice, it can also be distilled from barley, sweet potatoes, or other ingredients. The *imo-jouchu* that Sakura mentions is *shochu* made from sweet potatoes, but although the *take* in *take-jouchu* means "bamboo," it does not mean the *shochu* is made from bamboo. Rather, it refers to other types of *shochu* that are served in bamboo bottles.

Page 55: The cell-phone provider Willcom puts out a cell phone that is meant for the use of small children. It is called the *anshinda phone* ("peace of mind phone"), and it is designed to call certain pre-programmed numbers with the push of a single button. With it, a child can call a safe number such as a parent's. Rival company NTT puts out a similar but even simpler phone with only three buttons.

Page 56, Kudoyama: In 1600, Ieyasu Tokugawa had won the Battle of Sekigahara

and controlled essentially all of Japan. Having fought against Tokugawa, Sanada and his father were exiled to Kudoyama near Mt. Koya in Wakayama Prefecture, just south of Osaka. Sanada spent nearly a decade and a half exiled there until he managed to escape and join the last of the Toyotomi clan in Osaka.

Page 62: There is a Japanese saying, *hachi-bunme*, which means that it is healthiest to fill up your stomach to 80 percent, rather than trying to eat until you are full. Some research done on longevity in Okinawa seems to confirm this 80 percent idea. There is a saying with a similar sentiment in English: "Light suppers make long life."

Page 68: Mitsunari Ishida was a *daimyo* (great lord) even before he met Hideyoshi Toyotomi, but when he entered the Toyotomi government he became one of Hideyoshi's top administrators. His administrative abilities were reputed to be brilliant, but he was also reportedly very strict and tactless and made enemies. After Hideyoshi's death, he was one of the five regents who were tasked with governing Japan until Hideyoshi's son, Hideyori, came of age. Ishida was one of the main leaders of the resistance against Ieyasu Tokugawa and commanded the Toyotomi-loyal forces at the Battle of Sekigahara—a pivotal battle that Ishida and the Toyotomi forces lost. A few days after the battle, Ishida was found, brought to Kyoto, and executed.

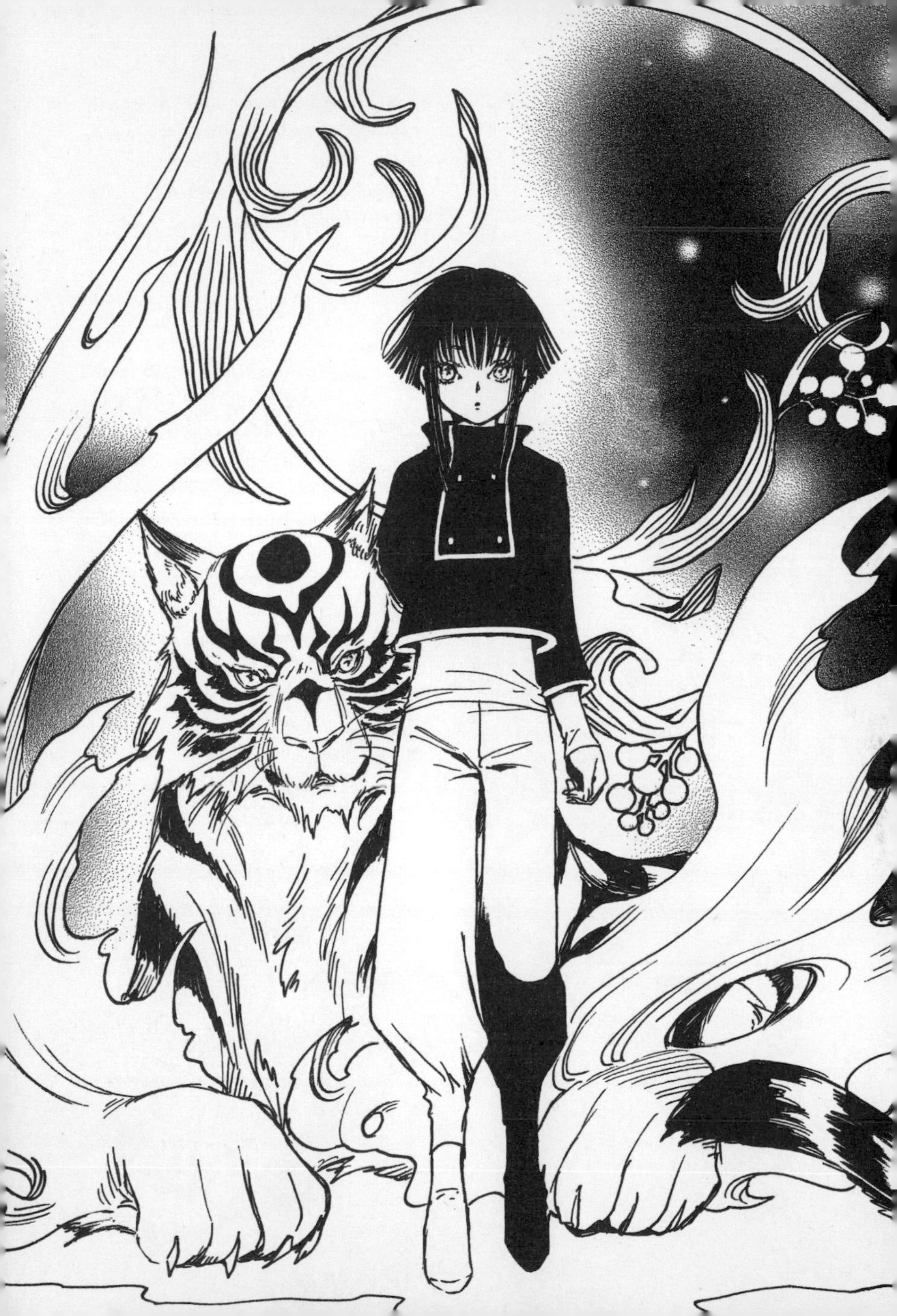

Page 69: Sakon Shima was one of Mitsunari Ishida's top lieutenants and a commander at the Battle of Sekigahara. He was wounded during the battle, later dying of those wounds.

Page 85: *Seiza* is the formal way to sit in Japan. You sit with your shins and feet tucked underneath your thighs and rear end, with your back as straight as if you were at attention. It is traditional, so the elderly in Japan are quite used to it, but modern Japanese young people hardly ever practice it. To those unaccustomed to it, *seiza* will cause a pins-and-needles feeling and

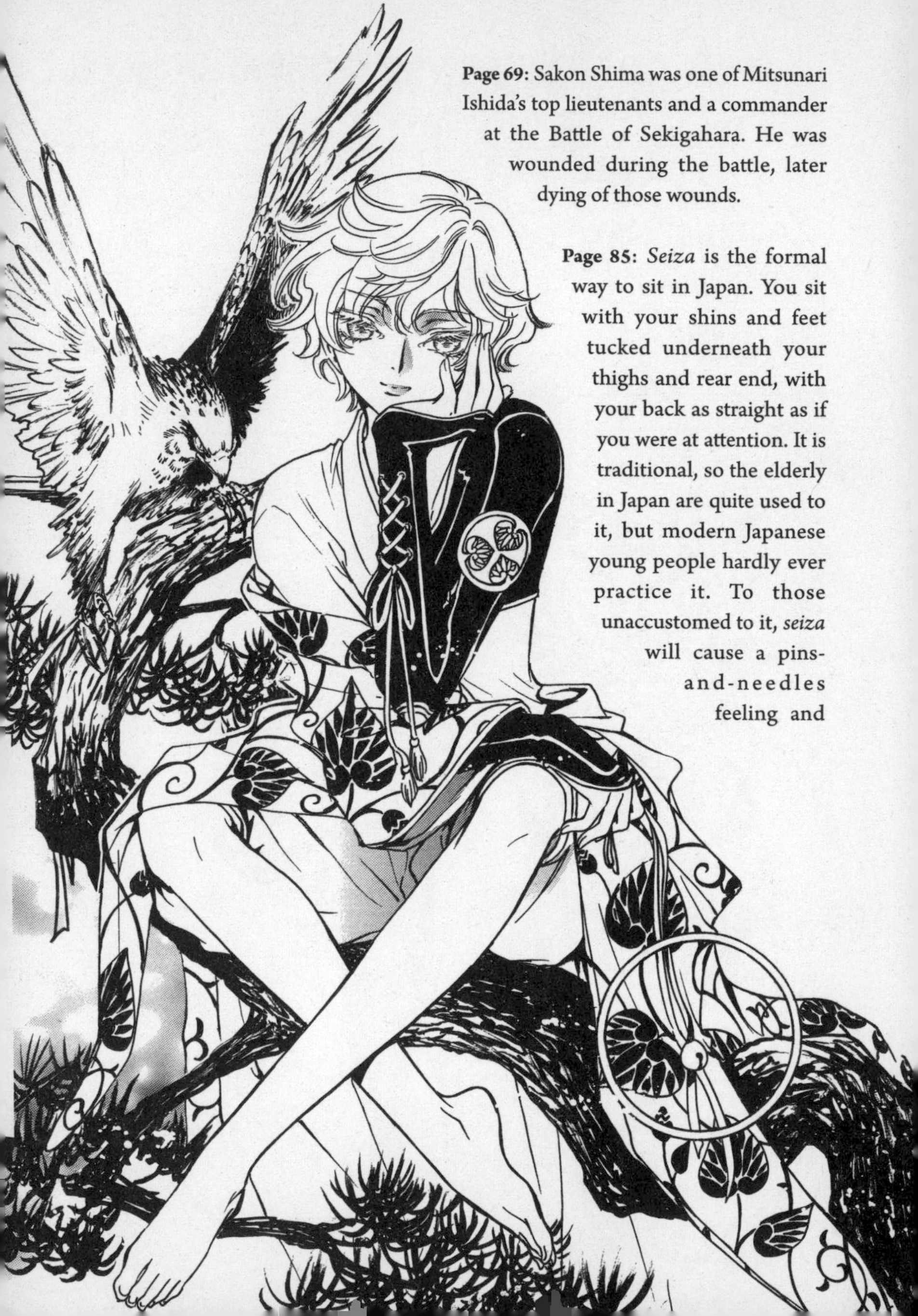

TANUKI: ***Raccoon dog. One of the standard magical creatures in Japanese folklore.***

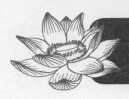

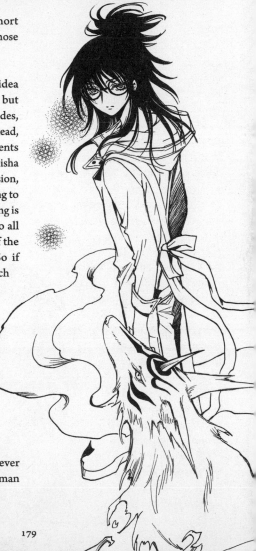

numbness in the legs after only a short while. It can also cause leg cramps in those without long practice.

Page 96, *maiko*: There is a Western idea that equates geisha with prostitutes, but although geisha certainly weren't prudes, their main selling point wasn't sex. Instead, it was their musical and dancing talents and conversational abilities. Being a geisha was (and is) a highly respected profession, and there is no shortage of girls striving to enter the profession. A geisha in training is called a *maiko*, and she is made to do all the chores assisting in the upkeep of the geisha under whom she studies. So if anybody needs help in the geisha-rich environment of Kami-shichiken, it's the *maiko*.

Page 100: Called *tanuki* in Japan, the raccoon dog, like the fox, is one of the standard magical creatures in Japanese folklore. There is an actual raccoon dog in Japan that resembles a raccoon or a badger, though it is a completely separate species. The mythological *tanuki* is a race of clever creatures that can shapeshift into human form or even possess people's bodies.

TSUNDERE can apply to anyone with a quick-to-anger personality.

Page 104: Upon completing a meal, especially when there is more than one person at the table, the standard phrase one says is *gochisô-sama deshita*, which means, "It was a feast." This is a way of thanking the cook (even if the cook is not present) and it is a ubiquitous phrase in Japan. Not nearly so ubiquitous is the cook's response phrase, *osomatsu-sama deshita*, which means, "Sorry for my poor performance." Since this is a standard phrase, the humble response is not necessarily taken by the diners at face value.

Page 108, *tsundere*: This word is a fairly recent addition to the Japanese lexicon, but it has spread quickly over the past decade until now nearly everyone in Japan knows what it means. It is derived from two onomatopoeia (sound words), *tsun-tsun*, which is the sound of being poked by something sharp, and *dere-dere*, one of the meanings of which is the sound of someone fawning all over someone else. The two together refer to a type of personality that is angry and prickly at one moment and loving the next. However, more recently it seems to apply to anyone with a quick-to-anger personality, regardless of whether the person is ever nice. Chikahito makes that clear when he responds that he's never seen Tachibana's *dere* side.

Page 122, *jibuni*: Reportedly a dish out of the historical tourist town of Kanazawa, it consists of duck that is thinly sliced,

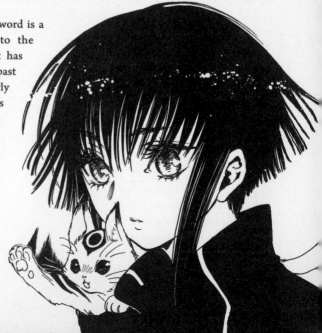

coated with flour or starch, and served up in a thick soy-sauce-based soup along with mushrooms and bamboo shoots. However, *jibuni* seems to have acquired a wide variety of ingredients and tastes as it spread out from its point of origin.

Page 132: The "princess" Sen-*hime* was the older sister of Iemitsu and daughter of the second shogun of the Tokugawa era, Hidetada. When she was seven she was sent off to be the wife of Hideyori, the juvenile heir to the Toyotomi clan. There she lived through the strife between her husband's Toyotomi forces and the forces of her grandfather Ieyasu Tokugawa. She was rescued from Osaka Castle before the castle fell to Tokugawa forces, but her Toyotomi husband and child weren't so lucky. They were killed or forced to commit suicide at the end of the siege. There is an unconfirmed legend that the man who rescued her from the castle tried to marry her himself, but he

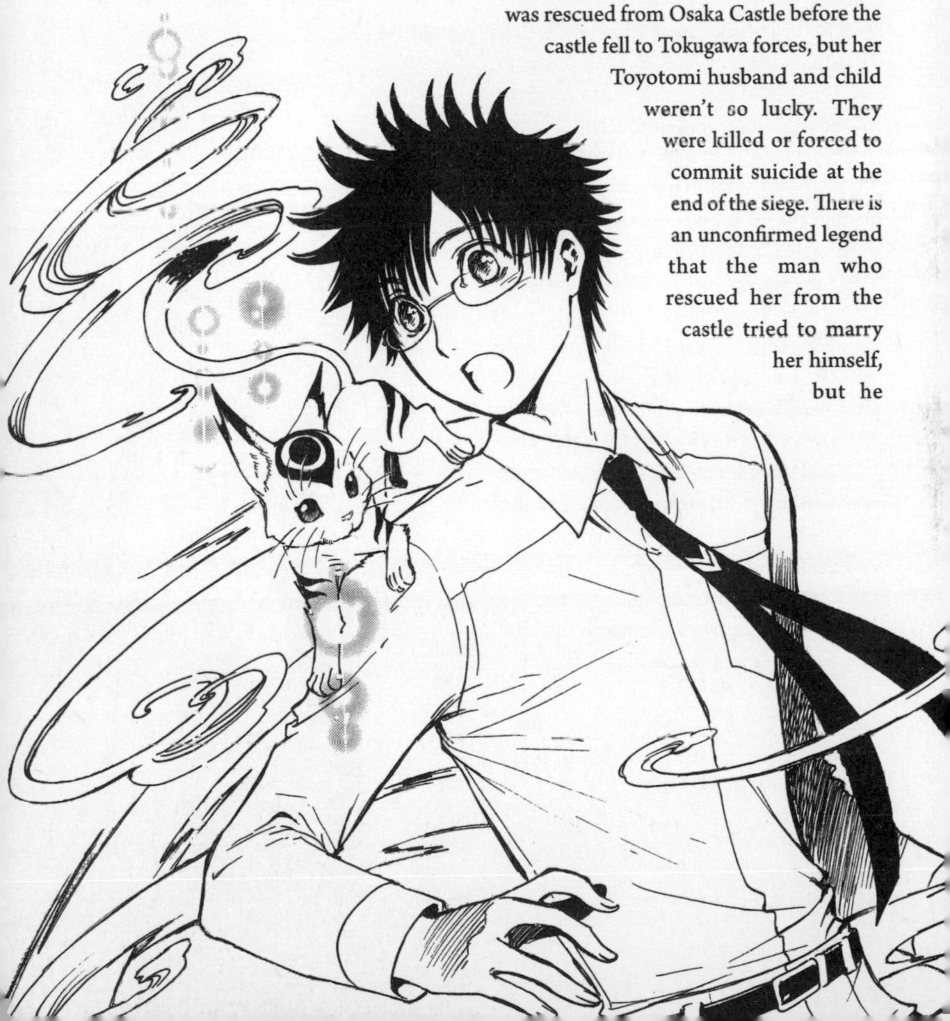

SAKURA: *"Cherry tree."* TACHIBANA: *A type of native Japanese citrus fruit tree.*

suffered a tragic death when his plan was uncovered. In the legend, Sen-*hime* had rejected the man's pleas anyway, preferring to marry the handsome Tadatoki Honda, sponsor of the famous swordsman Musashi Miyamoto. But Sen-*hime*'s luck was never good: her only son with Tadatoki died at the age of three, and Tadatoki himself died of tuberculosis when Sen-*hime* was twenty-nine years old. It was then that she cut her hair and took the life of a Buddhist nun.

Page 150: *Sakura* means "cherry tree," and *tachibana* is a type of native Japanese citrus fruit tree. "The twin trees" refers to the two older men of the Ura-shichiken. It also reminds Japanese readers of the *tachibana* and *sakura* trees that were planted in the emperor's garden (see the "Right Flank/ Left Flank" note in volume 1).

Page 166, *kazabana*: The name for this *myoho* technique is a combination of two kanji; the first is *kaza* or *kaze*, which means "wind," and the second is *hana*, which means "flower." (*Hana* changes to *bana* through linguistic rules.)

Page 170, *ennya*: The name for this *myoho* technique is made up of kanji for "fire" and "arrow."

GATE 7 PINUPS

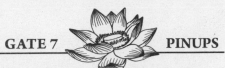

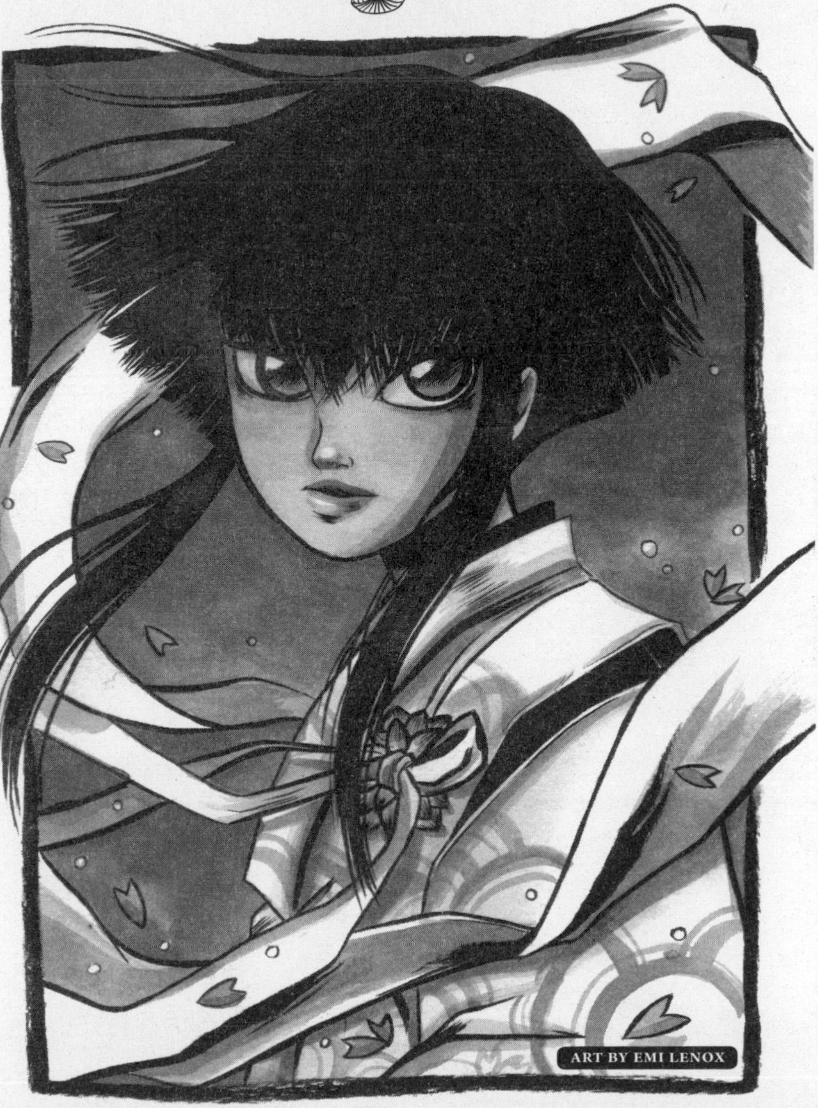
ART BY EMI LENOX

SOME OF *GATE 7*'s FANS ARE PROFESSIONAL ARTISTS THEMSELVES!
CHECK OUT THE PINUPS ON THESE THREE PAGES.

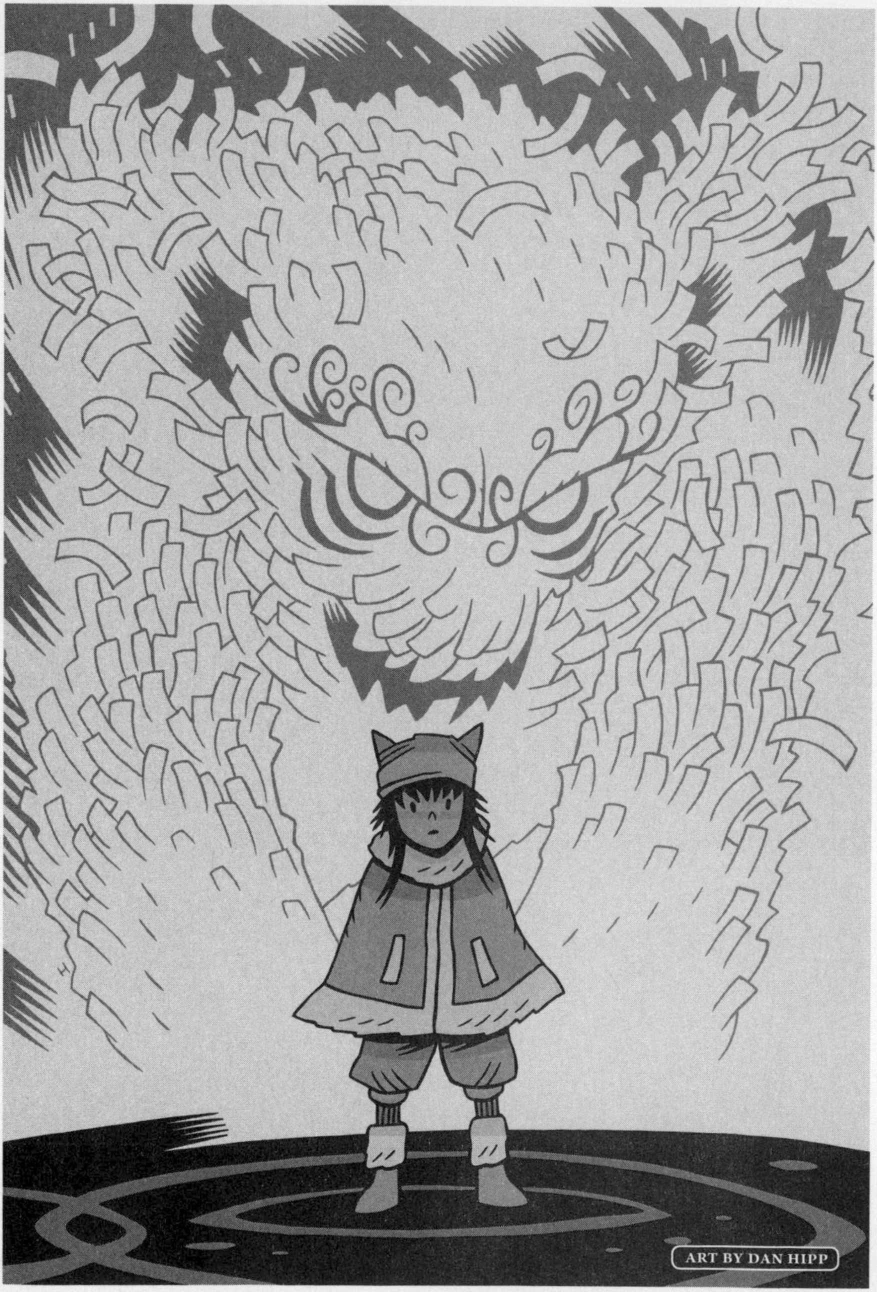
ART BY DAN HIPP

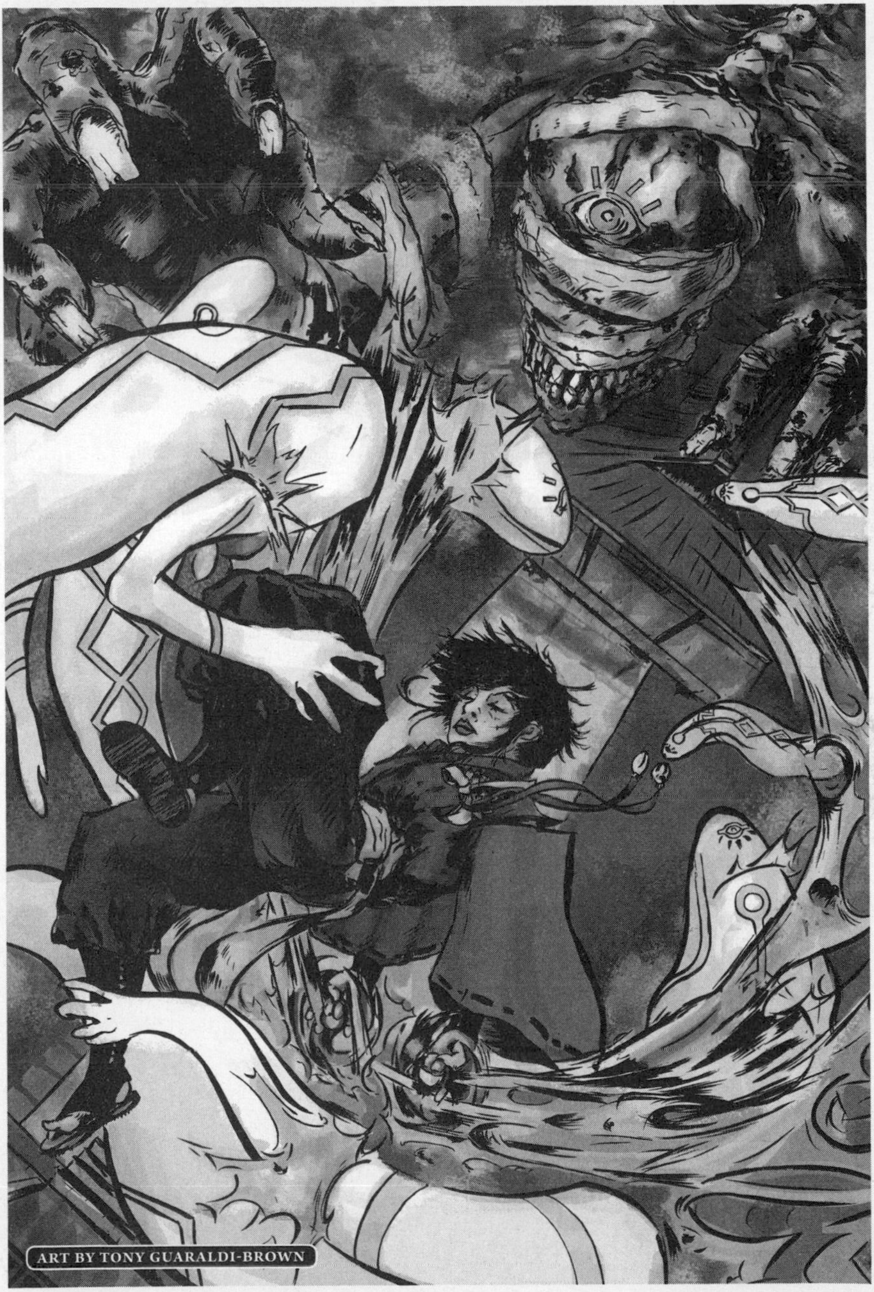
ART BY TONY GUARALDI-BROWN

GATE 7
ゲート セブン

BRAND NEW FROM CLAMP—COMING TO THE U.S. JUST MONTHS AFTER JAPAN!

An innocent sightseeing trip to a legendary shrine opens up a magical realm to shy high schooler Chikahito Takamoto! Chikahito finds himself in the mystical world of Hana and her comrades, and his immunity to their powers leads them to believe he's no ordinary, awkward teenager! Protecting our world from violent elemental beasts, Hana and her team welcome the confused and cautious Chikahito—who isn't quite sure that he wants to be caught in the middle of their war!

Volume One	Volume Two	Volume Three
ISBN 978-1-59582-806-4	ISBN 978-1-59582-807-1	ISBN 978-1-59582-902-3
		Coming in June

$10.99 each

C L A M P

Chobits
ちょびっツ

IN NEAR-FUTURE JAPAN,
the hottest style for your personal computer, or "persocom," is in the shape of an attractive android! Hideki, a poor student, finds a persocom seemingly discarded in an alley. He takes the cute, amnesiac robot home and names her "Chi."

But who is this strange new persocom in his life? Hideki finds himself having to teach Chi how to get along in the everyday world, even while he and his friends try to solve the mystery of her origins. Is she one of the urban-legendary *Chobits*—persocoms built to have the riskiest functions of all: real emotions and free will?

CLAMP's best-selling manga in America is finally available in omnibus form! Containing dozens of bonus color pages, *Chobits* is an engaging, touching, exciting story.

BOOK 1
ISBN 978-1-59582-451-6
$24.99

BOOK 2
ISBN 978-1-59582-514-8
$24.99

AVAILABLE AT YOUR LOCAL COMICS SHOP OR BOOKSTORE
To find a comics shop in your area, call 1.888.266.4226. For more information or to order direct: •On the web: DarkHorse.com •E-mail: mailorder@darkhorse.com •Phone: 1.800.862.0052 Mon.–Fri. 9 AM to 5 PM Pacific Time.

CHOBITS © CLAMP. Publication rights for this English edition arranged through Pyrotechnist, Ltd. All rights reserved. Dark Horse Manga™ is a trademark of Dark Horse Comics, Inc. All rights reserved. (BL 7093)

DARK HORSE MANGA
DarkHorse.com

Cardcaptor Sakura
カードキャプターさくら

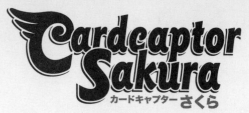

Story and Art by

CLAMP

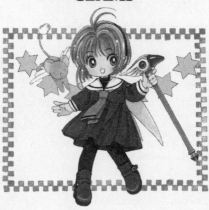

Fourth grader Sakura Kinomoto has found a strange book in her father's library—a book made by the wizard Clow to store dangerous spirits sealed within a set of magical cards. But when Sakura opens it up, there is nothing left inside but Kero-chan, the book's cute little guardian beast . . . who informs Sakura that since the Clow cards seem to have escaped while he was asleep, it's now her job to capture them!

With remastered image files straight from CLAMP, Dark Horse is proud to present *Cardcaptor Sakura* in omnibus form! Each book collects three volumes of the original twelve-volume series, and features thirty bonus color pages!

OMNIBUS BOOK ONE
ISBN 978-1-59582-522-3 $19.99

OMNIBUS BOOK TWO
ISBN 978-1-59582-591-9 $19.99

OMNIBUS BOOK THREE
ISBN 978-1-59582-808-8 $19.99

OMNIBUS BOOK FOUR
ISBN 978-1-59582-889-7 $19.99

DARK HORSE MANGA
DarkHorse.com

AVAILABLE AT YOUR LOCAL COMICS SHOP OR BOOKSTORE!
To find a comics shop in your area, call 1-888-266-4226
For more information or to order direct: • On the web: DarkHorse.com
E-mail: mailorder@darkhorse.com • Phone: 1-800-862-0052 Mon.–Fri. 9 AM to 5 PM Pacific Time

BRIDE of the WATER GOD

When Soah's impoverished, desperate village decides to sacrifice her to the Water God Habaek to end a long drought, they believe that drowning one beautiful girl will save their entire community and bring much-needed rain. Not only is Soah surprised to be *rescued* by the Water God instead of killed; she never imagined she'd be a welcomed guest in Habaek's magical kingdom, where an exciting new life awaits her! Most surprising, however, is the Water God himself, and how very different he is from the monster Soah imagined . . .

Created by Mi-Kyung Yun, who received the "Best New Artist" award in 2004 from the esteemed *Dokja-manhwa-daesang* organization, *Bride of the Water God* was the top-selling *shoujo* manhwa in Korea in 2006!

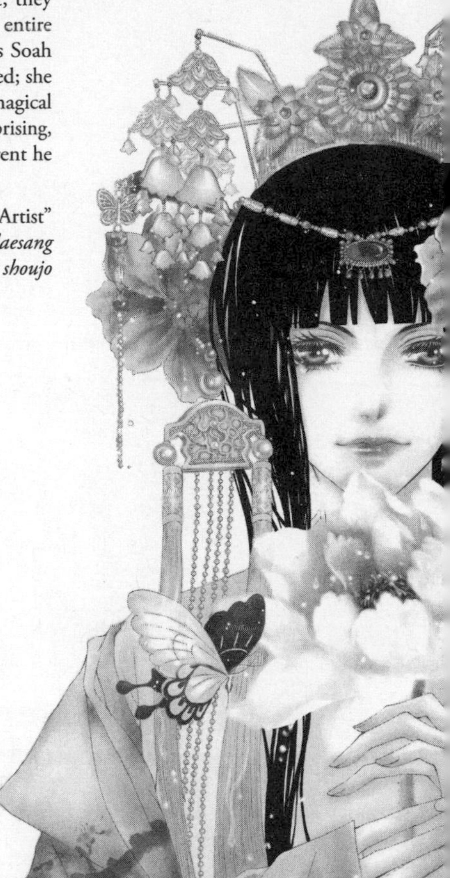

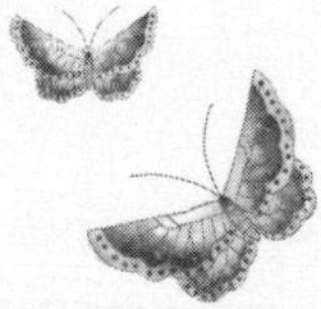

Volume 1
ISBN 978-1-59307-849-2

Volume 2
ISBN 978-1-59307-883-6

Volume 3
ISBN 978-1-59582-305-2

Volume 4
ISBN 978-1-59582-378-6

Volume 5
ISBN 978-1-59582-445-5

Volume 6
ISBN 978-1-59582-605-3

Volume 7
ISBN 978-1-59582-668-8

Volume 8
ISBN 978-1-59582-687-9

Volume 9
ISBN 978-1-59582-688-6

Volume 10
ISBN 978-1-59582-873-6

Volume 11
ISBN 978-1-59582-874-3

Volume 12
ISBN 978-1-59582-999-3

Volume 13
ISBN 978-1-61655-072-1

Volume 14
ISBN 978-1-61655-187-2

$9.99 each

Previews for BRIDE OF THE WATER GOD and other DARK HORSE MANHWA titles can be found at darkhorse.com!

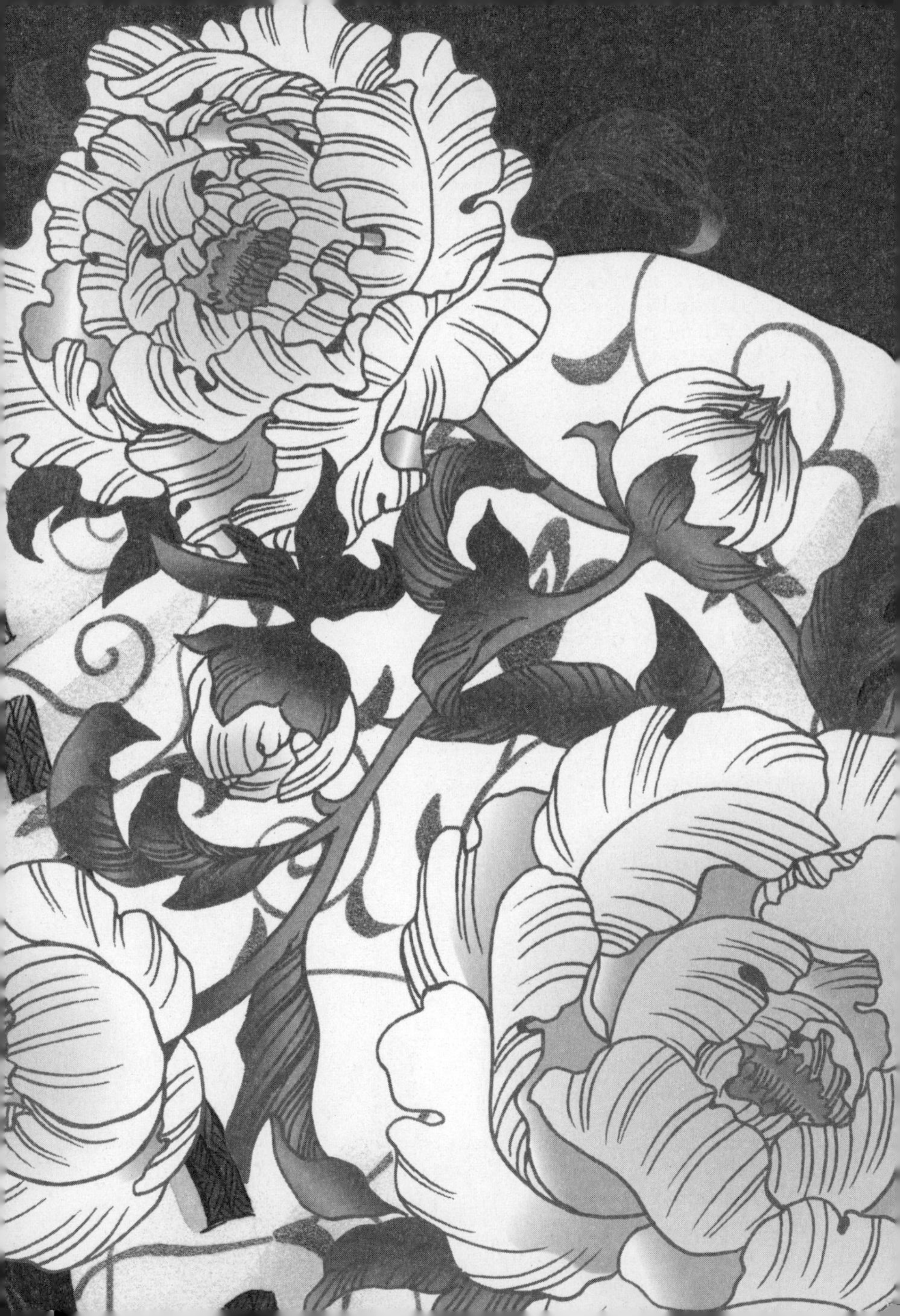

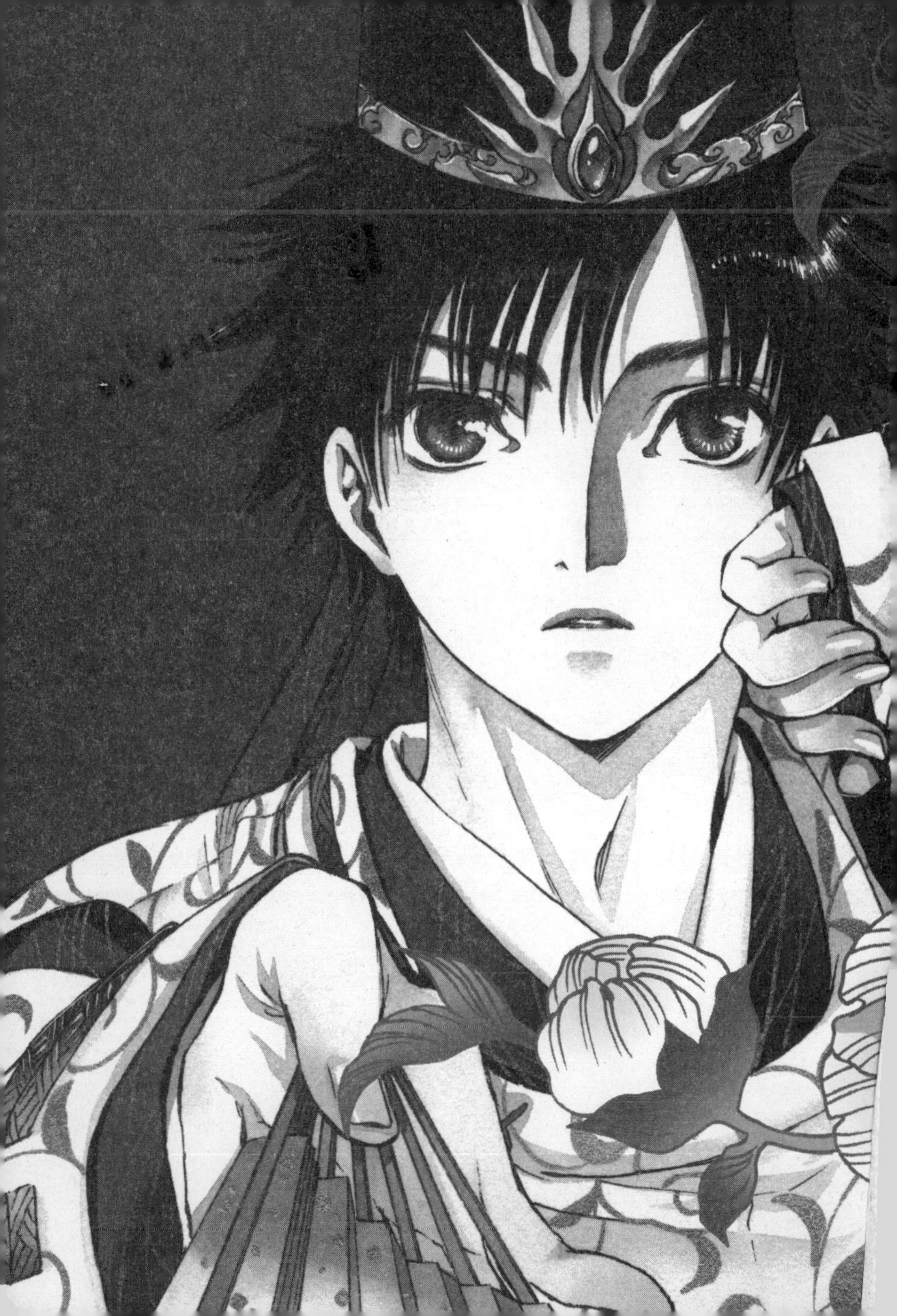

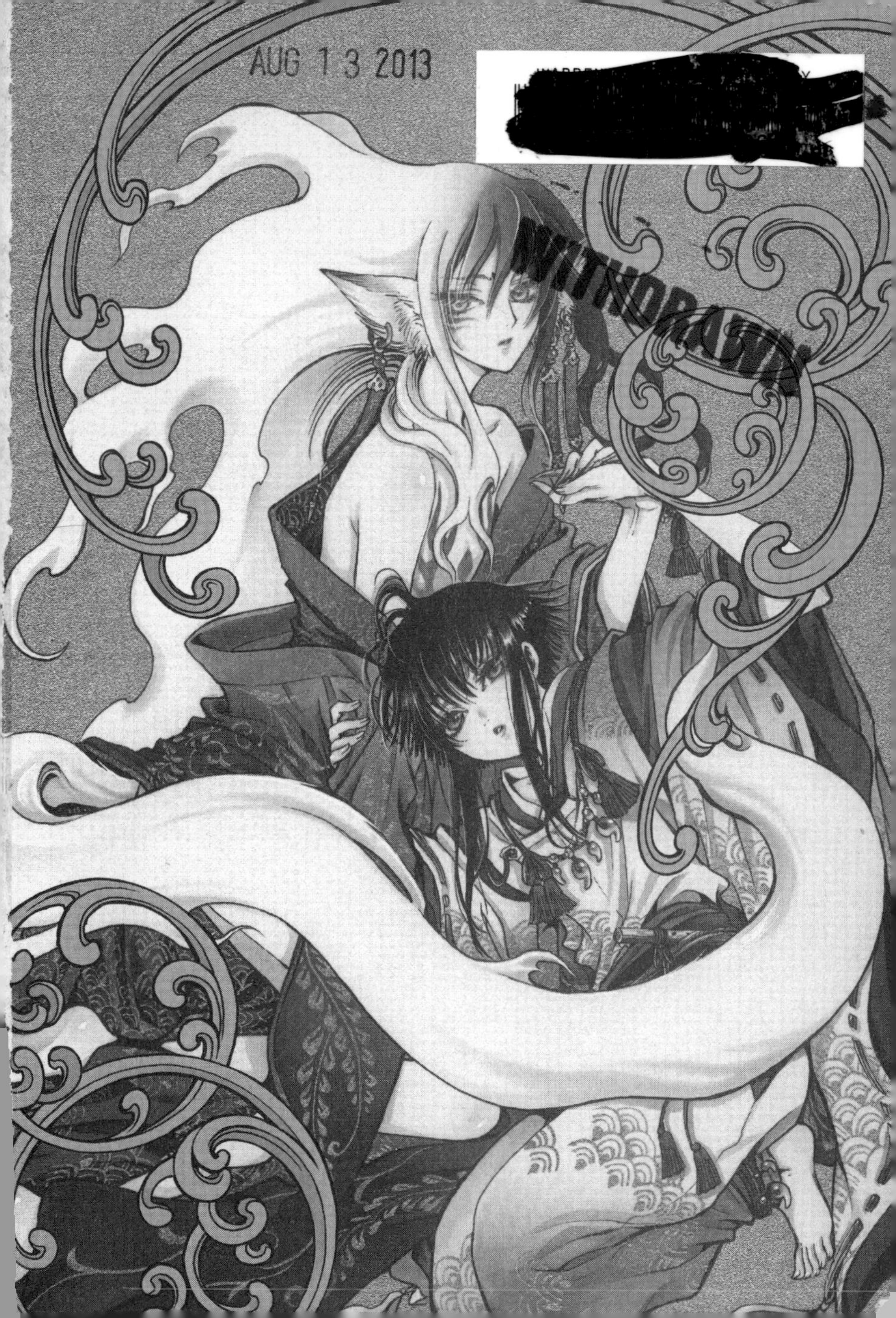